Picture This

Picture This

WORLD WAR I POSTERS AND VISUAL CULTURE

EDITED AND WITH AN INTRODUCTION BY PEARL JAMES

UNIVERSITY OF NEBRASKA PRESS · LINCOLN & LONDON

© 2009 by the Board of Regents of the
University of Nebraska
All rights reserved
Manufactured in the United States of America

Publication of this book was supported in part
by grants from the Office of the Vice President
for Academic Affairs at Davidson College,
Davidson, North Carolina, and the Office of
the Dean of the College of Arts and Sciences,
University of Kentucky.

Library of Congress Cataloging-in-Publication
Data

Picture this : World War I posters and visual
culture / edited and with an introduction by
Pearl James.
      p. cm. — (Studies in war, society, and the
military)
Includes bibliographical references and index.
ISBN 978-0-8032-2610-4 (pbk. : alk. paper)
1. World War, 1914–1918—Posters. 2. War
posters—History–20th century. 3. World
War, 1914–1918—Art and the war. 4. Visual
communication—History—20th century.
5. Popular culture—History—20th century.
6. World War, 1914–1918—Social aspects.
7. World War, 1914–1918—Propaganda.
D522.25.P53 2009
940.3′1—dc22
2009021118

Set in ITC New Baskerville.

CONTENTS

List of Illustrations   vii

Acknowledgments   ix

Introduction: Reading World War I Posters   PEARL JAMES   1

1. Imaginings of War: Posters and the Shadow of the Lost Generation   JAY WINTER   37

Part 1. WAR POSTER CAMPAIGNS AND IMAGES, COMPARATIVE READINGS

2. Barbaric Anti-Modernism: Representations of the "Hun" in Britain, North America, Australia, and Beyond
NICOLETTA F. GULLACE   61

3. Chivalrous Knights versus Iron Warriors: Representations of the Battle of *Matériel* and Slaughter in Britain and Germany, 1914–1940   STEFAN GOEBEL   79

4. Regression versus Progression: Fundamental Differences in German and American Posters of the First World War
JAKUB KAZECKI & JASON LIEBLANG   111

Part 2. ENVISIONING THE NATION AND IMAGINING NATIONAL AESTHETICS

5. Young Blood: Parisian Schoolgirls' Transformation of France's Great War Poster Aesthetic   MARK LEVITCH   145

6. Race and Empire in French Posters of the Great War
RICHARD S. FOGARTY   172

7. Images of Racial Pride: African American Propaganda Posters in the First World War   JENNIFER D. KEENE   207

8. Segodniashnii Lubok: Art, War, and National Identity
ANDREW M. NEDD   241

Part 3. FIGURING THE BODY IN THE CONTEXT OF WAR

9. Images of Femininity in American World War I Posters
PEARL JAMES 273

10. Humanitarians and He-Men: Recruitment Posters and the
Masculine Ideal   MEG ALBRINCK   312

11. Iconography of Injury: Encountering the Wounded Soldier's
Body in American Poster Art and Photography of World War I
JOHN M. KINDER   340

Epilogue   JEFFREY T. SCHNAPP   369

Selected Bibliography   377
Contributors   383
Index   387

ILLUSTRATIONS

1. Iowa potatoes, "the newest fighting corps"   7

2. Bicycle-boat bearing messages   10

3. James Montgomery Flagg's recruitment move   11

4. Bell ringers promote Liberty Loan bonds   12

5. U.S. Food Administration bonds billboard   13

6. Wagon displaying Food Administration poster   15

7. Anonymous, "Your Country's Call"   43

8. Anonymous, "Remember Belgium"   44

9. Anonymous, "Is *your* home worth fighting for?"   45

10. *Punch*, "Injured Innocence"   63

11. H. R. Hopps, "Destroy This Mad Brute"   69

12. Norman Lindsay, "?"   72

13. Lucian Bernhard, "Das ist der Weg zum Frieden"   82

14. Leo Schnug, "Kameraden zeichnet die VII^te Kriegsanleihe"   88

15. Fritz Erler, "Helft uns siegen!"   91

16. Anonymous, "Britain Needs You at Once"   99

17. Frederick Strothmann, "Beat Back the Hun with Liberty Bonds"   114

18. Paul Dienst, "U-Boot-Spende: Gebe jeder nach seinen Kräften!"   115

19. Richard Pfeifer, "Sammlung für ein Mutterhaus"   127

20. Anonymous, "All Aboard!"   129

21. Harrison Fisher, "I Summon You to Comradeship in the Red Cross"   134

22. Marthe Picard, "Mangez moins de viande"   146

23. Yvonne Vernet, "Economisons le pain"   147

24. G. Douanne, "Soignons la basse-cour"   148

25. Henri Villain, "Compagnie Algérienne 1920"   181

26. Lucien Jonas, "Compagnie Algérienne"   182

27. Maurice Romberg, "Compagnie Algérienne . . . Souscrivez" 193

28. Lucien Jonas, "Journée de l'armée d'Afrique" 199

29. E. G. Renesch, "Emancipation Proclamation" 216

30. E. G. Renesch, "True Blue" 223

31. E. G. Renesch, "Colored Man Is No Slacker" 225

32. Anonymous, "Dawn of Hope" 233

33. Kazimir Malevich, "A Sausage Maker came to Lodz" 254

34. Kazimir Malevich, "The French Allies" 255

35. Anonymous, "We are the Russians" 258

36. Kazimir Malevich, "An Austrian went to Radziwill" 260

37. Kazimir Malevich, "What a boom, what a blast" 261

38. Kenyon Cox, "The Sword Is Drawn" 279

39. M. Hoyle, "They Crucify American Manhood—Enlist" 286

40. Howard Chandler Christy, "Gee!! I Wish I Were a Man" 289

41. Women working for the Third Red Cross Roll Call 297

42. Exhibit at an Iowa fair 298

43. Lambert Guenther, "Join the Land Army" 299

44. Ernest Hamlin Baker, "For Every Fighter a Woman Worker" 300

45. Howard Chandler Christy, "The Motor Corps of America" 305

46. F. Foxton, "Men of Britain! Will you stand this?" 320

47. Savile Lumley, "Daddy, what did *you* do in the Great War?" 325

48. Laura Brey, "On Which Side of the Window are *You*?" 327

49. E. V. Kealey, "Women of Britain say—'*Go!*'" 328

50. Robert Baden Powell, "Are *you* in this?" 329

51. Albert Sterner, "We need you" 346

52. Institute for Crippled and Disabled Men, "Future Members of the Fourth Estate" 353

53. "Living Death" 361

ACKNOWLEDGMENTS

This project is proof that scholarship and teaching play equally important and mutually beneficial roles in the production of scholarly knowledge. I became interested in war posters many years ago when I was teaching a Yale College seminar on masculinity and war. My class visited the Yale British Art Center, where Elisabeth Fairmen shared artifacts and an account of curating a World War I exhibit. After her fascinating presentation one of my students decided to do a research paper on recruitment posters. We went together to the Yale Manuscripts and Archives collection, and although the student ultimately changed his topic, I was hooked. I became convinced that posters formed an important part of the world I was trying to understand in my research. As I have continued to teach images and texts from World War I and its aftermath, my students' questions have continued to push me in useful directions.

Many people have provided encouragement, support, and helpful criticism in the intervening years and have helped bring this project to completion. Jay Winter spurred the project along with suggestions for contributors, his model scholarship, and his infectious enthusiasm. Vivien Dietz and Scott MacKenzie both made strategic suggestions about locating contributors and funding at an early stage. I am grateful to Amanda Ewington, John MacKay, Steven Norris, and Karen Petrone for generously sharing their expertise in Russian culture. Their help made the volume more inclusive. Karen's vital contributions to the field of World War I studies are an inspiration.

While working on my own contribution to the volume, I received many useful criticisms from colleagues at the Modernist Studies Association conference, including Debra Rae Cohen. When I met with some of the contributors at the University of

Newcastle upon Tyne for a recent World War I conference, the enthusiasm from them, along with Jeffrey Reznick, Christian Maryska, Peter Sattler, and others helped me see the whole project with a fresh perspective. More recently, members of the University of Kentucky Social Theory working group made useful comments on my essay; I have greatly benefited from their collective interdisciplinarity and rigor. Steven Biel and David Lubin both took the time to read drafts and offered astute suggestions. Peter Kalliney's suggestions for the introduction made it a more interesting argument. Jeffory Clymer, Michael Trask, and other members of the UK English Department have provided me with a community that has sustained me during the final stages of *Picture This*. I thank them.

The nature of this project has led me into several archives, where the expertise and enthusiasm of conservators and staff have enabled some exciting discoveries. I am particularly grateful to the Yale Manuscripts and Archive Collection staff, Jonathan Casey of the Liberty Memorial, Lori Cox-Paul of the National Archives in Kansas City, and Janel Quirante of the Hoover Institution at Stanford University.

The cost of illustrating this volume has been generously supported by the dean of the faculty at Davidson College and the University of Kentucky's College of Arts and Sciences. The images are at the center of our inquiry, and the volume simply could not have gone to press without this support.

I have learned a great deal from the contributors to the volume. They not only have smart and original insights to offer individually but also worked hard to make this collective project come together on a schedule. I have been very privileged to work with them.

The University of Nebraska Press has been consistent in its support for this project, and its editors, editorial board, and very fine readers did everything I could have asked. Their ideas and criticisms influenced the volume for the better. Sally Antrobus's expert help clarified the volume's prose; we all thank her. I am grateful to Margie Rine, Elizabeth Demers, Bridget Barry, and especially Heather Lundine, for their interest and support.

I am grateful for support from family and friends in California, Illinois, and Maryland.

My deepest appreciation belongs to my best reader and best friend, Leon Sachs.

Picture This

war with a host of cultural certainties in place. Paul Fussell's by now aphoristic description of the prewar world as one of "prevailing innocence," in which "traditional moral action" could be "delineated in traditional moral language" reminds us that the war unfolded in an essentially nineteenth-century cultural landscape.[1]

Mass-produced, full-color, large-format war posters are at the crux of this contradiction. They were both signs and instruments of two modern innovations in warfare—the military deployment of modern technology and the development of the home front. In some ways the medium of the war poster epitomizes the modernity of the conflict. In addition to being sent to the front, they reached mass numbers of people in every combatant nation, serving to unite diverse populations as simultaneous viewers of the same images and to bring them closer, in an imaginary yet powerful way, to the war. Posters nationalized, mobilized, and modernized civilian populations. Through the viewing of posters, factory work, agricultural work, and domestic work, the consumption and conservation of goods, and various kinds of leisure all became emblematic of one's national identity and one's place within a collective effort to win the war. It was in part by looking at posters that citizens learned to see themselves as members of the home front.

Yet for all their newness, war posters constituted a political adaptation of a medium that already pervaded European cityscapes. They presuppose "the modern concept of the public— in which the members of a society are defined primarily as spectators and consumers" and imply an "urban, public space" that had already become "an arena of signs: the image- and word-choked façades and surfaces of the great modern cities."[2] War posters reflect the period's confusion of traditions and modernity. In war posters new national identities coalesce around nostalgic visions of the past. Women wear both traditional and nontraditional guises, appearing as old-fashioned mothers, wives, and damsels in distress but also as nurses, drivers, and munitions workers. Depictions of imperial subjects conform to some racial hierarchies but challenge others. Posters proffer a complex blend of folk art, traditional "high" art, and slick advertising sense. War put pressure on longstanding cultural traditions (the family, sentimentalism, the military hero, to name a few). Properly viewed, posters record both traditions and the pressures impinging upon them. These Janus-faced images look back to nineteenth-century empires and forward to modern bureaucratic nation-states.

Posters were "the medium for the construction of a pictorial rhetoric of . . . national identities"—identities upon which the waging of war hinged.[3] They not only functioned as illustrations of the war in popular understanding but also had an impact on the facts of the war, including its duration and its reach. Without the consent and material support of the home front, combatant nations would not have been able to sustain the huge losses a four-year war of attrition entailed.

These posters are preserved in several private collections and institutional archives in every combatant nation, and since the publication of Maurice Rickards's classic *Posters of the First World War* (1968), several volumes have brought their striking images to a wider public.[4] More recently, many archives, collectors, and vendors have published poster images online.[5] Often, however, the images are left to speak for themselves, raising more questions than they answer. Even when volumes provide impressive numbers of high-quality images, they often provide scanty accounts of the posters' production, distribution, and reception. (Rawls's *Wake Up, America!* and Aulich and Hewitt's *Seduction or Instruction?* are welcome exceptions.) Thus, although we might appreciate the images' visual power, our understanding of their importance to the generation who made and viewed them often remains vague. In contrast, the essays in *Picture This* offer specific interpretations of how posters functioned in various contexts at the time of their production. Contributors look backward to the nineteenth-century past and forward to the war's twentieth-century legacies in order to understand posters' meanings. Collectively, the essays consider posters from several combatant nations (Britain, France, Germany, Russia, and the United States) and work to define new aspects of the war's internationalism. This volume offers further reasons to call World War I, as many have done, "the poster war."

When World War I began in 1914, the poster was a mature advertising tool and artistic medium. It had evolved over centuries. According to Alain Weill, typographical posters were ubiquitous in European cities by the seventeenth century. With the invention of lithography (by Aloys Senefelder in the 1790s)—a process in which paper is rolled over a smooth stone that has been treated and inked, rather than engraved—it became relatively cheap to reproduce graphic images on paper. The invention of chromolithography (by Godefroi Engelmann in 1837) brought the welcome addition of color. But Weill traces the poster as we know it to the "stunning" intervention of Jules Chéret, an artist whose talent with color inaugurated the poster's French "Golden Age" (1880–1900). During this period art and advertising conspired to make posters "the fashion of the times." Chéret, Pierre Bonnard, Henri de Toulouse-Lautrec, and Alphonse Mucha, among others, brought painterly skill to the medium and established new standards of design and color. By the turn of the twentieth century, posters did far more than advertise. They were exhibited, collected, and recognized as an artistic medium with a proud tradition and an international market.[6] Although some communities (such as London in the 1890s) worried about the intrusiveness and vulgarity of outdoor advertising, posters became increasingly ubiquitous in urban landscapes in both Europe and America.[7] In the decades before the war, poster producers, advertisers, and billposters cooperated through their professional organizations to standardize poster sizes and outdoor displays (particularly for large, twenty-four-sheet billboards), seeking to become more efficient and to expand their share of the burgeoning advertising market.

Given these developments, the poster was poised to become the favored propaganda medium of the war. According to Maurice Rickards, it was "the one big instrument of mass communication" because it was "accepted and understood by the public at large; it was tried and tested—and it was cheap."[8] And if the poster was crucial to the waging of the war, so the war was "the critical moment in the history of the propaganda poster."[9] The poster industry capitalized upon the opportunity the war afforded by cooperating with governments and demonstrating both their patriotism and the effectiveness of their services. In the United States, for instance, the Poster Advertising Association donated designs, production, and display space. Industry leaders were canny about the return this patriotic investment would bring, assuring themselves in their trade papers that "the unprecedented use of posters . . . and the marvelous results attained by means of them, has impressed the power of the medium upon the world's population so forcibly that all doubt that may have existed as to its efficacy has been permanently removed."[10] Despite its bluster, this was not an overstatement. The industry's war work established its effectiveness and, just as important, its institutional legitimacy. The medium's instrumentality as a link between the state and the masses became a rule in most combatant nations.[11] If some governments—particularly those in Germany, Austria-Hungary, and Britain—had initially balked at using "crass" advertising methods to communicate with their citizenry, the difficulty of waging the war over four long years led them to reconsider.[12] Nor was the decision theirs alone to make. Images of soldiers and the war were used in privately produced posters for charities and interest groups and were used to advertise commodities such as soap and tobacco. The unprecedented numbers of posters produced and displayed across the combatant nations attest to the fact that governments, charitable and other private organizations, and manufacturers all perceived the medium as a crucial and effective link to the public.

War posters, then, constitute a complicated category. Before the war it would have been easy to differentiate between a public notice and a poster, according to James Aulich and John Hewitt. They point out that despite similarities—"both are pieces of paper and are printed with text to be exhibited in public space"—these two mediums did "different jobs" and "constructed their putative audience in specific ways: where the public notice informs, instructs or even commands, the poster persuades, seduces and even wheedles . . . the public notice constructs the 'readers' as citizens subject to the power of various institutions, while the poster constructs them as consumers who have the freedom to choose from what is on offer."[13] During the war, at least in some nations, this fundamental distinction became blurred, as governments tried to seduce, and as producers, sellers, and advertisers tried to annex the aura of official authority and public business that support for the war could confer.

A shop window display from a store in Maquoketa, Iowa, illustrates this overlap: shoppers were encouraged to buy potatoes at this store as part of a national campaign to conserve wheat and feed the troops (fig. 1). Their "Potatriot" display allowed shop owners Staack and Luckiesh to advertise not just their products but their own "100% Americanism" and

Fig. 1. Potatoes in Iowa become "the newest fighting corps" on the domestic front, ca. 1917–18. Photos in the introduction are from the U.S. National Archives and Records Administration, bearing record group (RG) and Archival Research Catalogue (ARC) numbers. Records of the U.S. Food Administration, 1917–1920, RG 4, ARC Identifier 283501, National Archives.

support for the war effort, as if to allay customers' suspicions about their German origins. In other words, to and for whom posters spoke was not always a simple matter. Midwestern violence toward Americans of German origin, itself a byproduct of war propaganda, may be the hidden but crucial context here. These merchants may have been fighting propaganda with propaganda and consolidating their membership in the emerging home front.

The Staack and Luckiesh display draws our attention to other interpretive complexities as well: how are we to reckon with the various elements, both visual and material, at work here? The unlikely transformation of potatoes to an artistic medium reminds us, in turn, of the materiality of both the home-made ("The Potato is a Good Soldier, Eat It Uniform and All") and mass-produced ("He is Fighting for you, You must save food for him") posters in this display. At least the hand-made posters are unique, if not in design or message, then in manufacture. This display suggests that posters need to be read both as images and as pictures, to introduce a distinction W. J. T. Mitchell has used to reconfigure visual analysis. "The picture," he tells us, "is a material object, a thing you can burn or break [or hang]. An image is what appears in a picture, and what survives its destruction—in memory, in narrative, and in copies and traces in other media."[14] We are more accustomed to reading posters for their images. We glimpse them in transit and expect them to disappear. We see them as mass-produced copies with no original, not as individual material objects. At the level of image, the display can be said to contain such familiar motifs as the stars and stripes and the figure of the lone soldier—motifs used repeatedly in other posters. "He is fighting for you" was obviously produced and distributed en masse by an anonymous, industrial producer of this and similar images, and as such addresses an equally anonymous mass audience trained, through practice, to read them: its long line of white tents refers to training camps but may also evoke the vulnerable home over which the lone soldier stands guard. But the photograph of this display invites us to read these posters also as material objects that were obtained by particular merchants, hung by a particular employee as part of a larger, self-produced three-dimensional display, and seen for a finite time in a particular location in Iowa. Three of the most prominent posters in the display were hand-made. In this process, the USFA

poster's relative anonymity—the generality of the injunction
to "save food" and the silhouetted, iconic soldier—has been
translated into and reinforced by a much more local idiomatic
message, wherein individual potatoes of all shapes and sizes become the means by which Maquoketa residents could "Spud
the Kaiser." Mass-produced posters provided a script but also
provided raw material for display makers to frame, emphasize,
repeat, save or discard. At each step individuals handled, selected, shared, and manufactured posters, sometimes at considerable private expense, and other times as the authorized
spenders of public funds.

As material objects, or as "pictures," in Mitchell's terms, posters took many forms. They were printed in a variety of sizes,
from small window cards to large single sheets, the very large
twenty-four-sheet billboards, and sizes in between. Newspapers included full-page inserts with poster images that could
be hung in the home. At least in the United States, individuals designed and displayed their own war posters, often in un-
conventional ways (as fig. 2 testifies). Posters were often incorporated into larger pageants, such as parades, rallies, tableaux
vivants, fair exhibits, and other events (see figs. 3, 4, and 5). In
England "many recruiting posters were drawn into a kind of
street theatre and became part of small, intense dramas usually lasting a fortnight and played out in the squares and thor-
oughfares of towns and cities."[15] Stefan Goebel's essay in this
volume describes how posters functioned in nail-driving rituals conducted by rural German communities to demonstrate
their fortitude during the war. How did such displays influence
viewers' responses to posters? Did they reinforce the impression that poster images were true to life? For such an intent often seems to be present: many ritualized displays invited viewers to become participants in the scene depicted by the poster,
and so to ratify or personalize its message. On the other hand,

Fig. 2. An advertising bicycle-boat built by U. S. Main was pedaled through the streets of Calexico, California, by his young son. Messages were changed from time to time. Records of the U.S. Food Administration, 1917–1920, RG 4, ARC Identifier 595357, National Archives.

such displays suggest that the poster by itself seemed insufficient, merely a backdrop for a more arresting spectacle.

Both as pictures and as images, posters infiltrated many places where advertisements had not gone. If commercial posters had been—and would again be—primarily aimed at urban consumers, war posters of all kinds were much more widely distributed, appearing not just on billboards or walls but also in shop windows, banks, schools, churches, libraries, town halls, factories, recruiting stations, offices, and homes; in cities, small towns, and rural settings. They redefined the boundaries of public space, bringing national imperatives into private or parochial settings. Hanging a poster in one's home was a way to become part of the war effort, and the incorporation such an object materialized was, in turn, amplified by the poster's other, immaterial aspect: its ubiquity as image. The same or similar images were

PEARL JAMES

Fig. 3. James Montgomery Flagg produced a life-size picture of the poster "Tell it to the Marines" in the New York Public Library to stimulate recruiting. Photo: Underwood and Underwood, July 1918. Records of the War Department General and Special Staffs, 1860–1952, RG 165, ARC Identifier 533472, National Archives.

reiterated elsewhere, in different sizes, alternatively in color or black and white, sometimes as graphic drawings and other times as photographs. Popular images were frequently reissued in different form, or evoked by another illustrator. As Susan Sontag observes, "The relation posters have to visual fashion is that of 'quotation.' Thus the poster artist is usually a plagiarist (whether of himself or others) . . . the stylistically parasitic trend in the history of the poster is additional confirmation of the poster as an art form."[16] Posters copy, parody, and otherwise repeat eye-catching, memorable, and significant imagery: quotation is arguably the most important aspect of their visual language, the one that allows them to convey so much so quickly and with such economical or simple designs.

Take, for example, one of the most popular posters of the war: Edward Penfield's poster, which implored its viewer to "Help the Women of France" and depicted three women pulling a plow across a field. Before Penfield made the poster, this image had been widely distributed as a photograph by the U.S. Food Administration (and other organizations) with a text by Dr. Alonso Taylor. That image inspired Penfield's design, which was taken up and reprinted in all sizes, addressed to "Women of Maine," "Women of Canada," and various other particular populations. In figure 6 (see p. 15) it was part of an appeal in the agrarian South. That region of the country showed "the most determined resistance to the World War I draft" (Keith, 5—see following note) and the highest desertion rates; there, according to Jeannette Keith, various hostile constituencies agreed in their opposition to the war: Southern Democrats

PEARL JAMES

Fig. 5. A U.S. Food Administration billboard hangs above a demonstration of the Foreign Legion during the fourth Liberty Loan drive, New Orleans, Louisiana, October 2, 1918. Records of the War Department General and Special Staffs, 1860–1952, RG 165, ARC Identifier 533665, National Archives.

opposed it as a campaign of Northern "militarism"; members of Christian sects rejected it on religious grounds; and populists, dirt farmers, and socialists—both black and white—argued against it as "a rich man's war, and a poor man's fight."[17] This poster's pastoralism addressed all of these constituencies simultaneously, insinuating that the war was a struggle for survival by hardworking rural farmers who shared much in common with southern ways of life across the racial spectrum. At the same time, abject French womanhood flattered white southern masculinity without depicting the (to some, threatening) possibility of uniforming and arming black men. The poster "transcends its utility in delivering [its] message" and exhibits "that duality" Sontag considers the medium's claim to art: "the tension between the wish to say (explicitness, literalness) and the wish to be silent (truncation, economy, condensation, evocativeness, mystery, exaggeration)."[18] Considered as an image, "Women of France" has multiple meanings. Looking at this photograph for evidence about this one poster's life as a picture is decidedly more challenging. The photograph suggests that the poster's imagery reflects not just its subject or its illustrator but its rural spectators as well. Though parodically mocked in at least one cartoon—where a leisured woman is portrayed as looking at this image while eating chocolates and murmuring, "How thrilling!"[19]—French peasant women would have been no laughing matter when viewed within agrarian communities. The photograph hints at the little-known consumption of posters in nonurban spaces. It reminds us that we will never know with precision where and by whom posters were *not* seen: this wagon's itinerant poster display tantalizingly illustrates the medium's mobility and ubiquity during the war.

The wider availability of poster images through book publications and on the web has coincided with an interdisciplinary turn in World War I historiography. World War I has in recent years become a much more complicated object of study than it once was: historians have discovered that while interest in the military aspects of the conflict never waned, the war's meanings as a cultural experience have been overlooked. Better understandings have emerged both through new attention to primary materials of all kinds, including mass-cultural ("low") artifacts such as war posters, and through reconsiderations of the sites, the participants, and the duration of the war. This change has led to new interest in posters and the connection they forged between the front and home front.

Posters belong to something of a twilight zone of evidence. They were produced by official governmental institutions and

Fig. 6. A wagon provided mobile display for a U.S. Food Administration poster tacked to its side in Mobile, Alabama, ca. 1918. Records of the War Department General and Special Staffs, 1860–1952, RG 165, ARC Identifier 533644, National Archives

unofficial private ones as well as by individuals. They were circulated en masse and undoubtedly had an impact on how people experienced the war, yet they were ephemeral. Martin Hardie and Arthur K. Sabin, editors of an early volume on posters titled *War Posters Issued by Belligerent and Neutral Nations 1914–1919*, understood the challenge this would present to later generations:

> The thought of the ephemeral character of the poster as such has in the first instance prompted the publication of this volume. A poster serving the purpose of a war, even of such a world cataclysm as we have witnessed during the past five years, is by nature a creation of the moment; its business being to seize an opportunity as it passes, to force a sentiment into a great passion, to answer an

immediate need, or to illuminate an episode which may be forgotten in the tremendous sequence of a few days' events. In its brief existence the poster is battered by the rain or faded by the sun, then pasted over by another message more urgent still. Save for the very limited number of copies which wise collectors have preserved, the actual posters of the Great War will be lost and forgotten in fifty years.[20]

Museums began to conserve posters, advertisements, and other ephemera, though as Aulich and Hewitt explain in their analysis of the Imperial War Museum, such material required curators to make unprecedented decisions about both what to keep and how to justify their choices to sponsors.[21] Like Britain's Imperial War Museum, the Liberty Memorial Association (the official American memorial to World War I) similarly began its collection by purchasing war posters.[22] Certainly many designs have been lost. But because of such early conservation efforts, the war's posters have not been entirely forgotten, as Sabin and Hardie worried they would be. However, although a sampling of the objects remains, their original displays are long gone. Interpreting them poses a challenge precisely because they cannot be studied in the surroundings in which they appeared, nor can their viewers be called to bear witness to them in any systematic way. Gauging a poster's relation to actual conditions in war time poses difficulties similar to those Roland Marchand identified in his study of another mass-media object, the advertisement: "Does the content of advertisements mirror the consumers' actual conditions and behavior—or their fantasies and aspirations? Or [do] the ads reflect . . . the particular values and preoccupations of advertisers, advertising agents, and copywriters? Of what value [is] a systematic analysis of the overt elements of the content of advertisements when subtle nuances often lay at the heart of their appeals?" he asks. These questions have their analogs in the study of posters, which, like ads, are produced by a small number of interested but often anonymous individuals and aimed at a mass audience. Marchand also cautions that gauging an ad's impact is extremely difficult, since "if sales increased during a particular advertising campaign, other factors in merchandising, distribution, economic conditions, or social fads might have triggered the response. Even if advertising could be isolated as the crucial factor in the 'merchandising mix,' the placement, frequency, special offer, or eye appeal of a given ad might have influenced customers . . . more than . . . its implicit or explicit social content."[23] The sheer number of variables makes interpreting such objects daunting. We know from contemporary accounts that governments perceived the posters as useful, but whether and to what degree such perceptions were accurate is another question. As Richard Fogarty wonders in this volume, "How effective were wartime posters, and what can they reveal about the mentalities of the people who made and saw them? This can be difficult to judge. There is 'no measuring instrument' of effectiveness, and conclusions based on intuition and 'post hoc reasoning' are not always totally reliable."[24]

Consider, for instance, the famous British recruiting poster that features a drawing of Lord Kitchener pointing to the viewer and captioned "Wants You." This poster, based on a design by Alfred Leete, was widely disseminated in Britain and inspired both imitations and parodies. Its iconography reappeared in recruiting posters in almost all combatant nations, in which artists replaced Kitchener with other appropriate national figures (such as Uncle Sam in the United States and common soldiers in Italian, Hungarian, and German posters). This poster can be read as a cultural hinge between the prewar past and the postwar future. Kitchener was nothing if not a figure of stalwart Victorian might. But, as some have noted, he may also have inspired George Orwell's chilling icon of bureaucratic war mongering, *1984*'s Big Brother. Carlo Ginzburg has argued that the poster's power stems from multiple sources: Lord Kitchener's popularity, use of bold color, and invocation of familiar "pictorial traditions" that use "frontal, all-seeing figures . . . with fore-shortened pointing fingers" to command authority. While he grants that "we'll never know how many people decided to volunteer under the impulse of Kitchener's image," his analysis teases out many reasons why the poster might have exerted a complex power over its viewer. For Ginzburg its own visual echoes of art historical tradition, coupled with the sheer number of imitators, provide tangible evidence of its influence.[25] But Nicholas Hiley's consideration of the same image and its imitators leads him to a different conclusion: he argues that the image (and the larger campaign of which it was a part) "provoked considerable . . . opposition," which was visible precisely through the proliferation of ironic parodies. For Hiley, the fact that the Kitchener poster has become an icon of the war tells us not about its success during its "first use in the recruiting campaign" but about its legacies, its "later ironic use." In Hiley's view we have inherited a "myth" of the poster's power.[26] Philip Dutton agrees, since a "straightforward correlation" between "known recruiting figures" and the poster's display yielded the "surprising conclusion" that "its widespread circulation in various forms did not halt the decline in recruiting."[27] Of course, one can never know if recruiting might have declined even more sharply in the poster's absence. Even where available, statistical analysis has its limits. Disentangling myth from history and situating posters in their complex historical contexts is the goal of *Picture This*.

Some methodological strategies do enable us to develop rich interpretations of war posters. Maurice Rickards developed one when he identified "discernible phases" and a common "sequence" of war poster themes that occurred across belligerent nations, a progression he compared to "the sequence of warfare itself." He identified a pattern that all national poster campaigns essentially followed: calling first for "men and money," then for help for the fighting man, then for "help for the wounded, orphans, and refugees," followed by calls for women workers, economy in consumption, and "austerity all the way around." In every nation, he noted, posters made periodic appeals for one "final" effort. He notes a "universality" of poster imagery and concludes that at a general level, all nations shared a "common strategy" in their use of posters.[28] In the present volume Fogarty articulates the warrant for claims based on the presence of such patterns: "Posters . . . often show a marked consistency in both their use of images and their messages, and this likely betrays a mentality or point of view that was more or less widespread. And repeated themes and motifs certainly reflected a vision that the works' sponsors, most often government officials, wanted the public to adopt." Moreover, in order to be persuasive, "the poster had to seek to exploit existing mentalities within its audience."[29] Identifying the patterns that underlie posters allows us to glimpse a commonly held vision, then, if only in an idealized form. It also allows us to appreciate the exceptions to the patterns and to understand what may have been truly unique in a particular poster or poster campaign.

Some contributors to *Picture This*, while working in similarly comparative contexts, define some of the perils that face those who draw conclusions based on "universal patterns" and "archetypes" appearing across posters, such as the ones Rickards identifies.[30] Stefan Goebel's comparative study of "almost identical visual imagery" in both German and British posters, for instance, reveals that "the same iconography carried fundamentally different meanings" in the two nations. He articulates a methodological principle shared by all contributors to this volume: posters need to be read not just visually but within a broader discursive context. "Iconographic evidence examined in isolation can be misleading. . . . Visual images . . . need to be located in their respective cultural settings." Iconography is incomplete without consideration of public rituals performed elsewhere and rhetoric found in written propaganda, public speeches, the press, postcards, and private letters, which in turn all drew upon longstanding cultural traditions. Jakub Kazecki and Jason Lieblang agree, arguing that when we place too much emphasis on universality, the poster's most relevant meaning for its contemporary audience can be missed.

Posters are designed to appeal quickly to a passing viewer and depend upon a certain instantaneous recognition. Successful posters achieve that instantaneous response through the visual medium, by clear design and color. Illustrations can reach people in a way written texts and performed speeches cannot, simply by virtue of the speed with which they communicate. As poster designers put it to themselves:

> The poster . . . must attract attention in the face of a thousand distractions and competitors for attention, and must make itself understood by people who are usually on the move. It calls for a large size, a forceful use of design and color and a simple presentation of its message with the medium of print. . . . It must tell its story forcefully and at once. It must be so designed as to be seen in its entirety from a passing motor car. If the message is rendered in a way too complex for this instantaneous view, there is too much in the design.[31]

Posters "should be single, clear, specific" and "must appeal to the emotions rather than to the intellect."[32] Yet a poster's ability to reach its viewer depends not only on its visual force but on its recognizability within an already familiar semiotic and linguistic world. Indeed, as Ginzburg's account of "Kitchener Wants You" demonstrates, visual force itself needs to be conceived as existing within a discursive tradition. Posters draw upon a complex of symbols, images, notions, and values already known to the viewer. David Crowley has argued that in order to reach the widest possible audience, posters rework common symbols and imagery within a widely understood repertoire—and that is certainly the case. On the other hand, posters are also nuanced.

We reject the idea that instantaneous intelligibility has, as its necessary corollary, unambiguous simplicity. To reason that "producers of graphic propaganda have tended not to overestimate the intellectual capacity" of their viewers, and that "the layers of meaning which make the study of a work of fine art so rich are not normally the feature of effective propaganda," is to underestimate the medium and its workings.[33] As Sontag puts it, "the point of the poster may be its 'message,'" but it "transcends its utility in delivering that message" through arts of evocation and suggestion.[34] It is not that the methods of analyzing fine art do not apply but that they are not in themselves adequate. Art historical methods are necessary and may yield rich insights in the case of some posters (as Ginzburg's analysis of the Kitchener poster proves). But art historical methods may not yield such rich results consistently. More important, the bureaucratic processes surrounding poster production and dissemination may intersect with the institutions of museums and fine art salons but do not necessarily do so. Despite the number of successful artists and illustrators who contributed to the war effort through poster design, many posters were issued anonymously and cannot be considered with reference to their designers. Moreover, because they are designed with mass consumption in mind, posters often resemble advertisements more than fine art objects. Hence, art historical methods of analysis serve as only one starting point. Posters refer to and act within a wider world, and reading them requires reconstructing that world. The contributors to this volume all embed the posters they interpret within widely drawn discursive contexts. Many contributors consider posters as they functioned within larger verbal propaganda campaigns; Stefan Goebel compares them to other wartime memorials and rituals; Mark Levitch examines posters that were part of a government-sponsored exhibit; I consider the way conservation posters were exchanged between a government agency and the women who displayed them; John M. Kinder compares images of wounded soldiers across posters, photographs, and antiwar albums of the 1930s. These examples reveal our commitment to situate posters within wider visual and verbal cultures.

Attention to particular contexts reveals that some posters may reflect their producers' visions to a larger degree than they reflect that of the public. That is, posters both reflect the views their audiences already hold and attempt to influence people. Two of the essays in this volume analyze British war posters and find in them different degrees of authentic public sentiment. Jay Winter notes that the poster producers were themselves members of the public. He argues that the "semiotics of solidarity" visible in some British posters "were a reflection rather than a cause of national unity in the First World War." Posters depicting the war as a threat to "the British way of life, a very local way of life, a life of pubs and clubs," allow us to see precisely what it was that British people fought to defend. By drawing connections between the arguments made in posters and other literary and cultural traditions extant in Britain in 1914, Winter argues that many images and their mottoes "illustrated but did not manufacture consent." Those who made the images "brought to the task personal experiences and recollections." As such, posters come down to us as traces of memories of "those who were there." He reminds us that our ideas of the war are informed by our knowledge of its unprecedented violence and catastrophe—a knowledge still unavailable to those making and seeing images in 1914 and 1915.

While Winter argues that posters reflect public feeling, Meg Albrinck considers them as instruments of coercion. She analyzes a gendered rhetoric of shame in British war posters, which developed in 1915 as the "solidarity" Winter describes began to deteriorate. She shares Winter's premise that the posters need to be read in relation to "other cultural discourses that were circulating about the war." But she focuses particularly on the Parliamentary Recruiting Committee (PRC), the governmental organization charged with filling the army's ranks. She detects a change in tone in its enlistment campaigns as the war dragged on and as numbers of volunteers diminished, and she asserts that the public did not always ratify the logic expressed in posters. We may confuse the goals of the campaigns with their results. She suggests that posters should be read as "proposed arguments for patriotic behavior," rather than as evidence that viewers accepted those arguments. Indeed, considering how campaigns changed during the course of the war reveals that poster producers were driven to experiment by the knowledge that their work was not a fait accompli. Poster producers continually had to develop ways to reach and persuade their audiences.

This question has its analogs in the other national contexts and campaigns under consideration in the essays. Each contributor brings different questions and evidence to bear upon a particular group of posters. In each case authors go beyond the presentation of images to analyze in detail the roles their selected posters played in the context of the war. They draw upon a wide range of available evidence, considering changes in poster campaigns, archival documents, trade magazines, periodical literature, exhibition catalogs, and the way poster imagery was reframed or challenged in subsequent years. Although the questions and examples vary considerably across the volume, a methodological commitment to contextualization undergirds the whole.

The analysis begins with Jay Winter's polemical claim that "in wartime, images overwhelm words." Winter reiterates his earlier call for a more "rigorous and critical history of the arts in wartime."[35] His current consideration of British recruiting posters, like his previous analysis of French *images d'Epinal*, supports his contention that images have played a special role— more important than that played by text—in the mythologization of the war and thus on the ways we do (and do not yet) understand it today. His point is not merely to impugn the dishonesty of propaganda. In his reckoning, posters often functioned as bona fide representations of people's memories. We may not see them as such precisely because they have become iconic parts of our "mental furniture"; they have been assimilated into our own partial vision of the war. For Winter, only after considering how they have been passed on and received by subsequent generations can we hope to understand how posters may have resonated with viewers in 1914.

The first cluster of essays read posters in comparative national contexts. Nicoletta F. Gullace considers the propagandistic portrayal of Germans as "Huns" in British, Australian, and American posters. Though she traces this imagery to a common source, she notes that depending upon national context, it looked different and meant different things. Viewers would have interpreted images of the barbarian Hun through a nationally specific configuration of racial tension and racial threat. Considering images of the Hun allows Gullace to redraw the world map of 1914–18 and to underscore different perceptions of war aims among allies and between allies and their imperial subjects. The relative brutality of American and Australian Hun imagery over that by the British, for instance, "reflects the difficulty of creating a vivid imperative to fight in countries where there existed no immediate threat." But other British colonial posters, though designed to appeal to similarly distant populations, avoid the brutality aimed at Americans and Australians. Gullace concludes that the depiction of the Hun in racialist terms that drew on negative stereotypes of Asian and African "primitiveness" would have had little appeal in those parts of the empire. Her analysis underscores the internationality of the First World War, in which posters functioned as messages sent from one nation to another and from colonial powers to their imperial outposts. The essay ends with an analysis of Germany's ironic reappropriation of its enemies' Hun imagery during the Second World War.

Stefan Goebel reflects on some of the ironies generated by the international exchange of propaganda posters. Many German posters use the icon of a mailed fist as "a symbol of somber resolve" to solidify their audience. But, as Goebel notes in his essay, that imagery "backfired on the Kaiserreich" when the imagery was transported abroad and viewed by others, who saw it instead a symbol of German barbarism. He concludes that while the same imagery appears across national boundaries, emphasis on "universal" imagery might cause us to miss what is lost in translation or what is deliberately *mis*translated in the context of political hostility.

Jakub Kazecki and Jason Lieblang identify and analyze fundamental differences between American and German posters, grounding their explanations in the two nations' different historical and art historical traditions and political situations. As Goebel does, they emphasize the German poster's recurrent use of an imagined medieval past as a way of consolidating viewers and cloaking the costs of modern warfare. They explain some of the crucial visual differences between German posters and American posters. They argue that the German nation needed past-oriented images of itself. A common history allowed Germans to see themselves as a homogeneous collective. The relatively future-oriented American self-image projected in posters, in contrast, reflected a more heterogeneous collective. And yet, they note, that heterogeneity had its crucial, boundary-defining limits: the American poster portrays comingling across class and gender lines but reinforces a racially hegemonic vision of American citizenship as a white prerogative.

All the essays in part 1 make a strong case for studying images across national contexts in order to understand their appeal. As these contributors take up that compelling claim from Rickards's *Posters of the First World War*, however, they elucidate the very different roles the same imagery plays in different national contexts.

Leaving international comparisons aside, part 2 is focused on singular national imaginaries as they were developed and contested through particular poster campaigns. Although posters were used to give visual coherence to the nation-at-war, they did not project internally uniform visions of given national communities.

Mark Levitch considers a vision of French solidarity elaborated in one particular campaign. These posters, produced by French schoolgirls between the ages of thirteen and sixteen, are unique among French war posters for their bright colors, disorienting perspective, and naive drawing. Levitch attributes their appeal not only to their visual qualities, however, but to the untapped national vitality viewers wanted to see in their creators. By examining evidence from the press, trade magazines, government documents, and exhibition catalogs, Levitch shows that the posters were celebrated both as the spontaneous outpourings of children and as the products of a new industrial arts educational program. The posters were billed as evidence that France was maintaining cultural strength despite the tolls of war.

Levitch argues that the gender of the artists was paramount to the posters' success. In the way their reception was guided and described, the posters were used to signify the strength of French womanhood. The fact that they were produced by girls allowed them to be heralded as "the creations of promising new French artistic blood": a generation of female artists who would survive the war and go on to take new places as women workers in the postwar economy. At the same time, the posters' small scale and domestic subject matter function to contain the threat that might be implied by women workers.

Turning from gender to race, Richard S. Fogarty argues in "Race and Empire in French Posters of the Great War" that war posters were instrumental in consolidating ties of solidarity between citizens of hexagonal France and French colonials. He considers a number of posters that focus on "the contributions of empire, both material and human, to the prosecution of the war. These images sought to reassure the French public that France had overseas support . . . and to remind viewers of the debt of gratitude they owed to the inhabitants of the colonies." Yet he shows that the posters portray colonial subjects in orientalist terms, as "irreducibly alien, primitive, and 'other.'" The posters reflect the "ambiguous status" of colonial troops, who were fighting for the nation but were not recognized as full members of it.

Jennifer D. Keene's "Images of Racial Pride" makes a similar discovery about American posters. She shows that posters illustrate imagined racial lines and were exchanged along and across them. Her research uncovers a debate that took place involving posters designed and produced *by* African Americans and those produced by the Committee on Public Information (CPI) *for* African American soldiers. After situating these little-known poster images within a larger national debate about black enlistment and civil rights, Keene describes how both official and private entities borrowed images from each other and in the process gave them new mottoes and meanings. In her essay, then, new historical research into the facts of poster dissemination emerges in support of an argument that engages larger cultural questions.

Even within a single nation, a given poster's audiences are diverse. Keene illustrates this eloquently in her analysis of the transformation that images of African American soldiers underwent as they were retitled and reframed for different locations and occasions. "Considering how these images were consumed," Keene concludes, "is as important as tracing how and why they were produced. Black and white communities each viewed governmental propaganda through the prism of their respective opinions about changing the racial status quo. The result was often a dramatically altered meaning for official propaganda." The debate taking place through the negotiation, appropriation, and interpretation of poster images "threatened to undo the very unity demanded by official propaganda posters."

The fourth essay in this cluster focuses on how posters functioned in the ongoing construction of Russian national identity. Andrew M. Nedd traces modernist visual motifs of Russian war posters to Russian folk art, demonstrating that some artists sought to reorganize national identity around indigenous and non-Western art forms. Nedd looks at the work of a particular group of artists, published together by the company Segodniashnii Lubok, who imitated the folk art form of the *lubok* in order to appeal to the masses. He situates their wartime work "within the nationalist, anti-Western discourses that artists participated in before the war," revealing the contested nature of Russian national identity as a product of often contradictory values ("high" and "low," "popular" and "official," "native" and "foreign"). The war put pressure on Russians to work together and on Russian propagandists to generate visions of a common—if imagined—Russian identity. The posters Nedd considers united Russians, but only for a time. The war exacerbated the perception of contradictions in Russian society. Using folk imagery to rally the masses to what was increasingly perceived as an imperialist war became less tenable. Nedd traces how the "reception of wartime *lubki* reveals the evolving nature of Russian national identity" on the eve of the Soviet revolution.

Part 3 is an analysis of how posters represent gender and the body. Many scholars have argued that the war fundamentally changed the way people imagined masculinity and femininity.[36] At a concrete level the war disrupted men's lives by mobilizing their labor in new ways, incorporating huge numbers of them into the armed forces, and, in extremis, wounding and killing them. Women's lives, too, changed in concrete ways during the war: they did new kinds of labor and were rewarded, by several combatant nations, with the vote. But as important as these concrete changes were, they need to be understood in relation to changes in how men and women *imagined* themselves as gendered and embodied subjects. Having a male or female body meant something different in 1918 than it had in 1913. A new host of realities and symbolic representations had been brought to bear on bodies during the war. For instance, the presence of wounded veterans made it difficult to ignore how vulnerable male bodies were in an age of industrial war. In the case of women, jobs in labor and the armed forces literally clothed them in new uniforms and in the process invested their labor and their laboring bodies with different significance. The war brought new meaning even to supposedly timeless female roles; for instance, motherhood was reckoned by some as a vital source of national renewal in the face of the war's human costs.[37]

Posters were instruments of these changes, linking the concrete world with the imaginary one. They conveyed information about how men and women could and should contribute to the war. In some cases they pictured men and women in new kinds of uniforms, doing new kinds of labor in new settings. In others they projected old-fashioned ideals to be maintained. But even when posters displayed traditional imagery, their mottoes and logic worked to forge imaginary alliances between individual bodies and the nation as a whole. Posters provided a new visual vocabulary for picturing men and women in relation to each other, the nation, and machines.

In my own essay I examine various contradictory uses of the female figure in American war posters. Women were depicted in a variety of incompatible ways, both to distinguish male participation as more vital to the nation and to invite unprecedented independent female participation. War posters register a profound confusion about women's place in the nation-at-war. But they also used images of femininity in order to negotiate questions that have little to do with women.

Meg Albrinck analyzes the importance of masculinity in British recruitment posters and describes how its depiction changed over time. Like Andrew Nedd, she focuses on the transformation of particular imagery, interpreting the change in one organization's campaigns as a response to public sentiment. When the rhetoric of national honor was no longer enticing, the government campaign moved to a rhetoric of coercion, using strategies suggesting that "the unenlisted man would suffer social embarrassment and personal guilt if he did not serve." This poster campaign sought to manipulate "popular conceptions of masculine duty." It provides an important, if distorted, mirror of what British poster makers projected as ideal masculine behavior.

John M. Kinder examines how American posters and other visual media were used to help soldiers and citizens assimilate one of the highest and enduring costs of the war: physical disability. He explores the gap between the hundreds of thousands of disabled veterans and their images in cultural productions, especially poster art, magazine illustration, and photography. He charts the various uses to which images of male wounds were put, finding that "they were almost always displayed for the consumption of the non-disabled" and used both to encourage and to frighten the public into espousing a range of attitudes toward the war. The bodies of injured veterans, then, were twice conscripted: first physically, and then symbolically.

Kinder's essay brings to a point one of the volume's overarching questions: how close do posters bring their viewers to the war's violence? His answer: not very close. He finds that although posters do make the wounds inflicted in wartime visible, they sanitize injuries and sentimentalize the afflicted soldiers. Posters distance viewers from the realities of wartime injury. His answer reiterates the findings of many contributors, and with them, he interprets the needs that led image makers to censor the war's violence. As Montrose J. Moses put it to his contemporaries in 1918, "rightly, there is reticence about the use of grewsomeness [sic] in posters; nothing should be suggested which would be either sickening or depressing."[38] Such an injunction places severe limitations on what one can show of war's central fact, killing. Posters operate according to the same mimetic principle Marchand identifies with advertising, that of the "Zerrspeigel, a distorting mirror" that enhances, selects, omits, and otherwise idealizes images.[39] Ads provide the public with a view not of the world as it is but as we wish it could be. "Ad creators"—and poster makers—"tried to reflect public aspirations rather than contemporary circumstances, to mirror popular fantasies rather than social realities."[40] This fictionalizing distortion does not render the poster useless as evidence. On the contrary, it means that posters provide windows onto how people imagined the war, how they wanted it to look.

For their part, poster makers often denied this element of distortion and claimed to be presenting factual information— the "realities" of war. A pamphlet issued by the National Committee of Patriotic Societies praised the poster's veracity in unequivocal terms: "The [U.S.] Government, following the example of France and Great Britain—has recently given commissions in the army to a number of artists who have been sent to the front to depict scenes and events which can be authoritatively presented to our people as a means of rousing them to the *realities of war*" (my emphasis).[41] Posters combined concrete reality (such as where to enlist) with fantasy ("Help Stop the Hun") in ways that their viewers might not always have appreciated. Their success in blurring the lines between fact and fantasy undoubtedly contributed both to their success at the time and to the surprising realization that we "still have not fully reckoned" with the war's "hardest truths"—the killing and death at its center.[42] As Jay Winter insists, posters—for all their ephemera—have become the iconic images on which we hang our vision of war.

All the essays in this volume take posters to task as visual evidence in new ways. One way of understanding what they are and what they did is by understanding what they are not, what they did *not* do. They did not show the war's human costs. Richard Fogarty analyzes a French poster that refers to fighting, "but in the most abstract way, avoiding any real evocation of the horrors that war actually entails." Jennifer Keene finds that "for all their radicalism on racial matters," privately produced African American posters "retained an inherently conservative perspective on the actual war" and "never departed from the storyline of official propaganda posters that portrayed the war as one in which individual soldiers could make a difference on the battlefield." Andrew Nedd's Russian posters depict "particularly violent acts" but do so in a humorous mode and set them in a mythic space, "reducing war to a kind of play." Albrinck's analysis of gender in British posters mirrors my American findings: they contain the war's violence through gendered imagery in which women seem vulnerable to attacks by the enemy and need to be defended by men, who seem relatively more secure. Once again, we are confronted with the Janus-faced nature of the poster medium: modern in its ability to reach a mass public but thoroughly old-fashioned in that, in Keene's words, it "avoided challenging viewers to reconsider what warfare entailed in the twentieth century."

In his epilogue Jeffrey T. Schnapp elaborates on the poster's myth-making role and contextualizes that role within the larger media landscape of World War I. He synthesizes the concerns and questions raised throughout *Picture This*. His evocation of the political poster's longer historical trajectory allows us to appreciate how exceptional World War I was, as a moment when the poster was widely displayed far beyond its traditionally urban milieu. As his meditation suggests, we have not exhausted the questions posters raise. Far from it. Instead, we hope these essays will provoke further engagement with these crucial if ephemeral texts.

Notes

1. Paul Fussell, *The Great War and Modern Memory* (Oxford: Oxford University Press, 1975), 23.

2. Susan Sontag, "Introduction" to Douglas Stermer, *The Art of Revolution: Castro's Cuba 1959–1970* (New York: McGraw Hill, 1970), n.p.

3. Steve Baker, "Describing Images of the National Self: Popular Accounts of the Construction of Pictorial Identity in the First World War Poster," *Oxford Art Journal* 13, no. 2 (1990): 24–30, quote from 24.

4. See Maurice Rickards, *Posters of the First World War* (New York: Walker and Company, 1968); Joseph Darracott, *The First World War in Posters from the Imperial War Museum, London* (New York: Dover, 1974); Peter Paret, Beth Irwin Lewis, and Paul Paret, eds., *Persuasive Images: Posters of the War and Revolution from the Hoover Institution Archives* (Princeton: Princeton University Press, 1992); Peter Stanley, ed., *What Did You Do in the War, Daddy? A Visual History of Propaganda Posters* (Oxford: Oxford University Press, 1983); Libby Chenault, *Battlelines: World War I Posters from the Bowman Gray Collection* (Chapel Hill NC: University of North Carolina, 1988); Rémy Paillard, *Affiches 14–18* (Paris: Rémy Paillard, 1986); Walton H. Rawls, *Wake Up, America! World War I and the American Poster* (New York: Abbeville Press, 1988); James Aulich, *War Posters: Weapons of Mass Communication* (New York: Thames and Hudson, 2007); and James Aulich and John Hewitt, *Seduction or Instruction? First World War Posters in Britain and Europe* (Manchester: Manchester University Press, 2007).

5. Two of the largest poster collections are in the process of being fully digitized and can be searched online: see Britain's Imperial War Museum, http://www.iwm.org.uk/; and the Hoover Institution at Stanford University, specifically their Political Poster Collection, http://www.hoover.org/hila/collections/. Other valuable online resources include Historial de la Grand Guerre/Museum of the Great War (Perone, France), http://www.historial.org/; Emory University's Great War 1914–1918, http://beck.library.emory.edu/greatwar/, which has scanned hundreds of World War I postcards; the U.S. National Archives Collection at http://www.archives.gov/research/arc/topics/ww1/; and the University of North Carolina's Documenting the South: North Carolinians and the Great War, http://docsouth.unc.edu/wwi/.

6. Alain Weill, *The Poster: A Worldwide Survey and History* (Boston: G. K. Hall, 1985), chaps. 2, 3, and 4, quotes from p. 50. For an account of the poster's development in Germany, see Jeremy Aynsley, *Graphic Design in Germany 1890–1945* (Berkeley: University of California Press, 2000).

7. For an account of the London poster controversy, see John Hewitt, "Poster Nasties: Censorship and the Victorian Theatre Poster," in *Visual Delights: Essays on the Popular and Projected Image in the Nineteenth Century*, ed. S. Popple and V. Toulmin (Trowbridge, U.K.: Flicks Books, 2000): 154–69.

8. Rickards, *Posters of the First World War*, 8.

9. David Crowley, "The Propaganda Poster," in *Power of the Poster*, ed. Margaret

PEARL JAMES

Timmers (London: Victoria and Albert Publications, 1998), 100–147, quote from 114.

10. "Poster Advertising and the Liberty Loan Campaigns," in *The Poster: War Souvenir Edition* (Chicago: Poster Advertising Association, 1919), 10.

11. See Jay Winter, "Propaganda and the Mobilization of Consent," in *Oxford Illustrated History of the First World War*, ed. Hew Strachen (Oxford and New York: Oxford University Press, 1998), 216–26.

12. On the situation in England, see Aulich and Hewitt, *Seduction or Instruction?*; on Germany, see David Welch, *Germany, Propaganda and Total War, 1914–1918* (New Brunswick: Rutgers University Press, 2000).

13. Aulich and Hewitt, *Seduction or Instruction?* 2.

14. W. J. T. Mitchell, "Visual Literacy or Literary Visualcy?" in *Visual Literacy*, ed. James Elkins (New York: Routledge, 2008), 11–29, quote from 16.

15. Aulich and Hewitt, *Seduction or Instruction?* 98.

16. Sontag, "Introduction," n.p.

17. Jeannette Keith, *Rich Man's War, Poor Man's Fight: Race, Class, and Power in the Rural South during the First World War* (Chapel Hill: University of North Carolina Press, 2004), 5, 7.

18. Sontag, "Introduction," n.p.

19. This image is held in the collection of the Food Administration, CN-1699, National Archives. It appears in Pearl James, "History and Masculinity in F. Scott Fitzgerald's *This Side of Paradise*," *Modern Fiction Studies* 51, no. 1 (Spring 2005): 8.

20. Martin Hardie and Arthur K. Sabin, *War Posters Issued by Belligerent and Neutral Nations 1914–1919* (London: A & C Black, 1920), 4–5.

21. See Aulich and Hewitt, *Seduction or Instruction?* chap. 1, "War Publicity, Posters, and the Imperial War Museum," 11–33.

22. Liberty Memorial Association, Minutes, 1920. Liberty Memorial Archive, Kansas City, Missouri.

23. Roland Marchand, *Advertising the American Dream: Making Way for Modernity, 1920–1940* (Berkeley: University of California Press, 1985), xvi.

24. On "post hoc reasoning" see O. W. Riegel, "Introduction," in *Posters of World War I and World War II in the George C. Marshall Research Foundation*, ed. Anthony R. Crawford (Charlottesville: University Press of Virginia, 1979), 13.

25. Carlo Ginzburg, "'Your Country Needs You': A Case Study in Political Iconography," *History Workshop Journal* 52 (2001): 1–22, quote from 12.

26. Nicholas Hiley, "'Kitchener Wants You' and 'Daddy, What Did You Do in the Great War?': The Myth of British Recruiting Posters," *Imperial War Museum Review* 11 (1997): 40–58, quotes from 53.

27. Philip Dutton, "Moving Images? The Parliamentary Recruiting Committee's Poster Campaign, 1914–1916," *Imperial War Museum Review* 4 (1989): 43–58, quote from 55–56.

28. Rickards, *Posters of the First World War*, 8–9.

29. Maurice Rickards, "Foreword," in Walton H. Rawls, *Wake Up, America!* 9.

30. Rickards, "Foreword," 9.

31. Matlock Price and Horace Brown, *"How to Put in Patriotic Posters the Stuff That Makes People Stop—Look—Act!"* (Washington DC: National Committee of Patriotic Societies, n.d., ca. 1917–18), 7.

32. Price and Brown, *Patriotic Posters*, 2.

33. Crowley, "The Propaganda Poster," 106.

34. Sontag, "Introduction," n.p.

35. See Jay Winter, "Nationalism, the Visual Arts, and the Myth of War Enthusiasm in 1914," *History of European Ideas* 15 (1992): 357–362, quote from 359.

36. On how the war influenced women's lives and femininity, see, for instance, Sandra M. Gilbert and Susan Gubar, *No Man's Land: The Place of the Woman Writer in the Twentieth Century*, 3 vols. (New Haven CT: Yale University Press, 1988); Margaret Randolph Higonnet, Sonia Michael, Jane Jensen, and Margaret Collins Weitz, eds., *Behind the Lines: Gender and the Two World Wars* (New Haven CT: Yale University Press, 1987); and Susan R. Grayzel, *Women's Identities at War: Gender, Motherhood, and Politics in Britain and France during the First World War* (Chapel Hill: University of North Carolina Press, 1999). On masculinity, see especially George Mosse, *Nationalism and Sexuality: Respectability and Abnormal Sexuality in Modern Europe* (New York: H. Fertig, 1985); Klaus Theweileit, *Male Fantasies*, 2 vols., translated by Stephan Conway in collaboration with Erica Carter and Chris Turner (Minneapolis: University of Minnesota Press, 1987); and Joanna Bourke, *Dismembering the Male: Men's Bodies, Britain, and the Great War* (Chicago: University of Chicago Press, 1996). On both masculinity and femininity in Britain, see Nicoletta F. Gullace, *"The Blood of Our Sons": Men, Women, and the Renegotiation of British Citizenship during the Great War* (New York: Palgrave Macmillan, 2002).

37. On motherhood, see especially Jennifer Haytock, *At Home, at War: Domesticity and World War I in American Literature* (Columbus: Ohio State University Press, 2003); and Susan Roberts, *Civilization without Sexes: Reconstructing Gender in Postwar France, 1917–1927* (Chicago: University of Chicago Press, 1994).

38. Montrose J. Moses, "Making Posters Fight," *Bookman* 47, no. 5 (1918): 504–12, quote from 509.

39. Marchand, *Advertising the American Dream*, xvii.

40. Marchand, *Advertising the American Dream*, xvii.

41. Price and Brown, *Patriotic Posters*, 6.

42. Stéphane Audoin-Rouzeau and Annette Becker, "Violence et consentement: La 'culture de guerre' du premier conflit mondial," in *Pour une histoire culturelle*, ed. Jean-Pierre Rioux and Jean-François Sirinelli (Paris: Seuil, 1997), 251–71. My translation, from 257.

Imaginings of War: Posters and the Shadow of the Lost Generation

L et me open this set of reflections on images of war with the assumption that what people see affects them more than what they read. In wartime, images overwhelm words. This simple fact dominated the most powerful and widely disseminated propaganda campaign to date, elements of which are preserved in collections of poster art in different parts of the world.

Collections of World War I posters provide a window onto a world that has largely vanished, but it has left behind so many iconic images that when we see them, we conjure up an entire set of representations of war. It is these that frame what Samuel Hynes has called our "war in the head," our mental furniture on which perch our images of war. These images are not memories—we were not there—but they are representations of the memories of others who were there. Many of those who designed posters brought to the task personal experiences and recollections. Many of those who viewed them during the war certainly linked them to memories of a personal kind. Now all we have are the traces of those memories, fixed onto canvas and paper, deposited in libraries and archives from the Hoover Institution in Stanford to the Bibliothek für Zeitgeschichte in Stuttgart and beyond. They conjure up second-order memories, our understandings of how the men and women of the Great War imagined and remembered the upheaval through which they lived.

Like all representations, posters have a life history. Their meanings are never fixed for all time. I want to offer an interpretation of some of these documents first in terms of a semiotics of solidarity. Posters were, I believe, a reflection rather than a cause of national unity in the First World War. I then describe a number of other ways in which societies at war, civilians and soldiers alike, imagined war, conjured up its dimensions and texture, and by and large justified its continuation, despite casualty levels the world had never seen before. Given the rich trove of images we find in World War I posters, I want to turn to a puzzling question. What happened to this grammar of consent in subsequent years and decades? Why, in the Second World War, were such images generally absent from poster art or indeed from broader imaginings of war? I propose an answer to this question, and thereby conclude that many poster images help us see aspects of the disenchantment of the twentieth century—the progressive retreat from these representations of war and warriors into more complex and compromised images. And this is not even to broach the topic of what images of Auschwitz and Hiroshima did to representations of war. In sum, what we of a later generation are left with is a mixed and shifting landscape of imaginings of war: some still heroic, others negative, troubled, unresolved, unsettled. And so it is bound to be, since that moral conundrum—how to imagine war without glorifying it—is with us still.

Social Representations of War before 1914

Posters are social representations of combat, combatants, and causes. As such in Britain they drew upon popular ideas of combat in a country with a formidable naval tradition but nothing remotely resembling what on the Continent is called "militarism." Militarism is the elevation and celebration of military virtues and values as admirable principles of national life. Generals on horseback stride across Europe throughout the nineteenth century and beyond, but they had virtually no place in British political culture in 1914.

Militarism was alive in British culture, though not primarily in Britain. The scarcely veiled iron fist of British power was evident in India, in Egypt, and, though battered by a relatively small force of Boer farmers, in South Africa. British power was a force of repression closer to home, too. In Dublin, the second city of the British Empire, the British Army was a force resented by a small but stubborn Republican movement. When Home Rule for Ireland became a real possibility, Protestants in the British Army made their displeasure known, but as usual, what applied to Ireland had little bearing on popular attitudes in mainland Britain. Ireland was always a world apart. And no one in Britain clamored for the army to clean up the stables of domestic politics as in Germany; no one in Britain juxtaposed the honor of the army to the right of an individual to justice, as in the France of the Dreyfus affair.

Militarism, if it existed at all in pre-1914 Britain, was isolated in small pockets of conservative thinking, voiced in London clubs or Oxford common rooms filled with pessimists gloomy about cities, about the working class, about everything that had happened since the industrial revolution. Such reactionaries wanted nothing of the twentieth century, and a reverie for Wellington and the armies that defeated Napoleon took the place of systematic political thinking.

The voice of Empire, though, was not at all unknown in prewar Britain. It was there in virtually every household that had a volume of Kipling on the shelves. Here was the source of many pre-1914 representations of warfare. In this quintessentially

Victorian rhetoric, combat had distinctly positive and gendered attributes: it was individual, heroic, and intensely masculine. This mixture is what gives Kipling's powerful poem "Gunga Din" its force as a distillate of military values. Riddled with bullets while warning through his trumpet of a sneak attack on a British garrison in India, Gunga Din earned the respect—indeed, the love—of his British superiors: "Though I've belted you and flayed you / By the living God that made you / You're a better man than I am Gunga Din."

Such notions about heroism and war were at the core of images of masculinity.[1] This linkage was evident in one extraordinary public display of mourning for fallen heroes before 1914. It followed the failure of Commander Scott's expedition to the South Pole and the death of Scott's team in 1913.[2] They had waged war on the Antarctic, and the elements had won. Through their effort the imperial assignment was sanctified. The Royal Geographical Society sponsored the voyage. The society chairman, Lord Curzon, formerly viceroy of India, affirmed that exploration was an imperial duty. It was a task British men had to do.

The fact that Scott's mission was a failure did not diminish its glory. The story was one of masculinity confirmed. You may recall the team seeing that they were not the first to arrive at the Pole. On the way back they were trapped in a snow storm, with no chance of escape and little hope of rescue. One of the team, Captain Oates, a good Cambridge man, was ill. He decided one morning to take a walk in the snow. He never returned. And then there was Scott himself—writing painfully with frozen fingers in his last letter, begging that something be done to provide for the families of the men who were dying. Here were the quintessential warriors before the war. They embodied what being a man entailed: stoicism, individual initiative, an acceptance of hardship—even death—without complaint.

I have often wondered about the uncanny flowering of these notions of heroism and sacrifice just months before the Great War broke out and gave them a terrible new meaning.

Wartime Imaginings of War

Poster art froze these representations in time and space. And necessarily so, since they provided the only mental furniture available to conjure up what war would be like. The revolutionary character of industrialized warfare was unanticipated by virtually everyone in Europe in 1914. The precedent of the United States Civil War was ignored, like most features of American developments, as no guide whatsoever to European affairs. Consequently, in September 1914, when the German invasion of France was stopped at the Battle of the Marne and the invaders dug in on the River Aisne, fifty kilometers to the north, and when the stalemate we now call the Western Front set in, older languages of heroic warfare, of individual combat and derring-do, were bound to flourish.

In Britain these images were no more unreal than elsewhere, but they had a different utility. Between August 1914 and January 1915, one million men volunteered for the army. Two million more joined up in 1915. All the other major combatants had conscript armies; men came forward by law or by convention, but in Britain a mass army was raised by consent.

Poster art helped bring them forward, but my view is that they would have come forth anyway. At this distance in time it is hard to see why the consensus was so strong that the war was just and had to be fought to the bitter end. Pacifists tried to batter at this consensus but got nowhere. The wall of support for the war was simply too solid.

What were its chief elements? On one level, the cause highlighted in posters was that of "poor little Belgium" and the sanctity of treaties; Britain was drawn into a war not of her own making and was fighting for "Right." These issues mattered intrinsically, but their power derived from the fact that they revealed a deeper and more immediate danger, one closer to home. That threat to Britain was German power, thrust into France and Belgium and soon camped on the shores of the English Channel itself. Posters such as "Your Country's Call" had little difficulty in pointing this out (fig. 7). Here was a clear and present danger to what contemporaries saw as the British way of life, a very local way of life, a life of pubs and clubs and a host of associations drawing people to activities of an astonishing diversity. Now in 1914 the strongest army in the world, the German Army, was at the gates. It was challenging a nation whose inhabitants unthinkingly believed that theirs was the preeminent world power, the envy of what Charles Dickens had called "Lesser Nations." In light of this threat, and in response both to the harshness of the treatment of Belgian civilians and to the high casualties among the professional army and the volunteers who served in the Territorial forces, public opinion in Britain was united behind the war effort (fig. 8). This was the milieu in which one million British men volunteered for military service in 1914 alone. Posters reflected an already existing and powerful consensus: they illustrated but did not manufacture consent.

National pride drew men to the colors in 1914, but so did a sense that the "nation" was a very local place (fig. 9). Popular culture—understood as the codes, gestures, and forms of voluntary associations, elaborated not through the state but in civil society and through the market—expressed these sentiments, and a host of entrepreneurs sold artifacts, songs, images, and entertainments that transmitted them.

This was where cultural codes and commercial strategies came together. Artists, actors, comedians, minstrels, and a host of others spoke to and for civil society in Britain. The state did

Fig. 7. Anonymous, "Your Country's Call," April 1915. A Scottish soldier gestures toward a bucolic image of village life, threatened by the menace of Germany. Political Poster collection, UK 218, Hoover Institution Archives.

not orchestrate their words or work or treat these people like puppets. And once millions of men had joined up, the armed forces drew on the same vibrant cultural life shared by their families at home. Posters and other wartime images are windows onto this world of thinking about war: they are signs of solidarity, not carriers of compulsion.

There is an important distinction to draw between recruiting posters and other forms of patriotic iconography. As Jim Aulich has argued, the poster art of the Great War broadcast one set of images of Britain at war. The advertising industry used other images and other inflections to sell both the war and the products their patrons paid them to sell.[3]

Fig. 8. Anonymous, "Remember Belgium," 1914. A woman and child fleeing from a village on fire show why men worthy of the name will join up to protect their families in England from a similar fate. Political Poster collection, UK 219, Hoover Institution Archives.

Here we can see a division of labor, informally set, between the recruiting campaign of 1914–16, which abjured class inflections, and the advertising campaign throughout the war, which celebrated them. When Oxo or Bovril or Mrs. Payne's remedies for whatever ailed you needed a plug, a group of enlisted men or working men and women provided the ideal forms and figures to get the message across. Thus the stylized classlessness of one form of wartime propaganda embedded in the recruiting campaign of the first half of the war must not be taken as proof that wartime images as a whole were innocent of the inequalities everyone lived with at the time. On the contrary, advertising naturalized the war by placing everyday commodities in wartime settings. Here are working-class faces

IS **YOUR** HOME
WORTH FIGHTING FOR?

IT WILL BE TOO LATE TO FIGHT
WHEN THE ENEMY IS AT YOUR DOOR
so JOIN TO·DAY

Fig. 9. Anonymous, "Is *your* home worth fighting for?" July 1915. A rallying call urges volunteers to reflect on the violation of domestic life by German brutality in France and Belgium. Political Poster collection, UK 515, Hoover Institution Archives.

and figures, in a society in which 80 percent of the population earned their living through manual labor. Ads used what Aulich terms the "vulgar modes of direct address" to make visual the local environment for which British men were fighting.

Given the shortage of paper in wartime, ads distilled a message both simplified and innocent. The war was naturalized, a part of everyday life, and fighting and winning it were naturalized too. There was no room here for the 'faux classical' diction of elite culture. Alongside the classless images of British recruitment, there were other ways to visualize what British men were fighting for. In the popular press most of these icons referred directly to the domestic sphere of working-class life, those peculiarities and idiosyncrasies of ordinariness that brought home to millions what being British was all about.

Front and Home Front

The second level on which to understand the meaning contemporaries attached to or derived from poster images is in terms of the maintenance of ties between front and home front. These works were not produced as accurate or realistic images but rather as visual codes of solidarity.

Historians are coming increasingly to the view that what kept the Great War going for so long was not just a rough balance of material power but also a rough balance between front and home front. That is, the reason men put up with the harsh conditions of military life was their love of their families, their towns, the simple rhythms of their way of life. Again "Your Country's Call" provides a case in point. Posters were small "snapshots" of these affiliations; they preserved elements of the prewar world soldiers had gone off to defend, each in his own way.

These posters had counterparts on the stage and in song. To some soldiers, music hall, popular songs, and theatrical displays were like ambulant posters. They did tend to trivialize the war and the hardships men faced at the front. But millions of other soldiers knew why they fought in part because their instinctive loyalties were touched by the sentimentalities of these voices and images. The message they took from songs and posters was clear. They could (and did) put up with the awfulness of trench warfare in part because of their commitment to the world they had left behind, a world conjured up in vivid terms by popular entertainments and in shorthand by poster art.

Here is the key to the history of popular culture in wartime Britain and among that part of the nation in action on the

Continent. A civilian army brought its civilian entertainments with it.[4] Music hall entertainments celebrated a code of ordinary life reminding soldiers that they were in uniform only "in parentheses," as it were.[5] In song and stylized stage buffoonery millions of soldiers saw the "before" and dreamed of the "after." Posters did the same; they were advertisements of continuity. The vast majority believed that this period in uniform was a hiatus in their lives, a period with a clear end: victory and demobilization. Defeat hardly entered their minds.[6] After the war they would return and resume the course of their lives. These men in effect never left home; they brought it with them in their imagination as cultural baggage that saw most of them through the worst of what they had to face.

From this perspective, prewar images of war were not discredited by the conflict as long as the war went on. Those prewar notions about combat and combatants were allusive rather than accurate. "Your Country's Call," with its picturesque hamlet and its landscape dotted with English cattle, illustrates, as many posters did, a *stylized* world, an *idealized* world, one remote from the trenches; one soldiers believed they were fighting to preserve.

Images of War in Cinema

Sooner or later ambivalence would replace acceptance as the dominant motif within representations of war. We can see this process beginning to unfold during the war itself. Cinema was the premier form of popular entertainment in wartime. It also had the capacity to capture the "reality" of the momentous events occurring just across the English Channel.

This power of verisimilitude lay behind the creation of one of the first film documentaries ever made. Remarkably, it was produced and aired during the Battle of the Somme, which lasted miserably from July 1 to November 30, 1916, and in which over one million men died while the line effectively moved not at all.

In London in September 1916 the filmic *Battle of the Somme* premiered while the real Battle of the Somme was still under way. Filmed at times under great personal risk by two cameramen, G. H. Malins and J. B. McDowell, *The Battle of the Somme* gave home audiences an unprecedented chance to see their troops in action. Intended as a morale booster, this pioneering film was a mixture of real and recreated events. Perhaps the most famous image of the war, showing soldiers going over the top and then disappearing into the fog of war, can be found in this film. It was staged.

Not that film goers knew—or cared—at the time. Audiences turned out by the hundreds of thousands, riveted by images on the screen that would be considered quite tame today. "I really thought that some of the dead scenes would offend the British public," confessed Malins. Theatre operators showing it questioned whether women should be submitted to the "actual horrors of warfare." One theatre manager refused to show the film altogether, declaring: "This is a place of amusement, not a chamber of horrors." While the film avoided the gruesome realities of the war, for people with little direct knowledge of the violence and vast scale of modern war it was as close a glimpse as they would ever get, and the film brought them out in droves, playing to thirty film theatres in London alone. "It was not a cheerful sight," another film goer wrote, "but it does give a wonderful idea of the fighting." In one London cinema the orchestra stopped playing when the subtitle announced "The Attack." One woman in the audience could not help screaming out, "Oh God, they're dead!" In the fall of 1916 the film ended its run, having been seen by an estimated twenty million people.[7] It was the most successful British film of all time. Perhaps half the population saw it in six weeks. Nothing before or since has matched it.

This film contains evidence of a critical change in the cultural history of the war. Until the Battle of the Somme, the British volunteer armies had formed and trained against the backdrop of conventional notions of the nature of war. After 1916 those representations of war began to fragment. This is one among a number of reasons why it is fair to say that Britain has never recovered from that battle. It is not only the lives thrown away but also the sense that something else was lost; something located in the symbolic universe those soldiers brought with them, which was blown apart and scattered in the wet soil of Picardy.

This loss of bearings about what war was did not occur at once, and not without countermovements shoring up older attitudes. Here the commercial film industry managed to undo some of the damage to heroic representations of war that documentary film had caused.

By the middle of the war the film industry emerged as the most important vehicle for projecting the meaning of the war as a struggle of Good against Evil. This cinematic effort took many forms, from comedy to melodrama to tragedy. Much of this film output was neither inspired nor organized through governments, though state funding was frequently involved. To be sure, the censor was active; but here again the private sector took the lead. On the screen, kitsch and popular entertainments came into their own, broadcasting messages with evident mass appeal about the Virtues of one side and the Villainy of the other. Music hall, melodrama, and the gramophone industry all chipped in, selling (at a profit) anodyne or uplifting images and songs to increasingly fatigued, anxious, and irritable populations.

No wonder film was so popular during the war. It satisfied

longings for the mundane at an extraordinary moment: it lampooned the dreariness of military life, and it added a large dose of outrage directed against the source of all the troubles—the enemy.

It is evident that the collision of representations of war began before the Armistice. As we have seen, the outlines of prewar notions about war began to change while the war went on. The film *The Battle of the Somme* was screened to intense public interest in what war was like. There was much more information available on the home front about combat and the awful conditions in the trenches than historians have hitherto assumed. There was the telephone; there were letters, irregularly censored to be sure, but filled with more than just Kipling-esque bravado. There were photographs. Many of these were taken without supervision and in remote corners of the war. They show the odd juxtaposition of the mundane and the bizarre—images of what Samuel Hynes has called "Battlefield Gothic." And if the telephone, letters, and photographs did not do the trick, there were the wounded, scattered throughout the country, convalescent images in their own right of the fact that war was no longer a contest between individuals, nor was it adventurous, nor even a test of masculinity. It had become very different from what contemporaries had been illustrating just a few short years before.

To return to the statement with which I began, that the visual mattered more than the written in wartime culture: there was a hidden advantage in this preference for images. Written propaganda was much more tied to a language riddled with assumptions about social class. The visual touched on these but frequently superseded them. When soldiers were shown, they were usually men in the ranks. A largely working-class army was represented not by its middle-class officers but by its working-class privates. Representations of home front work, though, had many more associations with class position. Appealing for women to do their bit by entering war factories thus described an innovation for middle-class women but a much simpler shift along the spectrum of manual labor for working-class women. By and large this meant that appeals on behalf of the army emphasized the classless character of the forces; appeals for solidarity at home were less universal. But whether directed at identifying the cause abroad or at home, visual propaganda escaped from much of the high-minded snobbery that riddled the countless pamphlets and sermons written on behalf of the Allied war effort. The written language brought out social class differences in a way that visual imagery usually managed to evade.

Postwar Representations

I have tried to identify the meaning and symbolic function of posters in terms of the ongoing engagement of front and home front in wartime. A question arises about the fate of these representations once the Armistice had been signed and demobilization had begun.

To find an answer to this question we need to elaborate a range of ambivalent wartime representations of the nature of war. Soldiers and their families accepted a prewar notation to describe the harsh conditions of their lives in part because they had no other choice. In wartime representations there endured prewar elements that soldiers recognized perfectly well as stylized and inadequate but that they did not succeed in either purging or transforming. The exceptions were the war poets, but their words were known to only a handful of people.

Once the war was over and the reckoning had come, there was little reason left to justify perpetuation of a code when its usefulness had come to an end. That is one reason why war poetry became iconic in the interwar period. It was the effort of men who tried to liberate language from the wartime codes that had constrained it during the conflict.

"Have we forgotten yet?" Siegfried Sassoon asked readers of his poetry as early as 1919. I wonder. But in part because of war poetry, our common ordinary language has not forgotten; our everyday speech carries traces of the Great War in a myriad of ways—"some desperate lie"; "the old lie"; "the bloody game." How far we have come from prewar representations of what John Keegan has called the face of battle.

Postwar Imaginings

It is important to recognize that alongside such subversive imaginings of war, there were others that preserved "the old lie" and affirmed that it was still an old truth. The long-term effect of the Great War on representations of combat is best conveyed not by pacifism or irony but by ambivalence. This ambivalence made it impossible for the notation of wartime posters to be used in the same way again. But elements of that code of solidarity never fully vanished.

This specifically British point of view is different from that evident in France and Germany after the war. In all three countries there were common elements. Here is French historian Antoine Prost's commentary on the subject of representations of war in postwar France:

> In the new representation of combat, death takes pride of place. Prior representations never denied the possibility of death in combat, but one did not dwell on it. After 1918, death is at the core of representations: the objective, even the very definition of combat. To make war is not to capture prisoners, take cities, conquer territory; it is to kill and to be killed. The semantic landscape is arranged around terms such as: "killing," "butchery," "carnage," "bloody horror." This set of representations is in war memoirs, in

soldiers' stories, in war memorials and in the ceremonies on 11 November, culminating in a vast funerary cult and pilgrimages to war graves cemeteries at the front.[8]

This was bound to affect the image of the soldier too. "To boast about his courage, his initiative, is to praise death," writes Prost. "His bravery, his tenacity, his sacrifice are not denied, but what war does, without his knowing it, is to insert inhuman instincts within these very qualities." The soldier is a death-giver, an agent of slaughter, *par excellence.*[9]

It is but a short step, Prost argues, from this kind of representation of war to a kind of paralysis. War must never happen again, French veterans said, because it is inhuman; but when in the 1930s war clouds returned, the likelihood of war was both recognized and rejected. That the phrase "entre-deux-guerres" was used so easily in the 1930s gives it away. War must not come, and yet war was coming. Is it at all surprising that successive French governments, and the electorate that put them in power, failed to prepare for war and failed to stand the course when it came? Representations of war had turned so negative that preparing for a war and fighting one became virtually impossible.

It is obvious that such a construction of representations of war had no purchase in postwar Germany. Militarism survived the transition to democracy, and disgruntled veterans provided the core of a movement that toppled the Weimar Republic in 1933. But what about Britain? Its political culture was remote both from that dominated by the pacifist veterans of France and that dominated by the bellicose veterans of Germany.

Instead of "never again" or "Germany arise"—representations of war with enormous significance in France and Germany—a different set of notions about war have dominated British cultural life. The term *Lost Generation* captures the British way of recasting nineteenth-century representations of war in a twentieth-century context.

One way to understand the images in poster art is to see them as symbols of a Lost Generation. That term has taken on a meaning at the heart of British notions of national identity in the twentieth century. The phrase has a life history, which opened in the war years and was then enshrined in commemorative ceremonies throughout Britain in the decade after the Armistice. Over time the term has wound up in normal language, in the notions that schoolchildren pick up from clichés, from comedy, from many sources obscure and mundane, about what being British means. In other words, different generations have constructed their own Lost Generation of the Great War from a set of icons that have changed over time but that still bear some resemblance to images drawn and painted and sculpted in wartime.

By attending to these cultural configurations, we can understand much about how in Britain, the 1914–18 conflict was converted from a victory into a disaster or, more precisely, into the iconic debacle of the twentieth century. Pre-1914 representations of war faded away, just as Britain's standing as a world power has faded too.

To be sure, the term *Lost Generation* describes something particular, something inescapably linked to the personal tragedies of three-quarters of a million truncated lives. But it is important to recall the second level I have evoked, a level on which the term operated powerfully in the two postwar decades. It was a phrase at first associated with the commemoration of the victory these men had paid for with their lives, with the obligation the living owed to the dead, and with the need for some kind of symbolic exchange to mark that irredeemable debt. Soon enough, though, the term took on a bitter taste, linked to the disappointments of the survivors as to the kind of world they had fashioned after 1918. What was lost to this generation was hope, the sense that history was moving forward to something better, the sense of a brighter future. The interwar depression and the renewal of international conflict in the 1930s put paid to such aspirations. By then the question had become: for what, if anything, did the Lost Generation die? This use of the term *Lost Generation* suggests a lack of closure, an unhealed wound in the survivors, a betrayal of trust between the living and the dead, an unbuilt future for their children. Here the second cluster of meanings of the term emerges, locating it in the divided, embittered postwar history of those who survived the war.

Paul Fussell and Samuel Hynes have captured this ironic turn in the remembrance of the Lost Generation. Both have spoken not only of monuments but of antimonuments, of the literary and visual forms through which the war was remembered. What marks these works is a sense of anger, of the betrayal of the young by the old, who sent young men off to fight and who stayed on to ruin the postwar world. Fussell has privileged the term *irony* as the emblem of this literary moment, when millions entered the long wartime journey from anticipation to outcome, from innocence to experience, from beauty and hope to ugliness and disillusionment. In the memoirs of Graves, Sassoon, Blunden, Mottram, and Ford, and in the poetry of Owen, Rosenberg, Sorley, and Gurney, this ironic vision has been preserved as the property of the nation as a whole. Through them it has become much more than a British vision; it is one we all share.[10]

There is a third level of usage for the term *Lost Generation*, which brings us to more recent times and adds one more dimension to what we glimpse in British posters from the Great War. On this third level the term moves away from the initial stages of mourning, and from the tone of postwar disillusionment, to take on a more general, metaphoric coloration. The *Lost Generation* is a term that has enabled people born long after the conflict to see the Great War as the moment when grand narratives broke down, when—in the words of the comic classic *1066 and All That*—history came "to a full stop."[11]

The sting in the tail of the joke should not be missed. Yes, the authors were having fun with the tendency of school textbooks to grind to a screeching halt in 1914, for purposes of convenience alone. But the authors of this parody—themselves veterans of the Great War—have disclosed something else about British cultural history. They suggest that what matters most about a nation's past is often concealed in its humor. And here it is a very special kind of gallows humor that has entered the language of everyday life, in the form of a set of jokes about insane generals, sardonic officers, and trapped infantrymen going over the top. Everyone growing up in England in the 1990s knew this scene—immortalized in the BBC comedy series *Blackadder.*

Why does it matter? Because it takes a tragic use of the term the *Lost Generation,* located in collective mourning earlier in the twentieth century, and turns it into an emblem of a shared catastrophe that defines what it means to be British in the later twentieth century, an emblem in the form of paper poppies that people wear in their lapels for a few days in November every year. This elision brings the loss of life in 1914–18 into contact with the loss of power and national independence in recent decades. The early disaster somehow stands for what was to come after. What Samuel Hynes has called the "myth" of the war—its narrative character—has thus become the myth of the decline of Britain in this century as a whole.

The late British poet laureate Ted Hughes once remarked that growing up in interwar Britain, he developed a sense that the Great War was a defeat around whose neck someone had stuck a victory medal. This captures much about the transformation of representations of war and warriors in the aftermath of the 1914–18 conflict.

"The true picture of the past flits by," wrote Walter Benjamin. "The past can be seized only as an image which flashes up at the instant when it can be recognized and is never seen again."[12] The poster art of the First World War discloses this landscape of art and ideas, a cultural landscape with much to commend it, but one that, like the small-scale world of social solidarities it celebrated, has virtually vanished from sight.

What remain are the language and the images of those unlucky men and women whose lives were indelibly marked by the Great War. What we make of them matters. They are traces of a world both very remote and very familiar. Even today we live with these images. In an almost automatic, semiconscious manner, the way we look at contemporary events returns over and over again to the war that defined the century and to the visual documents it left behind. Their power and their sadness makes me wonder whether we too form a part of the Lost Generation, a part of that vast population of men and women whose lives have been lived and whose imaginations have been formed, whether we like it or not, whether we admit it or not, in the darkening shadows of war.

Notes

1. George Mosse, *Nationalism and Masculinity* (New York: Howard Fertig, 1992).

2. For the full story, see Max Jones, *The Last Great Quest: Captain Scott's Antarctic Sacrifice* (Oxford: Oxford University Press, 2003).

3. James Aulich and John Hewitt, *Seduction or Instruction? First World War Posters in Britain and Europe* (Manchester: Manchester University Press, 2007); and Jim Aulich, "Advertising in Britain during the First World War," Canterbury conference on Justifying War, July 2008.

4. John Fuller, *Troop Morale and Trench Journalism among British and Dominion Forces in the First World War* (Oxford: Oxford University Press, 1990); and

Susan Grayzel, *Women's Identities at War: Gender, Motherhood, and Politics in Britain and France during the First World War* (Chapel Hill: University of North Carolina Press, 1999).

5. Fuller, *Troop Morale*, passim.

6. To judge by the language of the trench newspapers analyzed by Fuller, the word or notion *defeat* was not in the vocabulary of soldiers. Indeed, official documents show the same blithe ignorance of the possibility of defeat. The exception is among naval personnel in 1917 during the height of the U-boat campaign. They worried about food supplies being cut off, but at no other time in the war do Cabinet papers or other state documents use the word *defeat*. In the Second World War, the word (and the reality) recurred regularly.

7. Nicholas Hiley, "La bataille de la Somme et les médias de Londres," in *Guerre et cultures*, ed. J. J. Becker et al. (Paris: Armand Colin, 1994), 203.

8. Antoine Prost, "*Representations of War and the Cultural History of France*," chapter 4 in *Republican Identities in War and Peace: Representations of France in the 19th and 20th Centuries*, trans. Jay Winter (New York: Berg, 2002).

9. Prost, *Representations*.

10. Paul Fussell, *The Great War and Modern Memory* (Oxford: Oxford University Press, 1975); Samuel Hynes, *A War Imagined: The Great War and English Culture* (London: Bodley Head, 1991).

11. W. C. Sellar and R. J. Yeatman, *1066 and All That*, illus. John Reynolds (London: Methuen, 1930).

12. Walter Benjamin, "Theses on the Philosophy of History," *Illuminations*, trans. Harry Zorn (Boston: Shocken, 1990), Thesis V.

Part 1

War Poster Campaigns and
Images, Comparative Readings

2

Barbaric Anti-Modernism: Representations of the "Hun" in Britain, North America, Australia, and Beyond

The use of the word *Hun* as a derogatory term for "German" can be traced back to a speech given by Kaiser Wilhelm II at Bremerhaven in July 1900. During the Boxer Rebellion, Chinese nationalists murdered the German envoy to Peking and several German missionaries, prompting a punitive imperial expedition to reassert European commercial authority. "No quarter will be given, no prisoners will be taken," fulminated the kaiser. "Let all who fall into your hands be at your mercy. Just as the Huns a thousand years ago . . . so may the name of Germany become known in such a manner in China that no Chinaman will ever again even dare to look askance at a German."[1] The kaiser's speech was widely reported in the European press, establishing the trope that would be so deftly used against Germany during World War I. Wilhelm II imagined this imperial moment as a sort of barbarian invasion in reverse, where victory would fall to the European aggressors exacting revenge millennia after the original barbarian invasions shook the West. Despite attempts at damage control by the German government, the Germans would soon become the victims of their own bombastic rhetoric.[2]

The term *Hun*—long used to denote those engaged in savage or brutal behavior—emerged as a popular and even casual epithet for the Germans during World War I. While the term could be used either facetiously or ominously, it became iconographic shorthand, evoking themes of racial "otherness" and primitive atavism that recast a modern European adversary as something far more menacing. In the *Punch* cartoon "Injured Innocence" we see the "German Ogre" dressed as primitive man (fig. 10).[3]

The cartoon offers a vivid rendition of one of the most powerful propaganda motifs used during the Great War—that of an enemy bent on destroying European civilization and repudiating modern humanitarianism. The German Ogre's foot tramples the treaty securing Belgian neutrality while his bloody hands, primitive weapons, and the dead women and children strewn at his feet illustrate his barbaric indifference to the restraints of civilized warfare. Such values as international law, the sanctity of culture, and respect for "family honor"—all learned values that distinguished modern man from the primitive and the bestial—seemed to be swallowed up in the primal fury of an enemy able to harness modern technology to the objectives of savagery. One pamphleteer described the Germans as "barbarians grosser and more criminal than the Huns or Visigoths, or the hordes led by Yengis Khan [sic] or Tamerlane the Great."[4] The Huns of propaganda were savage, Asiatic, backward, and brutal—a European enemy metaphorically cast from the annals of the West.[5]

The poster functioned in conjunction with a variety of other media to render World War I as a war against the primitive, where heroic modern man battled to save European civilization from a return to savagery. Despite its imposing visual presence, the atavistic conceptualization of the enemy has enjoyed far less scholarly attention than the murderous implications of modern war. As Sandra Gilbert notes, "World War I was not just the war to end wars; it was also the war of wars, a paradigm

NICOLETTA F. GULLACE

INJURED INNOCENCE.

The German Ogre. "HEAVEN KNOWS THAT I HAD TO DO THIS IN SELF-DEFENCE; IT WAS FORCED UPON ME." (*Aside*) "FEE, FI, FO, FUM!"

[According to the Imperial Chancellor's latest utterance Germany is the deeply-wronged victim of British militarism.]

Fig. 10. "Injured Innocence," *Punch, Or the London Charivari,* May 31, 1916. The German ogre emerges from a door bearing the militaristic slogan "Weltmacht oder Niedergang" (World power or decline), yet insists he has acted in self-defense. Note the torn treaty underfoot, blood seeping from the door, and bodies of women and children. "Fee, Fi, Fo, Fum!" evokes "I smell the blood of an Englishman," conflating the barbarian with a fairy-tale giant hungry for English blood.

of technological combat, which with its trenches and zeppelins, its gases and mines, has become a diabolical summary of the idea of modern warfare—Western science bent to the service of Western imperialism, the murderous face of Galileo revealed at last."[6] While Gilbert shows that this bleak view of World War I had very different implications for women, she never questions the basic thesis that for the men who fought it, the Great War was murderous, ironic, and above all modern.[7] Contemporary artists, writers, and jurists, however, represented the war not as an exercise in modern annihilation but as a crusade against a foe who was the antithesis of modernity itself. The image of the Hun in British, American, and Australian war posters reveals the complex juxtaposition of the primitive and the modern in wartime iconography. While the modern was certainly recognizable in new technologies of war, a benevolent modernity—conceived of most fully in the enlightenment idea of limited warfare—seemed to offer the only hope of holding at bay an enemy that had allegedly reverted to a primal state.

The anti-modern nature of the enemy was frequently understood in racial terms. At their most basic level, Allied propaganda posters depicting the enemy tapped into a variety of contemporary concerns about race, empire, and otherness that linked British, Australian, and American images of the enemy. While domestic populations in different countries probably engaged with these images in various ways, the images themselves reveal both the international nature of war propaganda and the universality of racial fears among white imperial and settler societies. Repudiating the idea that Germans and British originated from a common white Anglo-Saxon stock, propaganda depicting the enemy drew on anthropology, history, and evolutionary biology to re-racialize the German as something other, hostile, and non-Western. "There may be force in the contention . . . that the Prussian is not a member of the Teutonic family at all, but a 'throw-back' to some Tartar stock," wrote J. H. Morgan, a lawyer investigating German atrocities in France.[8] "Germany is European in nothing but name, and is more completely alien to western ideals than the tribes of Afghanistan . . .. It is a hybrid nation [which] can acquire the idiom of Europe and yet retain the instincts of . . . some pre-Asiatic horde."[9]

While during the Napoleonic Wars the British conceived of their French enemy as a Catholic other defined against a Protestant Britain, during World War I enmity was conceived of in racial terms.[10] Given that the enemy was German, this could have been iconographically inconvenient. Cecil Rhodes, after all, had established the Rhodes scholarship for the explicit purpose of indoctrinating eugenically superior white men from America and Germany into the superiority of English culture at Oxford University.[11] Indeed, with the outbreak of World War I, the German Rhodes scholarships were promptly canceled in a move that paralleled the racial redefinition of Germany for propagandistic purposes.

The depiction of Germany as a land of Huns reveals much about the way the Allies contemplated their own engagement with modernity during Europe's first modern war. Whereas Gilbert and others tend to emphasize the destructive force of modernity, the Allies subscribed to a vision of modernity that encompassed enlightenment and liberal values and was characterized by contemporary faith in the benevolent power of progress. In this guise modernity meant restraint and, above all, a respect for international law and the limits placed on "civilized" warfare.[12] "In most parts of the ancient world, and among the semi-civilized peoples of Asia till very recent times, wars were waged against combatants and non-combatants alike," wrote the eminent jurist Lord James Bryce disapprovingly. "A reaction of sentiment caused by the horror of the Thirty Years' War, coupled with a general softening of manners, brought about a change."[13] Extolling the progress Europeans had made in humanizing warfare since the eighteenth century, Bryce lamented German methods of war, which constituted "a reversion to the ancient methods of savagery" and "a challenge to civilized mankind."[14] This juxtaposition of the civilized, restrained, modern soldier of the Allied European armies and the almost Neanderthal barbarism of the atavistic Hun constitutes a visual and literary trope that runs through much propaganda. In Raleigh's "Halt the Hun" we see the finely chiseled face of an American GI stepping in against a brutish, semihuman Hun about to violate a woman and her baby. The physical contrast between the two soldiers, and the affecting vulnerability of the woman and child, offer a stark comment on the issues at stake in a reversion to premodern forms of warfare.

If the past was marred by unrestrained warfare, however, previous generations had also produced some of the loveliest artifacts of European civilization. For cultivated Europeans, modernity involved not only a respect for human life but a reverence for the past and for Europe's cultural heritage. Vividly linking the actions of the German Huns of 1914 with the vandalism of their premodern namesakes, much World War I propaganda dwells upon acts of cultural destruction—particularly the shelling of the Gothic cathedral at Rheims and the burning of the famous medieval library at Louvain, landmarks of a humane tradition stretching from the emerging West to the present. For a twenty-first-century audience, the sheer volume of material on cultural destruction is overwhelming and even puzzling. The tremendous human toll of the war may make it more difficult to engage with the loss of cultural sites, many of which we have never known.

"Among all the black crimes of the German invasion of Belgium none is blacker than the sack and burning of Louvain, the fairest city of Belgium and the intellectual metropolis of the Low Countries," wrote the critic Logan Marshall.[15] Louvain was a city of unparalleled Gothic beauty, and it housed a fifteenth-century library that contained 150,000 volumes, many of them priceless medieval manuscripts. According to Frank Jewett Mather, a well-known American art critic, "Louvain contained more beautiful works of art than the Prussian nation has produced in its entire history."[16] Many pamphlets describing cultural crimes read like Baedekers of destruction, taking readers on tourist trips through the destroyed parts of historically valuable sites that they might have visited as actual tourists years before. "At the 'Seven Corners' Louvain reveals itself

NICOLETTA F. GULLACE

to my eyes like a luminous panorama in the glade of a forest," wrote Professor E. Gilson, of the University of Louvain. "The center of the city is a smoking heap of ruins. . . . The walls of St. Pierre [are] now a grinning silhouette, roof and belfry gone, the walls blackened and caved in. . . . Further on, the remains of Les Halles, entirely destroyed, except for the arcade . . . of the Salle des Pas Perdus. The library and its treasures are entirely gone."[17]

Such acts of cultural destruction adumbrated the irrevocable annihilation of historically and artistically significant parts of the European past. Acts of cultural destruction, perhaps more than any other legacy of war, are entirely irreversible. No new generation could ever rebuild the Gothic cathedrals or replace the medieval libraries. Such treasures could not be regenerated, as could human casualties, which would eventually be replaced by a new generation. This type of cultural loss gave tremendous force to the image of the Germans as Huns. Linking the modern German army with the fifth-century Huns of Attila, the destruction of European cultural sites seemed to replay the almost mythic moment when Europe was plunged into the Dark Ages. War posters evoked these themes by using background images of flames or architectural ruins. In "Help Stop This," an almost simian German soldier steps on the carcass of a dead woman as he admires, open mouthed, the remnants of a ruined Gothic cathedral. Similarly, "Beat Back the Hun" shows the menacing face of a bloodied German soldier peering over smoldering architectural ruins as he prepares to cross the waters to America.

Ironic juxtaposition of the "savage" and the "civilized" also appeared as a theme in war cartoons. "As Others See Us" (a cartoon of unspecified origins, reproduced in a 1915 atrocity pamphlet) depicts an African, satirically drawn with exaggerated lips, spear in hand, and a can on his head reading "king," poring over a war report from London, while his cauldron simmers in the background. His response to the news is, "UGH! The Dirty Heathen!"[18] The use of Africa as a point of comparison to Germany is not an isolated trope. As the Parliamentary Recruiting Committee reminded readers in its convenient summary of the Bryce Report on German atrocities, "These 240 pages of cold, judicial print make a terrible indictment against a so-called Civilized Power—and one, moreover, whose home is not in 'Darkest Africa,' but in the very heart of enlightened Europe."[19] The evocation of the image of the African reveals the deeply racialized sense of the boundaries of civilization. Germany, as a nation aspiring to imperial greatness, was derisively compared to those regarded as the most backward subjects of empire, undercutting both Germany's imperial aspirations and its very claim to be a Western nation. Instead, Germany, in an atavistic reversion to the past, metaphorically moved back beyond the Asiatic Huns of the early Middle Ages to the savagery of the primitive tribes of Africa.

This reversion to the primitive emerges in posters that go beyond the depiction of the German as an Asiatic barbarian, or even an African savage, and begin to depict him as not human at all—a Darwinian throw-back to the apes from which man descended. H. R. Hopps's "Destroy This Mad Brute," one of the most striking American posters issued during the war, vividly depicts this anti-evolutionary theme (fig. 11). "Destroy This Mad Brute" pictures a gorilla with a German helmet emerging on America's shores from a destroyed Europe. He carries a bloody cudgel reading "Kultur" and holds captive a tormented European woman who, like Fay Wray struggling against King Kong, finds herself in the throes of terror and despair. Evoking both the rape of conquered women and the rape of Liberty, the woman is the helpless victim of the "mad brute" of German militarism and its false sense of "Kultur." Anne Classen

NICOLETTA F. GULLACE

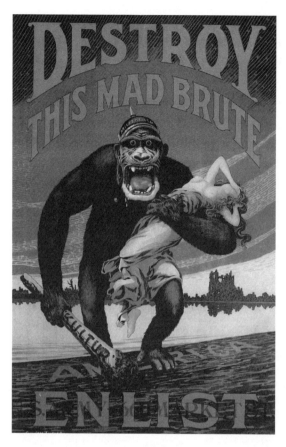

Fig. 11. H. R. Hopps, "Destroy This Mad Brute," ca. 1917. The primitive Hun has morphed into a savage gorilla in this highly sexualized rendition of German militarism. The phallic and bloody cudgel and the beast's power over the half-naked girl give urgency to the enlistment call. As the beast steps onto American shores, recruits are invited both to fight militarism and to vie for the eroticized figure of raped Liberty. Political Poster Collection, us 2003, Hoover Institution Archives.

Knutson has pointed out that in the United States the image of the ape was used at once to depict a German enemy and to raise the specter of miscegenation and racial tension.[20] More generally, to a public versed in popular Darwinism, the image of the ape evoked fears of a European civilization that had reverted back to a primordial state. It was in combination with such fears of the primitive that modernity itself began to take on more sinister meanings.

If modernity evoked the restraint and progress that had developed in Europe over the last several centuries, it also had another much more disturbing manifestation. Poison gas, aerial warfare, submarines, and the machine gun all revolutionized the First World War and, most terrifyingly, were weapons wielded by the enemy. What made Germany so frightening was that it possessed the "technology and destructive resources of the West combined with the ruthlessness and contempt of human life of the East."[21] In short, the primitive beasts were masters of modern technology. "It is like an intellectual savage who has learnt the languages and studied the dress and deportment of polite society, but all the while nurtures dark atavism and murderous impulses in the centres of his brain," wrote one critic.[22] The popular British cartoonist Will Dyson vividly illustrated this idea. As H. G. Wells wrote in a foreword to a collection of Dyson's cartoons, Dyson's work had been published mostly in a daily "labour" paper, but "its direction and appeal have been steadfastly to the ruler, the employer, and the responsible men."[23] It is not surprising that his work appealed to the great writer of science fiction, a genre richly tapped in Dyson's themes. In one cartoon, titled "Modern Science and Prehistoric Savagery," Dyson depicts a modern professor saying to an apelike Neanderthal man, "Together, my dear Herr Cave-dweller, we should be irresistible."[24] Dyson's work was both cheaply reproduced and exhibited in gallery shows, making his images widely available. In his most famous cartoon, "Wonders of Science," Dyson depicts a chimpanzee with a German helmet flying an airplane while his companion drops bombs on London. Both "Herr Cave-dweller" and the chimpanzees represent a primordial brutishness, rendered far more frightening by their mastery of modern technology.[25]

If the German Hun threatened to bring back an untamed past by destroying both the cultural legacy of the West and the modern rules of war put in place to preserve it, he was also a sexual predator who threatened the future of the race through violent attacks on women. Numerous images of the

NICOLETTA F. GULLACE

Germans evoke the mass rapes reported in Belgium and northern France. The French became so preoccupied with the threat of miscegenation that, as Ruth Harris has shown, some nationalists advocated abortion for French Catholic women impregnated by the enemy.[26] Images of rape and miscegenation, however, were not limited to the occupied territories but became a staple of recruiting posters in lands as far removed from the conflict as Australia and the United States. In J. S. Watkins's "Women of Queensland!" a violated women with hair streaming and breast bared stares up to the sky with clenched fists as her two dead children bleed at her feet. The flames of her village burn in the background and the poster reminds the viewer to "Remember how women and children in France and Belgium were treated. Do you realise that your treatment would be worse? Send a man to-day to fight for you."

Unlike "Destroy This Mad Brute," "Women of Queensland!" does not depict the enemy but rather allows the viewer to imagine the perpetrator of the crimes depicted in the image. Given the consistent depiction of the enemy, such visualization would not have been difficult. In fact Norman Lindsay makes a similar point in another Australian poster that could almost be the prequel to "Women of Queensland!" In "Will you fight now or wait for this," rather than seeing the burning village in the background, the viewer finds himself amidst the flames with a family being shot and beaten, while a monstrous square-jawed German rips off a woman's bodice and threatens rape. The image leaves nothing to the imagination, and the German threat, depicted periodically and written about even more frequently, is made explicit.

In the atavistic, though by no means linear, journey into the past taken by poster artists depicting Germany, the culmination perhaps came with Norman Lindsay's "?" (fig. 12). In this image, the Hun is no longer Asiatic, African, or apelike—but

Fig. 12. Norman Lindsay, "?" 1918. The image of a brutal, blood-soaked German monster about to tear into a globe uses powerful graphic design to represent Australia's fate as one with the world. Produced and distributed in secret for Australia's last recruiting campaign, the poster was placarded throughout the country on a prearranged night—Australians awoke to confront the arresting image at every turn. PST 3242, Imperial War Museum.

a monstrous ogre who defies earthly reality and is imaginable only as a personification of bloodlust. This Australian poster, which was imitated in the United States, offered yet another commentary on German militarism.[27] Evoking a bestial transformation, the monster, bloodied up to its elbows and dripping blood onto a world about to be grasped in its murderous claws, still wears a German helmet. Like a grotesque Mr. Hyde, the German monster looms larger than the earth itself. The poster's only text, its cryptic question mark, beckons Australians to step in and alter this imagined vision of a bloody future.

One is struck by the sheer brutality of later images like "?" and "Beat Back the Hun," which began to appear in the Allied countries most remote from the war: Australia and the United States. In Great Britain, which lay closer to the danger zone,

NICOLETTA F. GULLACE

and where extraordinary sacrifice was already being exacted, the visual images, if not the literary ones, tended to be tamer. While part of this difference may be stylistic, the brutality of the images also reflects the difficulty of creating a vivid imperative to fight in countries where there existed no immediate threat. Australia had no conscription, and Americans were deeply ambivalent about entering the fray at all. Tactically, artists trying to provoke a response from audiences attempted to make a distant threat seem immediate—both to reluctant recruits and to those who might buy bonds, give money, or encourage others to serve. American posters frequently depict the brutal Hun emerging from the water, while Australian images remind viewers of the possibility of invasion. Such images suggested that even an ocean could not protect isolated inhabitants from the threat of German militarism.

On a more psychological level, the image of the Hun drew upon racial fears endemic in societies anxious over racial mixing and white vulnerability. Overtly, the images played upon the soul of the individual, suggesting that those who refused to "Halt the Hun" or "Buy Liberty Bonds" were complicit in an unspeakable outrage. Yet the Hun also became a psychological trope, meant both to evoke the dark reality of a primal enemy and to suggest that responsibility for such evil lies with all who fail to act. Like D. W. Griffiths's famous *Birth of a Nation*, the image of the Hun conflated racial and sexual fears with the European war, recasting the enemy as a sort of stand-in for the threat of racial contamination in America and Australia. This is perhaps another reason that a settler society and a former slave society would share such vivid renditions of the meaning of a distant enemy.

Despite the particular resonance of the Hun for white Western audiences, Allied propaganda bureaucracies did not hesitate to circulate such images to the rest of the world. In "Sus

Bonos de la Libertad ayudarán á fin con esto" ("Your Liberty Bond Will Help Stop This"), F. Amorsota produced a bilingual poster for the Philippines depicting the crucifixion of a horrified American marine onto a tree by brutal German soldiers. Though circulated in Asia, the poster employs entirely Western iconography. Heroic American soldiers rush to the aid of their comrade, waving the Stars and Stripes, as the evil Germans prepare to run. Would the image have been resonant to Filipinos? Or would it have appeared to be yet another self-serving bit of propaganda depicting the glories of American military intervention? While reception is evasive, the image of Germany as primitive, barbaric, and other remained central in Allied propaganda shipped around the globe. "One way and another," wrote one former participant in the British propaganda endeavor, "literature in the appropriate languages reached the Seychelles, Mauritius, Madagascar, the Chatham Islands, Sandwich Islands, New Guinea, Iceland, the New Hebrides, Formosa, Belgian Congo and Fernando Po, while Wellington House pamphlets were reproduced in the newspapers of places so divers as Bogota, Switzerland, Tehran, Johannesburg and Patagonia."[28] Indeed, literally tons of such materials were shipped around the globe, taking advantage of the highly productive relationships among the British propaganda bureau, academic specialists, and the merchant marine.

One of the best documented campaigns to influence opinion outside the West was an attempt to win the hearts and minds of "Oriental" peoples with a fabricated report of a German "corpse conversion factory." News reports, based on the mistranslation of an article about the disposal of dead horses, alleged that the Germans shipped their war dead to industrial plants where they boiled them down for use in soap and lubricating grease.[29] The story, ominously prescient to a modern audience, was meant to revolt the Turks, to poison relations

NICOLETTA F. GULLACE

between Germany and India, and to shock the ancestor-worshiping Chinese. The Foreign Office noted that the Sepoy had revolted for less and hoped that by claiming some of the grease was used to lubricate bullets and to make margarine, propaganda could make the Germans appear to be cannibalistic, causing Muslims to revolt. The fabrication and mistranslation were quickly exposed, but the episode raises the question of how "Oriental peoples" responded to Allied atrocity reports that exalted the virtues of Western modernity.[30]

While the Chinese ambassador was apparently horrified by the corpse conversion factory story, other commentators were more skeptical about the effectiveness of atrocity stories outside the West. According to Captain M. D. Kennedy, the use of atrocity propaganda in Japan only "strengthened the undercurrent of national sympathies towards Germany." Although the Japanese were officially allies of the British in World War I, their remoteness from the war made a propaganda effort there necessary. As Kennedy points out, the Japanese officer corps was modeled on the German one and there was much sympathy for German discipline and military efficiency. "Instead of emphasizing the fine fighting qualities of our own troops," British propagandists emphasized "the iniquities of German 'frightfulness.'" "The fact that we resorted to such 'unsporting' methods was regarded . . . as proof positive that, man for man, the Germans were better fighters."[31]

Perhaps the difficulty the British had in creating a plausible anti-German narrative had less to do with being "sporting" and more to do with the fact that the anti-Hun campaign was so deeply implicated in upholding "Western Civilization," Western methods of war, and Western racial motifs. The vilification of an enemy depicted as Asiatic or apelike, in defiance of a common Western heritage, was perhaps unlikely to have garnered tremendous sympathy in the Orient. If the image of the Hun lacked resonance outside the West, however, it was certainly deeply felt by ethnic Germans. On the eve of World War II, midwestern farmers gave one journalist the impression that they were "waiting with shotguns to shoot down the first propagandist who mentions Belgian babies."[32] And in Germany itself, the Hopps poster was reissued during World War II to remind Germans of the hate-filled propaganda that had been used against them in the preceding war. In "The old hatred—the old goal!" a German poster from 1939, a reproduction of the Hopps image was glossed with the following message: "When they assaulted us 25 years ago, they wrote on their rotten slanderous poster: 'Destroy this mad beast'—they meant the German people!!!"[33] The evocation of World War I propaganda by the Nazis offers us one tangible clue about its reception. Whether or not it effectively elicited young recruits, accelerated the sale of Liberty Bonds, or poisoned global sentiment against Germany, it created a deep and abiding resentment among the German people, one that would be effectively tapped and manipulated in another far more brutal and monstrous war.

Notes

1. *Oxford English Dictionary Online*, "Hun," from *Daily News*, November 20, 1900.

2. "Kaiser Wilhelm II and German Interests in China," H-net Online, accessed June 4, 2008 at http://www.n-net.org/~german/gtext/kaiserreich/china.html.

3. *Punch*, May 31, 1916.

4. William Le Queux, *German Atrocities: A Record of Shameless Deeds* (London: George Newnes, n.d.), 65, 121.

5. Louis Raemaekers depicted the "Hun" in his cartoon "Germany's Pledged Word" with an Asiatic top-knot and slanted eyes as well as a German handlebar mustache. Louis Raemaekers, *Raemaekers Cartoons* (London: Hodder and Stoughton, n.d.), 1. Similarly, a somewhat crude Australian poster entitled "Always Huns [whether] A.D. 451 [or] 1915" juxtaposed the image of an Asiatic Hun with the image of a German soldier, unmistakably conflating the two "barbarians." Peter

Stanley, *What Did You Do in the War Daddy? A Visual History of Propaganda Posters* (Oxford: Oxford University Press, 1983), 28.

6. Sandra M. Gilbert, "Soldier's Heart: Literary Men, Literary Women, and the Great War," in *Behind the Lines: Gender and the Two World Wars*, ed. Margaret Higonnet et al. (New Haven: Yale University Press, 1987), 197.

7. For the classic account of the "modernity" of the Great War, see Paul Fussell, *The Great War and Modern Memory* (Oxford: Oxford University Press, 1975). Jay Winter has offered a compelling critique of Fussell in *Sites of Memory, Sites of Mourning: The Great War in European Cultural History* (Cambridge: Cambridge University Press, 1995). Winter argues that a faith in traditional values continued to motivate Europeans well into the interwar period.

8. J. H. Morgan, *German Atrocities: An Official Investigation* (London: T. Fisher Unwin, 1916), 52–53.

9. Morgan, *German Atrocities*, 56–57.

10. Linda Colley, *Britons: Forging the Nation 1707–1837* (New Haven: Yale University Press, 1992). Colley has usefully adapted Edward Said's notion of "otherness" to an understanding of representations of the enemy in European war. Edward W. Said, *Orientalism* (New York: Random House, 1979).

11. Six German Rhodes scholarships had been provided for in a 1901 codicil to Rhodes's will, in acknowledgment of German Teutonic racial unity with Britain. Shula Marks and Stanley Trapido, "Rhodes, Cecil John," *Oxford Dictionary of National Biography Online*.

12. For a discussion of cultural conceptions of international law during World War I, see Nicoletta F. Gullace, "Sexual Violence and Family Honor: British Propaganda and International Law during the First World War," *American Historical Review* (June 1997): 714–47.

13. Lord James Bryce, "A Fresh Examination of German War Methods," reprinted in Morgan, *German Atrocities*, 11–12.

14. Bryce, "Examination," 15.

15. Logan Marshall, *Horrors and Atrocities of the Great War: Including the Tragic Destruction of the Lusitania* (New York: L. T. Myers, 1915), 159–60.

16. Quoted in Marshall, *Horrors*, 159–60.

17. Quoted in Marshall, *Horrors*, 165–66.

18. In another obscure cartoon, Death is dressed as a Roman gladiator, dragging the prostrate female form of Europe back into "barbarism." Marshall, *Horrors*, 37, 147.

19. Parliamentary Recruiting Committee, *The Truth about German Atrocities: Founded on the Report of the Committee on Alleged German Outrages* (London: PRC, 1915), 4.

20. For a thorough discussion of the imagery in the Hopps poster and its contextualization within American anxieties over race and immigration, see Anne

Classen Knutson, "Breasts, Brawn and Selling a War: American World War I Propaganda Posters 1917–1918" (Ann Arbor: University Microfilms International, 1998), 39–76.

21. Morgan, *German Atrocities*, 56–57.

22. Morgan, *German Atrocities*, 57.

23. Will Dyson, *Kultur Cartoons* (London: Stanley Paul and Company, 1915), foreword.

24. Dyson, *Kultur Cartoons*, 11.

25. Dyson, "Modern Science and Pre-historic Savagery" and "Wonders of Science," in *Kultur Cartoons*.

26. Ruth Harris, "The 'Child of the Barbarian': Rape, Race and Nationalism in France during the First World War," *Past and Present* (October 1993): 191; Susan R. Grayzel, *Women's Identities at War: Gender, Motherhood, and Politics in Britain and France during the First World War* (Chapel Hill: University of North Carolina Press, 1999), 55.

27. Peter Stanley, *What Did You Do in the War Daddy? A Visual History of Propaganda Posters* (Oxford: Oxford University Press, 1983), 10.

28. Imperial War Museum, London (hereafter IWM), Department of Documents, Sir Campbell Stuart Papers, "British Propaganda during the Great War, 1914–1918," 7. Foreign Office records at the Public Record Office (now the National Archives) also elaborate on these far-flung propaganda efforts.

29. See for example, Anon., *A "Corpse Conversion Factory": A Peep Behind the Lines* (London: Darling & Sons, n.d.), and Fichte Association, "Confutation of the Lies about German Atrocities during the War" (Hamburg: Fichte Association, [1925]).

30. National Archives, Kew, FO 395/147, "miscellaneous General Files, 1917."

31. IWM, Department of Documents, papers of Captain M. D. Kennedy, "Memoirs 1912–1922" (1931), 194–98.

32. Anthony Rhodes, *Propaganda: The Art of Persuasion in World War II* (New York: Chelsea House Publishers, 1976), 139.

33. Peter Paret, Beth Irwin Lewis, and Paul Paret, eds., *Persuasive Images: Posters of War and Revolution from the Hoover Institution Archives* (Princeton: Princeton University Press, 1992), 145.

STEFAN GOEBEL

3

Chivalrous Knights versus Iron Warriors:
Representations of the Battle of *Matériel* and Slaughter in Britain and Germany, 1914–1940

T he First World War marked a turning point in the history of military conflict. The Great War of 1914–18 was not only the bloodiest but also the first industrialized mass war the world had seen. In the military service of Britain and Germany alone, three million men died; many of them were killed by machine-gun bullets and artillery shrapnel.[1] In this essay I examine and compare how these two outstanding features of the First World War—the enormous bloodshed on the one hand and the battle of *matériel* on the other—were culturally reconfigured in Britain and Germany during and after the 1914–18 conflict. I argue that the endurance test of the *Materialschlacht* and the soldier's "experience" of war dominated German representations, whereas British imaginings focused on the slaughter and the soldier's conduct in war. Interestingly, Britons and Germans mobilized an almost identical visual imagery to represent these two sides of the same coin: medievalist images of knights in armor proliferated in both countries, but the same iconography carried fundamentally different meanings in Britain and Germany.[2] While images of iron warriors helped to accommodate the shocking and novel experience of industrialized mass warfare in Germany, in Britain representations of chivalrous knights were employed to legitimize the carnage and to restore a sense of moral superiority.

This preliminary finding poses a methodological challenge to the study of visual images in the era of the Great War. Iconographic evidence examined in isolation can be misleading. In order to appreciate delicate nuances of representation in Britain and Germany, visual images of knights in armor need to be located in their respective cultural settings. In this essay I pay particular attention to the contexts that connected the visual and linguistic fields, concentrating on the process of memorialization in the aftermath of the Great War. War memorials combined visual with discursive and performative modes of representation; their iconography was incomplete without public rituals and rhetoric and vice versa. Memorial designs required interpretation, and agents of remembrance were anxious to clear up any ambiguities in the preliminary discussions, unveiling speeches, and newspaper articles.[3] Such representations of war were, of course, embedded in a longer tradition. Apart from sources relating directly to the construction and reception of war memorials, I also read memorials in relation to other visual objects that shaped commemorations, notably wartime poster art and picture postcards (both bearing the stamp of nineteenth-century medievalism), which function as what Daniel Sherman calls "registers of experience."[4] The imagery of visual propaganda, once freed from its wartime aggressiveness, offered a template or repository of images for the construction of memorials and memory after the catastrophe of 1914–18.

Representations of the *Materialschlacht*: Germany's Iron Warriors

The German dream of a crushing military victory in the early stages of the war failed to materialize. Commentators thus had to adjust their language to the reality of a stalemate. Notations of holding out or resilience instead of advance proliferated by 1915: "In the east and west, in the north and south we clench our enemies with an iron fist."[5] To be sure, the Russian retreat from Poland in summer 1915 aroused new excitement. Germans at home imagined that the Imperial "mailed fist hovered menacingly in the air for the ultimate, crushing blow."[6] The "iron fist"—an implicit reference to the story of Reich Knight *Götz von Berlichingen with the Iron Hand* (thus the title of Johann Wolfgang von Goethe's drama)—was firmly established in the corpus of propaganda. It symbolized the army's unbreakable determination to resist the enemy attack and to achieve a lasting "peace." "This is the way to peace—the enemy wills it so!" reads a 1918 poster by Lucian Bernhard advertising war loans. It depicted a clenched mailed fist as a symbol of somber resolve (fig. 13).[7] Propaganda of this kind backfired on the Kaiserreich. Abroad, the image of the iron fist—dating back to Wilhelm II's infamous "mailed fist speech" on the German occupation of Tsingtau in 1897—was identified with German barbarism. "Have you read the Kaiser's speeches? . . . They are full of the glitter and bluster of German militarism—'mailed fist,' and 'shining armour,'" said David Lloyd George in the winter of 1914.[8] Even years after the war, the frightful propaganda of Imperial Germany had not been forgotten. Remembrance ceremonies and war memoirs recalled the horror of the kaiser's "gory mailed fist."[9]

This imagery, however infamous abroad, had consolatory power in Germany. The *Materialschlacht*, the battle of *matériel* in the world war, put an immense and often intolerable strain on the combatants. Politicians and generals pushed their soldiers beyond the boundaries of endurance. Invocations of "cold steel" offered a symbolic compensation to Germans. Propagandists pictured the nerve-racking drumfire with iron willpower. Iron determination would overcome the enemy

Fig. 13. Lucian Bernhard used the image of a clenched iron fist to represent Germany's iron determination in wartime. "Das ist der Weg zum Frieden—die Feinde wollen es so! darum zeichnet Kriegsanleihe!" (This is the way to peace—the enemy wills it so! Therefore subscribe to the war loan!), 1918. Political Poster collection, GE 250, Hoover Institution Archives.

within: anxiety. The sociologist (and war propagandist) Werner Sombart illustrated the ideal of calmness by analogy with an armor-clad warrior resting stoically on his gigantic sword in the midst of battle.[10] Commemorations, both during and after the war, echoed Sombart's vision; the knight in armor represented the archetypal man of steel who was mentally and physically invulnerable.[11] This image informed a language the contemporaries devised to acknowledge the soldiers' achievement, a language that posited the soldiers' ability to abide unimaginable harshness. It is little wonder that after the war, veterans encouraged the use of this language. Both their special status in postwar Germany and their involvement in public rituals of

STEFAN GOEBEL

commemoration enabled them to do so. At the same time iron masculinity was the cure prescribed for disabled veterans. Time and again, orthopedic surgeons and technicians praised Götz von Berlichingen as a role model; a number of new designs for prosthetic arms bore Götz's name. The famous knight with his "iron fist" became the archetypal German warrior disabled by injury but sustained by his unbreakable spirit.[12]

Imposed on war cripples by medical experts, the notion of iron endurance also provided able-bodied but disgruntled veterans with a welcome collective myth that underscored their special status in postwar German society. British political culture, in contrast, was unprepared to assign a special role to ex-servicemen. Veterans were not usually party to the initiating committees, since war memorials were meant to be tributes from citizens to soldiers. The soldier's experience could rarely be fully articulated within the framework of communal commemorations, which were mostly managed by those who had remained at home.[13] As a consequence the British story lacks a precise analog to the German cult of the *Kriegserlebnis,* the mythical "war experience," and its "eyewitnesses."[14] Instead, the British First World War experience was encoded in a language of suffering and sacrifice that validated soldiers' vulnerability.[15] In the Anglo-Saxon world, the term *shell shock* transformed from a medical diagnosis to a metaphor of the experience of the First World War.[16] What is more, the imagery of "cold steel," discredited by the shadow of the kaiser's "mailed fist," was unavailable for the expression of the soldier's ordeal.

Knights in Armor

The German fascination with men of iron will materialize in the massive proliferation of war landmarks or *Kriegswahrzeichen zum Benageln* in 1915 and 1916. Throughout Germany (and Austria-Hungary), local communities erected wooden objects, and knights proved one of the most popular motifs. In the course of month-long celebrations these wooden statues or plaques were described or outlined by a series of nails. All citizens, young and old, male and female, rich and poor, were called on to hammer iron (and also silver and golden) nails into war landmarks. The organizers—generally committees composed of local elites—plastered towns and cities with posters (often of poor quality, complained the trade journal *Das Plakat*) that advertised nailing events.[17] The participants had to pay for the privilege by contributing to war charities, mostly in aid of war widows and orphans. Every participant received a "nailing certificate" depicting the war landmark as a token of his or her contribution. In addition picture postcards and an array of wartime kitsch were often on sale. Thus war landmarks contributed to both the cultural and financial mobilization of the population. Completed iron-nail figures visualized the unity of home and front; the nailing ritual acknowledged the soldiers' iron endurance and created an opportunity for the civilian population to do its bit—at least symbolically.[18]

The imagery of iron endurance and the nailing ritual did not imply indifference toward human life; the iron knight was no agent of the wartime "brutalization" of German society.[19] Take the "Iron Defender" unveiled in January 1916, the war landmark of Halberstadt in the Prussian Province of Saxony. The local press interpreted the body language of the figure as follows: "Not in an offensive posture, armed for battle, but the shield dipped and the sword in the scabbard; and yet clad in full armor to repel attacks directed against him. And in this state of calmness he is a model of steady strength."[20] Composure and not brutality distinguished this iron warrior. Halberstadt's "calm" knight was a typical idealization of the "age of nervousness."[21] Some observers of Western societies had been increasingly preoccupied with nervous disorders since the late nineteenth century. Doctors diagnosed a correlation between the acceleration in socioeconomic modernization and an increase in nervous complaints. Underlying their research was a pessimistic critique of the modern condition. The outbreak of war presented the medical profession with a new situation. Mental trauma—named war strain, neurasthenia, anxiety neurosis, or shell shock—spread rapidly among formerly healthy men, and effective treatment for nervous diseases under the conditions of industrialized warfare became a pressing military need.

The medical discourse of the war years has attracted considerable attention from scholars.[22] A feature worth noting is the popularization and vulgarization of the diagnosis in public ceremonies. War landmarks were commonly identified as "a symbol of iron will."[23] Note the slippage and oscillation between the material and the mental; metallic qualities became charged with psychic value. The war landmark provided a focus for rituals of exorcising nervousness and promoting calmness as a wartime virtue. The practice of hammering iron nails into wooden objects signified the steeling of nerves. Driving iron nails into oak meant, as Karl-Ernst Osthaus put it, "to greet and to peel the hard with the even harder [material]."[24] Wooden objects were thus turned into steeled figures. Communal action created a protective suit of iron. "Iron is the word of our time! Germany's power wears an iron garment"—thus Bremen sang the praises of its "Iron Roland" at the unveiling ceremony in July 1915 (the poem was later reprinted on a picture postcard of the figure).[25] The "iron garment" was a standard formula in ceremonies held at war landmarks.[26] The symbolism was most persuasive where iron nails were used to describe the figure or image of a medieval knight clad in a suit of armor, such as the *Wackere Schwabe in Eisen,* "Gallant Swabian in Iron," of Stuttgart.

Stuttgart's "Gallant Swabian" exemplifies the strength of regional traditions and identities in notations of endurance. Judging from its design (as can be seen on surviving posters and postcards), the war landmark of Stuttgart was nothing out of the ordinary: a conventional representation of a knight armed with a sword and shield. The figure was unveiled on September 2, 1915—Sedan Day. Sedan Day, *the* official national holiday, dramatized annually the founding myth of Imperial Germany, the formation of a national phalanx against France in the war of 1870–71. Although it was a celebration of national union, the flavor of the event differed among states and regions.[27] The unveiling ceremony of 1915 accentuated Swabian steadfastness in the ongoing conflict. The main speaker, the president of the Red Cross of Württemberg, highlighted the *Ausharren*, "endurance," of the soldiers at the front, which he related to the legendary *Schwabenstreiche*.[28]

The term *Schwabenstreich*, "Swabian trick," originally a mocking expression for a piece of folly, had been refashioned by Ludwig Uhland. In 1814 Uhland, a leading protagonist of German romanticism and a medievalist at the University of Tübingen, wrote the humorous poem "Swabian Intelligence" ("Schwäbische Kunde"). It tells the story of the "Gallant Swabian," a paladin of the crusader Frederick I Barbarossa, who always remains cool, calm, and collected in battle. He endures the assaults launched on him by the Turks (rather than the Arabs) with disdain and plays a passive role up to a point when he unexpectedly but vigorously strikes back with his sword: the *Schwabenstreich*. In short, the poem could be read as a tale of resilience or resilient humor. A local newspaper remarked on the iron-nail figure: "With an expression of humorous contempt, winking, twisting his mouth into a slight smile, he looks back over the massive shield which has blocked a few arrows; but with his right hand he grasps the good sword, and woe betide anyone who comes too close to him! He will taste what the *Schwabenstreiche* means."[29]

After the war the "Gallant Swabian in Iron," like many other war landmarks, fell into oblivion. During the socioeconomic crisis of the early 1930s, the figure, meanwhile transferred to a storeroom in Stuttgart's old castle, captured Swabian imagination once again. The castle was badly damaged by fire, but by a strange twist of fate the "Gallant Swabian" survived intact. In the aftermath of the fire disaster the discourse of iron endurance flared up temporarily, and the iron figure was once again pronounced a role model for the people. "Thus the 'Gallant Swabian' . . . has, in front of everybody, truly risen again from the fire ruin of the Württembergian mother castle as a wonderful symbol of Swabian toughness and victorious steadfastness," reported the bourgeois press.[30] The story of the miraculous survival of the "Gallant Swabian" was also spread by means of picture postcards showing the knight surrounded by the rubble of the castle. The caption stated that he "'gallantly' stood firm during the fire disaster of the Old Castle in Stuttgart. . . . Practically undamaged he rises from the rubble."[31]

The Steel-Helmeted Man

Iron was the icon of both the age of industrial modernity and the era of medieval knights. Iron-nail landmarks synthesized the modern and the archaic.[32] It is noteworthy that these monuments swept the country in 1915–16. The notion of iron resilience was born of the experience of a prolonged war of position and entrenchment at the Western Front in 1914–15. The symbolism of iron predated both Verdun and the Somme, the two battles that revolutionized the meaning of the word *endurance.* In the aftermath of the battles of *matériel* of 1916, a new icon of hardness proliferated alongside the established metaphors of medieval armor. The *Stahlhelm,* the distinctive flat-

Fig. 14. The *Stahlhelm* (steel helmet), the progeny of modern engineering, blends with medieval armor in Leo Schnug's "Kameraden zeichnet die VII^te Kriegsanleihe" (Comrades subscribe to the seventh war loan), 1917. Bibliothek für Zeitgeschichte, Stuttgart.

topped steel helmet, was introduced in January 1916 to replace the decorative but inefficient spiked *Pickelhaube*, a relic of the nineteenth-century army (fig. 14).

Although the *Stahlhelm* was the progeny of modern engineering, its shape conjured up archaic helmets. In *All Quiet on the Western Front* Erich Maria Remarque observed that cavalrymen "in their steel helmets resemble knights of a forgotten time."[33]

STEFAN GOEBEL

The editor of the magazine of the Kyffhäuser-Bund (the national umbrella organization of local veterans' societies) noted in an essay on the "Struggle at the Somme—The Emotional [*seelische*] Experience of a Front-Fighter": "But those soldiers! Those German soldiers with the German Siegfried helmet, with the fist on the hot rifle, with iron features of valor, love and horror . . . —those men at the Somme are the defenses in the most monstrous hurricane of this war."[34] Official war propaganda had probably set the tone; in poster art the steel helmet blended with medieval armor.[35] In the course of time the steel helmet evolved into the quintessential German symbol of the Great War. Countless war memorials featured "the German steel helmet in its wonderful, almost ancient form."[36] However, for some agents of memory the notions of hardness associated with the steel helmet had more radical, ideologically far-reaching implications. I turn now to this subdiscourse.

The steel helmet connoted the *Kriegserlebnis* of the frontline combatant. Not for nothing was a new veterans' organization named after the new helmet: the Stahlhelm, Bund der Frontsoldaten, the anti-republican "League of Front Soldiers," was founded in November 1918 (later, noncombatants and youngsters could also enlist in suborganizations of the Stahlhelm league).[37] Many veterans joined the Stahlhelm league in order to dissociate themselves from the boozy atmosphere of the traditional *Kriegervereine*, the veterans' societies established in the nineteenth century. No better emblem could have been found to outline a symbolic demarcation between the Great War and previous conflicts than the helmet of Verdun and the Somme. A new type of soldier, the "Verdun fighter," was hammered into being in 1916, as Bernd Hüppauf has argued.[38] Hardened by the battle of *matériel*, the front-fighter typified a dehumanized race, a war machine with an iron soul.

Externally, the "new man" was distinguished by the steel

helmet crowning his head, as can be seen on numerous war posters. It was the visual propaganda that first popularized the steel helmet as the new icon of military and masculine prowess. Notably, Fritz Erler's poster for the sixth war loan campaign of 1917 proved highly influential; in fact, it marked the belated breakthrough of the picture poster in wartime Germany (fig. 15).[39] It featured an infantryman wearing a steel helmet and with piercing eyes. Widely distributed during the final years of the war (and also reprinted on picture postcards), Erler's design established a recurring motif of (right-wing) political posters during the Weimar Republic and Third Reich, a motif that also entered the visual language of memorial design.[40] To be sure, memorial designers did not simply imitate the iconography of poster art but rather tapped into patterns of representation of the *Kriegserlebnis* on which graphic artists like Erler had conferred an air of authenticity.

The visual grammar of the "new man," crystallized in Erler's 1917 poster, was firmly established by the time Ernst Jünger immortalized in prose the new breed of warrior. To Jünger, the poet of the machine war, the steel-helmeted man appeared to be "the inhabitant of a new, mysterious and harder world."[41] Jünger's detached, clinical descriptions of the Western Front capture the imbalance between man and material. The soldier who endured hell on earth, the artillery's *Stahlgewitter*, "storm of steel," emerged as a new human species. There is a degree of resemblance between the writings of Jünger and German psychiatrists.[42] Doctors concerned with war neuroses pointed out the spiritually invigorating effect of battle on man's psyche. They envisaged war as a kind of therapy or cure, a *Stahlbad*, a "bath of steel."[43]

How widespread was the idea of a "new man" surfacing in the aftermath of the storm or bath of steel? A recent study of

STEFAN GOEBEL

Fig. 15. Fritz Erler's infantryman with piercing eyes popularized the new steel helmet as an icon of military might and masculine prowess in "Helft uns siegen! Zeichnet die Kriegsanleihe" (Help us win! Subscribe to the war loan), 1917. Political Poster collection, GE 364A, Hoover Institution Archives.

German war memorials suggests that monuments erected after about 1928, when mourning was supposedly on the decline, were vectors for the dissemination of notions of the new man.[44] The figure of the steel-helmeted man with a stern face was indeed a popular choice—perhaps the most popular choice—for figurative war memorials, especially regimental memorials, even before 1928. Notably, according to one contemporary expert, the sculptor Hermann Hosaeus modeled to perfection the soldier who "marched through the 'Storm of Steel'".[45] He regarded Hosaeus's monument for the town of Norden, Hanover, unveiled in 1927, as exemplary memorial art:

One glance at this face and one understands why the enemy must hate him and wants to bring him to his knees with diabolic cunning. Because one cannot cope with him in any other way. He is genuine, that is why one needs craftiness against him; he is deep and spiritualized [*verinnerlicht*], that is why one has to defame him; he is upright, that is why one has to humiliate him; he is steadfast against inner distress and outer threat, hard as iron and steel, solid as rock-steady stone, that is why one has to murder him. He can win, lead, fight and die. His power is strong and is as quick as a hammer raining down. His weapon is as safe as death. His faith is as true as his eye. His death is like an ancient epic of heroism and ruin. He is greater than the material of battle, because he embodies defiance, spirit and will.[46]

Even though the figure is located in a provincial town in East Friesland, it attracted national attention, for Hosaeus was one of the outstanding sculptors of Weimar Germany. Edwin Redslob, the Reich art custodian, showed an interest in the statue, which he identified as an image of Roland, the legendary paladin of Charlemagne and guardian of municipal sovereignty.[47] Redslob's finding, though incorrect, is revealing. The memorial clearly features a *Feldgrauer*, a German soldier of the First World War clothed in a "field-grey" uniform; a steel helmet crowns his head.[48] The accessories are distinctly modern, yet his posture is evocative of representations of Roland. The soldier stands erect with his legs apart, his hands clasping the barrel of a long rifle. The borrowings from medieval (and neo-medieval) Roland columns were deliberate. Hosaeus himself labeled his private photographs of the Norden memorial "The 'Roland' of Norden."[49] Modernized Rolands were a common motif after the Great War; Hosaeus designed similar figures for the city of Osnabrück, Hanover, and the town of Bleicherode, Prussian Province of Saxony.

STEFAN GOEBEL

Literary and visual representations of the steel-helmeted warrior complemented each other. They enshrined one particular facet of the First World War experience, namely operations in the frontline of the western battlefields. Ernst Jünger himself had joined one of the elite storm troop units formed in answer to the British bombardment on the Somme. These units were given full freedom of action. The new tactics relied on the storm trooper's aggressiveness and imagination and thus reinvented individualism in the middle of a mechanical war. Consequently, Jünger's experience of the conflict was anything but representative of the legendary front generation. Nonetheless, Jünger, one of the most prolific writers of his generation, was enormously influential in shaping the veterans' ideal of the frontline fighter, an ideal that excluded a significant proportion of ex-servicemen. The Weimar Republic saw a bitter wrangle over the question of who did and who did not belong to this exclusive group. Did army railroaders, for instance, share the front experience? Their association was anxious to stress the unity of "sword and track," which was the theme of their war memorial in the Berlin suburb of Schöneberg.[50] "Does it not take a whole heart . . . to drive the trains onto the battlefield in the storm of steel of the enemy artillery?" their leader asked. "The army railroad-service, full of privation, called for hearts and nerves of steel and iron fists."[51]

After the war, imagery of memorialization frequently borrowed and transformed imagery of wartime visual culture and discourses depicting the "metallization" of the German soldier. That imagery may have been bourgeois in its origin, since metaphors of iron determination and endurance reflected long-established fears about mental degeneration, fears that predominated among the middle classes. They were the instigators of iron-nail landmarks in 1915–16. But after the war such metaphors became most seductive among the minority of soldiers who joined in the Jüngerian chorus. The steeled superman was the brainchild of a counterrevolutionary elite, eagerly embraced by equally reactionary spokesmen of conservative veterans' associations and regimental societies.[52] In contrast, the silent majority of soldiers held themselves aloof from veterans' politics.[53] And although workers participated in the nailing rituals, the working-class press proved by and large immune to the mystique of metal.[54] Thus any understanding of the image of the iron warrior must take into account the specific moment and context of its dissemination and reception.

Representations of Slaughter: Britain's Chivalrous Knights

Ernst Jünger's *Storm of Steel*, first published in German in 1921, is now one of the most celebrated accounts of the experience of the trench war. However, prior to 1929 both the novel and its author were little known outside the *Reichswehr*, the veterans' camp, and radical nationalist circles. Jünger achieved overnight fame in the literary world when the distinguished publishing house of Chatto and Windus brought out the English-language edition of *Storm of Steel* in 1929. Within a year of publication the translation of Jünger's book not only went through five editions but was also given more—and mostly favorable—reviews than the German original(s) throughout the era of the Weimar Republic. British reviewers, though, demonstrated a conspicuous naiveté about Jünger's reactionary agenda.[55] In 1930 one critic commented on Jünger's *Copse 125* that in the publisher's announcement "we are told, the book 'is an epic of action, endurance, and courage.' I fail to see this. A greater part is concerned with reflections on the nobility of being noble and how noble it is to slaughter or be slaughtered for my country, right or wrong."[56]

Had Jünger fooled his British readership? Literary historian Hans-Harald Müller holds that the preface to the English edition of *Storm of Steel* was one factor in molding British readings of Jünger's oeuvre.[57] In the foreword Jünger shifts the emphasis from the German "war experience" to British conduct in war:

> Time only strengthens my conviction that it was a good and strenuous life, and that the war, for all its destructiveness, was an incomparable schooling of the heart. The front-line soldier whose foot came down on the earth so grimly and harshly may claim this at least, that it came down cleanly. Warlike achievements are enhanced by the inherent worth of the enemy. Of all the troops who were opposed to the Germans on the great battlefields the English were not only the most formidable but the manliest and most chivalrous.[58]

Jünger reiterated a British popular sentiment. Chivalry dominated British imaginings of the Great War. It was a commemorative trope that tended to obscure exactly the harshness of war captured in Jünger's writings. Britons showed little understanding of the kind of warfare the First World War epitomized, warfare that, according to the *Daily Chronicle*, "requires deathless endurance, but no chivalry."[59] The ghastliness of the war, however, did not diminish the glory of the warrior. "War is not glorious . . . but oftentimes in war men are," public commemorations reasserted.[60] Soldiers were deemed glorious when they adhered to the principles of chivalry. The centrality of chivalry in war remembrance points to the profound force of civil society in Britain. Memory work was by and large in the hands of middle-aged civilians who, in contrast to their German counterparts, lacked first-hand army experience (conscription had been introduced only in January 1916) as well as a militaristic socialization. Consequently, agents of remembrance failed to translate experiences of combat into a commemorative discourse, for they had little to say about the "war experience" and the virtue of iron endurance. Instead, they exalted their soldiers' chivalry, a code of conduct not specific to the First World War but firmly anchored in British public life.

Medieval Knights and British Gentlemen

The concept of chivalry was by no means an invention of the age of the Great War. Modernized chivalry had entered the arena of British high culture by the beginning of the nineteenth century.[61] The concept operated on two interrelated levels. On the one hand, chivalry manifested itself as an aesthetic phenomenon. The Eglinton Tournament, fancy-dress balls with Queen Victoria and Prince Albert, Sir Walter Scott's novels, or Pre-Raphaelite paintings offered aesthetic redemption to the perceived ugliness of the modern world. On the other hand, romantic images of chivalry were transformed into a normative force. Medieval knighthood constituted a resource for people who wanted to ennoble and better the existing world. The concept of the gentleman came into being in part as an adoption of the medieval idea of chivalry designed for modern everyday life.[62] The gentlemanly paradigm was in essence a code of behavior that prescribed a set of virtues, such as fairness, kindness, or loyalty. The ability to conform to these standards was seen as a function of character.[63] Character, in turn, demanded conquering one's weaker self. Modern knights were engaged in a permanent struggle; "life was a battlefield on which a gentleman had to fight impure thoughts in himself, injustice or ignorance in others," writes Mark Girouard.[64] The language of fighting permeated the gentlemanly community. The knights of Edwardian Britain, literary historians have pointed out, were mentally primed for combat when war broke out in 1914.[65]

An emphasis on character is the salient mark of languages of chivalry. It is the knightly or gentlemanly character that sets

STEFAN GOEBEL

the modern knight apart from ordinary mankind. The system of high diction in war remembrance that defined the chivalric character can be divided broadly into five categories: courage, duty, honor, fairness, and faith. All five elements together do not necessarily occur in any given memorial project. For example, at Redgrave, East Suffolk, stress was laid on "chivalry, courage, faith."[66] In aggregate, however, the five constituents stand out.

Convention dictated that knights were courageous, brave, gallant, or valiant—the four most popular adjectives in inscription lines and unveiling speeches. Fallen soldiers were remembered collectively as those "Whose dauntless courage / Was the living breath / Of freedom and of chivalry / And truth."[67] They were thus remembered individually as well: "a man of courage, unshakable and chivalrous as strong."[68] Memorial makers indulged in heroics. Nevertheless, Paul Fussell's argument that chivalry connoted total bravery, an idea that could not admit of human weakness, does not stand scrutiny.[69] Visual representations of knights were in many cases not stridently heroic. The figure of St George at Leeds, although victorious, has a pensive look on his face. His opposite number at Colchester, also sculpted by H. C. Fehr, bows his head as a sign of mourning.[70] Similar to depictions of the "Tommy" (the embodiment of the ordinary British soldier), knights "represented a nation drawn into war by necessity, not design."[71] Even official propagandists did not necessarily uphold the notion of total bravery. In a speech to an American audience on St. George's Day in 1918, John Masefield suggested that England's patron saint "went out, I think, as the battalions of our men went out, a little trembling and a little sick and not knowing much about it, except that it had to be done, and then stood up to the dragon in the mud of that far land, and waited for him to come on."[72]

The concept of courage was intrinsically tied up with the notion of dutiful service to the community. The dutiful aspect of service had been accentuated by wartime propaganda prior to the passing of the Military Service Act in January 1916. As Britain's war effort relied initially on voluntary recruitment, early propaganda appealed to men's chivalrous feelings. A well-known poster issued by the Parliamentary Recruiting Committee in 1915 proclaiming "BRITAIN NEEDS YOU AT ONCE" depicted St. George clad in armor fighting the beast (fig. 16).[73] The language of volunteering of 1914–15, however, lived on in the rhetoric of war remembrance in spite of conscription. A private from Chatteris, Cambridgeshire, was posthumously awarded the Victoria Cross "for most conspicuous bravery and devotion to duty."[74] He had been killed in action in France in 1917 after rescuing wounded comrades. Accordingly, his memorial window in Chatteris parish church features a knight in gleaming armor. Knights were supposed to have a rigid sense of duty and to be ready to serve. "The word knight . . . means 'servant,'" emphasized a wartime agitator.[75] Selfless service entailed the preparedness to die; that is, to make the supreme sacrifice: "Tranquil you lie, your knightly virtue proved," reads the famous stanza of "O Valiant Hearts" ("The Supreme Sacrifice").[76] John Arkwright's hymn set the tone of commemorations throughout the British Isles. It was obligatory to sing the hymn at remembrance services. In addition the text was inscribed on many war memorials.[77]

Failure to answer the call of duty courageously resulted in dishonor. A Welsh-language epitaph dedicated to a "true and very gallant Welsh gentleman" stated that it was "A thousand times better to die as a brave boy than to live as a cowardly boy."[78] The highest form of honor at which a soldier knight could aim was a "death of honour."[79] Honor was the knight's reward for sacrificial death for the sake of Britain's great crusade.

STEFAN GOEBEL

Fig. 16. Before conscription was introduced in Britain, domestic propaganda appealed to men's chivalrous feelings and sense of duty. This anonymous PRC poster depicts St. George in armor fighting the dragon. "Britain Needs You at Once," 1915. Bibliothek für Zeitgeschichte, Stuttgart.

At the same time, commitment to honor imposed a moral obligation on the soldier. He was not to hate his enemy but was bound, by the brotherhood of arms, to respect the enemy even while doing his best to kill his foe: "During one of the very few months of open warfare a cavalry private of ours brought in a captive, a gorgeous specimen of the terrific Prussian Uhlan of tradition. 'But why didn't you put your sword through him?,' an officer asked, who belonged to the school of Froissart less obviously than the private. 'Well, sir,' the captor replied, 'the gentleman wasn't looking.'"[80]

It is noteworthy that this quotation is taken from *Disenchantment* by C. E. Montague, first published in 1922. The author is a prime authority on the turn of mind produced by the war, according to Samuel Hynes.[81] Yet the title of the book is misleading, and Montague's attitude to the war is more nuanced than literary critics have admitted.[82] Some passages evince his bitterness and disillusionment; others convey his belief in the survival of personal morality. The common man is portrayed as a hero, the commander as a villain. Characteristically, the paragraph cited was reprinted in a volume containing uplifting prose and poetry for private remembrance on Armistice Day, thus converting an "anti-monument" (if it was one at all) into an affirmation of Victorian notions of chivalry and decency. Likewise, wartime posters depicting medieval knights displayed what one scholar called "a vision of individual masculine heroism that rose above the unspoken dehumanization and degradation of trench warfare."[83] Public commemorations after the war, too, assured the bereaved that the war dead were not bloodthirsty killers. Even though they spilled human blood, the dead remained untainted: "Not only were they gallant in action, they were chivalrous to their enemies."[84] Fairness toward the opponent was axiomatic in the chivalric code. Scrupulously fair conduct involved recognized formalities like straightforward attack and courtesies like kindness toward prisoners of war.

The chivalrous bearing of medieval warriors in battle testified to the fact "that you need not cease to be a Christian or a gentleman because you have to fight," underlined Bishop Arthur Winnington-Ingram in 1917.[85] Gentility rather than aggression marked the knight. The unwritten laws of chivalry resonated allegedly with Christian dogma. Chivalry and Christianity, it seemed, went hand in hand. Church propagandists even pictured heaven itself as a breeding ground for chivalry. Fanatical preachers did not shy away from calling Jesus "the one perfect chivalrous Gentleman that the world

STEFAN GOEBEL

has ever seen," or "the most perfect and knightly character in the whole history of chivalry."[86] Oxford theologian Henry Scott Holland conceived the Sermon on the Mount as "the book of Christian Knighthood"—the Gospel revisited.[87] Some outspokenly belligerent churchmen gave their blessing to the perpetuation of these images on the local level. A memorial plaque mounted by members of a soldiers' home in Avenmouth, Gloucestershire, honored those who by their sacrifice had "upheld the cause of justice and true Christian chivalry."[88] In figurative war memorials the iconography could establish a link between chivalry and faith. The connection is especially striking where knights are depicted holding a sword aloft but pointing downward. In that the sword, the prime symbol of chivalry, becomes a cross, as in the case of the Pearl Assurance war memorial by Sir George Frampton. At the unveiling ceremony in London in 1921, the chairman of the company commented on the memorial design that it

> is crowned by a figure of a chivalrous Knight, holding a shield on which is engraved the Cross of Christianity—the emblem of sacrifice. In the right hand aloft is the sword of glorious victory; at the feet lies a dead monster—the embodiment of all that is brutal, treacherous and unholy—slain and obliterated from our life, we fervently hope, for all time by those other 435 valiant and chivalrous knights [i.e., the killed employees] whose names are cut in everlasting granite, which will be a perpetual reminder to posterity and ourselves of our great indebtedness to them.[89]

Chivalrous Knights versus Iron Warriors, Civic Values versus Military Virtues

In the wake of the First World War every one of Britain's fallen soldiers could be regarded a courageous, dutiful, honorable, fair, and holy knight; the class dichotomy typical of the medieval revival in the previous period dissolved after 1914–18. To label this development chivalric egalitarianism or feudalization of war remembrance is to miss the main point. Crucial to an understanding of chivalric notation in war remembrance is the fact that the war dead were not only victims but also executioners.[90] Just as chivalric imagery in war posters had mystified the violence of trench warfare during the conflict, so chivalric notation provided one solution to the moral dilemmas of the postwar years. The soldiers of 1914–18 were both defenders and killers, mobilized by civilian society in their defense. Evocations of chivalry resolved doubts as to the moral character of the actions of the soldiers, both those who survived and those who had died in the war. Chivalric tropes in war posters and memorials reconfigured the act of killing as a bloody yet noble deed, a deed that followed a code of conduct deeply entrenched in the norms of civil society in Britain. The language of chivalry recognized the fact that the soldier had taken life but translated the slaughter of the Great War into a narrative intelligible to the British, a nation proud of its naval past but without strong military traditions.[91]

By contrast, scholars have noted that Germans had been socialized into a "nation-at-arms" through victory parades, veterans' societies, and compulsory military service in the late nineteenth century.[92] The fact that combat entailed killing did not come as a shocking revelation to the German public in 1914–18. Rather the enormity and novelty of the event as such had to be located in a symbolic order to make it tolerable. The *Kriegserlebnis*, the experience of industrialized mass warfare, became encoded in images of steely endurance; the iron knight preceded the gentlemanly knight. Notably, war landmarks conveyed German tenacity. In Dortmund, Westphalia, the iron-nail monument unveiled in September 1915 represented the city's patron saint, St. Reinoldus, in a suit of armor shouldering

STEFAN GOEBEL

a large sword. In 1920 a local clergyman compared the "Iron St. Reinoldus" to a fourteenth-century effigy of the warrior saint: "The Reinoldus created by the sculptor Bagdons . . . is of shattering force and steadfast warriorhood [*Reckenhaftig-keit*], whereas the saint of the church shall remain an exemplar of Christian faith and chivalrous devoutness."[93] Overall, there was a marked contrast between the prevalence of visual representations of knights—ranging from St. George to Roland—and the insignificance of chivalric diction in German representations of the Great War.[94]

The *Materialschlacht* (at the Western Front) revolutionized the connotations of endurance; the "storm of steel" put an immense and often intolerable strain on the combatants. Many Germans empathized with (or, in reactionary circles, eulogized over) the soldier's ordeal of battle: his iron endurance in the midst of a frenzy of destruction. In fact, the "eyewitnesses"— that is, the veterans—themselves assumed an active role in shaping the course of commemoration. Tommy's *Kriegserlebnis*, by contrast, met with silence at home (though translations of German war literature sold well in Britain). British discourses, predominantly conducted by civilians, dwelt on *conduct in* war (that is, the killing) rather than the *experience of* war (that is, the battle of *matériel*). In Britain, civilian agents of remembrance propagated the ideal of the chivalrous gentleman rather than the iron knight and civic values rather than military virtues. Chivalric diction, firmly anchored in prewar public life, translated the act of killing into a language that was comprehensible to an unmilitary society.

Notes

A research fellowship at Churchill College, Cambridge, enabled me to research and write this essay, and I would like to thank the Master and Fellows of the college for their support. Thanks are also due to Santanu Das for his perceptive comments on this essay.

1. On the demographic history of the war, see J. M. Winter, *The Great War and the British People* (London: Macmillan, 1986).

2. For extended discussion of medievalism in the commemoration of the Great War, see Stefan Goebel, *The Great War and Medieval Memory: War, Remembrance and Medievalism in Britain and Germany, 1914–1940* (Cambridge: Cambridge University Press, 2007); Stefan Goebel, "Re-membered and Re-mobilized: The 'Sleeping Dead' in Interwar Germany and Britain," *Journal of Contemporary History* 39 (2004): 487–501.

3. On agency in war commemoration, see Jay Winter and Emmanuel Sivan, "Setting the Framework," in *War and Remembrance in the Twentieth Century*, ed. Jay Winter and Emmanuel Sivan (Cambridge: Cambridge University Press, 1999), 6–39.

4. On visual propaganda and postwar commemoration, see Daniel J. Sherman, *The Construction of Memory in Interwar France* (Chicago: University of Chicago Press, 1999), 15, 49–64.

5. "Der Eiserne Roland in Bremen: Die Einweihungsfeier," *Bremer Nachrichten*, no. 195, July 16, 1915. Unless otherwise indicated, all translations are my own.

6. "Einweihung des 'Schmiedes von Essen,'" *Rheinisch-Westfälischer Anzeiger*, no. 205, July 26, 1915.

7. "Das ist der Weg zum Frieden," 1918, Plakatsammlung Erster Weltkrieg, 2.5/32, and "Deutsche Kriegsausstellung," 1916, Plakatsammlung Erster Weltkrieg, 2.6/1, Bibliothek für Zeitgeschichte, Stuttgart. The former poster is included in Peter Paret, Beth Irwin Lewis, and Paul Paret, eds., *Persuasive Images: Posters of War and Revolution from the Hoover Institution Archives* (Princeton: Princeton University Press, 1992), fig. 101.

8. David Lloyd George, "Through Terror and Triumph!" in *Through Terror to Triumph: Speeches and Pronouncements of the Right Hon. David Lloyd George, M.P., Since the Beginning of the War*, ed. F. L. Stevenson (London: Hodder and Stoughton, 1915), 10; on the speech of 1897, see Lothar Reinermann, *Der Kaiser in England: Wilhelm II. und sein Bild in der britischen Öffentlichkeit* (Paderborn: Ferdinand Schöningh, 2001), 180–81.

9. David Clark, "Rejoice!" unspecified press cutting, n.d., acc. 7216, vol. 2, Stewartry Museum, Kirkcudbright; G. K. Chesterton, *Autobiography* (London: Hutchinson, 1936), 246.

10. Werner Sombart, *Händler und Helden: Patriotische Besinnungen* (Munich and Leipzig: Duncker & Humblot, 1915), 131–32.

11. Aribert Reimann, *Der große Krieg der Sprachen: Untersuchungen zur historischen Semantik in Deutschland und England zur Zeit des Ersten Weltkriegs* (Essen: Klartext, 2000), 39–68, 280.

12. Sabine Kienitz, "Der Krieg der Invaliden: Helden-Bilder und Männlichkeitskonstruktionen nach dem Ersten Weltkrieg," *Militärgeschichtliche Zeitschrift* 60 (2001): 384–87.

13. Angela Gaffney, *Aftermath: Remembering the Great War in Wales* (Cardiff: University of Wales Press, 1998), 26–33; Adrian Gregory, *The Silence of Memory: Armistice Day 1919–1946* (Oxford: Berg, 1994), chap. 2; Mark Connelly, *The Great War, Memory and Ritual: Commemoration in the City and East London, 1916–1939* (Woodbridge: Boydell, 2002), 190. For a contrary opinion, see Alex King, *Memorials of the Great War in Britain: The Symbolism and Politics of Remembrance* (Oxford: Berg, 1998), 29, 90; Keith Grieves, "Common Meeting Places and the Brightening of Rural Life: Local Debates on Village Halls in Sussex after the First World War," *Rural History* 10 (1999): 171–92.

14. Bernd Ulrich, *Die Augenzeugen: Deutsche Feldpostbriefe in Kriegs- und Nachkriegszeit 1914–1933* (Essen: Klartext, 1997).

15. Laurinda S. Stryker, "Languages of Sacrifice and Suffering in England in the First World War" (PhD diss., University of Cambridge, 1992); see also Peter Leese, *Shell Shock: Traumatic Neurosis and the British Soldiers of the First World War* (Basingstoke: Palgrave, 2002).

16. Jay Winter, "Shell-Shock and the Cultural History of the Great War," *Journal of Contemporary History* 35 (2000): 7–11.

17. Hans Sachs, "Vom Hurrakitsch, von Nagelungsstandbildern, Nagelungsplakaten und anderen—Schönheiten," *Das Plakat* 8, no. 1 (1917): 3–21.

18. Stefan Goebel, "Forging the Industrial Home Front: Iron-Nail Memorials in the Ruhr," in *Uncovered Fields: Perspectives in First World War Studies*, ed. Jenny Macleod and Pierre Purseigle (Leiden: Brill, 2004), 159–78; Gerhard Schneider, "Zur Mobilisierung der 'Heimatfront': Das Nageln sogenannter Kriegswahrzeichen im Ersten Weltkrieg," *Zeitschrift für Volkskunde* 95 (1999): 32–62.

19. On the the brutalizing effects of the Great War, see George L. Mosse, *Fallen Soldiers: Reshaping the Memory of the World Wars* (New York: Oxford University Press, 1990), chap. 9; Klaus Theweleit, *Männerphantasien*, 2 vols. (Reinbek: Rowohlt, 1980); Modris Eksteins, *Rites of Spring: The Great War and the Birth of the Modern Age* (London: Bantam, 1989); Niall Ferguson, *The Pity of War* (London: Allen Lane, 1998), 357–66; see also the critique of the brutalization thesis in Richard Bessel, *Germany after the First World War* (Oxford: Clarendon Press, 1993); Dirk Schumann and Andreas Wirsching, eds., "Violence and Society after the First World War," theme issue, *Journal of Modern European History* 1 (2003).

20. "Die Einweihung des Eisernen Wehrmannes," *Halberstädter Zeitung und Intelligenzblatt*, no. 23, suppl., January 28, 1916.

21. Joachim Radkau, *Das Zeitalter der Nervosität: Deutschland zwischen Bismarck und Hitler* (Munich: Carl Hanser, 1998).

22. Radkau, *Zeitalter der Nervosität*, chap. 5; see also Paul Lerner, "Psychiatry and Casualties of War in Germany, 1914–18," *Journal of Contemporary History* 35 (2000): 13–28.

23. Sachs, "Vom Hurrakitsch," 10.

24. Karl Ernst Osthaus, "Die Kunst und der Eiserne Schmied in Hagen," *West-fälisches Tageblatt*, no. 214, September 13, 1915; see, in general, Reimann, *Krieg der Sprachen*, 48–68.

25. "Der Eiserne Roland in Bremen: Die Einweihungsfeier," *Bremer Nachrichten*, no. 195, July 16, 1915; see also "Der Eiserne Roland zu Bremen," postcard, n.d. (1915), 10-B-Al-875, Staatsarchiv Bremen.

26. *Der Eiserne Schmied von Hagen: Das Erste Jahr seiner Geschichte* (Hagen: Verlag des Eisernen Schmiedes, 1916), 3; "Im Zeichen des Sedantages: Der 'Wackere Schwabe' in Eisen," *Stuttgarter Neues Tagblatt*, no. 443, September 2, 1915.

27. On celebrations of Sedan Day in Württemberg, see Alon Confino, *The Nation as a Local Metaphor: Württemberg, Imperial Germany, and National Memory, 1871–1918* (Chapel Hill: University of North Carolina Press, 1997).

28. "Die Einweihung des 'Wackeren Schwaben,'" *Schwäbische Tagwacht: Organ der Sozialdemokraten Württembergs*, no. 205, September 3, 1915; "Einweihung des 'Wackeren Schwaben,'" *Stuttgarter Neues Tagblatt*, no. 444, September 2, 1915; see Carl Grüninger, "Der wackere Schwabe in Eisen zu Stuttgart" (1915), in *Plakate des Ersten Weltkrieges 1914–1918*, ed. Deutsches Historisches Museum, CD-ROM (Munich: K. G. Saur, 1996), P64/329.

29. "Im Zeichen des Sedantages: Der 'Wackere Schwabe' in Eisen," *Stuttgarter Neues Tagblatt*, no. 443, September 2, 1915.

30. Wilhelm Schussen, "Der Wackere Schwabe," *Stuttgarter Neues Tagblatt*, no. 277, June 17, 1932.

31. "Wackerer Schwabe," n.d. (1931), Postkartensammlung Stadtarchiv Stuttgart.

32. Goebel, "Forging the Industrial Home Front," esp. 174–75.

33. Erich Maria Remarque, *All Quiet on the Western Front* (London: G. P. Putnam, 1929), 67.

34. Otto Riebicke, "Ringen an der Somme—Das seelische Erleben eines Frontkämpfers" (1917; reissued 1928), in *Krieg im Frieden: Die umkämpfte Erinnerung an den Ersten Weltkrieg*, ed. Bernd Ulrich and Benjamin Ziemann (Frankfurt am Main: Fischer, 1997), doc. 21b.

35. "VII⁺ᵉ Kriegsanleihe," 1917, PST 3213, and "Brigarde Reinhard," n.d. (1919), PST 5985, Imperial War Museum, London (hereafter IWM).

36. Ludwig Kittel, "Heldenehrung in Ostfriesland," *Ostfreesland: Ein Kalender für Jedermann* 15 (1928): 101.

37. On the Stahlhelm league, see Volker R. Berghahn, *Der Stahlhelm: Bund der Frontsoldaten 1918–1935* (Düsseldorf: Droste, 1966).

38. Bernd Hüppauf, "Schlachtenmythen und die Konstruktion des 'Neuen Menschen,'" in *"Keiner fühlt sich hier mehr als Mensch . . .": Erlebnis und Wirkung des Ersten Weltkriegs*, ed. Gerhard Hirschfeld, Gerd Krumeich, and Irina Renz (Frankfurt am Main: Fischer, 1996), esp. 81–84; see also Mosse, *Fallen Soldiers*, 132, 184–85.

39. Barbara Posthoff, ed., *Plakatsammlung des Instituts für Zeitungsforschung der Stadt Dortmund*, microfiches (Munich: K. G. Saur, 1992), F7/15.

40. Detlef Hoffmann, "Der Mann mit dem Stahlhelm vor Verdun: Fritz Erlers Plakat zur sechsten Kriegsanleihe 1917," in *Die Dekoration der Gewalt: Kunst und Medien im Faschismus*, ed. Berthold Hinz et al. (Giessen: Anabas, 1979), 108–9; Paret et al., *Persuasive Images*, figs. 58, 152–57; George L. Mosse, *The Image of Man: The Creation of Modern Masculinity* (Oxford: Oxford University Press, 1996), 115–17.

41. Jünger, *In Stahlgewittern: Ein Kriegstagebuch*, 20th ed. (Berlin: E. S. Mittler, 1940), 97. The 20th edition is a reprint of the 16th edition (4th revised version) of 1935. Jünger revised his novel four times in the years 1921 to 1935. *Inter alia* he altered the wording of the passage cited, putting additional emphasis on the steel helmet.

42. Lerner, "Psychiatry and Casualties of War," 27.

43. As cited in Radkau, *Zeitalter der Nervosität*, 404.

44. Sabine Behrenbeck, "Zwischen Trauer und Heroisierung: Vom Umgang mit Kriegstod und Niederlage nach 1918," in *Kriegsende 1918: Ereignis, Wirkung, Nachwirkung*, ed. Jörg Duppler and Gerhard P. Groß (Munich: R. Oldenbourg, 1999), 336–37.

45. Karl von Seeger, *Das Denkmal des Weltkriegs* (Stuttgart: Hugo Matthaes, [1930]), 35, 148–49.

46. Von Seeger, *Das Denkmal des Weltkriegs*, 35.

47. Reichskunstwart Edwin Redslob to Edgar C. Kiesel, May 2, 1930, R 32/350, fol. 211, Bundesarchiv, Berlin.

48. Stadtbaumeister Dorner, "Kriegerdenkmal in Ludgeri-Kirche," memorandum, October 20, 1932, Dep. 60, uncatalogued files, Staatsarchiv Aurich.

49. "Der 'Roland' von Norden," photographs, n.d., Nachlaß Hermann Hosaeus, Ho 854, Hochschularchiv, Technische Universität Berlin.

50. Max Heubes, ed., *Ehrenbuch der Feldeisenbahner* (Berlin: Wilhelm Kolk, 1931), n.p.

51. Heubes, *Ehrenbuch der Feldeisenbahner*.

52. See the critique of Bernd Hüppauf's thesis by Benjamin Ziemann, "'Macht der Maschine': Mythen des industriellen Krieges," in *Der Tod als Maschinist: Der industriealisierte Krieg 1914–1918*, ed. Rolf Spilker and Bernd Ulrich (Bramsche: Rasch, 1998), 184.

53. Benjamin Ziemann, *Front und Heimat: Ländliche Kriegserfahrungen im südlichen Bayern 1914–1923* (Essen: Klartext, 1997), 419–20, 437.

54. Reimann, *Krieg der Sprachen*, 67–68.

55. Hans-Harald Müller, "'Herr Jünger Thinks War a Lovely Business' (On the Reception of Ernst Jünger's *In Stahlgewittern* in Germany and Britain before 1933)," in *Intimate Enemies: English and German Literary Reactions to the Great War*

1914–1918, ed. Franz Karl Stanzel and Martin Löschnigg (Heidelberg: C. Winter, 1993), 328.

56. "Copse 125," *Life and Letters* 5 (1930): 142; see Müller, "Herr Jünger," 334.

57. Müller, "Herr Jünger," 331.

58. Ernst Jünger, *The Storm of Steel: From the Diary of a German Strom-Troop Officer on the Western Front*, introduction by R. H. Mottram (London: Chatto and Windus, 1929), xii–xiii. The English edition is based on the 5th edition (2nd revised version) of *In Stahlgewittern* (1924).

59. Hall Caine, "The Coming of Peace," *Daily Chronicle*, no. 17304, August 3, 1917; see Reimann, *Krieg der Sprachen*, 46.

60. "Kirkcudbright Parish Church: War Memorial Unveiled," unspecified press cutting, January 16, 1921, acc. 7216, vol. 3, 11–2, Stewartry Museum, Kirkcudbright.

61. Mark Girouard, *The Return to Camelot: Chivalry and the English Gentleman* (New Haven: Yale University Press, 1981); see also Marcus Collins, "The Fall of the English Gentleman: The National Character in Decline, *c.* 1918–1970," *Historical Research* 75 (2002): 90–111.

62. Girouard, *Return to Camelot*, esp. 260–74.

63. On "character," see Stefan Collini, *Public Moralists: Political Thought and Intellectual Life in Britain 1850–1930* (Oxford: Clarendon, 1991), chap. 3.

64. Girouard, *Return to Camelot*, 281.

65. Girouard, *Return to Camelot*, 281; Michael C. C. Adams, *The Great Adventure: Male Desire and the Coming of World War I* (Bloomington: Indiana University Press, 1990), chap. 5; see also Allen J. Frantzen, *Bloody Good: Chivalry, Sacrifice, and the Great War* (Chicago: University of Chicago Press, 2004).

66. Faculty for memorial to Captain the Hon. Lyon Playfair, Redgrave, February 21, 1916, Redgrave with Boesdale Parish Records, FB 132, E 3/3, Suffolk Record Office, Ipswich.

67. Mountain Ash, Glam., 6777, National Inventory of War Memorials (hereafter NIWM) at the Imperial War Museum, London; and South Stoke, Oxon., as cited in Patricia Utechin, *The Trumpets Sounded: Commemoration of the War Dead in the Parish Churches of Oxfordshire* (Oxford: Robert Dugdale, 1996), 40.

68. Harrow, Middlesex, 18007, NIWM.

69. Paul Fussell, "The Fate of Chivalry and the Assault upon Mother," in *Killing, in Verse and Prose and Other Essays* (London: Bellew, 1990), 222.

70. Colchester Borough War Memorial Committees and Sub-Committees, minutes, 1919–25, acc. C4, Essex Record Office, Colchester.

71. J. M. Winter, "British National Identity and the First World War," in *The Boundaries of the State in Modern Britain*, ed. S. J. D. Green and R. C. Whiting (Cambridge: Cambridge University Press, 1996), 269–70; see also Alan Borg, *War Memorials: From Antiquity to the Present* (London: Leo Cooper, 1991), 50.

72. John Masefield, *St. George and the Dragon* (London: William Heinemann, 1919), 42–43.

73. "Britain Needs You," 1915, PST 4902, PRC 108, IMW. This poster is reproduced in Paret et al., *Persuasive Images*, fig. 66.

74. Faculty for window for G. W. Clare, Chatteris, May 4, 1918, Ely Diocesan Records, D 3/4C, 21-2 and D 3/5, Cambridge University Library; see also Lanhydrock, Cornwall, 1890S, NIWM.

75. Edward S. Woods, *Knights in Armour* (London: Robert Scott, 1916), 16.

76. John S. Arkwright, "The Supreme Sacrifice," in John S. Arkwright, *The Supreme Sacrifice and Other Poems in Time of War*, 2nd ed. (London: Skeffington, 1919), 17–18.

77. "Borough of Talbot: War Memorial in Remembrance of Those of this Borough Who Fell in the Great War," June 27, 1925, Ephemera Collection Memorials, K 3820, IWM, is an example.

78. Aberystwyth, Cardigan, 6977, NIWM.

79. Wisbech, Cambs., 3465, NIWM.

80. C. E. Montague, "Christmas 1914," in *Cenotaph: A Book of Remembrance in Poetry and Prose for November the Eleventh*, ed. Thomas Moult (London: Jonathan Cape, 1923), 102; C. E. Montague, *Disenchantment* (London: Chatto and Windus, 1922), 140; on chivalry and soldiers' attitudes toward military killing, see Joanna Bourke, *An Intimate History of Killing: Face-to-Face Killing in Twentieth-Century Warfare* (London: Granta, 1999), 67, 169–70.

81. Samuel Hynes, *A War Imagined: The First World War and English Culture* (London: Bodley Head, 1990), 307–10; Peter Buitenhuis argues similarly in *The Great War of Words: Literature as Propaganda 1914–18 and After* (London: B. T. Batsford, 1989), 149–51.

82. Keith Grieves, "C. E. Montague and the Making of *Disenchantment*, 1914–1921," *War in History* 4 (1997): esp. 44–45, offers a revisionist account of Montague's work.

83. Paret et al., *Persuasive Images*, 50.

84. "Pembrokeshire's War Memorial: Unveiling by Milford V.C.," *Pembrokeshire Telegraph*, no. 3575, September 7, 1921.

85. Arthur F. Winnington-Ingram, *The Potter and the Clay* (London: Wells Gardner and Darton, 1917), 62.

86. Woods, *Knights in Armour*, 25; see Albert Marrin, *The Last Crusade: The Church of England in the First World War* (Durham NC: Duke University Press, 1974), 153.

87. As cited in Alan Wilkinson, *The Church of England and the First World War*, 2nd ed. (London: SCM, 1996), 231.

88. Avenmouth, Glos., 7363, NIWM.

89. "Pearl War Memorial," *Insurance Gem* 12, no. 139 (1921); Peterborough [originally London], Northants., 3569, NIWM.

90. Jay Winter, "Representations of War on the Western Front, 1914–18: Some Reflections on Cultural Ambivalence," in *Power, Violence and Mass Death in Pre-Modern and Modern Times*, ed. Joseph Canning, Hartmut Lehmann, and Jay Winter (Aldershot: Ashgate, 2004), 212.

91. On the debate on militarism in Britain before 1914, see Winter, "Representations of War," 206–7; for a contrary opinion see Anne Summers, "Militarism in Britain before the Great War," *History Workshop* 2 (1976): 104–24; on the cult of the navy, see Jan Rüger, "Nation, Empire and Navy: Identity Politics in the United Kingdom 1887–1914," *Past & Present*, no. 185 (2004): 159–87.

92. Jakob Vogel, *Nationen im Gleichschritt: Der Kult der "Nation in Waffen" in Deutschland und Frankreich, 1871–1914* (Göttingen: Vandenhoeck & Ruprecht, 1997); see also Frank Becker, *Bilder von Krieg und Nation: Die Einigungskriege in der bürgerlichen Öffentlichkeit Deutschlands 1864–1913* (Munich: R. Oldenbourg, 2001).

93. Hans Strobel, ed., *Dortmund: Ein Blick in eine deutsche Industriestadt* (Dortmund: C. L. Krüger, 1922), 50–52; see Uwe Fleckner and Jürgen Zänker, eds., *Friedrich Bagdons (1878–1937): Eine Bildhauerkarriere vom Kaiserreich zum Nationalsozialismus* (Stuttgart: Gerd Hatje, 1993), 48–49.

94. Compare, by contrast, Frantzen, *Bloody Good*, 165, who relies entirely on iconographic evidence.

4

Regression versus Progression: Fundamental Differences in German and American Posters of the First World War

I n his classic *Posters of the First World War*, Maurice Rickards focuses on the universality of First World War poster language: on the similarities—thematic, visual, and linguistic—that pervade the war propaganda poster production of the time.

While not disputing the presence of such similarities as common archetypes, slogans, and images to which Rickards points, we argue there are nevertheless *fundamental* differences in the posters of the combatant nations. This is nowhere more apparent than in German and American posters created between 1914 and 1918 and is most clearly visible in those designs created after the United States entered the conflict in April 1917. German and American posters reveal underlying differences of historical, social, and national perspective, which are enforced, reinforced, and sometimes created through subject selection and manner of portrayal. A survey of the posters reveals two nations, constructed out of different historical narratives, that identify with and are formed by different ideologies, iconographies, and modes of linguistic appeal.

We highlight these differences in poster language through the comparison of a representative cross section of individual German and American examples taken from the twelve hundred posters we have examined. While certainly far from exhaustive, in our opinion the selection constitutes a survey sufficiently wide in scope to support our conclusions.[1] We organize our analysis of these differences around a central distinction between regressive (Germany) and progressive (United States) narratives, a distinction we explain in terms of divergences in the development of the medium, different attitudes toward propaganda, and a fundamental difference of ethos. This regressive/progressive distinction is not intended as a value judgment, nor are we referring to any political vocabulary. Rather, this opposition captures the different temporal, spatial, and social attitudes communicated through these posters.

Art-historical and technological developments of the poster medium partially explain the differences in poster production and design of Germany and the United States during the Great War. The invention of steam-powered rotary printing (1843) and photoengraving (1881) caused a poster production boom in the United States in the 1880s and '90s. American artists profited from the artistic freedom these inventions guaranteed, developing original poster art that diverged from the German traditions rooted in the decorative and academic style of the Düsseldorf Academy of Art, the *alma mater* of many early American poster creators.[2] A distinctly American school developed favoring dynamic and realistic designs executed with graphic vitality and expressed in true color. Posters in the United States were used primarily as vehicles of commercial advertisement and were shaped by the competition for market share between the periodicals they promoted.[3] Accessibility to the American public became important.[4]

German posters did not show the same degree of adaptability because Germany's social profile was not changing so dynamically. Unlike their American counterparts, German designers worked within a firmly established and homogeneous

JAKUB KAZECKI AND JASON LIEBLANG

cultural context and could also count on a high level of literacy. In addition, the commercial poster boom did not arrive in Germany until almost twenty years after America's "poster revolution": Lucian Bernhard and Ludwig Hohlwein created their first advertising posters during the period 1900–10, and these designs, influenced by Jugendstil illustration, shaped the form of the commercial poster in Germany up to the First World War.

The most important compositional differences between American and German propaganda posters stem from their respective prewar traditions. The employment of a broader color spectrum resulted from the availability to American artists of greater technological and economic resources. While not all American posters are vibrantly colorful, many exhibit a wider spectrum than do German posters. Whereas German poster artists drew from Jugendstil, from the abstract directions of the European avant-garde, and from the typographical and compositional developments of Bernhard and Hohlwein, American artists worked out of a homegrown painterly tradition stressing realism and narrative.[5] Although many German posters show human figures and scenes representing "reality," the limited colors, the employment of color in blocks, and greater abstraction in human representation foreground decorative rather than thematic aspects. A wide survey also reveals that purely textual posters and those using maps with accompanying text make up a far greater percentage of overall production in Germany. These posters incorporate a lot of information but are often too complicated for rapid comprehension.

Common also are German posters employing a single image, such as an eagle or flag, with little text or purely informative text, in a manner reminiscent of prewar *Sachplakaten* (object posters). Some posters incorporate literary quotations, and a few effectively employ short, complementary legends.

Overall, however, American posters show more sophistication
in their wording and the extent to which text complements
image: illustrations of pithy slogans such as "Hun or Home?,"
"Clear-the-Way!!" or "Treat 'Em Rough" are common in American posters; far fewer German designs exhibit the seamless in-
terface between slogan and image that American posters frequently achieve (fig. 17).

   More important to German artists than textual brevity or ap-
propriateness is typographical quality and artistic integration
of design elements. Bernhard's textual posters illustrate the

Fig. 18. With its central letter "U" forming a submarine's hull afloat in a sea of text, Paul Dienst's "U-Boot-Spende: Gebe jeder nach seinen Kräften!" (U-Boat Donation: Each According to Their Means!) exemplifies German poster artists' desire to integrate word and image aesthetically. Deutsches Historisches Museum, Berlin.

emphasis on textual rendering, while Paul Dienst's "U-Boot-Spende," with its dominant "U" forming the hull of a submarine displayed floating in a sea of text, highlights the German pursuit of integrating word and image. In contrast to the terse statements accompanying realistic images that make many American posters immediately comprehensible and highly emotive, Dienst's composition captures the gaze with its central "U" but demands closer attention if its championing of heroism and rational appeal are to be understood (fig. 18).

A further compositional difference is in manner of portrayal. American posters for all agencies and purposes exhibit a striking kinetic tendency of which Joseph Clement Coll's "The Tidal Wave" is exemplary.[6] Here an eagle leads an armada of new ships atop a surging wave. Clouds hover above, these containing a stylized image of fast advancing cavalry. While German soldiers, usually alone, sit in trenches or stand guard, their American counterparts, often pictured as a group, march, charge, leap out of trenches, or walk purposefully to enlist, donate, or board ship. Likewise, American posters favor kinetic portrayals of technology while German technology is usually stylized or symbolic.[7]

The German Situation: "Should an Army Be Raised by the Same Means as Customers for Jam?"

In August 1914 the Supreme Command of the Army did not acknowledge posters as either an appropriate or a necessary means of propagating a conflict that Germany's decision makers perceived in almost mystical terms. The war was interpreted as an event uniting all social classes in enthusiasm for German historical destiny and therefore required no further announcement. Advertising methods used for enlistment in Great Britain and the United States were criticized in Germany as not corresponding to the dignity of the goal: "Should an army be raised by the same means as customers for jam?" asked one commentator.[8]

Even if German officials had attempted to use American-style advertising, they lacked the commercial experience needed to market a product. The authorities "contented themselves with proclaiming the law from their specially reserved places."[9] The posters lacked the avant-garde boldness of the best achievements in German commercial graphic art from before the war. Although their creators contributed propaganda posters, with their stylistic innovations clear in certain designs, military censorship limited their thematic and aesthetic choices. Propaganda posters simply reverted to the "strict typographic sobriety" that was popular before the turn of the century.[10] Additionally, the invasion of neutral Belgium in August 1914 put

JAKUB KAZECKI AND JASON LIEBLANG

German propaganda almost instantly on the defensive, both at home and abroad. Its tactics relied heavily on the rational explanation of war goals, played down the expansionist character of the war, and stressed the historic mission of superior German culture. In expectation of imminent victory, *Durchhalten* (fortitude), obedience to authorities, and unity during difficult times became the dominant themes of propaganda on the home front. In the United States, a small, informal but well-financed pro-German organization went about affecting American public opinion, primarily through rational defensive arguments in the press.[11]

The "turnip winter" of 1916–17 with its worsening food crisis marked the turning point in German public opinion. Calls for further sacrifices—advertised by posters promoting war loans, saving food, and recycling raw materials—were no longer proving effective. To support the morale of both soldiers and German civilians, in July 1917, a few months after the United States entered the war, the Supreme Command of the Army launched a program of "patriotic instruction." Although propaganda methods differed slightly from the formulas employed before 1917, the program nevertheless continued to attach great importance to national sentiments and the value of obedience to the emperor and military leaders.[12]

The American Situation: "The World's Greatest Adventure in Advertising"

Although officially neutral until April 2, 1917, the United States was in reality anything but neutral. The country's elite favored the Allies from the war's first weeks, with this sentiment rapidly growing under the influence of highly effective British propaganda.

American private loans and steadily increasing munitions shipments made it possible for the Allies to continue waging war in Europe, while at home the call for military preparedness, passionately championed by former president Theodore Roosevelt and often justified by arguments of the imminence of German invasion, was gaining in influence. Although popular opinion on entry was still divided, the influence of the president's advisors on a leader leaning in favor of the Allies—in spite of public commitment to pacifism and neutrality—made American entry into the conflict inevitable.

This pervasive pro-Allies attitude among the country's most powerful forces manifested itself as a media profusion of anti-German rhetoric: spy hysteria gripped the nation, as espionage headlines and often entirely fabricated stories of German atrocities found nationwide dissemination through oratory, books, and film and especially in the press, which at the beginning of the war favored the Allies by a ratio of five newspapers to one.[13]

While enlistment posters for various agencies were produced before 1917 in the United States, more important was that the period saw the crystallization and distribution of narratives describing Germany as barbaric and militaristic, its leader as a demonic despot, and its army of blood-thirsty rapists as a direct threat not only to American ideals but also to U.S. soil. These narratives are highly significant to poster production after April 1917, as they provided ready-made, emotionally charged propaganda themes to make visual—as well as a mass audience already familiar with them.[14]

Specifically American realities made greater demands on American propaganda than was the case for the other belligerents. Politically, war involvement constituted a radical departure from the isolationist traditions of recent American diplomacy—a fact that needed obscuring. Further, the United States lacked the close geographical proximity to the peril of war that galvanized public opinion in the other combatant nations. Socially, in contrast to the relatively homogeneous societies of Britain, France, and Germany, the American population was an ethnically diverse mix of divided and often conflicting loyalties, dispersed over a vast area and lacking both a common history and the developed mythologies and iconographies available to propagandists in the European countries.

War entry saw those already actively engaged in Allied propaganda, notably the National Security League and the majority of the press, intensify their efforts, while President Woodrow Wilson, formerly so committed to neutrality, set about marketing the war in terms congenial to the American sensibility: this was "a war for democracy, a war to end war, a war to protect liberalism, a war against militarism, a war to redeem barbarous Europe, a crusade."[15] He created the Committee on Public Information (CPI) to churn out propaganda through every available medium. Its head, George Creel, later wrote of the agency, "In all things, from the first to the last, without halt or change, it was a plain publicity proposition, a vast enterprise in salesmanship, the world's greatest adventure in advertising."[16]

Part of the CPI, the Division of Pictorial Publicity (DPP) responsible for poster production, had at its disposal the nation's most talented illustrators and top publicity experts. Submitting seven hundred designs in total over the period from April 1917 to November 1918, the DPP contributed significantly in terms of both quality and quantity.[17] However, two thirds of the posters produced came from outside its jurisdiction, with the army, navy, marines, and Department of Labor all producing large numbers of their own. Many other designs were the product of competitions hosted by various patriotic societies. As Anne Classen Knutson suggests, poster production was probably less centralized than scholars have traditionally acknowledged.[18] Nevertheless, overall production proves consistent in the expression of the most salient features of American propaganda during the First World War: the active employment and further development of advances in advertising and an aggressive campaign of enemy vilification. (For more on depictions of the German enemy as the "Hun" in American posters, see Nicoletta Gullace's essay in this volume.)

Comparative Analysis of Poster Language

German posters of the First World War stress the need to defend Germany's past cultural and economic achievements. The lone warrior, whether mythological barbarian, medieval knight, modern soldier, or blend of these, embodies (often literally) the German imagined community, a community whose unity and consensus are givens. By contrast, American poster language, visual and textual, stresses progress and expansion.

1. We Stand Alone in Defense of the German Nation

One striking characteristic of German posters is their preoccupation with the past, which is imagined as a source of ideal societal organization models and ever-valid gender roles. While American propaganda portrays the German soldier as a beast, a "Hun" in the kaiser's military uniform (see fig. 11, chapter 2), German posters present a positive barbarian imaginary.[19] Icons of Germanic fighters are incorporations of values originating in Germany's tribal past but stretching continuously throughout its history.

The poster "The Last Blow Is the 8th War Loan" shows a man's figure posed as a half-naked ancient warrior, brandishing his sword.[20] The sword, the central element in the picture, constitutes a dominant sign in many German posters. In "3rd Army: 7th War Loan," a bare-breasted fighter swings to cut off the four heads of a dragon, each head representing one of the enemy allies.[21] The poem below him promises triumph

JAKUB KAZECKI AND JASON LIEBLANG

over "lies and deception," provided that "wallets be opened." In both posters Germanic warriors, through visual and textual presentation, are put into a contemporary context.

The presence of Germanic motifs in these posters is not coincidental. According to Michael Titzmann, the images of ancient Germanic societies developed in German literature and the fine arts in the nineteenth century—such as the images originating in the rediscovered medieval heroic epic *Nibelungenlied* (Song of the Nibelungen)—promoted the identification of contemporary society with an imagined ancient community. The identification justified the anti-democratic decision-making process of Wilhelminian Germany and helped the citizen to fit into the monarchical governmental system. The preservation and defense of the homogeneous social group became the central value. The imagined ideal way of decision making was by consensus reached only through unconditional obedience to the leader.

The utopian picture of a disciplined community, with a lonely hero as its most exposed representative, however, contradicts the sociopolitical reality of the late nineteenth and early twentieth century. The norm and value system expressed by the Germanic iconography of many posters obscures modern war, dominated by technology and a reduction of the role of the individual on the battlefield. By adopting the image of Germanic community as the ideal of societal order, the posters reject the social changes caused by the industrial developments of the nineteenth century, regressing into mythical, premodern tribal organization. German posters exhibit a fondness for weapons requiring the close physical proximity of the opponent and a "fair fight," and a relative absence of modern war technology in comparison with American designs: the sword, medieval armor, lances, and cannons figuring prominently in German designs.

The knight of the Middle Ages, also a popular figure in German design, expresses the same ethos. Here too, the possibility of keeping individuality in the conditions of "material battle" is expressed through regression into an idealized past (see also Stefan Goebel's essay in this collection). The armored defender and the series of medieval votive figures are realizations of the same collective dream that contributed to the creation of the ancient dragon slayer: a man of action characterized by *Treue* (loyalty to the community) and *Ehre* (honor derived from the community's confidence in him).

By connecting the Germanic and medieval worlds and wartime Germany, the posters establish the image of a strongly militant, anti-democratic, and hierarchical social order. A strictly prescribed function of each member of the society results in the fixing of roles that cannot be questioned or subverted: the authoritarian leader is ever present, his position never threatened. Hence, in contrast to Uncle Sam, the flexible central leadership figure in American posters, little possibility exists for socially recontextualizing the German military leader (e.g., Hindenburg or Friedrich the Great). German posters stress his presence and the purpose of his existence, whether through reinterpreting the war loan as the best personal birthday gift for the leader or through his portrayal as a supportive half-real father figure pointing out to the young soldier the meaning of battle.[22]

From the concept of complete unanimity within the group derives the understanding that any differences of opinion are potential threats to group integrity. Therefore the conflict of 1914–18 manifests itself as an attack on the group. The peace of the group must be restored; its unanimity—the warrant for peace—must be reestablished through the fight against an enemy who is easily definable: the enemy is the trouble maker, the line crosser. However, in contrast to American posters, German

JAKUB KAZECKI AND JASON LIEBLANG

defense is not defined as a preemptive "defensive strike," an oxymoron that allows America's war involvement to be justified in terms of progress and universal law, but rather through securing the peace and status quo of the community. *Durchhalten* (fortitude), stressed by the military authorities in the difficult war months, can be seen not only in terms of physical survival but also in terms of keeping and strengthening the shared values of the group. German soldiers in posters, unlike their American counterparts, do not "defend democracy" by fighting its opponents in order to educate them and thus integrate them into the democratic order; they do not "spread freedom" over state borders but rather secure the community against corruption, fight off the aggressor, and guard the border. In one of the most popular posters of the time, "Help Us to Win! Sign Up for the War Loan," a static soldier stresses the moment of tense silence and expectation of attack, keeping watch for the enemy, standing guard.[23] The border line, the barbed wire, is broken, and the gap has to be replaced by a human defender who watches over its continuity; his body marks the line of defense (as in the trenches), anticipating attack but not engaging in it. The concentration on the integrity of the group and on presenting the group and the hero as the center of interest has another consequence for German propaganda art: in comparison to American posters, the enemy is featured far less frequently in German designs. The visual language of German privately published postcards, in contrast to official posters, is much more aggressive in its treatment of the enemy, who is frequently humiliated, laughed at, and disparaged.[24] One possible reason could be the unwillingness of the German military commanders to vilify the opponent in government-authorized publications, as the Haag Convention of 1907 prohibited this.[25] The almost complete absence of the enemy from German posters suggests the importance of the relationships within the community over the hostile relations with the opponent.

Consistent with the dominant anti-modern imaginary, when German posters do show the effects of violent confrontation with the enemy, they mostly depict destroyed enemy technology or provoke the viewer with apocalyptic images of the adversary's technology devastating the peaceful German landscape. Physical encounters between soldiers are rare. Interesting in this context is the poster "We Beat Them and Sign Up for the War Loan!": it is unclear whether the pronoun *them* refers to the advancing enemy tanks or the enemy himself.[26] Modern war technology and the opponent (British soldiers) are identified with each other: dehumanized, they force Germans to defensive measures.

In contrast to this kind of metonymy, the bodies of German soldiers are pictured in both mythic and realistic ways. The nation is often identified with the physical shape of its members. Analyzing the development of national identity in history, Ross Poole notes that the concept of "person," of a self-conscious being who acknowledges a social role with its responsibilities, has usually been viewed in philosophy as privileged and subordinating other concepts of human self-understanding, among others the "man in a physical sense" or "natural man," understood as a form of organic life.[27] The idea of defining the organic existence of the individual from within the concept of national identity is manifested in German posters. The individual soldier is identified with the German nation—in a synecdochical process of figuration, in which the one (the soldier on the battlefield) stands for the whole (the collective of soldiers and civilians describing themselves as a nation) as well as for the space inherited by the collective. The individual assimilates the nation to the extent that its geographical limits (as drawn on the map) are the limits of the human body: the

JAKUB KAZECKI AND JASON LIEBLANG

skin becomes the German border, the blood metamorphoses into the rain and river water, the railways change into body nerves. When the group interprets the attack on its values as an attack on its physical existence, an act of violence against one member of the group is interpreted as an act of aggression against the whole nation. One bleeding German soldier means a wounded Germany; physical pain becomes one of the most prominent characteristics of national identity, but the sacrifice of health or life and the fulfillment of patriotic duty offer in reward the transcendental feeling of belonging to the Fatherland.

The incorporation of the Fatherland, where the whole country takes the bodily form of an individual, appears also in Luis Oppenheim's series of "comparative" posters from 1914. The portrayal of Germany's expenses on education, production of electric machines, new book editions, and international trade show the apparent material/physical domination of the Wilhelminian state over its enemies. The figures in these posters are the embodiment of Germany: Germany as factory worker, farmer, university teacher, writer, wife of a wealthy citizen, and child. Once again, the greatness of the nation is expressed in the form of the human body and the size of its members: Germany appears as a bigger man, both literally and metaphorically. Ironically, the direct relationship between numbers and body shape and size did not always correspond with the aims of officials, resulting, if the context were not considered, in subversion of the intended propaganda message. One poster presenting three soldiers from the belligerent nations for comparison asks, "Who is the militarist?" The fragile German is overwhelmed by enormous French and British statues.[28]

Oppenheim's posters also use national and gender stereotypes in order to solidify the roles of German citizens. The professions portrayed are exclusively practiced by men; even the hope of the nation, shown in the poster comparing population increase, is projected in the form of a boy playing war games—apparently preparing to carry out the future role of a soldier. The impression that every boy's dream role ought to be that of the heroic adult protector of the homeland can be acquired also from the poster "Sign Up for the 8th War Loan: Jungfried-Siegfried."[29] The warrior attributes (sword, helmet, and cannon), along with the commenting poem, draw a parallel between a German boy's youth, his future role as soldier, and the mythological figure of Siegfried. The quoted masculine role model originates in the nineteenth-century image of an ancient Germanic community and rematerializes in other posters, where man is portrayed as an agent, while woman is understood as an object to be protected from the enemy's aggression. Unlike in American posters, woman's role in German posters is limited to that of wife and child bearer. The moment of physical desire does not exist here; it is consistent with the almost masochistic renunciation of sexuality understood as the immanent characteristic of the Germanic hero.[30] All figures of women in German posters are desexualized, appearing either as young mothers or nurses—idealized motherly characters whose sole role is to care for soldiers, past, present, and future (fig. 19).[31]

2. Join the Crowd in Making the World Safe for Democracy (and Get the Girl in the Process)

American poster language emphasizes a historical mission of progress and expansion, what Brian Klunk describes as a "belief that along the American path lie freedom, democracy, peace, and prosperity, not only for themselves but for the whole world."[32]

This mission is rooted in both the theology of early American Protestantism and the Enlightenment ideals of America's early

JAKUB KAZECKI AND JASON LIEBLANG

Fig. 19. Richard Pfeifer's "Sammlung für ein Mutter- haus" (Collection for a Moth- erhouse; detail) is typical of the desexualized represen- tation of women in German posters. Deutsches Histori- sches Museum, Berlin.

political and intellectual leadership. By the end of the nine- teenth century, however, Americans took this mission overseas. Many American posters of the Great War project what Helmut Walser Smith identifies as a diffusionist narrative, one that jus- tifies American colonial expansion in terms of progressive so- cial evolution and sees world history as a circuitous journey of political institutions of freedom and self-government rooted in classical antiquity, which culminates in American rights and liberties. Consequently the narrative sanctions violence as a necessary means toward achieving the unity and homogeniza- tion of a free and just mankind under democratic principles. Posters that communicate the need for American war support through the use of classical motifs borrow this logic of historical "progress." This narrative contrasts with the barbarian/feudal historical continuity of German posters, which stress the need to defend the integrity of the group and its values rather than to spread them and which center on the noble warrior hero as the embodiment of this defensive struggle.[33]

While certain American posters evoke real dates, events, and people from the nation's history, far more significant is the imagined meta-narrative that justifies America's "mission" and, through it, her participation in the war. "American ideals" are figured as descending not only from classical antiquity but also from the French Revolution. Representations of Lady Liberty wearing the red Phrygian cap, directly echoing the famous Delacroix image *La Liberté guidant le peuple*, occur frequently, as do images of Columbia with her sword of justice. These female allegories tend to be static, masculinized, and heroic—extensions of the "City Beautiful" mural imagery of the turn of the century, which celebrated advanced Western technology, ideals, and civilization on walls all over the United States.

Leadership portrayal in American posters lacks the noble and authoritarian character that marks the German leader, who, whether fictional or real, inevitably stands alone, either statuesque or pictured in a defensive martial posture. While Washington, Lincoln, Pershing, and Wilson all appear, the most prominent American leader is the remarkably flexible Uncle Sam. Although capable of demanding obedience, as in James Montgomery Flagg's famous "I Want You," Uncle Sam is most often a populist figure portrayed among the people, leading by example in many guises and social contexts: as a naval commander but also as an advancing soldier, a doctor, a teacher, and even as a gardener and cashier.[34] It is hard to imagine a German leader being portrayed as engaged in such everyday tasks.

JAKUB KAZECKI AND JASON LIEBLANG

Fig. 20. Anonymous, "All Aboard! Liberty Bond Fourth Issue, Sept. 28–Oct. 19, 1918" is one of many posters stressing teamwork and cooperation. It evinces a preoccupation in American propaganda with building consensus within a socially, economically, and ethnically heterogeneous American population. Prints and Photographs Division, LC-USZC-8120, Library of Congress.

One image shows Uncle Sam as the driver of a "liberty truck" full of smiling people of different ages, both genders, and many professions, who have all jumped aboard to join in spreading freedom. An arrow signpost reads "to Berlin," signaling that through cooperation the spread of American ideals will embrace even the enemy (fig. 20). In another Liberty Loan poster, Sam is happily selling a bond to a middle-aged businessman, behind whom thousands wait in line. The viewer is encouraged to "Join the Crowd" of smiling people representative of American society: business and idealized labor, younger and older, man and woman are all shown united in enthusiastic support for the war.[35] Such collective enthusiasm is consistent with the positive tenor of American posters: civilians and soldiers are always smiling, having fun together, which contrasts strikingly with the somber and solitary representations that dominate German portrayals.

The populist employment of Uncle Sam exemplifies an emphasis on teamwork and cooperation, which reveals a preoccupation with "like-mindedness" in American society, the certainty of which German propaganda posters take for granted.[36] The demands of war made achieving this intrinsic desire for mass "commonality of mind" necessary, while growing ethnic diversity and class divisions made it increasingly problematic.

Although many posters stress the need for consensus in war support, they do so with little evidence of class or ethnic—let alone racial—difference. All displayed are Anglo-Saxon and middle class, evidence of the creation in American propaganda posters of "a world in which signifiers of difference and individuality . . . are suppressed."[37] This suppression constitutes an attempt to gain consensus among a socially and economically diverse population, which is deeply ironic, especially in light of America's justifying historical mandate to spread individual freedom worldwide.[38] Exceptions are posters employing languages and national historical icons specific to certain ethnic groups, such as a series appealing in Polish and English to America's large Polish community, which prominently displays Polish icons to encourage enlistment in the French Army.

American posters also understand war in terms of individual progress, though the chance for individual development is available only to the exemplary Anglo-Saxon soldier. Many enlistment posters stress practical educational opportunities, while others employ exotic fantasies to advertise war as an opportunity for overseas adventure and fun. Such portrayal is absent from German posters, where involvement is understood as duty to the national community without the attendant individual benefits American posters foreground. German posters never emphasize individual opportunity, which suggests that

JAKUB KAZECKI AND JASON LIEBLANG

individualism is threatening to group integrity. To pursue individual interests is to betray the group and thus to breach its
defenses, which are built on unanimity and identification with
a shared group history, relying on the notion of a fixed geographical area that the German nation inhabits. By contrast,
American posters portray the individual soldier's progress as
consistent with his group membership, the group's success,
and the global spread of its ideas and systems.

"A Chance Shot," which uses a photograph of muscular
young men working together to load a ship's gun for "a chance
shot" at a German submarine, is exemplary in combining the
physical, educational, and spatial ways American posters advertise individual progress: its text sells the war as a young
man's chance "to build [the] body, to learn a trade, to see the
world."[39] However, this and similar posters can simultaneously
be read as selling the war as an opportunity to gain or prove
masculinity. Another such example is Herbert Andrew Paus's
"The United States Army Builds Men," which clearly defines
what constitutes manliness: a doughboy stands staring at a large
globe topped with a statue of Nike/Victrix, the classical personification of victory.[40] Behind stand three stylized male figures, symbolizing "crafts," "character," and "physique." American masculinity, that of real "Men," involves a combination of
these, all of which can be gained, or tested, in the U.S. army
while enjoying worldly adventure and victories in the name of
spreading freedom.

Perceiving the military as a proving ground for masculinity
takes on special significance against the context of pre–World
War One America. A view that circulated widely involved male
sexuality being in crisis as a result of the increasing domination
of corporate capitalism over male life. Emblematic was Theodore Roosevelt's view that the once vigorous Anglo-Saxon race
had become overcivilized. If it was to carry out its God-given

mission to spread American values worldwide, the primitive traits of vigor, manliness, and audacity had to be reclaimed.[41] Many American posters speak to this perception, addressing anxiety over masculinity through presenting war as a test of manhood: the army is where the "Men" are: "The United States Army Builds Men." Such posters present a liminal space where masculinity can be reclaimed by an Anglo-Saxon upper and middle class that has grown effete: in Flagg's "Tell That to the Marines" a young businessman reads a headline about German atrocities and immediately rips off his suit jacket, presumably to rush off and enlist.[42] In Laura Brey's "On Which Side of the Window are *you?*" an effeminate suited young man stands in the dark watching a group of soldiers march by his window (see fig. 48, chapter 10).[43] Both have the opportunity to prove their masculinity through enlistment, as does the viewer who is likewise challenged.

Some more overtly sexual posters portray war as an opportunity to express virility, as in R. F. Babcock's "Join the Navy," where a sailor straddles a speeding torpedo as if riding a bucking bull.[44] Still others suggest homoerotic tension. Francis Xavier Leyendecker's "These Men Have Come Across" displays the gunners of "A Chance Shot" but emphasizes the situation's physicality and sexuality.[45] Two men are shirtless, their idealized physiques stressed under the strain of their task. Two sets of manly buttocks appear at the poster's center, while the sailor loading the long (phallic?) shell angles it directly at his partner's groin. Together these signifiers create a sexually charged image capable of arousing both homo- and heterosexual desire.

While practically absent from German posters, sexualized images, especially of women, are common in their American counterparts. Many American poster artists were recruited from popular magazines and newspapers, where their illustrations

JAKUB KAZECKI AND JASON LIEBLANG

were used as advertisements. They brought to propaganda the emerging ad industry's strategy of using females as sexual commodities to arouse male desire, in essence seducing men into purchasing the attainable visualized commodity with which the seductress is attached, this becoming endowed with the ability to resolve desire. Howard Chandler Christy, James Montgomery Flagg, and Harrison Fisher—all prewar magazine illustrators—employ such seductresses. Christy's posters frequently show beautiful, obviously vulnerable interpretations of Lady Liberty, their mouths opened enticingly (they could be moaning!), and wearing only white undergarments that gather provocatively at the groin. Ready to be ravaged, Christy's seductresses offer a sexual reward for enlistment or financial support, as does Fisher's sexy Red Cross nurse with her plunging neckline and expression of ecstasy (fig. 21). These sexualized tropes are especially striking when we acknowledge how commonplace they have become in today's advertising.

Generally speaking, American posters offer more diversity in female representation than do German ones. In addition to allegorical portrayals, both masculinized and sexualized, American posters also feature women in traditionally male roles.

The Question of Effectiveness: A Postwar Perspective?

Although scholarship and testimony together provide clues to the material circumstances and social climate of the time, hermeneutic distance makes it impossible to gauge the persuasive power these different explanations would have had on their specific target audiences at the moment of their appearance. The question of whether the narrative of progress or that of defense has proven more effective over time is also difficult to answer.[46]

Similarly, the practices by which to measure the effect of propaganda on the events of the First World War are closely

Fig. 21. American poster artists continued the prewar advertising industry's strategy of using females as sexual commodities to arouse the male viewer's desire, as in Harrison Fisher's "I Summon You to Comradeship in the Red Cross." Prints and Photographs Division, LC-USZC4-1281, Library of Congress.

linked with the discourse on the general importance of war propaganda. The special role attributed to propaganda after the war (emphasized by German politicians and military leaders in particular, with Adolf Hitler being the most established example) may be interpreted as resulting from a prescriptive rather than an inductive process; that is, coming not from the evaluation of the impact posters had on soldiers and the civilian population during the war but rather deriving from the simple fact of German defeat in the conflict.[47] The popular perception of propaganda as an effective tool that helps win military confrontations (and hence that the most effective propaganda techniques and motifs are those used by the winning side) is quite a problematic issue itself.[48]

JAKUB KAZECKI AND JASON LIEBLANG

In our opinion, the question of effectiveness must be viewed in terms of the popularization of the democratic model of government that came to dominate the Western hemisphere over the course of the twentieth century. As James Aulich suggests in his *War Posters: Weapons of Mass Communication,* the development of the officially sponsored public information poster in Western liberal democracies is closely linked with the activities of the advertising industry. The First World War and the financial demands it made on the governments involved accelerated the commercialization of public institutions that were previously marked as off-limits to commercial culture (such as poster advertising) and also questioned their special status within society. The clash between the conservative national state model—presented in German poster images throughout the First World War—and the visible crisis of a governmental model based on trust in leadership and the sanctity of official institutions rendered German propaganda posters as representative of the views of the society's elite and consequently unable to connect with the attitudes of the general public. This was surely detrimental to their overall effectiveness. Aulich remarks that the military command, despite the unfavorable results of its own market research (!), decided to continue reproducing "spectacular Wagnerian imagery."[49] Presumably the government did so in hope of forcefully imposing such imagery on the wider population, or as the result of a serious misunderstanding of the unique place the production, consumption, and reception of poster advertisement takes in a specific time and location. Whatever the reasons, this failure to capture the *zeitgeist* also rendered the posters less fit for further reproduction under the conditions of free-market democracy not bound by censorship control. The limited appeal of certain poster elements speaking to the military, land owners, and industrialists and not to other increasingly politicized groups (such as women and the working classes) differentiates German First World War posters from images present in the public spaces of other combatant nations. As Richard Fogarty elucidates in his contribution to this volume, French poster production fittingly reflects the existing mentalities, emotions, and desires of a broader range of citizenry and consequently proves effective in mobilizing audiences for the cause. As we earlier described, the diversity of representation in American posters functions similarly, targeting different ethnic groups and classes toward establishing consensual support for military engagement.

Accordingly, the longevity of American propaganda was due, first, to the broad employment of commercial advertising techniques that resonated with the wider audience emotionally and adjusted to the moods of the public dynamically and, second, to a balance between text and image appropriate to the poster medium. In his *Prop Art: Over 1000 Contemporary Political Posters*, Yanker notes that propaganda posters have no room for rational explanations. Posters lacking dynamic visual appeal fail to attract attention, as the passer-by has no time to concentrate on an elaborate message. The American propaganda posters of the First World War fulfill these conditions for effective modern propaganda. Further, the most popular tendencies in commercial and political advertisement of the twentieth and the twenty-first century—the premises of individual, physical satisfaction and of putting the viewer in a morally marked leadership position (as the propagator of democracy or as the figurehead of technological progress)—are already visible in American war posters, proving these were effective within a free-market democracy.

While a comparative analysis of German propaganda posters from the two world wars is beyond the scope of this discussion, we should note that Nazi propaganda posters clearly adopted the targeted modes of appeal and aesthetic sophistication that we have argued differentiated American from German posters of the First World War. In Nazi posters traditional Germanic icons such as the national eagle and the warrior figure, which tended to dominate earlier posters in which they were present, are incorporated along with the new symbols of German fascism in a far more sophisticated manner. Furthermore, attention is clearly paid to the effective incorporation of pithy slogans and to balancing text and image for maximum comprehensibility and emotive effect, while posters targeting specific segments of society (women, veterans, labor, and especially youth) abound.[50]

Another method of gauging effectiveness is to analyze the persistence of specific strategies and motifs that gained the status of iconic images. Such images function like memes, propagating themselves through cultural repetition. Once associated with a particular advertisement campaign that has been perceived as successful, they come back in various versions not because they keep their universal appeal but because their multiplication fixes these designs in the medium and causes their increased recognizability and, consequently, their effectiveness. The self-referentiality of poster designs doubtless contributes to their positive impact. One example is a poster for the European parliamentary elections of June 2004 that features Joschka Fischer replicating the famous pointing gesture of Lord Kitchener and Uncle Sam first employed in Allied posters more than ninety years ago and repeated in various advertising campaigns ever since.[51] The accompanying text exhorts: "It's Yourope—You Decide!" Since some poster motifs are historically marked as associated with the failure to persuade, Fischer is shown neither as a sword-wielding dragon slayer nor as the embodiment of unquestioned authority, as he would have been represented in the Germany of the First World War. To the winner—in the poster war as in other wars—go the spoils.

Notes

1. For estimates of total American poster production see Walton H. Rawls, *Wake Up, America! World War I and the American Poster* (New York: Abbeville Press, 1988), 12. See also George Theofiles, *American Posters of World War I: A Price and Collector's Guide* (New York: Dafran House, 1973), and Anne Classen Knutson, "Breasts, Brawn and Selling a War: American World War I Propaganda Posters, 1917–1918" (PhD diss., University of Pittsburgh, 1997).

2. See also Peter C. Marzio, *The Democratic Art: Chromolithography 1840–1900; Pictures for a 19th-Century America* (Boston: David R. Godine in association with the Amon Carter Museum of Western Art, Fort Worth, 1979).

3. See Frederick R. Brandt, "Introduction: Posters, Patrons and Publishers," in *Designed to Sell: Turn-of-the-Century American Posters in the Virginia Museum of Fine Arts*, ed. Frederick R. Brandt (Richmond: Virginia Museum of Fine Arts, 1994), 1–24.

4. Philip B. Meggs, "Turn-of-the-Century American Posters: Art + Technology = Graphic Design," in Brandt, *Designed to Sell*, 33–45.

5. Rawls, *Wake Up, America!* 23–25. See also Sabre Fierement Whitt, "The Role of World War I Posters in American Art" (MA thesis, University of Missouri, 1997), 5.

6. Joseph Clement Coll, "The Tidal Wave—July 4, 1918, 95 Ships Launched," 1918, Library of Congress, Prints and Photographs Division, Washington DC, LC-USZC4-9734.

7. For examples underlining this contrast compare the poster pair: Max Bernuth, *Denkt an unsere Krieger! Elberfelder Liebesgabentag*, 1915, Deutsches Historisches Museum, Berlin, GOS-Nr. PL002957, and Charles E. Ruttan, *A Wonderful Opportunity for You, U.S. Navy, Inquire at Recruiting Station*, 1917, Library of Congress, Prints and Photographs Division, Washington DC, LC-USZC4-2007.

8. Maurice Rickards, *The Rise and Fall of the Poster* (New York: McGraw-Hill, 1971), 25.

9. Alain Weill, *The Poster: A Worldwide Survey and History* (Boston: G. K. Hall, 1985), 129.

10. Weill, *The Poster*.

11. For a detailed discussion of German propaganda efforts in the United States during the war see Stewart Halsey Ross, *Propaganda for War: How the United States Was Conditioned to Fight the Great War of 1914–1918* (Jefferson: McFarland, 1996), 194–95.

12. David Welch, *Germany, Propaganda and Total War, 1914–1918: The Sins of Omission* (London: Athlone Press, 2000), 207–11.

13. See Ross, *Propaganda for War,* 194–95.

14. For a discussion of the propaganda themes of the years 1914–1916, see Ross, *Propaganda for War,* 145–213.

15. Ross, *Propaganda for War,* 51.

16. George Creel, *How We Advertised America* (New York: Arno Press, 1972), 4.

17. Rawls, *Wake Up, America!* 167.

18. Knutson, "Breasts, Brawn," 6.

19. H. R. Hopps, "Destroy This Mad Brute," 1916, Deutsches Historisches Museum, Berlin, GOS-Nr. PL003967.

20. Paul Neumann, "Der letzte Hieb ist die 8. Kriegsanleihe," 1918, Deutsches Historisches Museum, Berlin, GOS-Nr. PL003092.

21. Artl Clauss, "3. Armee: 7. Kriegsanleihe," 1917, Deutsches Historisches Museum, Berlin, GOS-Nr. PL003160.

22. Lucian Bernhard, "So hilft Dein Geld Dir kämpfen! Zeichne Kriegsanleihe!" 1917, Deutsches Historisches Museum, Berlin, GOS-Nr. PL003075.

23. Fritz Erler, "Helft uns siegen! Zeichnet die Kriegsanleihe," 1917, Deutsches Historisches Museum, Berlin, GOS-Nr. PL003076.

24. See *Der Erste Weltkrieg in deutschen Bildpostkarten* (Berlin: Deutsches Historisches Museum, 2002), CD-ROM.

25. See James Brown Scott and Carnegie Endowment for International Peace: Division of International Law, eds., *The Hague Conventions and Declarations of 1899 and 1907 Accompanied by Tables of Signatures, Ratifications and Adhesions of the Various Powers and Texts of Reservations* (New York: Oxford University Press American Branch, 1915), 116.

26. Lehmann, "Wir schlagen sie und zeichnen Kriegsanleihe!" 1918, Deutsches Historisches Museum, Berlin, GOS-Nr. PL003063.

27. Ross Poole, *Nation and Identity* (London: Routledge, 1999), 46–49.

28. Luis Oppenheim, "Wer ist Militarist?" 1914–18, Deutsches Historisches Museum, Berlin, GOS-Nr. PL002744.

29. S. Mayr, "Zeichne die 8te Kriegsanleihe! Jungfried-Siegfried," 1918, Deutsches Historisches Museum, Berlin, GOS-Nr. PL003067.

30. Michael Titzmann, "Die Konzeptionen der 'Germanen' in der deutschen Literatur des 19. Jahrhunderts," in *Nationale Mythen und Symbole in der zweiten Hälfte des 19. Jahrhunderts: Strukturen und Funktionen von Konzepten nationaler Identität,* ed. Jürgen Link and Wulf Wülfing (Stuttgart: Klett-Cotta, 1991), 120–45, esp. 140.

31. See Anne Schmidt, "'Kämpfende Männer-Liebende Frauen': Geschlechterstereotype auf deutschen Propagandaplakaten des Ersten Weltkrieges," in *Geschlecht*

und Nationalismus in Mittel-und Osteuropa 1848–1918, ed. Sophia Kemlein (Osnabrück: fibre, 2000), 217–53. See also Klaus Theweleit, *Männerphantasien 1+2,* vol. 1 (Hamburg: Piper, 2000), 131–45.

32. Brian Klunk, *Consensus and the American Mission* (Lanham: University Press of America, 1986), 2.

33. Helmut Walser Smith, "The Logic of Colonial Violence: Germany in Southwest Africa (1904–1907); the United States in the Philippines (1899–1902)," in *German and American Nationalism: A Comparative Perspective,* ed. Hartmut Lehmann and Hermann Wellenreuther (Oxford: Berg, 1999), 205–31.

34. James Montgomery Flagg, "I Want You for the U.S. Army Nearest Recruiting Station," 1917, Library of Congress, Prints and Photographs Division, Washington DC, LC-USZC4-3859.

35. Anonymous, "Invest Your Money with Uncle Sam! Join the Crowd—Buy a Liberty Bond!" 1917, Library of Congress, Prints and Photographs Division, Washington DC, LC-USZC4-8123.

36. David M. Kennedy, *Over Here: The First World War and American Society* (Oxford: Oxford University Press, 1980), 46.

37. Knutson, "Breasts, Brawn," 119.

38. Knutson, "Breasts, Brawn," 124.

39. Anonymous, "A Chance Shot: This Is a Chance Photograph of a Chance Shot at a 'Sub' by a Real Chance Taking American," 1914–18, Library of Congress, Prints and Photographs Division, Washington DC, LC-USZC4-7783.

40. Herbert Paus, "The United States Army Builds Men: Apply Nearest Recruiting Office," 191[9], Library of Congress, Prints and Photographs Division, Washington DC, LC-USZC4-3189. According to Rawls, the poster was probably created in 1917, although the Library of Congress dates the design to 1919.

41. Matthew Frye Jacobson, *Barbarian Virtues: The United States Encounters Foreign Peoples at Home and Abroad, 1876–1917,* 1st ed. (New York: Hill and Wang, 2000), 3–5.

42. James Montgomery Flagg, "Tell That to the Marines!" 1918, Library of Congress, Prints and Photographs Division, Washington DC, LC-USZC4-3181.

43. Laura Brey, "On Which Side of the Window are *you?*" 1917, Library of Congress, Prints and Photographs Division, Washington DC, LC-USZC4-9659.

44. Richard Fayerweather Babcock, "Join the Navy: The Service for Fighting Men," 1917, Library of Congress, Prints and Photographs Division, Washington DC, LC-USZC4-9568.

45. Frank X. Leyendecker, "These Men Have Come Across, They Are at the Front Now: Join Them—Enlist in the Navy," 1918, Library of Congress, Prints and Photographs Division, Washington DC, LC-USZC4-3185.

46. For two different perspectives on effectiveness see Erwin Schockel's *Das politische Plakat: Eine psychologische Betrachtung* (München: F. Eher, 1938), and Philip

M. Taylor's *Munitions of the Mind: A History of Propaganda from the Ancient World to the Present Era* (Manchester: Manchester University Press, 1995), 176–97.

47. See Troy R. E. Paddock, *Propaganda, Public Opinion, and Newspapers in the Great War* (Westport CT: Praeger, 2004), 115.

48. See Alice Goldfarb Marquis, "Words as Weapons: Propaganda in Britain and Germany during the First World War," *Journal of Contemporary History* 13, no. 3 (1978): 468–69.

49. James Aulich, *War Posters: Weapons of Mass Communication* (New York: Thames and Hudson, 2007), 13.

50. For example, see *Krieg auf Plakaten: Veröffentlichungen der Landesarchivverwaltung Rheinland-Pfalz* (Koblenz: Verlag der Landesarchivverwaltung Rheinland-Pfalz, 2000), 116, 122, 124.

51. Anonymous, *It's Yourope—Du enscheidest!* 2004.

Part 2

Envisioning the Nation and
Imagining National Aesthetics

5

Young Blood: Parisian Schoolgirls' Transformation of France's Great War Poster Aesthetic

I n May 1918 poster hangers plastered bakery and store windows, post offices, trams, metro stations, and innumerable walls throughout Paris and the provinces with yet another series of wartime illustrated propaganda posters. The series of sixteen small-scale posters urged the French to conserve materials such as meat, sugar, coal, and gas, all in desperately short supply in this, the fourth—and though few could have predicted it, final—year of the First World War. The conservation theme of the posters was unexceptional, but their designs, by French wartime standards, were unprecedented (figs. 22–24). Bright colors, disorienting perspective, and naive drawing and lettering marked a complete break from the erstwhile dominant wartime poster style—sober compositions in which color had been virtually banished in favor of a self-consciously artful hand-drawn line. Yet despite what was by 1918 an increasingly divided cultural-political atmosphere, both the popular press and specialized art publications across the spectrum acclaimed the innovative new posters—albeit not for their fresh designs alone. The posters were equally heralded for being the creations of promising new French artistic blood: Parisian schoolgirls between the ages of thirteen and sixteen.

The proximate cause of the government's poster project

Fig. 22. Marthe Picard (16 years old), "Mangez moins de viande pour ménager notre cheptel" (Eat less meat and save our livestock), 1918. Prints and Photographs Division, LC-USZC2-4058, Library of Congress.

was the need to boost morale amid Paris's desperate late-war material shortages, and it was exceptionally shrewd propaganda. If children could face the war's privations with the good-humored abnegation suggested in their cheerful posters, then certainly Parisian adults had no business complaining about restrictions. The posters also resonated, however, well beyond their short-term propaganda value. Stylistically they challenged the prevailing grave wartime poster aesthetic, which itself reflected deeper cultural ideas about what public art was appropriate during the war; children's art, with its seemingly unimpugnable sincerity, became the only acceptable method of

MARK LEVITCH

injecting color into what had been a virtually colorless visual culture. On a structural level, the posters—by virtue of their style and authorship—hinted at an imminent shift in the organization of French decorative arts, a branch in need of renewal if France were to compete economically with its German rival.

The posters resulted from a state-sponsored competition launched in early 1918. The minister of provisions, Victor Boret, had recently viewed the exhibition "Le dessin dans les écoles primaires municipales pendant la guerre" (Drawing in the municipal primary schools during the war), showing Paris work in the city's Musée Galliera in June 1917. The show had

Fig. 24. G. Douanne (16 years old), "Soignons la basse-cour. Je suis une brave poule de guerre. Je mange peu et produis beaucoup" (Let's take care of the poultry. I am a fine war hen. I eat little and produce a lot), 1918. Prints and Photographs Division, LC-USZC2-4064, Library of Congress.

generated great enthusiasm among both the public and the art elite, and the minister was convinced that using war-related children's drawings like those he had seen at the show "would be a profitable means of propaganda."[1] A few months later, with war-related shortages worsening and war weariness growing, Boret initiated "voluntary restrictions" to supplement the already extensive rationing program.[2] While intended to stretch limited home front resources further, thereby freeing unused materials for the war effort, the campaign was ultimately more moral than practical: launched amid the "patriotic gloom" that had set in after the workers' strikes and army mutinies of spring 1917, which represented the first serious cracks in the

MARK LEVITCH

public's ongoing support of the war effort, the new program was intended to remind restive civilians that the war's outcome depended on their continued steadfastness and that any sacrifice they were asked to make was less onerous than that being made by soldiers.[3]

Minister Boret approached the organizer of the Musée Galliera exhibition, Paul Simons, principal inspector of the teaching of drawing for the city of Paris, and requested that Parisian schoolchildren address the theme of voluntary restrictions in their primary school drawing classes. Simons directed students at schools across Paris to make conservation-related drawings, and from several hundred submissions, a jury headed by Simons chose sixteen to be translated into lithographs.[4] All bear the names of the student-artists who designed them and the school each attended, and most also include the student's age.

Several factors suggest the significance the government attached to this project: Minister Boret's direct intervention, the rapid turnaround from idea to execution (January to May), and the costs involved in transferring to lithographic stones and printing sixteen full-color posters—some with as many as seven colors—in runs that totaled hundreds of thousands.[5] Another sure sign of the government's sustained focus was the high-level press attention the posters received upon their public release. Within a month a leading daily newspaper, the most respected illustrated weekly, and the most popular humor magazine had prominently featured the new posters.[6] The coordinated coverage of such a non-news event—and the decision to send large numbers of the posters to France's allies—reflected government priorities.[7]

The children's posters marked an important stylistic break with the French war posters that had preceded them. French posters had lacked the attention-grabbing color that characterized most German, British, and American posters and had completely eschewed reductive, flat color designs like those favored by Germany's modernist *plakatstil* war poster artists. French artists instead privileged the "traditional" elements of draftsmanship and design, employing a seemingly old-fashioned line-drawing lithographic technique and a muted or monochromatic palette that highlighted the hand of the artist. France's foremost war poster designers—including Théophile-Alexandre Steinlen, Jules Abel Faivre, Jules Adler, and Adolphe Willette—used a black lithographic crayon as their primary, and sometimes only, drawing tool. This new, sober standard was set and recognized with the country's first illustrated posters in 1915:

> One perceives that a new tradition has installed itself because of the tragic events we are living through and the multiple emotions that shake us. Art has leant its support—no longer the exhilarating fantasies or graphic caprices designed to amuse us with their fanfare of colors; this has yielded to a graver, more tender expression. It has found, to represent the disasters that have arisen—in line with Jacques Callot's "The Miseries of War"—gestures of simple nobility and poignant significance.[8]

In 1917, even after hundreds more posters had been produced, an exhibition catalog described French war posters in similarly solemn terms: "pulling in passers-by with color is useless here, reality alone matters and is sufficient.... In the history of posters, this carnival of the walls, the great printed pages from when war began until it ends, will all recall a bleak and hazy Ash Wednesday."[9]

Almost overnight the war had given rise to a new visual culture privileging "reality," a semantically flexible term that during the war became intertwined with the decidedly masculinized discourse of renewed national purpose. Hallmarks of both the French modern poster and avant-garde art—color, fantasy, and boldly graphic rather than illustrative style—came to be seen as slick, artificial, and indulgent, telling visual signs of the nation's prewar decadence. Mirroring the larger wartime culture of abnegation and moral rectitude, French poster artists abandoned their quasi-modernist prewar styles and instead adopted a representational lexicon that was overloaded both stylistically and iconographically with connotations of directness and authenticity—connotations that ensured the posters would be construed as appropriate to, but also supportive of, the nation fighting for its very survival.

The conception of the children's poster project allowed an ideologically acceptable way to break out of the narrow stylistic confines of wartime realism, which had grown visually and intellectually monotonous, especially by 1918. The project emerged directly from the exhibition of children's drawing at the Musée Galliera a year earlier, and in some ways marked the culmination, the lasting product, of that temporary exhibition. Because most discussions about the posters refer to the earlier show, and reviewers used similar language to discuss both, we should first look at the exhibition itself.

The 1917 exhibition was conceived more widely than the later restrictions-related posters. Its goal, as explained by Alphonse Deville, president of the municipal council of Paris's fine arts commission, was "to try to make known the course followed in Parisian teaching of drawing, its results in the present and promise for the future, and also the evolution that had taken place in the spirit and taste of the children of Paris during the war with its complex and terrible consequences."[10] This immense show included more than a thousand drawings and a substantial display of decorative arts, nearly all of which featured military imagery. Colorful, bright, and infinitely patriotic, the drawings and designs reassuringly suggested that

Parisian children were facing the war squarely and bearing its burdens with aplomb.

The show also had another goal: to demonstrate that the "liberal" method of drawing recently implemented in Paris's primary schools was preparing the country for its postwar battle with Germany in the field of decorative arts. The debate over how best to teach drawing had been contentious in France since the mid-nineteenth century and was bound up with the nation's economic well-being. It took on added urgency in the aftermath of the Prussian defeat of France in 1870, when France's nearly monopolistic hold on craft production fell away precipitously in the face of challenges from mechanized production emanating from the newly unified Germany.[11] In 1883 Eugène Guillaume, a former director of the École des Beaux-Arts, nationally instituted a method for teaching drawing that was based on geometry rather than drawing from life. Guillaume wanted to establish drawing as a "regular language" but not something for "promoting the teaching of art."[12] Molly Nesbitt argues persuasively that Guillaume's emphasis on geometry and technical drawing actually created "a language of industry."[13] But in the early 1900s Guillaume's language came under attack for being too hard to translate. Critics argued that it was an inappropriate basis for craft production because it stressed a conceptual approach to design rather than a practical one, "producing designers who were fine artists, not craftsmen."[14]

In 1914 Paul Simons was appointed principal inspector of the teaching of drawing for Paris. With the nation distracted by the outbreak of the war, Simons moved forcefully to uproot vestiges of the old Guillaume program and its recent variants and to implement fully his own progressive agenda—all the while tying his reforms rhetorically to the wider war effort.[15] The 1917 Musée Galliera exhibition and the 1918 series of children's posters were the highly publicized first fruits of Simons's new program.

Simons described his method in detail in an issue of the decorative arts monthly *Les Arts Français* that was dedicated exclusively to the children's drawing exhibition. In a rhetorical nod to the conservative proponents of the Guillaume method, Simons said students would "of course" continue to learn from the past. But, he stressed, the new program was predicated on action, and "the spirit that will now guide our methods results from the form and the intensity of modern life."[16] Major components he enumerated were light, movement, and color. Students would study everyday objects rather than old plaster casts, and the centerpiece of the program would be decorative composition, an endeavor that would impassion children because it privileged color.

Simons's emphases on modernity, action, the study of everyday objects, and color ran counter to the more conservative method that his program replaced. A sensitive aspect of it, given the wartime context in which much modern art was branded *munichois* (a derogatory term used to denote Munich taste), was that Simons's ideas also sounded vaguely similar to what many observers took to be characteristics of the German approach to the decorative arts.[17] For instance, a 1912 French study of applied art education in Germany, aimed at making France more competitive, noted: "Two traits characterize the education and production of German schools without exception: everywhere there is a voluntarily and energetically practical and utilitarian tendency and, on the other hand, a willingness, when it comes to style—to getting away from the beaten track—an intense, constant effort toward liberation and renewal."[18] Simons's stress on the study of everyday objects, rather than classical casts, could be construed as leaning toward the "practical and utilitarian," and his privileging of action and modernity sounds similar to the Germans' "constant effort toward liberation and renewal." More concretely, Simons's insistence on the role of color associated his program with one of the regular criticisms leveled against German decorative arts and modern French decorative arts that were believed to have fallen under their sway—"abusing color," by which was generally meant the use and juxtaposition of bright colors.[19]

Simons was evidently cognizant that his program might invite comparisons with the so-called decadent, individualistic, and undisciplined French modern art that had been labeled German-influenced; to establish his call-to-order bona fides, he argued that his pedagogical program would blend old and new, bringing together "logic and expression, the aesthetic and construction," and "creativity and discipline."[20] Lest there be any confusion, he assured wary readers "we remain purely Latin. We remain French."[21] The goal of this method, moreover, as he pointed out in the concluding paragraph of the catalog for the show, was explicitly patriotic: "Primary school instructs the future artisans who will then nourish the Parisian ateliers. They, in their turn, have the mission of conserving for our industrial art the place of honor that it has always been accorded in the world."[22]

The 1917 children's show was seen as an outstanding success—a tour de force of decorative arts, including wallpaper, ceramics, posters, fabrics, fans, and notebook covers as well as freely painted compositions and smaller works by younger children. Several commentators, including Frantz Jourdain, president of the progressive Salon d'Automne and a defender of modern art against charges of Germanism, hailed the exhibition's "fresh air." Jourdain further promoted his modern agenda by linking the popular show to modern art, extending his thanks to the children's drawing professors "who, imbued with modern ideas, influenced . . . by Toulouse-Lautrec and Vuillard, have opened the eyes of the generation of to-morrow."[23] Léo Claretie, a longtime advocate of modernizing France's decorative arts, was struck "by the pronounced taste for decorative art" among the children, which he, among others, cast as auguring well for future competition with the "Boches."[24]

Astoundingly, the reactions to the show were overwhelmingly positive—almost nobody took issue with a liberal program that seemed ready-made to incite a modernist arts controversy. At least one critic was caught off guard by the unanimous acclaim, noting, "We are very agreeably surprised at the miracle of the *union sacrée* that this exhibit has produced. We see side by side, with the same enthusiasm for the color and its interpretation, authors who would seem to feel differently."[25] The critic was likely thinking of Alphonse Deville, president of the municipal council of Paris's fine arts commission. Deville had been a self-appointed watchdog guarding French art and taste against what he saw as nefarious German influences, but he nevertheless authored the laudatory lead article in the issue of *Les Arts Français* dedicated to the children's drawing exhibit.

In the article, however, Deville hedged his support for the prominence accorded to color in the Simons program—an issue, as we have seen, that was especially important in the discussion of German influence on French art. After expounding at length on the traditionalist refrain of the importance of composition, Deville explained that a "new" element under Simons was that "the student studying drawing should be led quickly to the idea and use of color, which will help with defining forms and especially the application of objects."[26] He then carefully couched his support of Simons's emphasis on color, thereby distancing himself from viewers drawn to the bright colors in the children's work: "If the Galliera show seduces with its shimmering and dazzling colors (which does not preclude it from presenting in portfolios the most interesting pencil drawings, which are in some way the skeleton of the color work), the exhibition shows that a child who has been familiarized with color at a young age knows, through its judicious use, how to dress up his drawing elegantly and harmoniously."[27]

Deville's support of color here is circumspect, at best. Color "seduces" and "dresses up" a work; it should be used "judiciously." To understand a work's essence, meanwhile, to see its "skeleton," one has to search out the uncolored line drawings accessible in the portfolios. Deville only grudgingly accepts an increased role for color; for him line and composition are still the touchstones of drawing instruction. Free to speak his mind, Deville might have agreed with the only negative review of the exhibit to surface—an anonymous review in *Le Dessin*, the journal for teachers of drawing, which said bitingly: "[If you] don't look for a sensation other than that born from the intense vibration of color, then you will be fully satisfied and happy."[28]

Deville's ultimate willingness to throw his support behind the new program despite his evident misgivings marks a significant moment in France's wartime cultural politics: for the first and perhaps only time during the war, traditional, conservative artistic forces ceded an issue of cultural import to more progressive elements. As Kenneth Silver has shown, the *union sacrée*—the wartime putting aside of partisanship in the name of national defense—effectively consolidated the right's traditionalist political and cultural agenda as state policy; the avant-garde, tainted as Germanic, withdrew from their most daring projects and instead, under the pressure of the war's all-encompassing nationalist fervor, embraced the qualities and often subject matter associated with a French-derived classicism: discipline, moderation, and order.[29] The children's drawing exhibition, on the contrary, jettisoned Guillaume's more classical method in favor of Simons's more modern and more Germanlike one.

Two factors likely contributed to the role reversal. On the one hand, it was imperative to establish a unified stance in the arena of French decorative arts. During the war the economic threat posed by Germany was painted in apocalyptic terms; as one commentator noted in an article about applied arts in February 1917, three months before the children's drawing exhibition opened, "the military war, brutally launched thirty months ago, will be followed, do not doubt it, by economic combat that threatens not to be less cruel than the combat in the trenches."[30] The French had to organize, and quickly, if they wanted to compete internationally with their neighboring enemy in the lucrative and prestigious decorative arts field—and the "arid" Guillaume method had done nothing to stem the steady loss of market share to Germany.

Second, using children was perhaps the only unimpeachable route available for reclaiming bold color as an inherently French, rather than German, artistic trait—one that was critical for short-term morale (and long-term success in decorative arts). Wartime imagery in France had been notoriously and monotonously monochromatic. Color, as noted, was suspect from a nationalist perspective; French decorative art *coloristes* were branded *munichois*.[31] Moreover, color had connotations of frivolity that were considered inappropriate during wartime. Indeed, the dominant color in French wartime visual culture was black—the black of mourning, the newly omnipresent black-and-white photos and newsreels, the quickly scrawled black ink or pencil *croquis* (rough sketches) that became the quintessential example of art from the Front.

Color, especially bold color, was in desperately short supply. It was most often seen in children's wartime books and magazines designed to entertain and educate through propaganda.

The only images aimed at adults that regularly featured striking colors were found in humor magazines and in prints called *images d'Epinal.* These naive and martially themed folkloric prints had been especially popular during the Napoleonic era and were revived upon the outbreak of war in 1914. They found an audience immediately receptive to their nostalgic, heroic, and utterly unreal construction of the all-too-real war at hand.

In contrast to the calculated naiveté of the *images d'Epinal,* which were deliberately crude constructions by professional artists or commercial firms that self-consciously employed color as a form of romantic escapism, the children's use of color was hailed as "authentic"—and authentically French—because it was innate and unmediated. Indeed, one irony of the children's art exhibition is that few critics directly acknowledged the influence of Paul Simons's teaching method on the works they so warmly embraced. The works were not admired for their skill but for precisely the opposite—their naiveté, spontaneity, and intuition. One critic, for instance, said the children's works displayed "admirable originality and sincerity" and "an instinct for décor."[32] Another said their drawings revealed that "free inspiration had burst forth from their brains like a force of nature" and, in a phrase echoed by many commentators, revealed "the genius of the race."[33]

Supporters and detractors of modern art united behind the children's brilliant coloring. Frantz Jourdain stressed the innately French rather than "studied" aspects of the brightly colored works, saying that one finds in them "the primordial qualities of our race: imagination, initiative, spirit, taste, originality and the *love of color.*"[34] Even Arsène Alexandre, a conservative critic one would expect to be wary of unbridled expression, praised the children's "instinct for color, at once full of vivacity and taste."[35] Jourdain and Alexandre, among others, argued that the children's use of color was instinctive,

MARK LEVITCH

that their "love of color" emanated from their very quality as French beings. Removed from the straitjacket of the arid Guillaume method and free to express their enthusiasm and sensations "sincerely" without being beholden to an abstract theory, the observers argued, French children were attracted to lively color. The centrality of color over line in Simons's drawing program could thus be presented as merely a "natural" outgrowth stemming from the French child's "sincere" expression of his or her French intuition. In the end, Simons's program reclaimed color as French and restored it rhetorically to what he and his supporters saw as its rightful and natural place in the French teaching of drawing.

The project for the conservation posters emanated from the 1917 exhibition and marked an attempt to present its lessons to a greater public. But the posters project also departed significantly from the exhibition: taking children's compositions out of the museum and putting them on the street injected them into a new setting with different valences; the conservation theme of the posters dictated the subject, or at least limited it; and whereas the gender of the children artists was a nonissue at the Musée Galliera show, it became central in the poster series. The girl-authored posters were imbricated in the contradictory notions of femininity that suffused wartime France—constructions that varied from traditional domestic roles to newly economically productive ones—and represented a potential model for reconciling these conflicting ideas.

Why was it decided to use only girls' compositions as the basis for the conservation posters project? It is inconceivable that the jury selected sixteen poster designs by girls, and none by boys, simply because the girls were better artists. Given the state's involvement in the poster project, the drawing and decorative arts background of the exhibition, and the changing nature of gender roles during the war, one must look beyond aesthetic considerations for an explanation.

The war caused severe economic and social dislocation in all the participating countries. As men marched off to the Front, women (and to a lesser degree, children) assumed jobs in heavy industry, agriculture, and public services that men would have held before the conflict erupted. Images of women in France during the war were as various and conflicting as the demands made on them. Mary Louise Roberts has suggested that the war polarized the cultural representation of women into two co-existing images—a good patriotic mother who protected the home front and a bad, pleasure-seeking woman who cavorted at home while her man suffered in the trenches.[36]

Needed for war work, especially in armaments, women who engaged in such occupations were portrayed as sexless or mas-culine.[37] The fear of a desexed female population who had left the hearth for the factory, in turn, played a role in the debate about French depopulation that preceded the war but had taken on new urgency during the conflict. France's declining birth rate, especially relative to Germany's quickly growing population, was seen as a straightforward national security is-sue: unless the French had more children, the disparity in size and strength of the French army relative to the German army would be impossible to overcome. Mothers and motherhood were lionized; bearing a child was held out as a duty equivalent to men's fighting at the Front. In 1916, for instance, French feminist Marguerite de Witt-Schlumberger argued that women had "two principal duties, to raise children without fathers and to give new children to the *patrie*."[38]

If the French were uneasy about a masculinized female work force, French soldiers in particular were concerned with an ob-verse image of their partners as pleasure seeking, frivolous, and ultimately promiscuous. In the face of the vast mental distance

MARK LEVITCH

separating the fighting front and the home front, many soldiers felt out of touch and out of control; some let their insecurities reign. As one soldier wrote, "Your imaginings depict your wife in the arms of another man."[39] Women's fashion, which changed dramatically during the war, was viewed as the outward manifestation of these feared behavioral and attitudinal changes, and the new shorter skirts and low-cut dresses were excoriated. One soldier noted, "Women have committed certain faults of frivolity, of carelessness, [and in] the skirts of 1916 look a little too much as though they have no cares in the world."[40]

These contradictory images of women were mediated through the more pliable images of girls. Girls were not women, but in wartime propaganda children often stood in for adults. Their image was frequently used to present the war through the filter of a child's presumed innocence—as in the many images of children playing war. (They were also used, of course, to evoke pathos, as in images of orphans.) And children were literally the nation's future for which the war was being waged—as suggested in the numerous images showing children learning about the war in French schools. In her study of French postcards during the war, Marie-Monique Huss determined that boys were frequently pictured in positions of action, especially as soldiers or as future soldiers, but girls, while occasionally depicted as nurses, were represented far less often and usually in support roles.[41]

In this particular wartime context the schoolgirls' conservation posters played several roles simultaneously, including some that are seemingly contradictory. All at once, the posters suggest that their makers be seen as courageous wartime participants, productive members of the anticipated peacetime workforce, and inevitably, future mothers.

Most discussions of the children's posters in the press mentioned lightheartedly that the artists were girls. An article in *L'Illustration*, for example, addressing all the competition's drawings, mentioned that "the girls are more precocious and their drawings—vexing detail for the strong sex—prove themselves much superior to those of the boys."[42] The critic Clément-Janin, in his postwar round-up of French posters, joked about whether revealing the ages of the schoolgirl artists would insult their modesty.[43]

This levity, however, only thinly disguised the serious issues that the girl-authored posters raised. The posters were unique—of the hundreds of French illustrated posters produced during the war, these were the only ones designed by women or girls. The compositions and objects created for the Galliera show, well received as they were, did not function beyond the exhibition. The posters, on the other hand, were concrete evidence that the children—and specifically, the girls—could contribute materially to the war effort through their decorative compositions, thus achieving the potential hinted at in the 1917 exhibition.

French authorities launched the girl-authored poster project in 1918 because they were then actively planning for a postwar world in which women would inevitably have to assume important roles, and they rightly saw the posters as a not-too-discomfiting vehicle for sensitizing the public to this new reality. The discussions about how to organize the country for future economic competition with Germany had to take into account the changed demographics that the war had brought about—starting with the nearly one and a half million Frenchmen killed in combat. Women had long played a prominent role in French decorative arts; in the 1890s French women—albeit the elite—were granted a central role in revitalizing national crafts.[44] But the decorative arts had undergone a "remasculinization" in the years just before the war—and by 1918 people were rethinking how to integrate women into the field.[45] Already in 1917, in conjunction with the Musée Galliera exhibit, the association for the development of technical teaching held a conference to discuss apprenticeships for young women in the "métiers féminins" (feminine crafts). Significantly, the conference recognized that working-class women would be integral to the development of France's postwar decorative arts. Municipal professional schools for young women "would not be useful" for bourgeois women who would not go on to professional jobs, they reasoned. Instead, pre-apprenticeships should be increased in working-class areas. It was also hoped that at the next exposition the French would find "a pavilion conceived, built, decorated and managed uniquely by women."[46]

In another sign that people were expecting women to play an increased role in the decorative arts, the Manufacture de Sèvres started admitting "young women" to its student body in 1918. Camille Bernard, writing for *Le Dessin*, expected an uproar, but she defended the new policy on the basis of changes caused by the war:

> With the terrible times we are passing through, an entire generation of young women at marrying age will not be able to do so, the war having terribly mowed down our male youth. . . . We must not leave any forces unproductive, and the war proves what resources of energy and force one finds in the collaboration of women. These are new times to get ready for; one must resolutely do his part . . . for the greatest good of our dear country.[47]

The choice of girls for the poster project, like these other state-directed changes, reflects the increased role for women in the war-transformed decorative arts fields.

The posters were a high-profile signal of greater female prominence in French decorative arts, but unlike the gender transgressions associated with the entry of women at Sèvres or the hope for a woman-constructed pavilion at the next exposition, the children's posters focused largely on domestic subjects that had long been considered a mother's domain. Nine of the sixteen posters, for instance, are food or drink related, most of them like still lifes. Of the remaining seven, five feature what could be construed loosely as domestic objects: a lamp, gasoline tins, coins spilling from a ewer, bank notes, and tobacco paraphernalia. One features a factory with three smokestacks, certainly not a domestic scene, but cropping suggests that it is being viewed from a window. The only poster that does not focus on an object instead prominently features a female figure—an Alsatian girl partly draped by the French flag.

The posters' focus on everyday objects also related a micro-history of the war that differed from the bombastic allegories or masculinized realist scenes that otherwise pervaded French wartime imagery and especially French war posters. Many of the items the schoolgirls depicted, moreover, were the modest but unmistakable daily signs of "France," such as coins, the confisserie, bread, grapes, and wheat. The objects are particularly striking because in many images they are oversized. In Louisette Jaeger's "Cultivons notre potager," the most simplified of the sixteen compositions, the carrots and lettuce stand out as enormous against an empty background. So do the steaming plate of potatoes in Yvonne Vernet's "Economisons le pain en mangeant des pommes de terre" (fig. 23) and, even more obviously, S. Vincent's gargantuan loaf of bread in "Ne pas gaspiller le pain est notre devoir."

This focus on objects associated with household economy encouraged some critics to circle back to a gender-based view of the posters. For instance, after extravagantly praising the children's posters as "a new genre" stylistically, the critic in *Les Annales Politiques et Littéraires* later referred to the artists as "future housewives" who must have applied themselves diligently to this new work.[48] *L'Illustration*, too, used the phrase "future housewives." Such terminology suggests how conflicted the issue of women's roles was during the war. Even as the girl authors demonstrated their ability to contribute mightily to the war effort, using skills with obvious postwar applications, most commentators could not construe the poster project outside the parameters of traditional domesticity. Faced with the slaughter of husbands and future husbands, French commentators clung even more tightly to a utopian postwar vision of the traditional French family. The posters' focus on domestic objects enabled them to perform double cultural work, embodying simultaneously two positive but seemingly contradictory wartime constructions of the French woman: woman as war worker and woman as (future) wife and mother.

The "unexpected modernism" of the posters by Parisian schoolgirls issued an unprecedented, and yet strangely nonthreatening, challenge to the sober paradigm of French propaganda posters.[49] Schoolgirls were perhaps the only artistic group who would not risk reprisal for inserting what could be perceived as foreign-influenced bold graphics and strident coloring into their works. The posters were so warmly received precisely because their colorful and naive style was viewed as "sincere." As the conservative critic Clément-Janin noted, "At a time when 'being naive' is the preoccupation of so many graybeards, one can't help but have a taste for the real naiveté of these truly young people."[50] Significantly, Clément-Janin attributed the modernist "look" of the posters to the work's source. Unorthodox avant-garde styles were anathema because they trafficked in artifice, but the "modernist" children's posters were heralded because they were perceived as direct, authentic expressions of the French race.

On the face of it, the schoolgirls' seemingly amateurish efforts had little in common with the hundreds of accomplished posters, most by noted French artists and illustrators, that preceded them. But if their look and authorship were strikingly different, the students' posters nevertheless shared stylistically with their more professional wartime antecedents an emphasis on the individual artist's hand in the creative process that was unparalleled in the posters produced in other belligerent countries. The self-conscious artfulness of French war posters and the consequent glorification of the artist had a particular resonance during the war, when French art and artists were held up on the home front as a national, even a racial, symbol—a sure way to differentiate the cultured French from the barbaric Germans in the clash-of-civilizations discourse that accompanied the war. Heralded for spontaneously embodying the artistic instincts of their race, the schoolchildren's posters, despite their striking formal differences from their predecessors, could in the end be subsumed into this larger, quasi-essentialist construction of the French as artists and could even be held out as its culmination.

Several commentators suggested that schoolchildren be given other poster assignments. Commissions had already been doled out, however, for what would be the final national loan drive, launched in October 1918.[51] But if the poster project was short-lived, its influence was still apparent at the lavish Exposition Internationale des Arts Décoratifs et Industriels Modernes held in Paris in 1925. The exposition, which introduced the term *art deco*, was intended to showcase France's postwar recovery and its return to international primacy in the decorative arts. Germany was excluded, and Paris's pavilion was entirely decorated by male and female students from the city's primary and professional artistic schools, who were described as "an army of workers who will replace the legions that the terrible torment [the war] laid in the tomb."[52] In tracing the genesis of the pavilion, the city's exposition guide gave pride of place

MARK LEVITCH

to the children's wartime poster project: "Who still doesn't have before their eyes the vision of these posters that lived as witnesses of an epoch at once tragic and glorious—where the soul of young generations infused with the emotions and anguishes of the country expressed itself."[53] The guide ascribed to the posters every positive moral and aesthetic quality imaginable, including bright harmonious coloring, sincerity, ingenuity, a rare faculty of balance, elegance, common sense, and an astonishing sense of art.[54] The pavilion, which featured entire rooms, boutiques, and a model school designed, decorated, and furnished by the schoolchildren, was implicitly cast as the "applied arts" fruition of the modern drawing method embodied in the posters—and, like the posters before it, the pavilion was hailed for exemplifying the French race's "wondrous reserves of innate taste and instinct for art."[55]

Gender, interestingly, was not the salient issue at the student-designed Paris Pavilion that it had been with the posters seven years earlier. Perhaps because girls and women had been largely integrated into the country's decorative arts structure in the immediate postwar period, authorities did not highlight female students' contributions apart from those of their male counterparts. More important rhetorically was that the pavilion was the work of artistically talented children, who, whether male or female, would lead the French decorative arts charge against the enemy across the Rhine. Moreover, in the postwar period, more controversial gender-related reforms were grabbing headlines; in 1924, for instance, the French education minister made secondary school curricula identical for both sexes, thus allowing women equal access to higher education for the first time.

The girl-authored conservation poster series upended wartime expectations with lasting consequences. Visually, the posters brought color and a "sincere" modernist sensibility to bear on an otherwise extremely sober poster aesthetic, opening the door, amid the discursively dominant return to order, to a stylistically daring redefinition of French national style. Structurally, the posters simultaneously represented a radical but ultimately reassuring model for integrating women into the decorative arts—and, by implication, into the postwar economy as a whole. Stylistically unprecedented, the posters potently demonstrated how girls could contribute uniquely and effectively to the war effort, even as the posters' small size and insistently domestic themes meant that the posters and their authors were construed within a framework of traditional women's roles. The publication of the girl-authored posters, and their uniformly positive reception as evidence of French artistic taste, marked a rhetorically unprecedented expansion of the race-based view of French artistic prowess expounded during the war, which in turn set the stage for greater female participation in the decorative arts in the interwar period.

Notes

1. Louis Lumet, "La Lettre illustrée," *La Baïonnette* 4:151 (May 30, 1918), 326.

2. Given its timing, it is possible the direct catalyst for the poster campaign was the imminent onset of bread rationing at the end of January 1918. Sugar had been rationed since March 1917, and the allocation was reduced in September 1917 to one-third of the average prewar consumption. In 1917 and 1918 controls were implemented to limit or halt consumption of butter and milk in cafés and restaurants. And "meatless days," set at two per week between May and October 1917, were extended to three between May and July 1918. Additionally, the prices of almost all food staples—except bread, which was controlled—rose dramatically over the course of the war; after spring 1917 sugar, milk, and fats were out of reach for most buyers, and meat and potatoes were extremely expensive. Thierry Bonzon and Belinda Davis, "Feeding the Cities," in *Capital Cities at War: Paris, London, Berlin 1914–1919*, ed. Jay Winter and Jean-Louis Robert (Cambridge: Cambridge University Press, 1997), 318.

3. Jean-Jacques Becker, *The Great War and the French People*, trans. Arnold Pomerans (New York: St. Martin's Press, 1986), 248.

4. The costs were sponsored by the Union française's "comité national de

prévoyance et d'économies" (national committee for foresight and thrift). Posters were commonly sponsored by private associations that, in practice, worked closely with the government. On the history of the project, see Noël Clément-Janin, *Les estampes, images et affiches de la guerre* (Paris: Gazette des Beaux-Arts, 1919), 77.

5. Paul Simons, *La composition décorative dans les écoles primaires de Paris*, from the series L'Art Décoratif Moderne, published under the direction of Louis Lumet, inspector of fine arts (Paris: La Connaissance, 1922), 41.

6. *Petit Journal*, a leading Parisian daily, reproduced "*Nous saurons nous en priver*" (We know how to sacrifice), featuring children standing outside a confiserie, on its front page on May 1, 1918; *L'Illustration*, the leading illustrated weekly, ran a long article on May 18, 1918; and *La Baïonnette*, the leading humor magazine, dedicated its entire issue of May 23, 1918, to the children's compositions for the competition.

7. Simons, *La composition décorative*, 41.

8. L. Roger-Milès, "Les affiches de l'emprunt," *L'Illustration*, November 27, 1915, 558.

9. Maurice Guillemot, "L'art de l'affiche" (introduction to a catalog for a poster exhibition in Neuilly), *Le Carnet des Artistes* 9 (1917): 18.

10. Alphonse Deville, "Le dessin et la municipalité parisienne," *Les Arts Français* 8 (1917): 113–14.

11. Exports of French jewelry, ceramics, and furniture contracted sharply after 1873. Between 1873 and 1889, exports of furniture from France dropped by one-third and from Paris by two-thirds. Deborah Silverman, *Art Nouveau in Fin-de-Siècle France: Politics, Psychology, and Style* (Berkeley: University of California Press, 1989), 54.

12. Molly Nesbit, "Ready-Made Originals: The Duchamp Model," *October* 37 (Summer 1986): 55.

13. Nesbit, "Ready-Made Originals," 59.

14. Nancy Troy, *Modernism and the Decorative Arts in France: Art Nouveau to Le Corbusier* (New Haven: Yale University Press, 1991), 55.

15. Simons, *La composition décorative*, 48. A national commission charged with evaluating the instruction of drawing proposed in 1908 that France jettison the rigid Guillaume method in favor of a process—sometimes called the "intuitive method"—that encouraged children to find joy in art rather to study it as a science. The proposals were formally adopted at the end of the year, but their implementation was effectively blocked by personnel unwilling or unable to adopt the new method. Paul Simons was an avid backer of the new drawing pedagogy and had particular ideas for how to implement it in Parisian schools.

16. Simons, *La composition décorative*, 140–41.

17. The term *munichois* derives from the exhibition of Munich decorators at

the 1910 Salon d'Automne. See Kenneth Silver, *Esprit de Corps: The Art of the Parisian Avant-Garde and the First World War, 1914–1925* (Princeton: Princeton University Press, 1989), 171–74.

18. François Monod, "L'Enseignement de l'art décoratif en Allemagne et en France à propos d'un congrès récent," *Art et Décoration* 34 (August 1913): 1–4, cited in Troy, *Modernism and the Decorative Arts*, 62.

19. Troy, *Modernism and the Decorative Arts*, 72–73.

20. Paul Simons, "Les écoles primaires municipales à Galliera," *Les Arts Français* 8 (1917): 146–47.

21. Simons, "Les écoles primaires," 141.

22. Paul Simons, *Le dessin dans les écoles primaires municipales pendant la guerre* (Paris: Musée Galliera, 1917), 11–12.

23. Frantz Jourdain, "L'Exposition de dessins du Musée Galliera," *Les Arts Français* 8 (1917): 125.

24. Léo Claretie, *L'Evénement*, June 10, 1917.

25. The *union sacrée*, or sacred union, refers to the wartime putting aside of partisan interests for the sake of national defense. P. Vagnier, "La question du dessin," *Le Dessin* 61 (December 1917): 53.

26. Deville, "Le dessin et la municipalité parisienne," 114.

27. Deville, "Le dessin et la municipalité parisienne."

28. "Musée Galliera," *Le Dessin* 60 (September 1917): 49.

29. Silver, *Esprit de Corps*, 26.

30. Charles Plumet, "L'enseignement technique des arts appliqués," *Le Carnet des Artistes* 1 (February 1, 1917): 11.

31. Raymond Koechlin, "L'Art français moderne n'est pas 'munichois,'" *L'Art Français Moderne* 1 (1916): 31–2.

32. "La Jeunesse et la France," *Renaissance*, June 9, 1917, cited in "Les Arts et la vie," section 3 of *Les Arts Français* 8 (1917): 60.

33. *Les Annales politiques et littéraires*, July 8, 1917, cited in "Les Arts et la vie," section 3 of *Les Arts Français* 8 (1917): 61.

34. My emphasis. Jourdain, "L'Exposition de dessins du Musée Galliera," 124.

35. Arsène Alexandre, *Figaro*, May 31, 1917, cited in "Les Arts et la vie," section 3 of *Les Arts Français* 8 (1917): 59.

36. Mary Louise Roberts, *Civilization Without Sexes: Reconstructing Gender in Postwar France, 1917–1927* (Chicago: University of Chicago Press), ix–x.

37. Roberts, *Civilization*, 69.

38. Marguerite de Witt-Schlumberger quoted in "L'Action sociale et morale en faveur de la maternité," *La Française*, March 25, 1916, cited in Susan Grayzel, *Women's Identities at War: Gender, Motherhood, and Politics in Britain and France during the First World War* (Chapel Hill: University of North Carolina Press, 1999), 104.

39. *Le Camouflet*, June 1, 1916, cited in Stéphane Audoin-Rouzeau, *Men at War, 1914–1918: National Sentiment and Trench Journalism in France during the First World War*, trans. Helen McPhail (London: Berg, 1992), 131.

40. *La Marmite*, March 1916, cited in Audoin-Rouzeau, *Men at War*, 133.

41. Marie-Monique Huss, *Histoires de famille, 1914–1918: Cartes postales et culture de guerre* (Paris: Noesis, 2000), 167.

42. Louwyck, "Sur quelques affiches d'enfants," *L'Illustration*, May 18, 1918, 496.

43. Clément-Janin, *Les estampes, images et affiches de la guerre*, 77.

44. Silverman, *Art Nouveau in Fin-de-Siècle France*, 196.

45. David Cottington, *Cubism in the Shadow of War: The Avant-Garde and Politics in Paris, 1905–1914* (New Haven: Yale University Press, 1998), 67, 178.

46. Georges-Eugène Bertins, "Pour l'apprentissage des jeunes filles," *Le Carnet des Artistes* 9 (1917): 16.

47. Camille Bernard, "Commentaires sur l'art industriel," *Le Dessin* 62 (1918): 6–7.

48. Sergines, "Affiches des écoliers de Paris," *Les Annales Politiques et Littéraires*, October 6, 1918, 298.

49. Sergines, "Affiches des écoliers de Paris."

50. Clément-Janin, *Les estampes, images et affiches de la guerre*, 78.

51. Frantz Jourdain, president of the progressive Salon d'Automne, apparently first suggested the students be given future poster commissions. Jourdain's open letter was reprinted in an editorial that lamented the generally poor quality of French war posters and echoed Jourdain's call that schoolchildren be given future commissions. "Opinion," *Le Petit Messager des Arts et des Artistes, et des Industries d'Art* 60 (September–October 1918): 1. Another article critical of the recent loan posters quoted an unnamed painter as asking, "Why didn't we call on the talented children who executed the charming little posters that we see on the metro?" "Le Salon de la Rue," *Carnet de la Semaine* (November 10, 1918): 10. The Association l'Art de France adopted Jourdain's proposal and asked the Ministry of Finance to consider commissioning posters from the schoolchildren, but the ministry responded that they had already commissioned the next (and last wartime) posters. *Bulletin de l'Association l'Art de France* 27, reprinted in *Le Petit Messager des Arts et des Artistes, et des Industries d'Art* 60 (September–October 1918): 5.

52. René Weiss, *La participation de la ville de Paris à l'exposition internationale des arts décoratifs et industriels modernes* (Paris: Imprimerie nationale, 1925), 45.

53. Weiss, *La participation*, 75.

54. Weiss, *La participation*, 76.

55. Anon., "L'exposition des écoles primaires dans le pavillon de la ville de Paris," *L'Illustration*, October 31, 1925, 473.

Race and Empire in French Posters of the Great War

The French colonial empire and its inhabitants played an important role in the Great War, a role often portrayed in official propaganda posters. The colonies provided labor and natural resources essential to waging modern industrialized warfare, and from the first weeks of the war thousands of soldiers came from France's overseas possessions to defend the metropole. Many of these soldiers were nonwhite colonial subjects, known as *troupes indigènes*, or indigenous troops,[1] and by the end of the war more than 500,000 of these men had entered the French army. This reliance upon the empire and, even more, the presence of hundreds of thousands of North African, West African, Madagascan, and Indochinese men in uniform and on French soil confronted many in France with fundamental questions about France's colonial relationships, race, and national identity. Troupes indigènes, after all, were colonial subjects, not citizens with corresponding rights and privileges. Yet they were shouldering one of the most important burdens of national belonging, making great sacrifices to defend France from the German invader. What place, then, did these men, and the lands from which they came, occupy in the French nation? How could one integrate men from such very different and diverse cultures into commonly accepted conceptions of nationhood? More important, how could one consider as French these soldiers who possessed very different racial characteristics from the average white French person of European descent? In short, contributing to the war effort, even fighting and dying in the struggle against a common enemy, associated the colonies and colonial subjects intimately with the French nation, yet at the same time perceptions of their distinct racial and cultural features held them apart.

The official response to this difficulty was to stress the ideal of assimilation. A pillar of French colonial ideology, assimilation held that the goal of French colonialism was to raise conquered peoples up to the intellectual, technological, and cultural level of France. In return for these benefits, colonized peoples would owe their French masters gratitude and, if necessary, more concrete returns such as military service. At the end of this process of assimilation, and the fulfillment of its attendant reciprocal duties, colonized peoples would have attained a sufficient level of advancement and culture to be admitted as full members of the French nation. Such an ideology was the product of France's strong republican tradition, born in the Revolution of 1789, which professed egalitarian and universalist ideals.[2] In practice, however, essentialist notions of racial difference made full assimilation at the very least problematic, and in the minds of many impossible. Thus France's colonial empire occupied an uncertain rhetorical and legal space in French national life.

This ambiguous status is reflected in wartime images of empire and of troupes indigènes. The support of the colonies and the presence of colonial subjects in the national army defending the metropole confronted French officials with a need to define more carefully their place in the nation, and official propaganda posters reveal the tension between republican assimilationist ideology and stereotypes placing these different lands and peoples outside the French nation. A number of posters evoking colonial themes focused on the contributions of empire, both material and human, to the prosecution of the war. These images sought to reassure the French public that France had overseas support, to communicate the usefulness of empire, and to remind viewers of the debt of gratitude they owed to the inhabitants of the colonies. These posters propagated the myth that France was *la patrie* (the fatherland) of both troupes indigènes and their white French comrades. Such posters stressed solidarity between France and its "children" from the colonies and even suggested the duty of France and its citizens to aid the indigènes who sacrificed so much. Yet many images presented in these same posters, and others, portray a romanticized and stereotyped vision of the colonies, their peoples, and the troupes indigènes, clearly depicting them as irreducibly alien, primitive, and "other." In short, French wartime posters reveal the republican vision of France and its colonized peoples struggling together toward a common goal—the expulsion of the German invader, which would benefit metropole and colonies alike—and the simultaneous difficulty of effectively integrating these racially diverse peoples into French conceptions of national identity.

Wartime Posters in France and Their Influence

Before examining specific portrayals of empire and race in the posters themselves, it is important to understand both the context in which the images were produced and the way the French public is likely to have responded to them. The lithographed art poster, of which the war posters were direct descendants, originated in France during the nineteenth century, and the form reached its apogee in its "golden age" just before the Great War, around the turn of the century, with the works of Eugène Grasset and Henri de Toulouse-Lautrec.[3] Thus it was not surprising that France would turn to that medium to mobilize its population for the unprecedented demands of modern war. Though many later commentators have been critical of the artistic qualities of wartime posters in general, at least some aspects of French productions were noteworthy.[4] French posters often made appeals to the glorious republican and military past, following the heroic and romantic style of nineteenth-century salon painting.[5] Even with this relatively constraining style, however, the emotional content could be powerful. Comparing French depictions of Marianne, the symbol of the Third Republic (1870–1940), with representations of the female figure in the posters of other nations, Maurice Rickards has noted: "But where Britannia posed and Italia postured, Marianne weighed in without reserve . . . Marianne is rough, tough, and real; her clothes are in attractive disarray and she is bawling her head off." Contrast this, he continued, with an example from an Austrian poster and "we can see the difference between France and all the rest; almost without exception, France's posters have a vigour and emotional impact that raise them far above their counterparts. With this air of unselfconscious spontaneity, the inherent unbelievability of the subject is made almost credible. The Austrian girl, we feel, did not exist; Marianne maybe did."[6] This dramatic romanticism combined with realism also rendered depictions of battle more realistic in French posters than in those produced by the British and the Americans.[7]

This realism and emotional candor is helpful as one tries to interpret the meanings behind these images. However, there are certainly problems associated with this interpretation. First of all, the intent of the artists who made the posters is often difficult, if not impossible, to discern with any exactitude, and in any case artists did not always exercise exclusive control over their productions. Artists had employers, whether the government or private businesses or organizations, so posters rarely spoke with one voice. Hence far from providing an uncomplicated guide to past mentalities, "posters raise questions."[8] The second problem associated with the interpretation of these messages from the past is how to gauge their reception by the public at which they were aimed. How effective were wartime posters, and what can they reveal about the mentalities of the people who made and saw them? This can be difficult to judge. There is "no measuring instrument" of effectiveness, and conclusions based on intuition and "post hoc reasoning" are not always totally reliable.[9] But the problem is not entirely insoluble. Posters addressing certain themes often show a marked consistency in both their use of images and their messages, and this likely betrays a mentality or point of view that was more or less widespread. And repeated themes and motifs certainly reflected a vision that the works' sponsors, most often government officials, wanted the public to adopt.

But beyond these considerations, there is good reason to believe that many posters struck a familiar chord within contemporary viewers. As "an instrument of persuasion," the poster had to seek to exploit existing mentalities within its audience.[10] As one scholar has put it, "To be effective, to be believed, a poster's message had to play upon broad ideas and feelings already current."[11] Put another way, posters must "utilize a code which corresponds, barely removed, to one of our intimate codes."[12] Contemporaries were well aware of this. A wartime American official remarked: "Again artists are working with and for the government of their people, at work which the people can understand, for if they cannot it is worthless."[13] Governments invested a great deal of money and effort in these poster campaigns, and they were unlikely to waste time introducing novelties to their audiences. The unfamiliar would provoke no response, so posters relied on stereotypes and exploited

RICHARD S. FOGARTY

the prejudices at large in the societies of the belligerent nations. Poster propaganda avoided "the new and unfamiliar" and instead appealed to "familiar ideas and images, conventional wisdom."[14] Of course, generalizations about prejudice and mentalities obscure the diversity of opinion and personality present in all societies. We cannot assume everyone in these societies was receptive to these messages, but we can assume that many people were.

This receptivity is not surprising, given the commercial origins of poster art, where seduction and manipulation were the primary goals. The French government official who launched the highly successful poster campaign for national loans declared: "Let us do as in commercial advertising." In other words, war posters should play upon emotions and desires to get people to part with their money not for the latest consumer product but for the sacred cause of national defense.[15] Comparing commercial advertising with war posters, one scholar has noted that "the political message, the war poster . . . speak[s] still more directly."[16] The war posters' message—"Sacrifice!"—was much more urgent than the commercial posters' "Buy!" As one scholar points out, "posters helped to raise substantial numbers of recruits and extremely large sums of money."[17] And in 1923, an observer who had recently lived through the great French poster campaigns of the war remarked: "The poster is the cry of the street, the speech in the open air; if it is well done, if it is sufficiently widespread and launched at the right moment, it will become a piece of advice listened to and will be able to cause the most surprising movements of opinion."[18] Given the interest of artists and their sponsors in playing to existing feelings and ideas within their societies, and given the ability of propaganda to influence public opinion, one can assume that wartime posters can reveal widespread attitudes. In using posters as a guide to the mental world of past societies, historians must nevertheless treat the images with caution and keep in mind that if posters serve as a "mirror of history," this mirror is both "faithful and distorting," though even the distortions can tell us something.[19]

This applies particularly to presentations of empire and race in French posters of the Great War. The images certainly represent a vision of the colonies and their inhabitants that military and political officials wanted the public to share, but they also represent a vision that was already part of many French people's worldview. It is not just the nature of propaganda that suggests this conclusion but also the fact that these mentalities were revealed in the words and actions of government officials, army personnel, and the broader French population.

Empire

One can see two main themes concerning France's colonial empire in wartime posters. The first evoked the contributions of the colonies to the war effort. These images sought to convey the usefulness of the empire in sustaining the metropole in its desperate struggle against the German invaders. The second theme focused on the debt France owed to its colonial populations in return for the enormous material and human sacrifices they made to aid the "patrie." Such posters sought to play both upon the pity viewers should have for wounded troupes indigènes and upon the sense of paternal responsibility French people should have for the well-being of their colonial "children."

Posters stressing the contribution of the empire to the war effort reassured viewers that France was not alone in the fight. Since their humiliating defeat in the Franco-Prussian War of 1870–71, many in France regarded Germany's larger population and great industrial strength with anxiety. One remaining source of hope, however, was France's huge colonial empire,

RICHARD S. FOGARTY

with its natural material wealth and millions of inhabitants. Some even argued that France, if one meant by that "la plus grande France," or France plus its colonies, in fact possessed a much larger population than Germany. Thus the French could remain confident in the face of a showdown with Germany, the eventuality of which very few doubted prior to 1914.[20]

That French officials recognized the importance of help from the colonies, and that they wanted all French people to recognize it, was apparent in a number of ways. To celebrate the colonial contribution, the Section Photographique et Ci-nématographique of the French army sponsored an exhibition highlighting "The Aid of the Colonies to France." The poster advertising the event made the exhibition's point simply and powerfully. It consisted of a drawing of French soldiers, guns at the ready, packs on their backs, marching across a battlefield crossed by trenches and strewn with the debris of war. On the extreme left, close up, one can see the distinctive profile of a *poilu* (French infantryman) following his comrades into the distant fields and, one assumes, victory. Superimposed on and interrupting this scene is a panel in the center of the composition, with text announcing the exhibition and two images. Below is a small depiction of Marianne, symbol of the republic, militant, defiant, and as always beautiful. Above her is a portrait of an African in uniform, standing at attention and holding his rifle upright beside him, bayonet fixed. The background is ambiguous—it could be somewhere in the colonies or on the Western Front—as is his equipment—the bayonet could just as easily be the tip of a spear, and the portion of his headgear showing could be either a helmet or a headband. The look on his face, however, is not at all ambiguous: his broad nose and grinning countenance convey the message that though he may be a bit primitive and perhaps also childlike, he is nonetheless happy to do his duty for his "adopted fatherland" (a term French officials used repeatedly throughout the war). Marianne watches over all her children, the poilus who march to defend their homes and the indigènes who support them.[21]

This reassuring sense that France could rely upon its colonies in the war found expression in the most prolific genre of French war posters, those advertising national war loans.[22] The government continued to raise these loans into the immediate postwar years, as reconstruction of the devastated occupied areas in the northeast was enormously expensive. In 1920 the Crédit Foncier d'Algérie et de Tunisie advertised the latest national loan with a colorful poster celebrating the various Mediterranean countries where it did business and upon which France could rely to subscribe to this vitally important loan. The poster featured seven flags fluttering together in a rejuvenating wind under a pointed Arab arch. Out in front was the French tricolor, and to the left and below were the flags of Algeria, Tunisia, and Morocco. Below and in the background, between the pillars supporting the arch, one can see the characteristic whitewashed buildings, narrow streets, and palm trees of a North African city. After having given so much of their treasure, both human and material, the inhabitants of such a city, along with the French of the metropole, would certainly wish to help complete the French victory by contributing to national reconstruction. The message was unity, teamwork, and idealized images of the French colonial empire.[23]

Some posters were much more direct in their portrayal of just how the colonies contributed to the war effort. Two more advertisements for the same 1920 loan made the point by depicting the hustle and bustle of ports during the war. One showed Algerian sailors, recognizable by their dark skin, white robes, and traditional headgear, shuttling goods in rowboats from a cargo ship to the dock of a French port. In the foreground one

Fig. 25. Henri Villain's depiction of a busy Algerian port, designed to raise money for a 1920 national loan floated by the Compagnie Algérienne, emphasizes the material contributions of the colonies to the war effort. POS-FR .v473, no. 1, Library of Congress.

sees an Algerian at work, his powerful back and arms straining with effort. In the distant background, one can see smoke rising from countless smokestacks. The message would be clear to viewers: the raw materials and brawn of the colonies fueled the metropolitan industry that was essential in waging modern war.[24] The second poster was similar but even richer in its imagery (fig. 25). In it a French ship is docked at a port in Algeria. In the background French sailors carry sacks onto the deck. One can assume that these sacks contain wool, as in the foreground is a flock of sheep with Algerian shepherds. In the immediate foreground three adults are in various states

of repose on the pier, watching the activity on the ship. Their backs are to the viewer, and their heads turned away, so one sees only their flowing robes and head coverings. In front of them is both the flock and the only indigène with a recognizable identity. He is a child, dressed all in white. The symbolism is striking: the anonymous, exotic indigenous masses; the natural wealth of the colonies at the disposal of the metropole; the industrious French workers preparing to make effective use of that wealth; and, near the middle of the composition and in the middle distance, that which the contributions of both the indigènes and the French seek to preserve, an innocent child, and less concretely, the future.[25]

Even posters that sought to evoke a somewhat different theme

RICHARD S. FOGARTY

often contained explicit references to the material contributions of the empire and made clear the nature of the relationship between the colonies and the metropole. A 1918 poster soliciting subscriptions to the latest war loan was set in an Algerian *souk* (marketplace), and featured a *tirailleur algérien* (native Algerian soldier) greeting his wife and child upon his return home (fig. 26).[26] Striking a familiar theme for such posters, the caption advised, "Subscribe, it will hasten his return with Victory." The drawing is highly stylized and idealized and ignores entirely the reality that as more than half of Algerians who served were conscripted, many would no doubt have preferred not to have left in the first place. Once again the child, this time with his mother, represents the ostensible goal of the war: a secure future where men can perform their highest peacetime duty, raising a family. As is often the case in posters of the Great War, the child is linked to the fighting but in the most abstract way, avoiding any real evocation of the horrors that war actually entails: he holds in his hand a string connected to a toy cannon, playing at war while his father goes away to fight a real one. In the background is a crowd of people, native Algerians in their robes mixing happily together with bourgeois white French settlers and even a priest. At the edge of the crowd stands a man selling oranges from baskets on the back of his donkey. The messages are multiple and clear. The colonies provide both soldiers and the bounty of nature, and life in the French empire is one of harmony, despite the great sacrifices of the moment. And in the colonies as in France, men fight and work for a future in which children will only play at war.[27]

Such posters sought to remind viewers of the sacrifices that the war entailed. They addressed both French people and, to some extent, colonial subjects, for although the majority of potential subscribers to these loans would have been comparatively well-off white European settlers or mainland French, these images could also resonate with the families of troupes indigènes (though most could not have been eager to add the sacrifice of their savings to that of their fathers, husbands, or sons). The imagery was also designed to reassure the public that mainland France did not face the hardships alone, that though it needed a little help to triumph, "la grande France . . . cannot lose."[28] A small poster featuring the tirailleurs sénégalais (native West African soldiers) made this point.[29] Several of these men stand guard in the Jardin du Luxembourg in Paris, watching over a moored zeppelin. Their bearing is not especially soldierly—they are standing at ease, leaning on a fence, and talking with one another. On the sidewalk just outside the park walks a blinded French soldier, guided by a Red Cross nurse. The soldier is a proud but tragic reminder of the price of the war, while the Africans remind the viewer that the colonies provide further manpower resources. The casual poses of the Africans also reassure the viewer of the essential simplicity and good nature of France's "children" in the colonies. These are the kind of soldiers who can be of use but need guidance and are still essentially different from white French soldiers.[30]

If images of troupes indigènes could be reassuring, artists could also mobilize such images to evoke pity and sympathy in the viewer, and this was part of the larger goal of conveying the debt the French nation owed to such men and all the inhabitants of the colonies. During the war the government and private citizens' organizations sponsored expositions, lotteries, or *journées* to benefit soldiers from the colonies. Often posters publicizing these events depicted wounded soldiers. An advertisement for a 1917 exposition of Moroccan art, held to raise funds for the war effort there, showed a Moroccan soldier leaning on a crutch, watching an artist at work painting arabesques on pottery. Similarly, a poster announcing a lottery to benefit

RICHARD S. FOGARTY

Moroccan soldiers featured two men in traditional dress, one with his arm in a sling and a cane in his other hand. Both of these images served to remind viewers of the sacrifices colonial subjects were making and the duty of everyone to contribute to their care.[31]

These images were evocative of both exoticism and sacrifice, but some posters made the point in a much more didactic, even heavy-handed way, employing long, exhortatory texts, sometimes even to the exclusion of any images at all. This was an increasingly rare approach so late in the war. At the beginning of the conflict, posters featuring long texts, such as the order for mobilization or important speeches by famous leaders, appeared on walls in the cities and towns of France. Even the first posters advertising war loans simply conveyed the advantages and terms of the loans in words and numbers. As the war went on, however, propagandists preferred simple, powerful images, with a brief, easy-to-remember slogan. As one historian has put it, after 1915, "the great period of the illustrated political poster was born: an image, a slogan."[32] In this respect war posters were merely catching up with developments that had appeared years earlier in commercial posters, which employed clear symbols, "something to be quickly perceived rather than pondered."[33] Yet apparently, when it came to communicating the special debt that France owed to its colonies, designers of posters sometimes felt the best way to reach their audience was by confronting it with a text spelling out exactly what this debt entailed.

At the beginning of 1917 two posters appeared announcing a "Journée de l'Armée d'Afrique et des Troupes Coloniales." Neither contained any images, just a decorative border surrounding text. One advertised a lottery to benefit soldiers and their families, listing the price of tickets and the prizes on offer, while the other contained a text of several hundred words. This second poster reminded viewers that from the very beginning of the war, troops from all of the colonies in France's empire, "fired by the purest and most ardent patriotism, rallied to the holiest of causes: the defense of the greatest moral being there is in the world, just as our illustrious Gambetta proclaimed, immortal France."[34] These soldiers from the colonies, all worthy of their illustrious predecessors who had fought for France in the past, "and whose incomparable bravery has become legendary, have held on to prove before the Universe that, having received from the hands of France the benefits of liberty and civilization, they want to conquer or die out in front and next to their older brothers [i.e., native Frenchmen]." Connecting the past with the present, a technique more common in French war posters than those of other nations, the author listed the famous battles in which these soldiers had fought since 1914 and the many famous nineteenth-century battles in which colonial troops had fought.[35] Praising their "élan," the author also connected them with the glory of the empire and their predecessors in the French army, who had "assured the magnificent colonial empire of France," and whose spirits were now saying to the heroes of the Great War: "You too have been well-deserving of the Patrie: Thank you." The government saw it as a sacred duty to pay homage to these men, and to enlist the French public to help show indigenous families that France valued their contributions. The paternalism, pride in empire, and faith in the genius and civilizing mission of France in the world could not be clearer.[36]

A 1918 poster made the same points with more flair. Combining a moderately long text with a dramatic drawing of a mounted North African cavalryman at full gallop, robes billowing and the French tricolor flag held aloft on a pole bearing a crescent and star, the poster simply sought to convey "What we owe our colonies." The text and the palm trees and cacti that

RICHARD S. FOGARTY

framed the image suggested the wild territories brought under French control, while the horseman evoked the proud warrior tradition of North Africans, tamed and employed to the civilized ends the French flag represented. But it was the text that made explicit the responsibility accompanying empire.

> What we owe our colonies. Before the war, everyone did not understand France's need for colonies or protectorate territories. We all know now what we owe to the thousands of indigenous volunteers who have fought for well-loved France with as much courage as the French themselves, or who have rendered the most precious services on the home front. We all know in what prodigious quantities our possessions in Africa, Asia, the Americas, Oceania have sent us their produce: without them, our resupply would have been much more difficult. In common effort will grow yet more common affection.

The French owed a debt to the inhabitants of the colonies, but of course there were limits. The poster reminded the reader that native Frenchmen themselves also fought, and their courage set the standard for the indigènes. Supplying the war effort would have been much more difficult, but not impossible, without contributions from the colonies. The text also purveyed a comforting conception of the colonial relationship, calling the troupes indigènes "volunteers," when in reality many were conscripted and many others enlisted to escape the poverty and hopelessness that the colonial regime engendered in their homelands.[37] Still, readers were to come away with a sense of paternal responsibility, secure in the knowledge that native French people and colonial subjects had waged the war as a "common effort" but cognizant that continued support of France's colonial mission would enhance the affection that the indigenous peoples of the empire clearly felt for their protectors.[38]

Race

If official French discourse about empire was clear from Great War posters, so were common understandings of race. For many in France the most striking aspect of the presence of troupes indigènes was their very different racial identity. They were indeed an important part of the common effort to repel the German invader, and this associated them intimately with the nation, but they were also visibly and culturally different from their white French counterparts, and thus their racial identity set them apart. This ambiguous status was clear in many wartime depictions. One can also see in posters featuring troupes indigènes the specific attributes many French people believed were inherent in the character of non-European peoples. Stereotypical images appeared often, and one can get a sense of racial characteristics that many in France held to be specific to different groups of indigènes.[39]

Though French forces during the war included soldiers from Indochina and Madagascar as well as North and West Africa, images of soldiers from these more distant colonies rarely appeared in posters. This was in part a question of numbers: about half of troupes indigènes who served during the war came from North Africa, and about one-third came from West Africa. Moreover, only a small number of Indochinese and Madagascan soldiers served in combat; most of them were relegated to noncombat support roles. Thus the more numerous and more visible North and West African combat soldiers came to symbolize, in the minds of poster artists and the French public, the colonial contribution to fighting the war at the Front.

Depictions of North Africans usually focused on Algerians (a large majority of the troops recruited in this area came from Algeria) and exploited a number of common themes.[40] One of these was exoticism. As we have seen, images of Algerians

in the posters advertising national loans portrayed indigènes
in traditional costume, flowing robes and dark skin emphasizing their differences from Europeans. Very often, the indigènes lacked individuality; they were symbolic of the teem-
ing masses that made up the great reservoirs of support on
which France could depend to defend itself from German
aggression. Landscapes were equally stylized, also calling to
mind the essential difference between France and the exotic
locales of the empire.

To these evocations of the exotic other were added—in the
case of Algerian soldiers, specific martial attributes. On the one
hand, many French officials had doubts about the suitability
of Algerians for modern European warfare. This had a great
deal to do with the image the French had of Algeria and of the
kind of warfare they themselves encountered there in conquering that colony. The wide open spaces alternating with rugged
mountains constituted terrain particularly well suited to quick
cavalry raids, hit-and-run tactics, and savage frontal assaults.
Combined with this was a prevailing stereotype of Arab fighters as duplicitous, undisciplined, and prone to pillage.[41]

On the other hand, there was a parallel and opposite discourse about the martial qualities of Algerians, deeming them
warlike and fairly good soldiers, given the proper guidance.
This stemmed in part from the difficulty the French had in
conquering Algeria, a process that required more than thirty
years of hard fighting. Military, political, and colonial officials
routinely referred to Algerians' "naturally warlike" sentiments
or nature, which only required the proper training and leadership in order to be of great service to the French army. A 1915
report on recruitment made the prevailing attitude clear: "Algeria is not simply, as some have put it, a reservoir of men. The
Arab and Berber races constitute, like the French, a warrior
people. War for them is not an accident, something unforeseen

and fearsome. They accept it as a normal event, chronically recurrent. They can, it is true, meet death by it, but who has ever escaped that? Sooner or later, it will come. Fatalism makes good soldiers."[42]

Another report on conscription in Algeria made much the same argument, praising Algerians as intrepid and brave, acknowledging their endurance and disregard of danger, and recalling the legendary exploits of the "turcos" (as Algerian soldiers had been nicknamed) in France during the Franco-Prussian War. Noting their value as "shock troops," a designation common to most troupes indigènes that emphasized their role in offensive operations, the report claimed that an additional 300,000 Algerians in the ranks in 1914 would have turned the balance against the Germans, transforming the battle of Charleroi into a French victory and preventing the invasion of the northern départements.[43]

These same contradictory attitudes about Algerian soldiers are apparent in the poster art of the period. One poster evoked the wild, untamed people and landscape of Algeria, now controlled and at the disposal of France in the current conflict. The illustration was a dramatic rendering of a nineteenth-century battle in the scrublands beneath a mountain. On one side, marching beneath the French tricolor is a host of indigènes in white robes and head coverings. Facing them is a group of as yet unconquered Algerians. Leading the French-allied forces is an Algerian on horseback, sword aloft, urging his comrades forward. The action is dramatic and of sweeping scope and sought to remind the viewer of the past support and martial exploits of native Algerians who aided in the conquest of their own land. Now all that warlike ardor was directed toward reconquering the German-occupied areas of France. The figure on horseback recalled an earlier, now vanished warrior ethos: the selfless individual hero who could alter the outcome of a battle through force of will and bravery. That the trenches of the Western Front had ended this kind of war forever (and in fact any kind of war on horseback) was not important to the myth making at work here. The point was to inspire the viewer. And another important and useful myth was embodied in the caption: "Pour la patrie, souscrivez à l'emprunt" (For the fatherland, subscribe to the loan). Exhorting the viewer to subscribe to a national loan "pour la patrie" reinforced the official and popular conception of Algeria not as a separate colony but as an integral part of the French nation itself. (Unlike other colonies, Algeria, with a large European settler population, was administratively integrated into the French nation: divided into three départements on an equal footing with those of mainland France and represented by deputies elected to the French Parliament by the white settlers.) After all, the scene of the battle was across the Mediterranean, not in France. Moreover, the slogan reinforced the idea that Algerians who fought in the colonial wars and in the Great War fought for their "adopted fatherland," France.[44]

The figure of the lone, courageous, and proud Algerian warrior on horseback was a popular motif in many posters. One advertising the Journée de l'Armée d'Afrique et des Troupes Coloniales in 1917 employed this symbolism, the cavalryman on horseback in the background, horse rearing and robes billowing out behind him. In the foreground under the tricolor march determined Algerian infantrymen, with fierce countenances and bayonets fixed, reminiscent of the patriots who marched off in 1792 to defend the Revolution and the new First Republic (1792–99) from foreign invasion and monarchical tyranny. This was a powerful symbol of the place of troupes indigènes in the French nation. Here they were, recognizably different through their exotic costumes and distinct facial features, but also fighting under the French flag and clearly in the great French republican tradition. Acceptance of French republican principles was one of the most important elements of the French ideal of assimilation, which in theory opened the door of citizenship to anyone, regardless of race or ethnicity. However, Algerians and other colonial peoples, the assimilation and "civilization" of whom was one of the main justifications for French imperialism, remained in practice outside the nation, their distinct ethnic identity, here symbolized by their dress and appearance, setting them apart.[45]

One of the most dramatic images of an Algerian warrior on horseback, Maurice Romberg's 1918 poster for the Compagnie Algérienne and its loan campaign of that year, emphasized this theme even more clearly (fig. 27). Against a bright yellow background and in the midst of a brilliant flash of light rides a cavalryman in traditional dress, which billows out behind him. His horse at full gallop, the man stands in the stirrups and beckons with an outstretched hand. The dual implication is that he calls both for his men to follow him into battle and for viewers to subscribe to the loan. Each is an important action that will hasten the victorious conclusion of the war. Everything about the image speaks of exoticism, from the horse's decorated harness and the ornate dagger in the man's belt to the look on his face, at once desperate, proud, and furious. The image was certainly meant to inspire, and in that sense the viewer was to take away a positive impression of admiration and awe in the face of such courage, but the man at the center of the composition is still irredeemably different. One might be proud to fight alongside such a man, but there is very little question of whether he was really French. One could identify with an image of a poilu in the trenches but not with this exotic other.[46]

Images of tirailleurs sénégalais, black men from West Africa, differed from depictions of white French soldiers too,

RICHARD S. FOGARTY

Fig. 27. Maurice Romberg's dramatic and highly stylized portrayal of an Algerian soldier on horseback is a 1918 poster advertising a war loan. The image drew on stereotypes of Algerians as exotic desert warriors. POS-FR .R65, no. 3, Library of Congress.

but there were also important differences between portrayals of West and North Africans.[47] These differences not only highlighted the specific racial characteristics many French people believed marked the West Africans but also revealed the distinctions the French often made among indigènes from various parts of the colonial empire. Despite North Africans' exoticism, their cultural differences (symbolized most potently by Islam), and their irreducible otherness, many in France found it easier to identify with North Africans than with West Africans. Muslim identity did seem to erect a cultural barrier between North Africans and both the secular republican and the Christian heritage of the French, and Islam often seemed an insuperable obstacle to the French project of civilization and assimilation. Yet some French people still felt a closer racial affinity with generally lighter-skinned Arabs and Berbers than they did with black Africans. It is significant that Charles Lutaud, governor general of Algeria during most of the Great War, remarked both that Algerians were "perfectible whites" like the French, and that "pure Islam still appears, in fact, like a bronze wall which, despite the repeated assaults of civilization, has not yet been seriously shaken."[48] Moreover, though many regarded Islam as anti-modern and a sort of atavism, no one denied the former greatness and real achievements of the remarkable Muslim civilizations of the past.

In the minds of many in France, however, black Africans were not even the inheritors of a fallen civilization. Though many West Africans were in fact Muslim, many others followed traditional indigenous animistic faiths, and the advanced kingdoms that had existed in the area were either unknown or deemed inferior to the great Muslim civilizations of the past. Simply put, in the minds of many French people West Africans were primitive savages. This characterization produced a dual vision of West African soldiers. On the one hand, according to the stereotype, these men were possessed of limited intelligence, combined with a childlike simplicity and innocence that bred in them a fierce loyalty to their French protectors. On the other hand, the tirailleurs sénégalais were reputed to be ferocious warriors who, though ill-prepared for modern forms of combat, could be very useful in assaults if properly led. These two main strains of thought about West Africans coexisted easily and reinforced each other. Tirailleurs sénégalais found that French people they encountered often treated them patronizingly, as one would treat small children, while at the same time expecting from them the most savage behavior

RICHARD S. FOGARTY

on the battlefield. One West African soldier recalled that upon the arrival of his unit in France, crowds of people cheered him and his comrades as they paraded through the streets, some of the spectators shouting to the Africans, "Cut off the Germans' heads."[49] Both Algerians and West Africans made a considerable impression upon the French public from the beginning of the war, and many images celebrated their courage, "but they charge 'with fury' or demonstrate an 'infernal fierceness,' in a way that betrays their fearsome savagery."[50]

The predominant view of West Africans as savage children was reflected and reinforced in wartime posters. The most famous depiction of a tirailleur sénégalais, during and after the war, was in publicity for the hot breakfast drink Banania. Beginning in 1915 a smiling African, in the distinctive uniform of the tirailleurs sénégalais, appeared on posters and packaging for the product. The association with the tirailleurs proved enormously successful, playing as it did on the popularity of the soldiers among the French public, but the images were clearly stereotypical. The overdrawn smile reflected the standard view of black Africans as good-natured and simplistic, and the overall effect was overtly paternalistic and racist. Reacting to the continued use of these images long after the war, Léopold Sédar Senghor, the great African poet and first president of an independent Senegal, wished he could tear posters featuring the insulting visage of the tirailleur from the walls of Paris.[51] But it was not merely the image that carried a racist message. The slogan "Y'a bon!" that accompanied the ad campaign and became intimately bound to Banania even after the images of the tirailleur disappeared in the late twentieth century, was inspired by the distinctive pidgin French spoken by the West Africans.[52] French military officials did nothing to discourage this and other ungrammatical expressions; in fact, they encouraged their use by institutionalizing pidgin French as the preferred language of training and command in West African units. This stemmed not only from expediency—the need to train quickly soldiers who spoke no or little French—but also from the idea that learning proper French was too taxing for the simplistic mentality of the tirailleurs.[53] This poor French served to reinforce the view many in France held of black Africans as primitive and unintelligent, and the Banania slogan gave the image wide currency in French society.

The stereotype present in both the images and the language appearing in publicity for Banania—the cheerful and simple child—found its way into other contexts as well. A 1918 advertisement for the fourth of the government's national loans featured a close-up of the face of a tirailleur sénégalais wearing the distinctive headgear of these soldiers, the *chéchia*. His features and smile an exaggerated caricature, the tirailleur made a direct appeal to the viewer, "Frenchmen, subscribe!" This message, entirely typical of all such advertisements for national loans, was elaborated in a caption beneath the picture. In broken and accented French, the caption had the soldier say, "'Tirailleur' fait une offre avantageuse: 'Mon Z'ami, ti donner tes sordis et tirailleur fait reste!'" Like other examples of the "tirailleur language," as many in France called this distorted form of French, the statement is impossible to render accurately in English and is full of the grammatical errors and phonetic pronunciation that marked the tirailleurs' spoken French. Nevertheless, like the Banania advertisements, this appeal played upon the undeniable popularity of the West African soldiers. Many French people were sympathetic to these men, even if such attitudes grew out of a paternalistic and racist sense of superiority. And the message, once one got beyond the pidgin form in which it was conveyed, was that the West Africans were doing their duty, and so the French public could at least do theirs. Give your money, we'll do the rest.[54]

RICHARD S. FOGARTY

The reference to "doing the rest," hinted at the other aspect of the stereotypical view of West Africans: the primitive and savage warrior upon whom France was fortunate to rely in the desperate struggle against the Germans. Such a view, however, did not preclude a persistent emphasis upon the inferiority of blacks to whites. Though the tirailleurs sénégalais were renowned for their alleged aggression in battle, white French leaders still needed to guide and channel such impulses. These views prevailed where it counted most, at the Front. French officers, in a position to decide when, where, and how the West Africans fought, were thoroughly imbued with these ideas about the men whom they led. Though opinions sometimes varied on the overall degree to which the West Africans were useful in modern European warfare, there was a general consensus about the nature of their strengths and weaknesses. One general wrote in 1916 that negative opinions among his subordinate officers who commanded tirailleurs sénégalais often resulted from the officers making an unfair comparison between black and white troops, a "comparison which leads them inevitably to lament the absence among the sénégalais of certain essential qualities of the European soldier, from which [stems] a reduction of confidence in the unit entrusted to them." The real question, he argued, was whether the West Africans could be useful in modern combat, and he thought that they could be if used as shock troops. West Africans, "naturally warlike and ready to fight," had the essential qualities for offensive warfare: "bravery, élan, quickness in action."[55] The contents of this and the other reports make plain the racial stereotypes that shaped the attitudes of French officers toward the tirailleurs. A battalion commander summed up these stereotypes, claiming that the West African soldier was brave and "a good marcher" who loved to fight, preferred hand-to-hand combat, and was disciplined, but who was capable only of short bursts of violence and needed prompt rest after an effort, feared "what he does not know," and reacted reflexively to events, being dominated by his animal instincts rather than "by will or reflection."[56] Other officers cited West Africans' limited intellectual capacities, their complete lack of initiative, their susceptibility to cold weather, and their childlike fear of bombardments. Thus it was clear that black troops, with all these deficiencies, could not replace white troops. However, with the proper leadership, a sufficient number of Europeans to perform specialized tasks beyond the capacity of the West Africans, and essential support from neighboring units of white soldiers, West Africans could constitute "a contribution permitting [us] to spare a certain number of European lives during attacks."[57]

This blunt statement reveals the dangerous implications for the tirailleurs of these racial stereotypes and the tactical doctrines that resulted from them. Fighting primarily during offensive operations exposed the West Africans to an increased probability of death. Whether West Africans served as "cannon fodder," as critics of their exploitation by the French have charged, has been the subject of some scholarly debate.[58] Whatever the case, there is no question that French army officials routinely referred to tirailleurs sénégalais as "troupes de choc" (shock troops) and often used them as such. This meant that West Africans most often found themselves on the attack, with the correspondingly increased risk of death or injury. That these views reached at least some of the French public was indicated by the reputation the West Africans had for raiding trenches and cutting Germans' heads off with large knives.[59]

One way the stereotype of the West African as primitive savage reached a wider audience was through one of the war's best known posters featuring troupes indigènes, Lucien Jonas's advertisement for the 1917 Journée de l'Armée d'Afrique et des

RICHARD S. FOGARTY

Fig. 28. One of the war's best known posters to feature troupes indigènes, Lucien Jonas's advertisement for the 1917 Journée de l'Armée d'Afrique et des Troupes Coloniales reflected and reinforced stereotypes of black West Africans as savage and primitive warriors. Political Poster collection, FR 642, Hoover Institution Archives.

Troupes Coloniales (fig. 28). The poster portrayed tirailleurs sénégalais, along with white French troops, assaulting a German trench. The most striking feature of the colorful drawing is a charging African soldier, one hand raised in a clenched fist and the other brandishing his rifle. Overwhelming the other figures in the action beside and behind him, he is frozen in the act of leaping into the enemy trench, an expression of uncontained fury and aggression on his face, his mouth wide open in a shout. Everything about him, even his tattered clothes, suggests primitive, uncontrolled violence. To be sure, the face of the white French soldier nearby is also expressive of determination, rage, and martial aggression, and he too is yelling. Of course, the French can also be justifiably proud of their own reputation for élan in the attack. But the Frenchman is in the background, and the viewer's eyes are drawn irresistibly to the African in the center of the composition. The action is dramatic, and the tirailleur seems as if he is about to leap right out of the poster, as his rifle extends beyond the frame of the drawing and indeed beyond the edge of the paper itself. At the extreme left of the picture is a tree in full springtime bloom, an improbable sight on the ravaged battlefields of the Western Front but symbolic of the hope, renewal, and promise of victory that the infusion of warlike troupes indigènes promised for the French war effort. The poster sought to remind the French public that together with their French comrades, the tirailleurs sénégalais would bring victory. It also reminded viewers that black Africans were very different from white French people, and a large part of that difference stemmed from Africans' primitive and savage nature.[60]

Conclusion

French posters depicting colonial themes during the Great War reveal a great deal about official and popular attitudes toward both empire and race. Officials sought to demonstrate to the public that the imperial adventures providing France with the second largest colonial empire in the world were now paying off. The metropole could count on the aid of the colonies to help withstand the German invasion and eventually to triumph. To be sure, this help came at a price, and several posters reminded the French that they had an obligation to recognize the value and sacrifices of the empire and its peoples. In portraying these peoples, posters resorted to images that would resonate with the racial stereotypes and prejudices abroad in French society. These images are so noteworthy because of the dramatic ways

RICHARD S. FOGARTY

in which they embody the ambiguous place colonial peoples occupied in the French nation, an ambiguity made all the more acute in that colonial subjects serving as soldiers were certainly participating in national life in the most basic and dramatic fashion. Speaking of imagery common to all the combatant nations of the Great War, Maurice Rickards has noted the "persistence of universal archetypes: the square-jawed handsome hero," among others. The soldier, if he is "ours," has "nobility of bearing, the same immediately likable, thoroughly decent air of right and might. . . . Not one of us—not one of 'ours,' at least—is ugly, stupid, nasty, or wrong."[61] Troupes indigènes fit somewhere in between these stereotypes: one of "ours" and "not one of us" at the same time.[62] Certainly not on the wrong side, they were still not quite as noble of bearing as the native white Frenchman. Fighting in a common cause, the right and just cause, associated these colonial subjects intimately with the French nation, but at the same time their allegedly primitive and savage natures, so clearly expressed in images of Algerian and West African soldiers, set them apart.

Notes

The author would like to thank in particular the staffs of the Hoover Institution Library and the Hoover Institution Archives for their help.

1. Of course, as soon as these troops set foot outside the colonies they ceased to be "indigenous." However, the French used this term to designate colonial subjects in the French army no matter where they were, and I retain this use for consistency and expediency. It is important to remember that, since the French Colonial Army and the Armée d'Afrique contained native Frenchmen as well as indigenous soldiers, calling them "colonial soldiers" would be inaccurate.

2. On the ideal of assimilation and the "civilizing mission" in French colonial policy, see Raymond F. Betts, *Assimilation and Association in French Colonial Theory, 1890–1914* (New York: Columbia University Press, 1961); Alice Conklin, *A Mission to Civilize: The Republican Idea of Empire in France and West Africa, 1895–1930* (Stanford: Stanford University Press, 1997); and Martin D. Lewis, "One Hundred Million Frenchmen: The Assimilationist Theory in French Colonial Policy," *Comparative Studies in Society and History* 4, no. 2 (1962): 129–53.

3. The "golden age" designation is Alain Weill's; see his *L'affiche française* (Paris: Presses Universitaires de France, 1982). For the broader history of posters and poster art, see Alain Weill, *L'affiche dans le monde*, 2nd ed. (Paris: Somogy, 1991); and Laurent Gervereau, *La propagande par l'affiche* (Paris: BDIC–Syros-Alternatives, 1991).

4. One writer has noted the "old-fashioned and academic style" of French World War I posters, which "seem untouched by the avant-garde movements" of the day, attributing this to the close relationship between the French government and the conservative École des Beaux-Arts. Even the paper, ink, and typography was often of low quality. This contrasted sharply with the careful composition and lively, innovative images and techniques found in French posters in the prewar years. Paula Harper, *War, Revolution and Peace: Propaganda Posters from the Hoover Institution Archives, 1914–1945 (An Exhibition Organized by Paula Harper and Marcia Cohn Growdon)* (Stanford: Hoover Institution on War, Revolution and Peace, 1971), 9. See also Alain Weill, "L'affiche de guerre," in Alain Weill et al., *Les affiches de la Grande Guerre* (Péronne, Somme: Martelle; Historial de la Grande Guerre, 1998), 8–15.

5. Harper, *War, Revolution and Peace*, 9.

6. Maurice Rickards, *Posters of the First World War* (London: Evelyn, Adams and Mackay, 1968), 25.

7. O. W. Riegel, "Introduction," in *Posters of World War I and World War II in the George C. Marshall Research Foundation*, ed. Anthony R. Crawford (Charlottesville: University Press of Virginia, 1979), 8.

8. Peter Paret, Beth Irwin Lewis, Paul Paret, eds., *Persuasive Images: Posters of War and Revolution from the Hoover Institution Archives* (Princeton: Princeton University Press, 1992), vi–ix.

9. Riegel, "Introduction," 13.

10. Maurice Rickards, "Foreword," in Walton H. Rawls, *Wake Up America! World War I and the American Poster* (New York: Abbeville Press, 1988), 9.

11. Rawls, *Wake Up, America!* 12.

12. Max Gallo, *L'affiche: Miroir de l'histoire, miroir de la vie*, 4th ed. (Paris: Parangon, 2002), 9.

13. Rawls, *Wake Up, America!* 13.

14. Riegel, "Introduction," 6–7.

15. Alain Gesgon, "Emprunt et propagande," in Weill et al., *Les affiches de la Grande Guerre*, 61.

16. Gallo, *L'affiche*, 11.

17. Joseph Darracott, ed., *The First World War in Posters from the Imperial War Museum, London* (New York: Dover, 1974), ix.

18. Gesgon, "Emprunt et propagande," 72–73.

19. Gallo, *L'affiche*, 12.

20. Charles Mangin, who became one of the most prominent generals to lead troupes indigènes during the war, was a particularly outspoken advocate of compensating for France's smaller population vis-à-vis Germany by drawing on the manpower resources of the colonies. See especially his *La force noire* (Paris: Hachette, 1910). On the general anxiety caused by a declining population, see John C. Hunter, "The Problem of the French Birth Rate on the Eve of World War I," *French Historical Studies* 11 (1962): 490–503; Joseph Spengler, *France Faces Depopulation* (New York: Greenwood Press, 1968); and Joshua H. Cole, *The Power of Large Numbers: Population, Politics, and Gender in Nineteenth-Century France* (Ithaca: Cornell University Press, 2000).

21. Hoover Institution Archives poster collection (hereafter HIA), FR 1369: G. Capon, "Section Photographique et Cinématographique de l'Armée Française, L'aide des colonies à la France" (Paris: Affiches Nouvelles, 1914–18?). The Hoover Institution Archives contain hundreds of Great War posters from many nations, a number of which have been published in Paret et al., *Persuasive Images*. One can also find many Great War posters, including some of those reviewed in this essay, in Rickards, *Posters of the First World War; 14–18 affiches: La Grande Guerre d'Est en Ouest* (Conservation Départementale des Musées de la Meuse, 1992); Rémy Paillard, *Affiches 14–18* (Reims: Matot-Braine, 1986); and Weill et al., *Les affiches de la Grande Guerre.*

22. On war loan posters, see Gesgon, "Emprunt et propagande," and Joëlle Beurier, "Pour une Union Sacrée des intérêts," in Weill et al., *Les affiches de la Grande Guerre*, 38–73.

23. HIA, FR 871: Anonymous, "Crédit Foncier d'Algérie et de Tunisie, Emprunt national 1920" (Paris: Devambez, 1920?).

24. HIA, FR 894: C. Boiry, "Crédit Foncier d'Algérie et de Tunisie, Emprunt national 6% 1920" (Paris: Devambez, 1920?).

25. Library of Congress (hereafter LOC), POS-Fr .v473, no. 1: Henri Villain, "Emprunt National 1920—Compagnie Algérienne" (Paris: Devambez, 1920).

26. *Tirailleur*, literally meaning "skirmisher" or "rifleman," was a term the French applied to all colonial infantrymen, adding *algérien* for Algerians, *sénégalais* for West Africans, and so on.

27. LOC, POS—Fr .J65, no. 7: Lucien Jonas, "Compagnie Algérienne. Souscrire, c'est hâter son retour avec la victoire" (Paris: Devambez, 1918).

28. Marie-Pascale Prévost-Bault, "Les collections de l'Historial," in Weill et al., *Les affiches de la Grande Guerre*, 24.

29. Soldiers from French West Africa were known generically as "sénégalais," even though Senegal represented only a tiny portion of this vast territory.

30. HIA, FR 17: Jean Le Prince, "Paris pendant la Grande Guerre: Le Petit Luxembourg (La Défense contre Avions)" (Paris: Éditions André Lesot, 1918?).

31. LOC, POS—Fr .N49, no. 1: Joseph de la Néziere, "Exposition d'art Marocain"

(Paris: B. Sirven, 1917); HIA, FR 736: Jean de la Néziere, "Loterie au profit des oeuvres d'assistance aux soldats marocains" (Paris: B. Sirven, 1917).

32. Gesgon, "Emprunt et propagande," 61.

33. Rawls, *Wake Up, America!* 19. See also Prévost-Bault, "Les collections," 21.

34. Léon Gambetta was a great republican hero of the unsuccessful struggle against the Germans in 1870.

35. Harper, *War, Revolution, and Peace*, 10.

36. HIA, FR 512: H. de Varoquier, "Journée organisée sur l'initiative du gouvernement au profit des oeuvres d'assistance de l'Armée d'Afrique et des Troupes Coloniales, 10 juin 1917. Tambola . . . " (Paris: Crete, 1917); FR 602: "Journée organisée sur l'initiative du gouvernement au profit des oeuvres d'assistance de l'Armée d'Afrique et des Troupes Coloniales, 10 juin 1917" (Paris: Crete, 1917).

37. For a recent and particularly illuminating discussion of colonial subjects' motivations for joining the French army, see Gregory Mann, *Native Sons: West African Veterans and France in the Twentieth Century* (Durham NC: Duke University Press, 2006).

38. HIA, FR 208: V. Prouve, "Ce que nous devons à nos colonies" (Paris: Berger-Levrault, 1918).

39. For a broader discussion of racial stereotypes in a comparative context as they applied to troupes indigènes during the First World War, see Richard S. Fogarty, *Race and War in France: Colonial Subjects in the French Army, 1914–1918* (Baltimore: Johns Hopkins University Press, 2008).

40. The most complete examination of Algerian participation in the Great War is Gilbert Meynier, *L'Algérie révélée: La guerre de 1914–1918 et le premier quart du XXe siècle* (Geneva: Droz, 1981).

41. Patricia Lorcin, *Imperial Identities: Stereotyping, Prejudice and Race in Colonial Algeria* (London: I. B. Taurus, 1995), 17–34.

42. Centre des Archives d'Outre-Mer (hereafter CAOM), DSM6: "Rapport de M. Delphin, Recrutement des indigènes en Algérie," December 15, 1915.

43. CAOM, DSM6: "Études Algériens, L'Administration des Indigènes: La Conscription," undated.

44. HIA, FR 430: G. Clairin, "Crédit Foncier d'Algérie et de Tunisie. Pour la patrie, souscrivez à l'emprunt" (Paris: Devambez, 1914–18?).

45. LOC, POS—Fr .F68, no. 4: D. Charles Fouqueray, "Journée de l'Armée d'Afrique et des Troupes Coloniales" (Paris: Lapina, 1917).

46. LOC, POS—Fr .R65, no. 3: Maurice Romberg, "Compagnie Algérienne. Souscrivez. Emprunt de la Libération" (Paris: Devambez, 1918).

47. The standard work on French West Africa's participation in the Great War is March Michel, *L'appel à l'Afrique: Contributions et réactions à l'effort de guerre*

en *AOF, 1914–1919* (Paris: Publications de la Sorbonne, 1982). Other works on the tirailleurs sénégalais include Joe Lunn, *Memoirs of the Maelstrom: A Senegalese Oral History of the First World War* (Portsmouth: Heinemann, 1999); Myron Echenberg, *Colonial Conscripts: The* Tirailleurs Sénégalais *in French West Africa, 1857–1960* (Portsmouth: Heinemann, 1991); Charles John Balesi, *From Adversaries to Comrades in Arms: West Africans and the French Military, 1885–1918* (Waltham MA: Crossroads, 1979); and Shelby Cullom Davis's classic *Reservoirs of Men: A History of the Black Troops of French West Africa* (Geneva: Chambéry, 1934).

48. Archives du Minstère des Affaires Étrangères, G1671: CIAM, Séance 19, 20 janvier 1916.

49. Bakary Diallo, *Force-Bonté* (Paris: F. Reider, 1926), 113.

50. Laurent Gervereau, "La propagande par l'image en France, 1914–1918: Thèmes et modes de représentation," in Laurent Gervereau and Christophe Prochasson, eds., *Images de 1917* (Paris: BDIC, 1987), 124.

51. For Senghor's reaction and more on Banania and images of the tirailleurs, see Anne Donadey, "'Y'a bon Banania': Ethics and Cultural Criticism in the Colonial Context," *French Cultural Studies* 11 (February 2000): 9–29. See also Jean Garrigues, *Banania: Histoire d'une passion française* (Paris: du May, 1991); John Mendenhall, *French Trademarks: The Art Deco Era* (San Francisco: Chronicle Books, 1991); Anne-Claude Lelieur and Bernard Mirabel, *Negripub: L'image des noirs dans la publicité depuis un siècle* (Paris: Société des Amis de la Bilbliothèque Forney, 1987).

52. Difficult to translate into English, "Y'a bon!" could be rendered literally as "There's good!" Perhaps a more accurate way to think of the phrase in English is to imagine someone saying, "Is good!" with a heavy foreign accent.

53. See, for example, *Le français tel que le parlent nos tirailleurs sénégalais* (Paris: L. Fournier, 1916), a manual for training French officers to use this pidgin French with West Africans under their command. See also Gabriel Manessy, *Le Français en Afrique noire: Mythe, stratégie, pratiques* (Paris: L'Harmattan, 1994), chap. 6: "Français-tirailleur et français d'Afrique," 111–21; and Richard S. Fogarty, *Race and War in France*, chap. 4: "Race and Language in the Army."

54. HIA, FR 9: A. Dolk, "L'emprunt de la libération du territoire (4e emprunt de la défense nationale). Français, souscrivez!" (Supplement to *La Revue Mauve*, September 29, 1918). Perhaps the closest translation of the caption would be, "'Tirailleur' makes an attractive offer: 'My friends, you to give your monies and tirailleur do rest.'"

55. Service Historique de l'Armée de Terre (hereafter SHAT), 16N196: General Dessort, Cdt le 16e DIC to Berdoulat, September 12, 1916.

56. SHAT, 16N196: "Rapport du Chef de Bataillon Trouilh, Cdt le 5e BTS, sur l'emploi des Sénégalais," August 13, 1916.

57. SHAT, 16N196: 1er CAC, E-M, 3e Bureau, "Rapport sur l'utilisation et le rendement des Sénégalais dans la guerre européen," September 18, 1916.

58. Most recently historian Joe Lunn has argued that in some ways West Africans did indeed suffer a higher proportional casualty rate than did white troops. However, the debate over this issue is fairly inconclusive, as all parties can cite valid statistics in their defense. See Lunn, *Memoirs*, 140–47; Michel, *L'appel*, 405–8; Balesi, *From Adversaries to Comrades*, 101–2; Echenberg, *Colonial Conscripts*, 46.

59. Germans shared this belief in the fundamental savagery of West Africans fighting for France. French officers noted that "a nearly irrational fear of our black contingents" afflicted German soldiers in the field, while the kaiser's government made alleged atrocities—ranging from rape to summary execution of prisoners and mutilation of corpses—the primary focus of an international diplomatic and propaganda campaign to protest French violations of the rules of war by introducing such an uncivilized element into civilized Europe. See SHAT, 7N2121: 10e Division Coloniale, Note de Service, "Objet: Utilisation des Sénégalais," October 19, 1916. See also Diallo's description cited above; Michel, *L'appel*, 344–50; and German white paper, "Völkerrechtswidrige Verwendung farbiger Truppen auf dem europäischen kriegsschauplatz durch England und Frankreich," July 30, 1915, Archives du Minstère des Affaires Étrangères, G1668.

60. One can judge the popularity and apparently wide diffusion of this poster both from the large number of collections in which it appears and from the frequency with which it has been reproduced since the war. This reproduction is from HIA, FR 642: Lucien Jonas, "Journée de l'Armée de l'Afrique et des Troupes Coloniales" (Paris: Devambez, 1917).

61. Rickards, *Posters of the First World War*, 29.

62. Laurent Gervereau has made a similar observation about the overtly sexualized images of tirailleurs sénégalais that appeared in many illustrations and postcards during the war. The "bestiality" that these men displayed in combat "is converted into superabundant virility, which fascinates," and the African is "supermanly (surmâle), without really being a man." Laurent Gervereau, "La propagande par l'image," 124.

RICHARD S. FOGARTY

7

Images of Racial Pride: African American Propaganda Posters in the First World War

During World War I governmental agencies in the United States produced thousands of posters that targeted both the entire country and specific segments of the population, including the African American community. These posters encouraged black citizens to do their part for the war effort by buying war bonds, conserving and producing food, and supporting troops in the field. Official wartime propaganda sought to tap into the patriotism and racial pride of African Americans to secure the enthusiastic support of this vital minority community. To achieve these goals the government successfully enlisted active support from a host of black newspapers, businesses, churches, and fraternal organizations, all of which helped bring the government's message into the black community by reproducing and displaying these posters.

African Americans, however, had additional goals besides winning the war. Many saw the war as a chance to advance the civil rights agenda. Here was an opportunity to prove their mettle in battle and to demonstrate both the key role they played in the economy and their willingness to sacrifice and die to ensure their nation's security. In return for their wartime service African Americans expected to receive long-overdue recognition of their civic and social rights, namely a dismantling of Jim Crow and an end to disenfranchisement. The African American community did not simply publicize these post-war goals through the printed word. A thriving private poster industry that marketed positive, uplifting images of African American soldiers emerged alongside the official propaganda poster campaign. Many of these privately produced posters expanded the meaning of wartime patriotism and bravery by linking these themes to specific expectations of an improved postwar democracy.

Rather than simply establishing two parallel propaganda campaigns, over the course of the war the government and the African American community used visual imagery to engage in an ongoing conversation over the ultimate significance of valorous wartime service. This dialogue took many forms. Similar images were copied and reused for different purposes, either to contest or reinforce government propaganda. Images allowed private citizens to both show support for and criticize various government campaigns. Through this exchange both the government and its citizenry tried to exercise control over the messages that images of racial pride conveyed. At times the government and blacks appeared in agreement about the need to assert African American economic, military, and physical agency by underscoring the important role that black workers and soldiers played in the war effort. By extension, many in the black community saw this governmental focus on their duty to support the nation in time of crisis as official recognition of their status as citizens. At other moments, however, similar images were employed in drastically different ways, with the army, for instance, turning a privately produced image of a proud black man leaving his sweetheart to go to war into one that emphasized the importance of obedience to army regulations requiring prophylactic treatment after illicit sex. In many privately produced posters, images of heroic black soldiers offered a subversive critique of racial discrimination within the military, in stark contrast to the official propaganda campaign, which used these same images simply to encourage uncritical support of the nation during a time of war. If governmental propaganda did not go far enough in the eyes of African Americans to address their specific grievances, to southern white newspapers that disseminated this propaganda, it went too far. Their independent dialogue with the government consisted of diluting the generally uplifting tone of wartime propaganda by imbuing it with conventional racial stereotypes to underscore southern whites' resistance to recognizing any kind of black power. Depending on the context, therefore, images of valiant African American soldiers and loyal black workers conveyed quite different messages.

Unlike official posters, commercially produced posters aimed at the black community devoted an equal amount of attention to the present and the future. Winning the peace, they suggested, was every bit as important as winning the war. This contrasted sharply with the intended consequences of similar images reproduced in official propaganda, which aimed merely to stimulate African American support for the war without opening up the Pandora's box of American race relations. African Americans intended to use their contributions, and by extension the posters and images that advertised their involvement, as leverage in an ongoing fight for civil rights and social recognition. The impact of the war on the future of American race relations was contested terrain during the First World War, and propaganda posters formed an important part of this debate.

Official Poster Propaganda: Sacrificing for the Cause

The Committee on Public Information (CPI) distributed the vast majority of governmental propaganda during the war, and over the course of the war, the CPI's Division of Pictorial Publicity designed nearly seven hundred posters for fifty-eight governmental agencies requesting artwork for their various propaganda campaigns. America's polyglot population forced the CPI to go further than simply creating a one-size-fits-all propaganda program. With one in five soldiers coming from an immigrant family, the CPI immediately recognized the need to disseminate posters, pamphlets, and films in foreign languages or risk ignoring a significant portion of the American population. Early in the war, the CPI sponsored two films that targeted African American audiences, *Our Colored Fighters* and *Colored Americans,* but overall the CPI produced few posters specifically for the black community.[1] The country was at war for nearly a year before the CPI began focusing on ways to mobilize support within an increasingly demoralized black community, shaken by governmental decisions to place the vast majority of black soldiers in noncombatant positions, reports of widespread mistreatment of black soldiers within the armed forces, and a violent race riot in East St. Louis. Emmett J. Scott, the special assistant who advised Secretary of War Newton E. Baker on issues pertaining to black soldiers, lobbied long and hard to convince the CPI that the people giving talks to black audiences on the government's war aims needed speeches that addressed the specific concerns of the black community. (The speakers were called the "Four-Minute Men" for the time it took to change film reels.[2]) Besides writing talks and pamphlets to distribute to black audiences, the CPI eventually organized a committee of a hundred influential ministers, educators, businessmen, and editors to head patriotic committees in black neighborhoods throughout the country.

The few extant CPI propaganda posters for the African American community emphasize the importance of supporting black troops in the field by purchasing war bonds or thrift stamps. A National Safety Council poster portrayed an African American railroad man licking a thrift stamp to place in a booklet under a caption that urged black workers to "do your 'two bits' daily . . . Loan your money to the government" and pay attention to safety on the job.[3] This poster aimed at black railroad workers linked together an array of desirable actions: helping out the war effort, ensuring that needed manpower was not lost because of work-related accidents, and maintaining a thrifty lifestyle. Although the poster put the emphasis on loaning private funds to help the war effort, the government primarily devised the thrift and war stamp campaign in the fall of 1917 to dampen demand for increasingly scarce consumer goods and to lessen the competition for raw materials between consumer- and defense-oriented businesses.[4] The key word in the campaign, therefore, was *thrift*. Taking out of circulation the surplus money that rising wartime wages placed in workers' hands was a way to reduce the consumption of unnecessary luxury goods without reverting to rationing. The government made it easy for even low-paid workers to defer spending any little extra they received as wartime wages rose. A thrift stamp cost twenty-five cents, and when a purchaser had accumulated sixteen stamps on a Thrift Card, he could exchange the four-dollar card for a war stamp that was redeemable for five dollars after five years. Overall, the government collected more than a billion dollars through the sales of thrift and war stamps.

During the Fourth Liberty Loan campaign, the CPI also made a special appeal to the African American community. Like the thrift and war stamp campaigns, the Liberty Loan campaigns had several purposes. One was clearly to pay for the war through voluntary subscriptions rather than relying solely on taxation. Like thrift stamps, war bond campaigns encouraged Americans to save and earn interest on their money rather than using it to fuel inflation in the goods-scarce wartime economy. Liberty Loan campaigns also helped involve ordinary citizens in the war effort. Officials estimated that nearly one third of the entire population purchased at least one Liberty Bond. The fourth and final Liberty Loan campaign ran in September–October 1918. These bonds paid 4.5 percent interest and matured fully in 1938. This final war bond drive was also the largest of the war, as a record number of subscribers purchased $6 billion in bonds, a particularly striking result because the drive took place at the height of the influenza pandemic of 1918. In an effort to contain the virus, cities throughout the nation closed the normal public meeting places where patriotic speakers made their most effective sales talks.[5] With fewer opportunities to pitch war bonds to movie audiences, posters played a particularly important role in inducing Americans to purchase yet another round of war bonds.

These posters reflect the government's effort to design posters that would encourage black citizens to support the war effort. Yet from the very moment that the CPI finally made the decision to reach out to the African American community, the intention of black newspaper editors to open up a dialogue with the government became clear. In 1918, by holding a meeting with black editors in Washington DC, the CPI took its first substantial step to enlist help from black newspapers in delivering the government's message of wartime unity.[6] The assembled editors pledged to help publicize the ways blacks could aid the war effort, but only after they outlined some of the key grievances circulating among black civilians, notably the failure to prosecute anyone for seventy-one lynchings that had occurred since the beginning of the war, discrimination against skilled blacks trying to secure wartime appointments, and the federal government's failure to eliminate Jim Crow train cars when it took over running the railroads.[7]

In sharp contrast to the rather limited efforts of most government agencies to reach out to African Americans, the Food Administration undertook a substantial campaign to ensure that

JENNIFER D. KEENE

its propaganda reached black farmers and consumers. Food Administration propaganda contained a message of sacrifice wrapped in imagery and words that explicitly recognized the key economic role that black citizens played. This was also the only propaganda campaign directed toward African Americans in which black governmental agents played a substantial role. From within the government, these African American administrators tailored a message of conservation and production that showered attention on black America's economic vitality. To disseminate this propaganda, the Food Administration created a productive partnership with privately run black newspapers. For most of the war A. U. Craig headed the Food Administration's Negro Press Section, with Ernest T. Atwell, a business professor at Tuskegee Institute, taking over when the section was reorganized a month before the Armistice. Taking advantage of the government's policy of relying on donated advertising space, Craig urged black newspapers to reproduce Food Administration posters freely in their pages. Many of the Food Administration's most famous propaganda posters urging citizens to conserve sugar, wheat, and meat appeared as advertisements in black newspapers. Among the twenty or so reduced-size posters appearing in a May issue of the *Baptist Leader*, for instance, only one, "'Garden Sass' Saves Wheat for Soldier Boys," portrayed an elderly African American woman looking proudly over the victory garden she maintained to feed her family.[8] The other advertisements contained generic admonitions such as "save a loaf a week," "fats are fuel for fighters: bake, boil and broil more, fry less," "eat more corn," and "Little Americans do your bit: eat corn meal mush . . . leave nothing on your plates." To encourage Americans to substitute corn for wheat products, the Food Administration constantly circulated corn-based recipes and reminded citizens that wheat traveled overseas better than corn. Press releases directed at the black press specifically addressed the prejudice that some blacks might have against incorporating corn into their daily diet. "Corn, once upon a time, was always on the table either as a cereal, bread, vegetable or desert. . . . As a child we remember the humiliation we felt at having to eat corn bread, but how times have changed! In exclusive tea rooms . . . we find a large demand for corn bread, corn griddle cakes, mush, etc., and little or no call for pastry made of wheat, or wheat bread," proclaimed one press release.[9]

All available surfaces were fair game for spreading the word to conserve food. The Negro Press Section encouraged barbershops and shoe-shine parlors to draw patriotic red, white, and blue slogans on their mirrors. Suggested ways to let "the mirror help win the war" included stenciled warnings that "U-Boats Sink Ships Loaded With Sugar; Slackers Leave Sugar in Their Cups" and "Make One Spoon of Sugar Do the Work of Two, Every Day Until the War is Through."[10] Restaurants posted signs advertising their establishments' compliance with Food Administration guidelines on wheatless Mondays and Wednesdays, meatless Tuesdays, and porkless Saturdays.[11] In a similar vein, black fraternal organizations throughout the country placed large signs with key food conservation slogans on their buildings as a show of support for the war effort.[12]

The Food Administration and U.S. Department of Agriculture also developed propaganda to address black farmers' key role as producers, not just consumers, of food. "HOE THE WORLD TO VICTORY! This slogan if placed in large head lines across our papers would carry the message to the readers," advised A. U. Craig in one press release.[13] In April 1918 black Alabaman demonstration agents for the Department of Agriculture (government employees who offered clinics in effective farm techniques) formed a U.S. Saturday League Club as part of a "Win the War by Working Six Days per Week" campaign.

The league provided stores and newspapers with posters entreating farmers to "Rest and keep it Holy" on Sunday while devoting the rest of the week to "Work!" In a letter accompanying the posters, Robert R. Moton, the principal of Tuskegee Institute, urged black farmers to consider "what you lose when you stop on Saturday" and how much money was wasted on Saturday entertainments. Self-interest and community responsibility both required producing more food. "May it never be said of any one of us, that our men at the front suffered because we would not feed them," Moton concluded.[14]

Both the CPI and Food Administration depended on cooperation from the black press, black businesses, and black fraternal and religious organizations to convey the message of wartime sacrifice to the African American community. This dependence by necessity opened up a dialogue between the government and the African American community over how to construct messages of particular appeal to black citizens, and how to use cooperation in the propaganda campaign as leverage to address other pressing civil rights issues. Both in the images projected and in the key role that African Americans played in constructing and disseminating this propaganda, official propaganda offered more than a portrait of an African American community able and willing to sacrifice for the cause. It also opened up the possibility of parlaying appreciation of that community's economic clout into recognition of social and political equality, a theme addressed directly in privately produced propaganda posters.

In one such poster, "Emancipation Proclamation, September 22, 1862" (created by E. G. Renesch), a portrait of President Lincoln is surrounded by snapshots of African American accomplishment (fig. 29).[15] In this poster a large eagle (the symbol of the United States) and six American flags drape the framed portrait of Lincoln, who holds a speech quoting these

Fig. 29. E. G. Renesch, "Emancipation Proclamation, September 22, 1862." The economic, intellectual, and military contributions of African Americans to the war effort became the basis for demands that the nation fulfill Lincoln's promise to ensure all Americans equal rights. Beinecke Rare Book and Manuscript Library, Yale University.

words from the Declaration of Independence: "All men are created equal that they are endowed by their Creator with certain unalienable rights, that among these are life, liberty, and the pursuit of happiness." Portraits of the writers Paul L. Dunbar and Frederick Douglass flank the image of Lincoln. On the left, Lady Liberty stands with one arm around a white boy and the other around a black boy, telling them "Look forward! There is room enough under the eagle's wings for great achievements by both." To the right of the portrait stands Booker T. Washington, the founder of Tuskegee Institute, who championed the economic contributions that blacks made to the South. Dressed in a suit and holding a speech, Washington points to

JENNIFER D. KEENE

a farmer plowing a well-kept field and a steamboat chugging up a river and says: "We have cleared the forests, reclaimed the land and are building cities, railroads, and great institutions." Below Washington, a well-dressed man stands with his fashionably attired wife before a group of children at play near a solid brick schoolhouse, where a couple in an automobile talk to their son. The man tells his wife: "Our children are being educated and will become useful citizens and a power in all affairs of life." The role of black soldiers takes its rightful place alongside these substantial accomplishments. On either side of Lincoln hang portraits of two black officers from the 370th Infantry, Lt. Col. Franklin A. Dennison and Lt. Colonel Otis B. Duncan. The 370th regiment served with the French during the war. Dennison was relieved of his command and replaced by a white officer soon after his arrival in France. Many black soldiers and civilians immediately challenged the official explanation that Dennison lost his command because of ill health. Duncan went on to lead his troops into battle, fighting not just the Germans but General Staff doubts about the ability of black officers to command troops effectively. In the lower left corner of the poster black soldiers carrying the flag advance against a German trench, with comrades falling to the ground as they go. The caption to this scene reads: "The bravest of the brave in defence of his country."

This crowded poster reflects the array of competing strategies for advancement circulating within the black community, an attempt to appeal to all spectrums of political opinion. The poster offers a healthy antidote to the one-size-fits-all governmental approach in appealing to the black community. In marked contrast, this poster portrays both the Talented Tenth, whom W. E. B. Du Bois exhorted to lead the race to full civic and social equality, and Booker T. Washington's emphasis on black laborers becoming the economic backbone of the South. The poster balances Du Bois's insistence on full academic schooling for African American children with more traditional images of black farmers working in the cotton fields. These various vignettes are all tied together by Lincoln's words. In their economic endeavors, educational abilities, dedication to their country, and ability to produce great men, blacks are every bit the equal of whites. Finally, this poster transforms the Food Administration's emphasis on the black community's economic contributions to the war effort into a demand that African Americans' economic and educational achievements be rewarded with full recognition of their rights as citizens.

Privately produced posters went to great lengths to underscore for viewers the link between the present war and the future of civil rights in the United States. In a poster entitled "Colored Men: The First American Who Planted Our Flag on the Firing Line," black soldiers are advancing victoriously against German troops under the watch of Abraham Lincoln, whose statement "Liberty and justice shall not perish" is inscribed under his portrait. The quote obviously had two meanings for black civilians, one for the present war overseas and another for the struggle against Jim Crow at home.[16] Both this poster and "Emancipation Proclamation, September 22, 1862" suggest that the link between the battlefront and home front encompassed more than economic support from civilians for troops in the field through war bond purchases and food cultivation or production. In addition, the achievements of black soldiers on the battlefield would translate into a stronger case for full recognition as American citizens at home. "Don't cut the rope," urged one Food Administration slogan to underscore the importance of civilian support for troops in the field, an admonition that private posters molded to serve the black community's civil rights agenda by emphasizing how the exploits

JENNIFER D. KEENE

of soldiers overseas also served to legitimize civilian demands for greater inclusion in the American polity. In this reformulation civilians and soldiers provided each other with mutual support during the war, each group contributing in their own way both to the greater cause of winning the war and to ending Jim Crow at home. United in these goals, black soldiers and civilians never came close to cutting the ties that created such a strong psychological bond between the home front and battlefront for the duration of the war.

Contested Meanings: Interpreting the Image

Active cooperation with the official governmental propaganda campaign and unofficial responses to the government's emphasis on the economic clout of the black community formed two important aspects of the wartime dialogue between the government and African American citizens. In addition, official governmental posters and propaganda proved open to a myriad of interpretations, revealing yet another way these images served as a medium in the ongoing conversation between the government and its citizenry over the ultimate costs of securing cooperation for wartime fiscal and conservation policies. Considering how these images were consumed, therefore, is as important as tracing how and why they were produced. Black and white communities each viewed governmental propaganda through the prism of their respective opinions about changing the racial status quo. The result was often a dramatically altered meaning for official propaganda. The government, however, proved as willing as private citizens to twist the interpretation given to borrowed images to suit its particular needs. The direct sharing of public and private propaganda images during the war revealed yet another way that the government and the African American community engaged in a thriving cultural exchange during the war.

African Americans derived a host of meanings from a Fourth Liberty Loan poster that contained a photograph of black troops under review in Alsace above a caption that read: "While their band plays stirring music, these sturdy negro soldiers, who have beaten the Germans every time they have faced them, are lined up for rifle inspection in an Alsatian village. These men are adding fresh laurels to those won by colored troops in the Civil and Spanish Wars."[17] The reference to continuing a soldierly tradition begun in the Civil War was a popular theme in posters targeting the black community. For black audiences this poster contained other important and familiar details concerning the black soldier experience. Black newspapers wrote often about the fame that African American bands, especially the one led by James Europe of the 369th Infantry Regiment, had garnered in France for their skilled playing of ragtime and jazz. Stories about the success of several black regiments in pushing the Germans back in Allied summer counteroffensives and fall offensives also received wide circulation in the black press. The poster then went on to link these well-known particulars to the general message that the Treasury Department was sending to all Americans: "Lend the way they fight. Buy Liberty Bonds to your utmost."

While the poster was clearly intended to arouse pride in the achievements of black soldiers, there was little chance of it convincing black civilians that their troops were being given opportunities to excel within the military. This poster fails to mention a pertinent piece of information likely known to most contemporary viewers, namely that the African American units amassing these honorable combat records were serving under French, not American, command, and the "laurels" these troops had received were mostly the French *croix de guerre*, not American military decorations.[18] To a savvy viewer, therefore, this poster suggested an alternative message beyond Emmett

Scott's exaltation in opening the Fourth Liberty Loan campaign at Howard University that "we who remain at home are in duty bound to lend the limit of our aid to those who have gone abroad to bare their breasts to shot and shell in defense of our flag and the sacred ideals for which it stands."[19] Instead, it reinforced the feeling that prejudice and discrimination within the American army left the vast majority of African American troops digging ditches or unloading ships, while the single black combatant division under American command went without the training and officers it needed to succeed in combat.

Sometimes, however, it was whites rather than blacks who provided an alternative, and by implication more subversive, interpretation of official governmental propaganda. Food Administration propaganda designed to underscore the key economic role that black cooks played in controlling food resources throughout the South provided official recognition of black women's power within the southern economy—recognition that blacks championed and whites dismissed. After conducting a wide-ranging survey of southern town mayors to collect the names and addresses of movie theaters that either catered exclusively to black audiences or accepted them as patrons, the Negro Press Section regularly sent these theaters slide lectures to display at each show.[20] One illustrated lecture detailed the deprivation overseas, before discussing what to eat and how to substitute for meat and fat in daily cooking.[21] In the closing weeks of the war Atwell also prepared speeches for Four-Minute Men to deliver in movie theaters or other public places. "In no vocation, in no activity, can the colored people of this country find opportunity to do their part more than by adopting the program of food conservation," read one script. "This is true not only in their own households but in addition they control the food in the homes of a very large proportion of other races."[22] In addition the Food Administration paid particular attention to churches and fraternal organizations as places where large numbers of blacks could take pledges to conserve food. Craig devoted particular attention encouraging county food administrators to organize patriotic Fourth of July celebrations for black communities throughout the nation, going so far as to prepare acceptable programs of music, lectures, cooking and canning demonstrations, and prayers.

Recognizing that large numbers of African American women were employed as cooks for white families, the Food Administration attempted to channel propaganda intended for black women through their white female employers. White newspapers that publicized the official campaign to conserve food, however, went to great lengths to demean the intelligence of domestic servants to avoid providing any sense of empowerment or importance to black women. In particular, in bringing this message to their white readership, some southern newspapers dramatically shifted the emphasis away from championing black women as linchpins in the conservation effort and instead sought to convey the same message of conservation through conventional racial stereotypes. "Mammy Must Learn to Conserve Food," announced the headline of one newspaper advertising an instructional meeting for waiters, cooks, and butlers in Jacksonville, Florida. This particular meeting included two films, one offering instruction in canning and substitution and the other showing "the troubles of an old darky cook in learning food conservation."[23] For cooking demonstrations organized by Women's Committees of the Council of National Defense, another white newspaper made less inflammatory announcements partly intended to convince black women that they would protect their jobs by following Food Administration recipes and guidelines. This emphasis on white women's role as employers, however, indirectly became another way to

Fig. 30. E. G. Renesch, "True Blue," 1919. This seemingly conservative portrait of a patriotic African American family raised fears among southern whites that material progress and wartime sacrifices were responsible for the new "insolence" and militancy evident in the civil rights movement. Records of the U. S. Post Office Department, RG 28, Entry 40 (Records Relating to the Espionage Act of World War I, 1917–1921), Folder B-584, National Archives.

reassure southern whites that the power to direct what went on in their kitchens lay with them.

White commentators also offered alternative readings of propaganda posters privately marketed to the African American community during the war. "True Blue" shows a wife standing with her three children before a portrait of the husband and father in uniform (fig. 30). In the poster a flag with a blue star hangs in the window to signal to passersby that someone from the home is serving in the military.[24] The two girls point to their father, while the son sits and contemplates his father's manly demeanor. The soldier's portrait is draped with two American flags and hangs above a mantel that also contains framed pictures of George Washington and Woodrow Wilson. To the right above the father hangs a somewhat larger portrait of Lincoln. The inclusion of Washington and Lincoln continues the well-established practice in propaganda aimed at the African American community of reminding viewers that the democratic vision of these two leaders remained relevant. Including Wilson in this pantheon of great American presidents suggests the resonance that his rhetoric for democracy had throughout the country. By making this "a war to make the world safe for democracy," Wilson continued the tradition established by Washington and Lincoln of giving war a transcending purpose that went far beyond specific territorial or political aims. Instead, war became a way to perfect and purify America's democratic values.

A warm fire burns in the fireplace, and the room is tastefully decorated with typical middle-class wallpaper, furnishings, and ornaments. Two vases filled with fresh flowers and a cat sleeping before the fire complete this scene of domestic bliss. The representation of a middle-class man who has provided well for his family and is now serving his country was standard fare for wartime propaganda, seemingly containing little that would invite controversy. Nonetheless, a postmistress in Melbourne, Florida, sent this poster along with two issues of the *Favorite Magazine* to the postmaster general to ask if he considered these seditious materials banned from the mail by the Espionage Act of 1917. Noting the "considerable insolence from the negro element lately," this postmistress lumped "True Blue" together with articles in the *Favorite Magazine* titled "'The White Problem,' A Discussion of the White Man as a Problem," and "How Colored Girls are Ruined in Mississippi."[25] Although she left unstated her exact objections to "True Blue," one could surmise that the pictured family's material success and the implication that wartime sacrifice entitled them to inclusion in the democratic vision championed by Washington, Lincoln, and Wilson served for this white woman as further

JENNIFER D. KEENE

Fig. 31. E. G. Renesch, "Colored Man Is No Slacker." Official government agencies and private publishers freely shared and exchanged images during the war, attaching captions or placing them within a context that dramatically altered an image's meaning. This privately produced poster, which initially underscored African Americans' voluntary contributions to the war effort, was transformed by the government into an image of a venereal disease–free soldier returning home to his family. Courtesy of the author.

evidence of "insolence." In some respects, official posters that encouraged black workers to save rather than spend their extra wartime earnings, such as the National Safety Council Thrift Stamp poster discussed earlier, served to allay white concerns that a frenzy of war-fueled consumption by African Americans would threaten the racial status quo; "True Blue," in contrast, raised that threat.

Along with its black and white citizens, the government also engaged in the practice of reinterpreting images to suit its own purposes. In one instance the army even went as far as explicitly recasting a commercially produced poster to alter its original meaning significantly. The privately produced E. G. Renesch poster "Colored Man Is No Slacker" originally portrayed a black soldier bidding his virginal sweetheart farewell as he prepares to join the unit marching by the house holding the American flag high (fig. 31).[26] The title gives this poster its meaning, suggesting that black men are eager to fight to defend the country and are not "slackers" who are intentionally looking for ways to avoid military service. It conveys a symbolic rather than literal truth, since it was not possible for much of the war for black men to demonstrate this willingness by voluntarily enlisting in the army. During the First World War, the American government implemented an immediate draft to avoid sapping the civilian economy of needed workers and leaders. For a short time the ranks were open to volunteers, but ultimately 72 percent of the army was conscripted. Within this short window of time to enlist, the handful of units reserved for African American soldiers quickly filled. Many eager applicants were turned away and told to wait for the draft to select them.

The importance of a motto in giving a propaganda poster its meaning becomes crystal clear when examining how the government took this same image and incorporated it into an anti–venereal disease lecture designed for black soldiers in stateside training camps. The line between private and public was not hard and fast during the war. Just as newspapers and citizens in the private sector could alter the meanings of official governmental propaganda, in this case the government borrowed a popular commercial image, removed the caption, and placed the scene of a soldier and his sweetheart in a context that dramatically altered the message.

During the war the army instituted a major campaign against venereal disease, designed to curb any unnecessary reduction in troop strength and to reassure the public that military service would not ruin the moral character of the fine, upstanding men eager to join the war effort. Progressive reformers working through the Commission on Training Camp Activities

JENNIFER D. KEENE

(CTCA) developed a multilayered campaign that targeted both women in the vicinity of training camps and soldiers themselves.[27] For soldiers the CTCA urged abstinence and provided a host of athletic activities to help them burn off excess sexual energy through wholesome pursuits. At the same time the CTCA and medical officers designed vivid sex education programs that informed soldiers about the debilitating effects of venereal disease and the types of prophylactic treatments available. One army lantern-slide lecture developed specifically for black troops by the Instruction Laboratory of the Army Medical Museum reveals the importance of context for understanding the full significance of patriotic images of soldiers.[28]

Only about half of some fifty slides for this lecture remain, but from them it is possible to piece together a general outline of the themes the lecture covered. The presentation began by posing the question: "Why should a man expect a woman to be decent if he is not?" After considering the double standard that allowed men to sow wild oats but labeled women who engaged in risky sexual behavior as whores, the presentation quickly moved to key mistakes that caused men to contract venereal disease. A parade of "Heeza" vignettes followed. One slide showed a character named "Heeza boozer," who makes the mistake of going home with a prostitute after a night of drinking, while another told the story of "Heeza wiseguy" about a young man who is crippled from venereal disease after refusing to listen to warnings about the risks of sleeping with prostitutes. Heeza wiseguy learns the hard way that "whiskey makes men weak, whores cause the 'bad leak.'"

After outlining the lifestyle habits that caused men to fall victim to diseased prostitutes, the lecture then focused on convincing men who indulged in risky sexual encounters to avoid compounding the mistake by turning in desperation to the "cures" sold by disreputable pharmacists. "What Fools These Mortals

Be," proclaims one lantern slide above the scene of a hobbled venereal disease victim buying "fixisit," a potion claimed to cure gonorrhea in five days. The images subsequently grew quite graphic to teach soldiers how to identify venereal disease sores and what cleansing treatments were available in army medical facilities immediately after risky intercourse. Some slides even offered a demonstration of how to inject a purifying solution into one's penis.

Medical officers, however, had no intention of ending the lecture on the positive note that some treatment was available. Instead, the final slides hit hard to lay out all the arguments against sleeping with prostitutes. Where do prostitutes come from, asks one slide? The business constantly requires new recruits—are you willing to sacrifice your sweetheart or sister? Another image shows the devil keeping a scorecard of how many innocent babies were born blind and how many women were infected by men who had had extramarital intercourse with prostitutes. Each soldier, the lecture concluded, owed it to his father, mother, sweetheart, and himself to stay clean for the duration of the war.

For the image of the sweetheart, medical officers slightly cropped the scene portrayed in "Colored Man Is No Slacker" and removed its original caption. Now this poster symbolized a clean-living soldier returning home to his sweetheart disease-free, a man of whom his sweetheart, comrades, and nation can be proud. The image loses its value as a depiction of a man who is willing to serve and becomes one of a man who can be assured of a warm welcome for his exercise of self-discipline during the war. In a similar fashion, the lecture appropriated the ubiquitous "Uncle Sam Wants You" poster. This time Uncle Sam points his finger at the viewer next to a caption that reads, "Uncle Sam wants your pep, punch and patriotism," to illustrate the point that soldiers owed it to their country to stay free of venereal disease during the war.

Images of Racial Pride: Challenging the Racial Status Quo

In the case of "Colored Man Is No Slacker," the government appropriated a privately produced image to construct a message vastly at odds with the one originally intended by the commercial artist. This exchange worked both ways, however. Some commercially produced propaganda adopted the prevailing official propaganda image of the brave and valiant soldier to express distrust of the government and to challenge discrimination within the armed forces. The subversive message contained within these images of a proud and vital race standing up for itself threatened to undo the very unity demanded by official propaganda posters. Whether one's loyalty was to one's country or to one's race became yet another dimension of the wartime debate waged between official and unofficial propaganda posters. Yet for all their radicalism on racial matters, these posters retained an inherently conservative perspective on the actual war. By viewing the war in traditionally romantic terms, privately produced posters never departed from the storyline of official propaganda posters that portrayed the war as one in which individual soldiers could make a difference on the battlefield.

Like the Treasury Department, private philanthropic groups used propaganda posters to raise funds. "German shells draw no color line," announced one poster for the Crispus Attucks Circle for War Relief, urging contributors to "help the negro people help their own" by building a hospital for wounded troops.[29] By naming itself after the first black man killed in the American Revolution, this organization evoked a legacy of heroic service that extended back to the creation of the republic. At the same time, however, the poster's message that the black community would have to take care of its own fighting men in a privately funded hospital suggested that African Americans could not count on the government to care for wounded or ill black troops properly. German shells draw no color line, the poster emphasizes, but white Americans certainly do. Realizing that "colored soldiers were apparently unwelcome at places of amusements" in Philadelphia, a group of black citizens decided to form the Crispus Attucks Circle because they believed "the colored soldier would not receive equal treatment with the white soldiers in medical treatment," the group's attorney explained.[30] Pursuing their idea to offer black soldiers quality private medical care, the Crispus Attucks Circle agreed to raise $110,000 to expand Mercy Hospital, a small private facility with twenty-eight beds. To raise funds, the Crispus Attucks Circle placed copies of this poster in storefronts and hired professional fundraisers to visit black businesses and homes. Contributors received a membership card and a button announcing "I am a Member" of the Crispus Attucks Circle for War Relief. At least one white businessman objected to the avowed purpose of the group. In a letter to the American Red Cross Institute, Aldwin Moore charged that the Crispus Attucks Circle was raising money under false pretenses because the government would indeed provide rehabilitation services to all soldiers. "Why not tell these people that they do not need to raise such a fund?" Moore queried.[31] The hundreds of Philadelphia companies and individuals who made donations totaling more than ten thousand dollars to the Crispus Attucks Circle clearly believed otherwise.

In the spring of 1918 the group found itself under investigation by the Military Intelligence Division (MID) and the Justice Department for possible ties to German saboteurs.[32] Many government officials, especially those within MID, stubbornly persisted in attributing black grievances about prejudice and discrimination to German operatives stirring up trouble within the African American community. MID approached the problem of worrisome morale within the black community by putting nearly every civil rights leader, organization, and publication under surveillance. The government's investigation of the Crispus Attucks Circle failed to find any links to German operatives, but federal agents did conclude that it was both a professional fundraising operation designed to defraud subscribers of their money and a group intent on stirring up race hatred. The Justice Department based this conclusion not on the provocative suggestion that the government would leave wounded black soldiers to their own devices but on one meeting that an agent attended which "started out to explain the merits of the circle, but soon twisted itself into [a] negro suffrage affair."[33] Pressured by the Justice Department, the Mercy Hospital severed its ties with the Crispus Attucks Circle in August 1918.[34]

The disgraced Crispus Attucks Circle was not alone in suggesting that private charitable donations were needed to ensure adequate care for ill or wounded black troops. "All Together Push!!!" urged a Circle for Negro War Relief poster inviting residents to the Manhattan Casino for a benefit to purchase an ambulance for black troops stationed at Camp Upton, New York.[35] The board for the New York–based Circle for Negro War Relief included the leading lights of the civil rights movement, among them National Association for the Advancement of Colored People officials W. E. B. Du Bois, Arthur Spingarn, Moorfield Storey, and James W. Johnson. "Help Our Coloured Solders. Do It Now!" entreated another Circle for Negro War Relief poster, because "one-tenth of our Army are Negroes."[36] The Circle for Negro War Relief emphasized the sizable contribution black soldiers were making to the war effort, which was even larger than this poster suggested. African

Americans actually composed 13 percent of the army even though they were only 10 percent of the civilian population. The racism of local draft boards and the limited number of slots for black volunteers contributed to the overdrafting of black men. By the end of the war the army had inducted one third of all black registrants, as compared to one fourth of all white registrants.

Besides offering criticism of army policies, privately produced posters also contained a measure of skepticism about the promises of the Wilson Administration to make this a "war for democracy." Civil rights leaders already had their doubts about Woodrow Wilson, who had given federal government agencies the option of segregating their offices and refused until late in the war to issue a statement denouncing lynching. Most commercial posters contained a more overt plea that the country adopt Lincoln's original dream of interracial democracy as part of its wartime mission.

The poster "The Dawn of Hope" (published by B. W. Brittain) was forthright in announcing the war as an opportunity to fulfill Lincoln's promise of equality for all (fig. 32). This poster shows a grandfather and grandson in a cotton field watching the rising sun together.[37] "My Boy!" declares the grandfather, "I waited 50 years for the realization of Father Abraham's wish, but in vain. Your brethren are now fighting to maintain Uncle Sam's liberty, and in hopes for equality and justice for the black man." The willingness of black soldiers to defend the nation takes on the dimension of repaying an old debt in the banner at the bottom, which proclaims, "You fought in 1865 for us, we are fighting now for USA [in] 1918." At the same time, however, the poster draws a rhetorical link with the Civil War to underscore the need to create a true interracial democracy in the United States. To the left of the pastoral scene of the grandfather and grandson each raising an arm in salutation to greet the rising

Fig. 32. Anonymous, "The Dawn of Hope," 1918. Challenging the government to make the war for democracy meaningful for African Americans was a common theme in posters privately marketed to the African American community during the war. Beinecke Rare Book and Manuscript Library, Yale University.

sun stands a statue of Lincoln with a plaque that reads: "The book of justice and the hand of freedom, 1865." To the right is a statue of a black soldier with his pistol drawn. The plaque at the base of this statue is more demanding and less hopeful about Lincoln's words becoming a reality. "Uncle Sam," the plaque reads, "We are still fighting for that freedom promised us making all men of equal standing. But never in the history of the black man has he been justly judged by all." Black soldiers are fulfilling their duties as citizens, this poster proclaims, even though the nation refuses to accord them the rights that are their due as men, as citizens, and as patriots.

Yet for all the radicalism inherent in these critiques of the government, it is also crucial to appreciate how conservatively they depicted warfare along the Western Front. The overall acceptance of the official emphasis on individual heroism and the romantic glory associated with victorious warriors unmasked the limits of the criticism offered in these privately produced posters. "Our Colored Heroes" depicts the well-circulated story of Henry Johnson and Needham Roberts, whose feats the poster portrays in a broad romantic style.[38] The poster shows two young men, each surrounded by hordes of German soldiers. In the back, Roberts bayonets a German assailant, while in the foreground Johnson stabs a German soldier with a dagger. Wounded German soldiers whom the two Americans have already dispatched writhe on the ground, while in the distance a rescue party carrying a large American flag hurries to save them. The encounter occurs on a moonlit night in the middle of the woods, with nary a hint of No Man's Land or artillery in sight. In conceiving of this scene, the illustrator took tremendous liberty with the facts. Sitting in an isolated listening post in No Man's Land on the night of May 14, 1918, Roberts and Johnson were part of a party of five on the lookout for an enemy attack. Noticing movement outside their post, the two discovered an enemy patrol and gave the alert. "The Germans cut us off from retreating and we had to fight. It was 25 against us 2," Roberts wrote in a letter home. "Having thrown all my grenades, I was wounded and put out of the fight. But my comrade Johnson resisted and drove them away all alone."[39] Johnson fired his rifle at the first German attempting to enter their shelter and, with his rifle empty, then had no choice but to club down the second German with his rifle butt. Glancing behind him, Johnson saw another two Germans carrying a heavily wounded Roberts off as a prisoner. Johnson sprang up and stuck his bolo knife so hard into the shoulder "of that ill-fated Boche, the blade of the knife was buried to the hilt through the crown of the German's head," attested his commanding

JENNIFER D. KEENE

officer, Captain Arthur Little.[40] Another charging German soldier wounded Johnson, who nonetheless managed to bring this enemy soldier down with his knife as well. "The enemy patrol was in a panic. The dead and wounded were piled upon stretchers and carried away," Little reported.[41] A critically injured Johnson harassed the retreating Germans by lobbing grenades after them. The official investigation concluded that the two had killed four German soldiers and driven off five times as many. "I saw them when they brought them back. Neither one of them could walk . . . they had two guys carrying Johnson, and Johnson, his legs was gone, his legs was hanging," James Jones later recalled.[42]

"Our Colored Heroes" celebrated the bravery of Johnson and Roberts by placing them in a scene that did not exist along the Western Front. The uniqueness of their story suggests the limited possibilities for individual feats of heroism in the industrial slaughter taking place across No Man's Land. It takes nothing away from the scale of their accomplishment in fighting off this raiding party to point out that the military value of their actions was quite small, as was nearly every other act of individual heroism in a war dominated by heavy artillery. To remind viewers of this reality by accurately depicting frontline conditions would rob the story of its ability to evoke the romance of past pivotal encounters on the battlefield where individuals truly made a difference. By placing these two in a pastoral scene that viewers would immediately associate with heroic possibilities, this poster avoided challenging viewers to reconsider what warfare entailed in the twentieth century. This poster had other things for viewers to reflect upon. To a society and military doubting black men's ability to fight and placing most of them in noncombatant laboring positions, this poster offered a strong retort. In this respect the poster presented a truth that many white Americans would rather have ignored.

Conclusion

In the United States during the First World War, both the government and private publishing companies designed and distributed propaganda posters intended to influence wartime behavior and shape popular perceptions about the meaning of black participation in the war effort. The basic themes of duty, bravery, and patriotism were present in both official and private posters aimed at the black community. Privately produced ones, however, often incorporated an undercurrent of doubt and concern that the contributions of black citizens and soldiers were not receiving the full recognition they deserved. Unlike official posters, these unofficial propaganda posters linked the nation's struggle against Germany to the campaign for improved civil rights at home.

All wartime propaganda emphasized the key role that blacks played in the domestic economy and highlighted their heroism on the battlefield. The ultimate significance of these wartime contributions for the future hopes and aspirations of African Americans remained contested terrain during the war, a debate evident through the steady exchanges between the various branches of the government (the CPI, Food Administration, Treasury Department, army) and black and white citizens who played a pivotal role in the creation, dissemination, and consumption of wartime propaganda. A dialogue that encompassed contested interpretations, the sharing of specific images, a white press that muted some parts of the government's message, and a black press that attached specific conditions to secure its cooperation all revealed the give and take that shaped the wartime propaganda campaign aimed at African Americans.

JENNIFER D. KEENE

In the end the government received the support it desired from the African American community with African Americans seemingly receiving little in return. Rather than ushering in an era of improved racial justice, the postwar years developed into one of the worst periods of racial violence in American history. Yet images of racial pride and the explicit critique of the government within privately produced posters helped lay the foundation for the more militant and racially conscious spirit that infused the civil rights movement in the postwar era, a new attitude encapsulated by W. E. B. Du Bois's call for African American soldiers to "return fighting."[43] Refusing to see themselves solely through the eyes of others represented an important component of this new determination to fight back against white supremacy. Controlling the image became a way to begin shaping their own futures as proud black Americans with fully recognized civic and social rights.

Notes

1. Walton H. Rawls, *Wake Up, America! World War I and the American Poster* (New York: Abbeville Press, 1988), 167.

2. Emmett J. Scott to Dr. Robert R. Moton, Tuskegee Institute, June 7, 1918, folder "M," box 1, Entry 96, Record Group 470, National Archives, College Park MD (hereafter NA).

3. National Safety Council poster, call no. ppc 70121B, Princeton University Poster Collection, 1863–1948, Archives Center, National Museum of American History, Smithsonian Institution, Washington DC (hereafter cited as Princeton Poster Collection, Smithsonian Institution).

4. Rawls, *Wake Up, America!* 215–22.

5. Rawls, *Wake Up, America!* 195–226.

6. Mark Ellis, *Race, War, and Surveillance: African Americans and the United States Government during World War I* (Bloomington: Indiana University Press, 2001), 72.

7. "Address to the Committee on Public Information," folder "Misc.—unidentified," box 2, Entry 96, Record Group 470, NA.

8. *Baptist Leader*, May 31, 1918, unlabeled folder, box 589, Record Group 4, NA.

9. Press Release No. 9, unlabeled folder, box 589, Record Group 4, NA.

10. "Let the Mirror Win the War" promotional literature, unlabeled folder, box 589, Record Group 4, NA.

11. Negro Press Section to J. H. Bowman, Bowman's Café, Vicksburg, Mississippi, March 15, 1918, unlabeled folder, box 588, Record Group 4, NA.

12. Negro Press Section to George M. Cook, Washington DC, April 17, 1918, "Administration" folder, box 588, Record Group 4, NA.

13. Press Release No. 12, March 4, 1918, unlabeled folder, box 589, Record Group 4, NA.

14. "Win the War by Working Six Days per Week" literature and posters, folder 12HMA3, box 589, Record Group 4, NA.

15. E. G. Renesch, Chicago, "Emancipation Proclamation, September 22, 1862," #1718, Randolph Linsly Simpson African-American collection, Beinecke Rare Book and Manuscript Library, Yale University.

16. Chas. Gustrine, Chicago, 1918, reproduction number LC-USZC4-2426, Library of Congress Prints and Photographs Division, Washington DC.

17. "Inspection of Our Negro Troops in Alsace" poster, call no. 043.09633, Princeton Poster Collection, Smithsonian Institution.

18. For a description of these troops' service with the French, see Stephen L. Harris, *Harlem's Hellfighters: The African-American 369th Infantry in World War I* (Dulles VA: Brassey's, 2003), and Arthur E. Barbeau and Florette Henri, *The Unknown Soldiers: African-American Troops in World War I* (New York: Da Capo Press, 1996).

19. Emmett J. Scott, *Scott's Official History of the American Negro in the World War* (Chicago: Homewood Press, 1919), chap. 25.

20. For letters to southern mayors asking for theaters that blacks could attend, see "Negro State Directors, Theaters" folders, arranged by state, box 590, Record Group 4, NA.

21. All the following are in Record Group 4, NA: Illustrated Lecture on Food Conservation, in "Associations, Conventions, etc." folder, box 590; Letter to theater owners, unlabeled folder, box 589; "Organizing the Church for Food Conservation," in "Administration" folder, and "Negroes Offer Assistance to Food Administrator," unmarked folder, both in box 588; for sample Fourth of July programs and lectures, see "Program and Promo Material" folder, box 591.

22. "Don't Cut the Rope" lecture, "Negro State Directors—Division of Four Minute Men" folder, box 590, Record Group 4, NA.

23. "Mammy Must Learn to Conserve Food," unmarked clipping, "H. Q. Organization, Education Division, Negro Press Section, Press Clips" folder, box 590, Record Group 4, NA. This file includes other articles announcing meetings for cooks.

24. "True Blue," E. G. Renesch, Chicago, file B-584, box 80, Entry 40, Record

Group 28, NA. Walter S. Bodle, "The Black Soldier in World War I," *Social Education* 49, no. 2 (1985): 129–32.

25. Alma P. Carmichael, Postmaster, Melbourne, Florida, to Postmaster General, August 5, 1919, file B-584, box 80, Entry 40, Record Group 28, NA.

26. E. G. Renesch, Chicago, "Colored Man Is No Slacker," poster in author's possession. A copy is also available in the Military poster collection, Art and Artifacts Division, Schomburg Center for Research in Black Culture, New York City Public Library.

27. For an overview of the CTCA program see Nancy K. Bristow, *Making Men Moral: Social Engineering during the Great War* (New York: New York University Press, 1996).

28. A basic history of the Instruction Laboratory's development of instructional materials is provided in Robert S. Henry, *The Armed Forces Institute of Pathology: Its First Century 1862–1962* (Washington DC: Office of the Surgeon General, 1964), 170–87. The venereal disease instructional lantern slide lecture is located in World War I Lantern Slide Training Sets, Set F-C3, Otis Historical Archives, National Museum of Health and Medicine, Walter Reed Army Medical Center, Washington DC.

29. "Help the negro people help their own" poster, call no. ppc 65234B, Princeton Poster Collection, Smithsonian Institution.

30. Crispus Attucks Circle for War Relief Investigation, June 12, 1918, file #OG 98505, roll 475, Record Group 65, NA.

31. Aldwin N. Moore, Colonial Trust Building, to William M. Russie, American Red Cross Institute, July 13, 1918, file #OG 98505, roll 475, Record Group 65, NA.

32. Ellis, *Race, War, and Surveillance*, 267.

33. Report filed by agent W. S. Carman, June 11, 1918, file #OG 98505, roll 475, Record Group 65, NA.

34. Crispus Attucks Circle for War Relief report, August 1, 1918, file #OG 98505, roll 475, Record Group 65, NA.

35. Circle for Negro War Relief poster, pamphlets, and stationary. Unmarked Folders, box 589, Record Group 4, NA.

36. "Help Our Coloured Soldiers" poster, call no. ppc 76529B, Princeton Poster Collection, Smithsonian Institution.

37. B. W. Brittain, "The Dawn of Hope," #1717, Randolph Linsly Simpson African-American collection, Beinecke Rare Book and Manuscript Library, Yale University.

38. "Our Colored Heroes," Military poster collection, Art and Artifacts Division, Schomburg Center for Research in Black Culture, New York City Public Library.

39. Controle postal, IV armée, Rapport de la Correspondance de ou pour

l'etranger du 26 Mai au 1 juin 1918, 16n 1409, Service historique de l'Armée de terre, Château de Vincennes, Paris.

40. Arthur W. Little, *From Harlem to the Rhine: The Story of New York's Colored Volunteers* (New York: Covici, Friede, 1936), 195.

41. Little, *From Harlem to the Rhine*, 196.

42. James Jones interview in *Harlem Hellfighters*, film by George Merlis and Roscoe Lee Browne (New Video Group; A&E Home Video, History Channel, 1997).

43. W. E. B. DuBois, "Returning Soldiers," *Crisis* 18 (May 1919): 13–14.

8

Segodniashnii Lubok:
Art, War, and National Identity

Soon after the outbreak of war in 1914, Russia's imperial government organized an exhibition of patriotic posters called "War and Publishing," which was held in Petrograd in 1914. Many publishers were represented in this exhibition, but the series put out by a company called Segodniashnii Lubok (Today's Lubok) was singled out by critics as, in the word of one commentator, "the most amusing and probably the most ingenious."[1] The Moscow publisher Mikhail Gordetskii had established the Segodniashnii Lubok to produce propagandistic anti-German posters and postcards in support of Russia's war effort. The artists of Segodniashnii Lubok appropriated the formal properties of the *lubok* (plural *lubki*), or the Russian popular print, which at that time was considered the most uniquely Russian form of "folk" art. Today these artists are identified as leaders in the prerevolutionary Russian "avant-garde": Kazimir Malevich, Vladimir Maiakovskii, Artistakh Lentulov, Ilia Mashkov, David Burliuk, and Vasilli Chekrugin.

In this essay I examine the posters designed by the artists of Segodniashnii Lubok, asking how Russian folk art forms, particularly the lubok, were used by both artistic and social elites as part of a nationalist discourse that defined "Russianness" through the artistic forms of its pre-Petrovine, preindustrial past. In the Russian context the culturally distinctive art forms of peasant populations were perceived as relatively uncontaminated by Western, cosmopolitan influences—thus the icon and the lubok became part of a national heritage to be manipulated by governmental, social, and artistic elites. This deliberate manipulation of Russia's past is an example of what Eric Hobsbawm calls "invented traditions," the phenomenon of constructed "traditions" used by government or social elites to create a modern sense of community in response to new social situations.[2] In this case folk art was used by both avant-garde artists and social elites to create, in the guise of "recapturing," Russian national identity.

Along with such deliberate manipulations of Russia's artistic heritage, I argue that the wartime lubki produced by Russian avant-garde artists reveal the contradictory nature of early modernism: a tension between forward- and backward-looking tendencies. Russian primitivism, drawing on folk art and popular culture with the intention of creating a new art, contained within it both radical and conservative currents. As Jill Lloyd notes in her revisionist history of German Expressionism, "The tendency to describe the genesis of modern art in this period as a separate and isolated history, characterized solely by its forward-looking initiatives and formulated in opposition to the conservative forces operating in society as a whole, needs to be redressed."[3] My analysis of these wartime images highlights the inconsistencies that histories of the Russian avant-garde have ignored, by asking how these patriotic lubki fit within the contradictory discourses of modern Russian society, including those that look to the West as a symbol of progress and those that look inward, or "backward," to rejuvenate society.[4] I look at what Russian folk art forms, particularly the icon and the lubok, meant to a generation of artists who

ANDREW M. NEDD

called themselves Futurists, primitivists, and "national" artists. My aim is to analyze the structure of their images and symbols to see how they appealed to viewers and to place them within the nationalist, anti-Western discourses in which artists participated before the war. Such an analysis reveals the contested nature of Russian national identity, which was the product of complex and often contradictory values (e.g., high and low, popular and official, native and foreign). For a brief time, the artists of Segodniashnii Lubok succeeded in employing folk art forms in order to encourage popular support for a campaign that was defined by the imperial administration's military ambitions. However, the suspension of such contradictions could not be maintained for long.

To limit the focus of discussion, I deal with three motifs in the posters of Segodniashnii Lubok: first, how these posters represent real battles, or the reality of battle—my contention is that the posters are "mythic" images downplaying the disappointments of the Russian army; second, how these artists represented the Russian "peasant soldier," imbuing him with the values of the "truly Russian" *narod,* or "folk"; and finally how this concept of Russianness was defined through images of Russia's racial "Other," who could be represented in the guise of a foreign enemy. The purpose of these posters was to unite all Russians against a common enemy, but they did so by using a definition of Russianness that simplified some distinctions and exaggerated others. As Sam Keen argues in his survey of modern war posters, the purpose of propaganda is to "paralyze thought, to prevent discrimination, and to condition individuals to act as a mass."[5] The folk posters of Segodniashnii Lubok do indeed appeal to this sort of mass thinking.

The circle of Russian artists working for Segodniashnii Lubok was not unique in appropriation of folk art forms. By the beginning of the twentieth century artists of the Russian avant-garde employed "native" artistic traditions both as a stylistic source for their art and as part of a discourse that contrasted French academic and modernist conventions with distinctively Slavic and Orthodox Russian culture. Natalia Goncharova, in the introductory essay to her first solo exhibition in 1913, expressed this idea: "Hitherto I have studied all that the West could give me. . . . Now I shake the dust from my feet and leave the West. My path is toward the source of all arts, the East. The art of my country is incomparably more profound and important than anything that I have known in the West."[6] Turning to the East as "the source of all arts," Goncharova not only rejected the influence of Western art in Russia but also participated in nationalist discourses concerning her country's identity. In particular, Goncharova refers to the ideas of the Slavophiles, a group of thinkers who, beginning in the middle of the nineteenth century, revolted against the westernization begun by Peter the Great and espoused the belief that through a "return to native principles" Russia would discover its "superior nature and historical mission."[7]

At the center of this anti-Western artistic discourse were such native art forms as the lubok and the icon. Aleksandr Shevchenko, in his 1913 book *Neo-Primitivism*, affirmed the power of "the lubok, the primitive art form, [and] the icon" to inspire the avant-garde because in them artists discovered "the most acute, most direct perceptions of life."[8] To Shevchenko, and to other artists whom he identified as neoprimitives, the lubok and the icon distinguished Russia from the West and heralded a new self-consciously Russian school. Thomas Crow, writing on the relationship of mass culture and modernism, argues that the avant-garde fulfills the function of "necessary brokerage between high and low" through the packaging of fringe culture for an elite, self-conscious audience.[9] In Russia this turning to "low" art forms took on a nationalist tone,

ANDREW M. NEDD

defining Russianness through "authentic" native art forms and contrasting them against those of the West. The appropriation and manipulation of folk art conventions by the artists of Segodniashnii Lubok are a continuation of this process, particularly since the six artists who produced these images were among the vanguard of Muscovite futurists and primitivists.

Despite the avant-garde's insistence on the uniquely Russian character of the lubok, these printed pictures were actually introduced into Russia by German merchants in the sixteenth century. In his history of Russian popular literature Jeffrey Brooks demonstrates that originally these "popular" pictures were referred to as "German sheets" and were primarily produced for upper-class audiences. By the eighteenth century, however, as Peter the Great introduced other Western art forms in Russia, elite audiences turned away from such prints, and the lubok "began a long descent to lower levels of Russian society." Lubki usually had short texts at the bottom of the picture and were often the first printed materials to enter the homes of common people.[10]

As popular audiences embraced the lubok, the prints deviated from the German model, becoming more simplified and satirical.[11] By the nineteenth century the term *lubochnaia literatura*, or "popular literature," referred primarily to the lively and colorful lubki, which were similar to European broadsides, such as English chapbooks or French *images d'Epinal*. While early lubki were religious in origin and were produced for an elite audience, by the last half of the nineteenth century this literature became largely secular and satirical. The nineteenth-century social reformer Alexander Radishchev observed this change and commented that "if Hogarth had been born among us, he would have found a wide field for his caricatures."[12] Indeed, by the time of the revolution in 1905, Russian artists began to criticize the regime in satirical lubki, lampooning the bourgeoisie and the imperial government. Even as lubki became largely secular and satirical, they retained something of their religious aura and were used to elicit nationalist feelings, especially during times of war.[13]

Prints depicting scenes of war were particularly popular and were hung in people's homes alongside spiritual images in an area traditionally called "the red corner." Vladimir Denisov, a contemporary critic who wrote on the relationship of war and popular images, commented on the fact that "war lubki took this place in the red corner by no accident. In popular thought war was endured, like universal and cosmic events, like manifestation of the omnipotence of God, who sends death, famine, and earthquakes . . . in fulfillment of His divine will."[14] The artists of Segodniashnii Lubok saw the function of popular images in the same way as Denisov—the conflation of war, religion, and "popular thought" was intended to imbue a national war with a religious aura. Appropriating the traditions of the popular art forms came to serve both aesthetic and ideological goals.

The reception of wartime lubki reveals the evolving nature of Russian national identity in the late imperial period. Popular representation of war served as an important rallying point around which Russian national identity could be defined and renewed. As Geoffrey Hosking argues, Russian "nation-building" involved the process of "eliciting loyalty and commitment of the population, which is usually achieved by fostering the sense of belonging, often by the manipulation of culture, history, and symbolism."[15] In earlier periods Russian national identity was focused on the imitation of European manners and traditions. In the wake of Napoleon's expulsion in 1812, Russian patriotism increasingly stressed Russian particularity through such themes as faith, loyalty, and the determination of the "Russian spirit."[16] Along with defining itself against a

ANDREW M. NEDD

foreign Other, Russian identity was increasingly identified with the Russian peasant, the Cossack, and "mother Russia," leaving behind traditional emblems such as the czar and church. Russian "patriotic culture," to borrow a phrase from Hubertus Jahn, responded to these events by celebrating the traditions and culture that made Russia unique.[17]

Interest in Russia's antiquities began in the eighteenth century when the Russian Academy of Sciences undertook archeological and ethnographic surveys of remote regions such as Siberia and the Caucasus. Eventually artists took part in these explorations. The railway magnate Savva Mamontov, who founded an artists' colony at his estate Abramtsevo, further stimulated interest in folk art on the part of Russian painters in the early 1880s, and this was followed by Princess Tenisheva organizing a similar colony at Talashkino.[18] Leading artists came to work and study at these colonies, which in turn were supported by small workshops that produced woodcarvings, pottery, embroidery, and other craft items for sale. Mamontov himself believed that art "will play an enormous role in re-educating the Russian people; and that Russian society, and morally regenerated art, are perhaps destined some day to serve as a light and a source of spiritual renewal for Western Europe."[19]

Also in the 1880s, the lubok was first recognized as a form of folk art when Dimitrii Rovinskii published the first major reference work on the subject.[20] Not long after, Viktor Vasnetsov, a graduate of the Saint Petersburg Academy who made his reputation as a realist painter, discovered folk art traditions and employed them in high art painting. Vasnetsov explored these ideas with his work at Abramtsevo, where he designed costumes and stage sets for Mamontov's "Russian Private Opera" and participated in the exterior and interior planning and decoration of the church at Abramtsevo. For the first time in the history of Russian high art painting, Vasnetsov borrowed directly from the iconography of the lubok in a series of works depicting birds of omen from Russian mythology.[21] Vasnetsov's painting *A Song of Joy and Sorrow* (1896), for example, is a direct reference to Alkonost and Sirin, the birds of paradise that were favorite characters in Russian folk art, particularly lubki.[22] Vasnetsov's appropriation of low art forms is an example of Crow's idea of cultural brokerage between high and low, or "between legitimate and illegitimate."[23] Its "illegitimate" status was demonstrated when Vasnetsov showed his mythical and epic paintings at the group show of the Peredvizhniki (Wanderers), members of which were staunch supporters of Russia's realist genre tradition. The group's leaders, despite their break with academic art and their espousal of national themes, were scandalized by the artist's rejection of conventional forms of representation.[24]

The colonies of Abramtsevo and Talashkino were breeding grounds for the cultural cross-fertilization of high and low, and of East and West, that the next generation of avant-garde artists would eventually use. However, as John E. Bowlt has argued, artists such as Vasnetsov and Nikolai Roerich tended to "aestheticize" popular culture for their elegant and sophisticated patrons, whereas Russia's Futurists and Primitivists used them as more direct attacks on the status of high art conventions.[25] Increasingly, these attacks became part of an anti-Western discourse that challenged the authority of foreign cultural values through a search for Russia's ancient pre-Petrovine past.

The messianic study of Russian art forms at Abramtsevo and Talashkino provides a direct link to the neoprimitivist culture of the Russian avant-garde. For instance, by 1911 Natalia Goncharova could write: "The significance of these works is infinitely great for the future of Russian art. Great art cannot help but to be national. Deprived of connection with the past, Russian art is cut off from its roots."[26] Russian national identity and independence were expressed in these assertions of Russian artistic uniqueness. Furthermore, the national artistic rhetoric that came to surround Russian folk art became an attempt to delegitimize the impact that Western cultural values had in Russia. Goncharova again argued in 1913, "if Eastern influences reached us in a roundabout way, then this does not prove anything—its path was from the East, and the West, as now, served merely as an intermediate point."[27]

Like Goncharova, Malevich too fell under the influence of the nationalistic discourses that celebrated Russian peasant art. In the first chapter of his memoirs, Malevich describes the impact that folk culture had on his own work and on the artists of his circle: "I felt something wonderful in them that was close to me. I saw in them all of the Russian people and their emotional creativity. I was reminded of my childhood: the cats, flowers, and roosters of primitive paintings and wood carvings. I felt a connection between peasant art and icons—icon painting being the supreme cultural form of peasant art."[28] Malevich's deliberate conflation of peasant art or traditional folk crafts with icons, a form that relied on literary sources and established guidelines, reveals an intentional reinvention of the Russian past. In fact, the neoprimitivist overlapping of such concepts as "national," "folk," and "popular" in the term *naraodnoe iskusstvo* is the result of the belief that the primitive arts should serve as a source of inspiration for Russian art.

Indeed, artists became increasingly interested in archeological and ethnographic discoveries, turning to prehistoric, archaic, and non-Western art forms in search of what they called the primitive. Russian Futurists specifically employed indigenous art and craft forms to resurrect Russia's imaginary, preindustrial, primitive past.[29] In opposition to Italian Futurism, which emphasized contemporaneity and rejected the past, Russian Futurists such as Larionov and Goncharova looked to the distant past as a way to declare their independence from the hegemony of Western culture. Russia's avant-garde adopted a notion of rupture that looked backward rather than forward, to draw from a mythic, prehistoric, timeless past.

This sense of rupture was evoked in 1912 by a group of Futurists who attempted to revive Russia's primeval past when they adopted the name Hylae, the ancient Greek name for the Crimea, the region Herodotus described in *The Histories* as the homeland of the Scythians.[30] In his memoir *The One and A Half-Eyed Archer*, Benedikt Livshits described this circle, which met at the summer home of the Burliuk brothers and which included the poets Maiakovskii, Kruchenykh, and Khlebnikov as well as artists such as Larionov.[31] The title of this book refers to Scythian mythology, to the "wild men" who roamed the Crimean steppe. Livshits described what this region meant to his friends: "Hylae, the ancient Hylae, trod upon by our feet, took the meaning of a symbol and had become a banner."[32] By emphasizing Russia's primitive roots, the Hylae circle linked the present to a primeval past—"by-passing," in Susan Compton's words, "the western European classical inheritance by joining up with their own pre-classical primitivism."[33] Archeology helped artists in this quest for the primitive since, around the turn of the century, many Scythian artifacts were uncovered by archeologists and displayed in museums and private collections. Artists who had access to these collections studied Scythian objects and incorporated the images into their work.

Besides these references to Scythian artifacts, the Hylaeans evoked Russia's ancient origins in a series of books they published that involved collaboration between artists and poets. The combination of image and word was one of the primary characteristics of these books, and this prefigures the union of text and image achieved by Segodniashnii Lubok. Furthermore, this collaboration of artist and poet recalled the manner

ANDREW M. NEDD

in which lubki were often bound together in book form, with the images and the texts together expressing the narrative. Another example of Russian Futurists referring to the mythical primeval past rather than to the mechanized can be found in a hand-made book titled *Mirskontsa* (World backwards), created in 1912 by the poets Khlebnikov and Kruchenykh in collaboration with Goncharova and Larionov. The title *Mirskontsa* (in Russian literally "world from the end") looks forward to the end of the world but also backward, as Susan Compton notes, to "the beginning of the world, the prehistoric world, long before the civilized world we know had begun."[34] Russian Futurism was a commentary on what Margarita Tupitsyn has called the "Petrovian rupture," with its inherent inclination toward the West, and proposes a rupture "backward," away from the authority of Western Enlightenment values and toward an imagined Russian past.[35]

While artists such as the Russian Futurists assimilated what they called the primitive in their work, breaking down the barriers between art and popular culture as part of their critique of Western values, Russian primitivism was also an appropriating device that reaffirmed the conservative values maintained by elite culture, particularly those values that defined Russia and contrasted it with the West. Whether Russian primitivism mocked or appealed to an educated and sophisticated audience or spoke to a more widespread audience, the pattern of defining Russia in terms of the traditions of Russia and the "East," and against Western artistic innovations, reflects larger discourses concerning national identity. The artists of Segodniashnii Lubok participated in these same discourses, employing the subversive traditions of Russian popular culture to mock Russia's enemies. In addition these same artists could draw upon a centuries-old tradition of popular imagery in order to promote Russian victory.[36]

In *War and the Lubok* Denisov argued that the origins of the wartime lubok could be traced back to the "Patriotic War," which culminated in Napoleon's invasion of 1812. This war, writes Denisov, "left a great impression on Russian life," and lubki from this period "impressed the style and subjects of 1812 on proceeding wars."[37] Denisov observed that contemporary artists, including those working for Segodniashnii Lubok, had at their disposal a variety of popular representational traditions from the Napoleonic era.[38] Significantly, the artists of Segodniashnii Lubok expressed national identity with the image of the common peasant rather than with traditional symbols such as the czar and Orthodoxy.

In the late imperial period national identity was in great flux—rapid industrialization and urbanization resulted in the fragmentation of Russian national consciousness. Additionally, as a number of scholars have argued, Russian national identity was plagued with the problem of creating a sense of common identity in a far-flung, multiethnic empire.[39] For example, Jeffrey Brooks claims that in the late nineteenth century Russians developed a new type of national identity and a new popular conception of their empire. In the view of ordinary Russians, argues Brooks, the empire was detached from the czar and the Orthodox Church and was worthy of celebration in its own right for its diversity and potential for bolstering Russian pride vis-à-vis "inferior" peoples.[40] The traditional symbols of Russian nationalism (czar, faith, and fatherland) were replaced in these years with newer forms of Russianness that celebrated the *narod*, the common Russian peasant. Russian national identity, furthermore, was defined in opposition to a foreign enemy in order to express the idea of popular unity.

The year 1913 was a watershed for the revival of Russian folk art. Two exhibitions in Moscow organized by artists celebrated the icon and the lubok: Nikolai Vinogradov displayed

ANDREW M. NEDD

both icons and lubki at a show held at the Moscow school of painting in February, and in March Mikhail Larionov held his "Exhibition of Original Icon Paintings and Lubki" on the premises of the Artistic Salon on Bolshaia Dimitrovka Street in Moscow.[41] That same year also saw the tercentenary of Romanov rule in Russia, commemorated by two exhibitions of Russian folk art and handicrafts, among many other events. In Saint Petersburg the Ministry of Rural Industry and Land Affairs brought together a variety of crafts, from hand-painted icons to wood carvings, at the Second All-Russian Exhibition of Handicrafts.[42] The Imperial Archeological Institute displayed icons, woven goods, and works in silver in its Exhibition of Ancient Russian Art held in Moscow.[43]

When war broke out the next year, aesthetic and nationalistic discourses converged in the posters produced by Segodniashnii Lubok. The appropriation of primitive art forms was inextricably linked to Russia's search for national identity and helped to form one definition of Russianness. The artists of Segodniashnii Lubok were eager to celebrate the popular images of a century earlier since in these images they could see a form of Russian national identity that celebrated Russianness at the same time as lampooning foreign values. Malevich's "A Sausage Maker came to Lodz," for example, is a two-paneled image that depicts an encounter between the German kaiser and a typical Russian peasant (fig. 33). In the left-hand panel the kaiser, referred to in Maiakovskii's text as Sausage Maker and represented as a large figure, leads his army across a hilly field. He is greeted by a jovial Russian peasant with the words "Welcome Sir." In the second image of this poster, the Russian peasant strides off triumphant, his back to the Germans, while the kaiser is shown in tattered uniform and with what Maiakovskii calls a "bruised bottom." The mocking character of text and image in this poster recalls the subversive techniques the

Fig. 33. Kazimir Malevich, "A Sausage Maker came to Lodz, and we said 'Welcome Sir,' and at Radom, next door to Lodz, he left with a bruised bottom," 1914. Costakis Collection, Greek Ministry of Culture, State Museum of Contemporary Art–Thessaloniki.

neoprimitivists used in their parodies of Russia's westernized bourgeoisie. In addition, representing the kaiser as an oversized figure refers to an old Russian tradition—the German as butcher, or sausage maker.[44] Just as some Russian neoprimitivists employed "grotesque realism," to use Bakhtin's term, to lampoon Russia's westernized bourgeoisie, Malevich relied on stereotype to mock the kaiser.

In Malevich's posters there is a refusal to view the Germans as a serious threat. In response to the initial victories of the Russian army against German forces, this circle of artists celebrated Russian military prowess and disregarded the threat of the German foe. Malevich expresses this idea by exaggerating the size of the figures of both allies and foes. For instance, in his poster "The French Allies have a wagon full of defeated Germans," a giant soldier on the left in a red uniform, identified by Maiakovskii's text, pulls a cart filled with the Germans

ANDREW M. NEDD

У союзниковъ французовъ
Битыхъ нѣмцевъ полный кузовъ,

А у братцевъ англичанъ
Драныхъ нѣмцевъ цѣлый чанъ.

Fig. 34. Kazimir Malevich, "The French Allies have a wagon full of defeated Germans, and our English brothers have a whole tub of them," 1914. Costakis Collection, Greek Ministry of Culture, State Museum of Contemporary Art–Thessaloniki.

he has gathered. The text also explains that "our English Brothers [in yellow] have a whole tub of them" (fig. 34). As Richard Cork notes, the Germans in this poster retain an element of expression in their faces, but only enough to show that they are startled to be treated "with no more dignity than would be accorded a heap of potatoes in a cart."[45] Along with this devaluation of the German army, Malevich further plays down the threat of German militarism by setting his scene in what Cork calls "innocent regions" with "pantomime flowers and clouds."[46]

This same landscape runs through all of Malevich's posters, as does exaggeration of the figures; thus Malevich scenes are set in a mythic space.[47] The world described in Malevich's posters is an innocent region that simplifies the complexities of war, reducing it to a kind of play. The same can be said of many of the Segodniashnii Lubok posters, which for the most part portray warfare as a playful experience. In Maiakovskii's "Come, German, come, come" toylike airplanes drop bombs on a miniature version of Berlin, which appears more like a medieval town than a modern city, while German soldiers fall on their way to Paris. And in another poster depicting a battle on the Vilna River, German soldiers scurry away under the organized charge of the Russian cavalry. Likewise, in "Ah! how terrifying and how forceful was the fat German who was walking on the Vilna" Russian cannons and artillery at the Battle of Osovets decimate the Germans, who in Maiakovskii's text are "sheared like sheep."[48] One poster showing the battle of Avgustova illustrates several particularly violent acts: in the center background a German soldier is skewered on the bayonet of a Russian mounted soldier, and in the foreground we see another soldier blown apart by a cannonball. Despite these horrors, the unknown artist of this poster retains an element of humor in the depiction of bodies floating in the River Nemen and in the way German infantrymen fall in rows like toy soldiers, recalling Malevich's colossal Russian peasant who reaps enemy soldiers.

Galicia was the site of several early victories for the Russian army fighting the Austrians, and the Segodniashnii Lubok posters depicting these battles are equally mythic in character. The unknown artist of one of these posters shows the Austrians scattering under the Russian cavalry's assaults at Lvov, which appears like a toy model of a medieval city. Significantly, the artist represents battle as a mythic event in that lances and sabers replace the cannons and guns of real warfare. Similarly, in a poster of a battle set in the Carpathian Mountains, the Russian cavalry charge is unhindered by Austrian cannons, which fall to the ground. According to Maiakovskii's text the Austrians, a "gang of dumbfaces," only "screamed their heads off" and

ANDREW M. NEDD

were then "chased across all of Galicia." This poster in particular refers to a traditional lubok motif, the mounted Russian officer leading the charge with his saber raised. This type appeared in countless lubki of martial scenes. The manipulation of Russian iconographic traditions reveals the evolving nature of Russian national identity. During the course of the nineteenth century Russian patriotism increasingly stressed Russian particularity through such themes as faith, loyalty, and the determination of the "Russian spirit."[49] Along with defining itself against a foreign Other, Russian identity was increasingly identified with the Russian peasant, the Cossack, and "mother Russia," leaving behind traditional emblems such as the czar and Church.

In contrast, the Segodniashnii Lubok posters that represented the reality of battle were not all entirely innocent. For example, the image titled "Germans! Although you are mighty, you will not see Warsaw" shows particularly violent actions. In the center a German soldier is skewered on a bayonet, and on the left a Russian soldier brings down his saber on the fallen enemy, while exploding shells all around remind the viewer of the threat of German artillery. Nevertheless, the ease with which the Russian army pushes back the German assault maintains the sense of myth that characterizes all the Segodniashnii Lubok posters.

The Russian army's fortunes declined after its initial successes as shortages of arms and ammunition and mismanagement by the czar and his ministers began to make themselves felt. After Hindenburg failed to take Warsaw he launched an attack that resulted in serious losses for the Russians, and following the shattering defeats at Tannenberg and the Masurian lakes in 1914, the Russians were forced to retreat from Poland. These battles cost Russia not only enormous casualties but also a great loss in weapons. In fact, up to 25 percent of

А нашего то полку прибыло
Ой Дидъ ладо прибыло

А нашего то полку убыло
Ой Дидъ ладо убыло

Fig. 35. Anonymous, "We are the Russians and there are more and more of us. We are the Germans and there are less and less of us," 1914. Costakis Collection, Greek Ministry of Culture, State Museum of Contemporary Art–Thessaloniki.

Russian soldiers were sent to the front unarmed, with orders to retrieve what they could from their dead comrades.[50] Thus the Segodniashnii Lubok poster "We are the Russians and there are more and more of us/We are the Germans and there are less and less of us" is truly a mythic image that ignores the serious reality of Russia's military problems (fig. 35). On the left a jovial Russian peasant marches with six other figures representing Russia's allies. His arms rest on the shoulders of Russia's two most important allies, the English and the French. On the right the kaiser limps along, supported on one side by his Austrian counterpart (carrying a crutch) and on the other side by a diminutive figure representing the Turks. The tightly organized formations of the Allied troops in the background contrast with the disorganized retreat of the enemy's armies.

In this poster the figure leading the enemy forces is the kaiser, who was customarily portrayed with broad whiskers and in

ANDREW M. NEDD

a military uniform, according to the traditions of "Russian pa-triotic folklore."[51] Significantly, at the center of the group that makes up the Allies, Russia is represented not by Czar Nicho-las II but by a jovial Russian peasant. This poster records a shift away from an older form of Russian nationalism toward a more popular definition of Russian national identity—expressed in the doctrine of "Autocracy, Orthodoxy, and Nationality."[52] As Hugh Seton-Watson has commented, the concept of "Official Nationality" fueled popular national movements and far-reach-ing romantic concepts of Slavdom that stressed Russian partic-ularity. Thus in the posters of Segodniashnii Lubok the Rus-sian peasant soldier came to represent the best characteristics of the Russian *narod*, or folk. For example, Malevich's poster "A Sausage Maker came to Lodz" opposes the satirical figure of the kaiser with the rugged figure of a Russian peasant, who comically salutes the kaiser and then sends him on his way. Just as the Russian avant-garde looked to "authentic" Russian folk culture to oppose ideas they perceived as foreign, similarly the artists of Segodniashnii Lubok employed the image of the Rus-sian peasant as a symbol of the unique resourcefulness of the Russian people. In addition, recalling Russia's "timeless" prim-itive past as described by Futurist artists, the posters are set in the eternal, timeless world of the Russian peasant.

Maiakovskii's poster "A red-haired, uncouth German flew over Moscow" exemplifies these attitudes. In the left-hand panel a Cossack soldier named Danilo the Savage pierces the side of a German zeppelin as it passes over a Russian village and the pilots of the craft fall to the ground with looks of astonish-ment on their faces. In the right panel, in a display of Russian ingenuity, Danilo's wife Pauline sews pants out of the material that made up the zeppelin. The message of this poster is that native Russian resourcefulness overcomes German material and technical superiority.

Fig. 36. Kazimir Malevich, "An Austrian went to Radziwill and landed right on a peasant woman's pitchfork," 1914. Costakis Collection, Greek Ministry of Culture, State Museum of Contemporary Art–Thessaloniki.

Malevich in his "Below Warsaw and Grodna we smashed the Germans left and right" repeats this narrative. Again a Russian peasant brings down a German soldier. Recalling the humiliation of the German who falls from the zeppelin, a Russian soldier spanks the enemy as if he were a naughty child. The image of the right panel demonstrates Maiakovskii's text, "our womenfolk are not bad at getting rid of the Prussians." Another Malevich poster, "An Austrian went to Radziwill," again focuses on the resourcefulness of the Russian peasant woman (fig. 36). In this astonishing image an Austrian soldier is skewered on the woman's pitchfork. The fearful expressions on the faces of the slain soldier and of another behind him are countered with the fierce grin of the Russian peasant. This image is rife with contradictions. On the one hand, Malevich's representation of the Russian female peasant recalls the neoprimitivist

Ну и треснъ-же, ну и громъ-же
Былъ отъ нѣмцевъ подлѣ Ломжи

Fig. 37. Kazimir Malevich, "What a boom, what a blast the Germans made at Lomza," 1914. Political Poster Collection, RU/SU 160, Hoover Institution Archives.

artists' "monumental" treatment of peasant themes, particularly those showing women dancing and working. Goncharova, for example, often exaggerated the size of the hands and feet in her paintings of peasant women at work, which provided a sense of monumentality to her figures. On the other hand, the cruel grins and the bulky forms of Malevich's women recall the deliberate "coarseness" that the artists of Segodniashnii Lubok employed and upon which critics commented. Either way, the Russian "peasant soldier" and his wife were imbued with qualities that best represented the Russian *narod*.

One measure of the success of these images is recorded in the critical response they evoked. One of the most fascinating of these wartime lubki appeared in the journal *Lukomorye*, in conjunction the "War and Publishing" exhibition: Malevich's "What a boom, what a blast the Germans made at Lomza" (fig. 37). In this print Malevich drew upon many of the formal characteristics of the lubok, including simplified color patterns applied in flat areas, exaggerated sizes for the figures, and a composition that, when read left to right, conveys the narrative without words. In this case the Russian peasant in Malevich's image flails the German troops, reaping them as if he were harvesting wheat and leaving behind their fallen bodies.

While the artists of Segodniashnii Lubok intended their images to be easily readable visually, the texts that accompanied the images, all written by Maiakovskii, are also meant to be clearly intelligible to a popular audience. In particular, Maiakovskii's verse resembles those that accompanied the *raek*, a traditional fairground amusement consisting of a lubok mounted in a box with magnifying glasses and commented on by a narrator.[53] Critics noted the way Maiakovskii's texts complemented the popular style of the images. "Only the Futurists," wrote one critic in his review, "have created authentic lubki. Only in their work is there the coarseness and keen character of the lubok, only they could have united such sharp-witted language with pictures."[54]

Malevich, in a letter to his friend Mikhail Matyushin, who felt that Malevich's backer would be shocked by the content of Maiakovskii's verses, justified the deliberate "crudeness" of the texts on the basis that they were intended to have a direct appeal to "the folk": "I have come up with some popular prints that are purely folk, but if the words sound a little crude, tell her not to worry, for this is exactly what folk art is: the people have a different aesthetic concept."[55] Malevich's comment on folk art reveals that his "authentic lubki" were addressed to a particular audience, one that was "different" from the usual constituency of the artists and that would appreciate this "crudeness." Specifically, Malevich and Maiakovskii sought to achieve the primitiveness of Russian folk art traditions that they appropriated, imitating both visual and textual forms, making

ANDREW M. NEDD

them, in Malevich's words, "purely folk." Another critic noted that despite the boastful nature of these prints, "the gay foolery and exaggeration in the spirit of folk tales and the curious primitiveness of these drawings amuse."[56]

Underneath the amusing surface, however, the primitive qualities of Segodniashnii Lubok's posters reveal the tensions that existed between official interpretations of national identity and popular concepts of Russianness. This conflict can be traced back, recalling Denisov's observations concerning the origins of the patriotic lubok, to Napoleon's invasion. After 1812 Russia's imperial administration was reluctant to embrace the populism that the war provoked. Russian authorities were confronted with a dilemma: how to manipulate the story of 1812, which relied on the belief that the expulsion of Napoleon was a "people's victory," while maintaining imperial authority. While the idea of Russianness was expressed in popular images representing the heroism and cleverness of the average Russian peasant, the official response was to stress the role of Alexander I in bringing about the "divine victory" over the French. Indeed, as Richard Wortman argues, beginning in 1813 Alexander I encouraged a "myth of national sacrifice and unity woven around the events of 1812" that played on the perceived alliance between the czar and the masses.[57] While the Patriotic War of 1812 continued to be regarded as a people's victory, the imperial administration employed the arts to stress the role of the czar and his closest commanders as the architects of Napoleon's downfall. But this myth of unity had collapsed by 1914. The primitivizing character of Segodniashnii Lubok's prints was a unique response to this dilemma. Malevich and his colleagues harnessed folk art traditions in order to promote Russia's participation in a war that had little to do with the interests of the common Russian.

Although the lubok-inspired poster fell out of favor with the

Russian imperial administration, the idea was revived soon after the October Revolution. In September 1918 the Russian Telegraph Agency, ROSTA, hired the artist Mikhail Cheremnykh to design posters that were hung in shop windows and on walls of public buildings along Moscow's Tverskaya Boulevard. He was soon joined by Maiakovskii, the artist Ivan Maliutin, and the writer-artist Dmitrii Moor. The posters were intended to spark popular support of the Red Army during the Civil War (1919–22). ROSTA posters were duplicated by teams of workers using cardboard stencils, and the images were placed around the city and soon in forty-seven cities around the country.[58]

According to Maiakovskii's biographer, Victor Shklovsky, before the poet-artist joined Okna ROSTA (ROSTA Windows), each window poster was presented as an isolated unit. Maiakovskii, drawing on his experience with Segodniashnii Lubok, introduced poster designs that consisted of four to twelve different frames telling a story through connected rhyming texts.[59] The posters illustrated current events in sequences of brightly colored images that reduced the current struggle to a metaphorical battle of good and evil.

Recalling the deliberate crudeness of Segodniashnii Lubok posters, the ROSTA posters employed shifting scale, simplified figures, and a bold color palette to appeal to a largely illiterate audience. For those who could read, each poster included a narrative text that often rhymed in the manner of folk tales. The Lubok form was adapted to a new set of exigencies, and as Nicoletta Misler observes, the ROSTA window posters succeeded: "Maiakovskii and his colleagues tried to standardize a few key figures within their new vocabulary, just as the old *lubok* had done, such as the red worker or the fat, green capitalist, in order to facilitate the prerequisites of multiple production (even though these early posters were generally handmade), rapid information flow, and ease of communication."[60] ROSTA

ANDREW M. NEDD

continued to publish posters until 1922, when the need for these images evaporated with the end of the Civil War. However, the lubok-inspired poster was revived in the 1940s by the artist collective Kukryniksy in creating similar posters for the Telegraph Agency of the Soviet Union, or TASS.

The patriotic lubki published by Segodniashnii Lubok were produced from August of 1914 until the first months of 1915. After an initial outburst of patriotism, the public mood began to show disgust with the war. As enthusiasm for the war declined the tone of patriotic posters changed, particularly those that drew upon folk traditions like the lubok. As one commentator noted, "The success of our army in the first months of the war provided rich material for lubki, and there wasn't an event or advance that was not reflected in one or another sheet . . . but as soon as we retreated from Galicia, the lubki became reserved and then grew silent. Now many consider them superfluous and wrongly boastful."[61] The social unity that patriotic popular culture presented during the first months of the war turned out to be a fiction that hid the failures of the Russian army and the disunity of Russian social life. Hubertus Jahn argues that the rapid decline of the "exaggeratedly heroic pictures and satirical attacks on the enemy" in Russian lubki was inevitable in the face of military defeat and social disintegration.[62] While Russian patriotic culture retreated into the realms of fantasy and romance, the lack of a "commonly accepted national figure" meant that "a unified national identity remained elusive."[63]

Notes

1. G. Magula, "Voina i narodnye kartiny," *Lukomorye* 30 (1914): 17.

2. Eric Hobsbawm, "Inventing Traditions," introduction to *The Invention of Tradition*, ed. Eric Hobsbawm and Terence Ranger (Cambridge: Cambridge University Press, 1983), 1–8. Benedict Anderson, in *Imagined Communities: Reflections on the Origin and Spread of Nationalism* (London: Verso, 1983), argues that

the modern nation is an "invented" category, a recent cultural artifact. As Anthony D. Smith argues, "imagery has long played an important part in the creation of national consciousness: the figure of the French Marianne or British John Bull, the symbolism of the double-headed Tsarist eagle . . . all suggest the uses of evocation in constructing the modern nation"; see his "The Nation: Invented, Imagined, Reconstructed?" *Millennium: Journal of International Studies* 20, no. 3 (1991): 353–68, quote from 353.

3. Jill Lloyd, *German Expressionism, Primitivism and Modernity* (New Haven: Yale University Press, 1991), vi.

4. Few art historians have dealt with the role that popular images played in the culture of imperial Russia. One exception is John E. Bowlt. See his essays "Nineteenth-Century Russian Caricature," in *Art and Culture in Nineteenth-Century Russia*, ed. Theofanis George Stavrou (Bloomington: Indiana University Press, 1983): 221–36; and "Art and Violence: Russian Caricature in the Early Nineteenth and Twentieth Centuries," *20th Century Studies: Politics in Cartoon Caricature* 13–14 (December 1975): 56–76. Several literary and political historians have dealt with the role that lubki played in Russia. See Jeffrey Brooks, *When Russia Learned to Read: Literacy and Popular Literature, 1861–1917* (Princeton: Princeton University Press, 1985); E. I. Itkina, *Russkii rizovannyi lubok knotsa XVIII-nachala XX veka* (Moscow: 1992); Stephen M. Norris, "Depicting the Holy War: The Images of the Russo-Turkish War, 1877–1878," *Ab Imperio* 4 (2001): 141–68; Susan Layton, *Russian Literature and Empire: Conquest of the Caucasus from Pushkin to Tolstoy* (Cambridge: Cambridge University Press, 1994); Susan Layton, "Nineteenth-Century Russian Mythologies of Caucasian Savagery," in *Russia's Orient: Imperial Borderlands and Peoples, 1700–1917*, ed. Daniel R. Brower and Edward J. Lazzerini (Bloomington: Indiana University, 1997): 80–99.

5. Sam Keen, *Faces of the Enemy: Reflections of the Hostile Imagination* (San Francisco: Harper and Row, 1988), 25.

6. Natalia Goncharova, "Preface to Catalogue of One-Man Exhibition," in *Russian Art of the Avant-Garde: Theory and Criticism, 1902–1934*, ed. and trans. John Bowlt (New York: Thames and Hudson, 1988), 55–56.

7. Nicholas V. Riasanovsky, *A History of Russia* (New York: Oxford University Press, 1977), 402.

8. Aleksandr Shevchenko, *Neo-primitivizm: ego teoriia, ego vozmozhnosti, ego dostizheniia* (Moskva: n.p., 1913), 46.

9. Thomas Crow, "Modernism and Mass Culture in the Visual Arts," in *Modernism and Modernity: The Vancouver Papers*, ed. Benjamin H. Buchloh, Serge Guilbaout, and David Sokin (Halifax: Press of the Nova Scotia College of Art and Design, 1983), 253.

10. Alla Stytova, *The Lubok: Russian Folk Pictures, 17th to 19th Century* (Leningrad: Aurora, 1984), 5–7.

11. Brooks, *When Russia Learned to Read*, 63–64.

ANDREW M. NEDD

12. Quoted in Marina Peltzer, "Imagerie populaire et caricature: La graphique politique antinapoleonienne en Russie et ses antecedents petroviens," *Journal of the Warburg and Cortauld Institutes* 48 (1985): 191.

13. One of the most fertile periods for these wartime lubki was during the Russo-Turkish War of 1877–78. As Stephen M. Norris observes, such lubki "depicted the bravery of the Russian troops," "depicted the Turks as savage enemies, capable of committing incredible acts of brutality," and "praised the Russian spirit that had brought victory against the enemy, a spirit embodied in the common Russian soldier." See Stephen M. Norris, "Depicting the Holy War: The Images of the Russo-Turkish War, 1877–1878," *Ab Imperio* 4 (2001): 147, 148, 154.

14. Vladimir Denisov, *Voina i lubok* (Petrograd: Novago zhurnal dlia vsekhex, 1916), 3.

15. Geoffrey Hosking, *Russia: People and Empire, 1552–1917* (London: Harper Collins, 1997), xix.

16. See Hans Rogger, *National Consciousness in Eighteenth-Century Russia* (Cambridge: Harvard University Press, 1960).

17. See Hubertus Jahn, *Patriotic Culture in Russia during World War I* (Ithaca: Cornell University Press, 1995), 2–4.

18. Simon Karlinsky, "The Early Twentieth-Century Cultural Revival and the Russian Merchant Class," in *Theater in Revolution: Russian Avant-Garde Stage Design 1913–1935*, ed. Nancy van Norman Baer (New York: Thames and Hudson, 1991), 25–33.

19. Quoted in Evgenia Kirichenko, *The Russian Style* (London: Laurence King, 1991), 143.

20. D. A. Rovinskii, *Russkiia narodnye kartinki*, 5 vols. (St. Petersburg: Top. Imp. Akademii nauk, 1881–93).

21. Kirichenko, *The Russian Style*, 150.

22. Stytova, *The Lubok*, 58–59.

23. Crow, "Modernism and Mass Culture," 254.

24. Kirichenko, *The Russian Style*, 148.

25. John E. Bowlt, "A Brazen Can-Can in the Temple of Art: The Russian Avant-Garde and Popular Culture," in *Modern Art and Popular Culture: Readings in High and Low*, ed. Adam Gopnik and Kirk Varnedoe (New York: Museum of Modern Art, 1990), 136.

26. N. S. Goncharova, "Mneniia o s'ezde," *Protiv techeniia*, December 24, 1911, quoted in E. F. Kovtun, "Izdatel'stvo *segodniashnii lubok*," *Stranitsi istorii otechestvennogo iskusstva, vipusk II* (Saint Petersburg: State Russian Museum, 1993), 58.

27. Bowlt, *Russian Art of the Avant-Garde*, 58.

28. Quoted in "Detstvo i iunost Kazimira Malevicha: Glavi iz avtobiografii khudozhnika," in *The Russian Avant-Garde/K istorii russkogo avangarda*, ed. Nikolai Khardzhiev (Stockholm: Hylaea Prints, 1976), 117.

29. See Vladimir Markov, *Russian Futurism: A History* (London: Macgibbin and Kee, 1969), 28.

30. Anthony Parton, *Mikhail Larionov and the Russian Avant-Garde* (Princeton: Princeton University Press, 1993), 100–1.

31. Benedikt Livshits, *The One and a Half-Eyed Archer*, trans. John Bowlt (Newtonville: Oriental Research Partners, 1977), 184.

32. Livshits, *One and a Half-Eyed Archer*, 184.

33. Susan B. Compton, *The World Backwards: Russian Futurist Books 1912–16* (London: British Library, 1978), 13.

34. Compton, *World Backwards*, 19.

35. Margarita Tupitsyn, "Collaborating on the Paradigm of the Future," *Art Journal* 52 (Winter 1993): 19–21.

36. During the reign of Nicholas II (r. 1894–1917) the imperial administration sought to revive the same pre-Petrovine heritage that the Russian avant-garde was exploring. This resulted in a series of ceremonies and celebrations that employed seventeenth-century cultural forms in order to connect the contemporary court to ancient Muscovy. In 1903, for example, pre-imperial cultural forms were evoked during a ball in Saint Petersburg for which the emperor and his court donned seventeenth-century robes and jewelry. Beginning in 1909, with the jubilee of the battle of Poltava, a number of ceremonies, celebrations, and exhibitions were organized that evoked the reign of Michael Romanov, who became Russia's czar in 1613. This culminated in the tercentenary celebrations of 1913. See Richard S. Wortman, *Scenarios of Power: Myth and Ceremony in Russian Monarchy*, vol. 2: *From Alexander II to the Abdication of Nicholas II* (Princeton: Princeton University Press, 2000), 421–80.

37. Denisov, *Voina i lubok*, 19.

38. See V. A. Vereshchagin, *Russkaia Karikatura*, vol. 2: *Otechestvennaia Voina: Terebenev', Venetsianov', Ivanov* (St. Petersburg: Tip. Sirius, 1912), 34.

39. See, for example, Hosking, *Russia*; Theodore Weeks, *Nation and State in Late Imperial Russia: Nationalism and Russification on the Western Frontier, 1863–1914* (Carbondale: Northern Illinois University Press, 1996); and Vera Tolz, *Russia: Inventing the Nation* (London: Arnold, 2001).

40. Brooks, *When Russia Learned to Read*, 244–45.

41. M. Larionov, *Vystavka ikonopicnix podlinikov i lubkov* (Moskva: Bolshaia Dimitrovka, 1913). N. D. Vinogradov, *Pervaia vystavka lubkov, Organizovana N. D. Vinogradovym, 19–24 fevralia: Katalog* (Moskva: n.p., 1913).

42. Glavnoe Upravlenie Zemleustroistva i Zemledeliia, *Russkoe narodnoe iskusstvo na vtoroi vserussiiskoi kustarnoi vystavke v Petrograde v 1913 g.* (Petrograd: n.p., 1914).

43. Imperatorskii Moskovskii Arkheologicheskii Institut, *Vystavka drevne-russkogo iskusstva, ustroennaia v 1913 gody v onamenovanie chestvovaniia 300-letiia tsarstvovania Doma Romanovyx* (Moskva: n.p., 1913).

44. Jean-Claude Marcadé, *Malevitch* (Paris: Casterman, 1992), 107.

45. Richard Cork, *A Bitter Truth: Avant-Garde Art and the Great War* (New Haven: Yale University Press, 1994), 58.

46. Cork, *Bitter Truth*, 52.

47. In Barthes's words, myth "abolishes the complexity of human acts, it gives them the simplicity of essences, it does away with all dialectics . . . and it organizes a world which is without contradictions because it is without depth." See Roland Barthes, "Myth Today," in *Mythologies* (London: J. Cape, 1972), 143.

48. Many of the images described here are reproduced in the following sources: Serge Fauchereau, *Malevich* (Barcelona: Ediciones Poligrafa, 1992), and Donald Karshan, *Malevich: The Graphic Work, 1913–1930* (Jerusalem: Israel Museum, 1975).

49. See Rogger, *National Consciousness*.

50. Riasanovsky, *A History of Russia*, 464.

51. See Jahn, *Patriotic Culture*, 134–37.

52. In 1832, in the aftermath of Napoleon's invasion, Count Sergei Uvarov, Nicholas's Minister of Education, proposed the doctrine of "Official Nationality," according to which the realm would be organized around these three principles. Initially the Czarist government resisted this idea, but by the reign of Alexander III (1881–94) it became official policy. See Nicholas V. Riasanovsky, *Nicholas I and Official Nationality in Russia, 1825–1855* (Berkeley: University of California Press, 1959), 359.

53. E. F. Kovtun, "Izdatel'stvo *segodniashnii lubok*," in *Stranitsy istorii otechestvennogo iskusstva, vipusk II*, ed. E. N. Petrova (Saint Petersburg: State Russian Museum, 1993), 82.

54. S. Isakov, "Otvet chitateliam," *Novyi zhurnal dlia vsekh*, no. 2 (1915): n.p.

55. Quoted in Alla Povelikhina and Yevgeny Kovtun, *Russian Painted Shop Signs and Avant-Garde Artist* (Leningrad: Aurora Publishers, 1991), 134–35.

56. Magula, "Voina i narodnye kartiny," 18.

57. Richard S. Wortman, *Scenarios of Power: Myth and Ceremony in Russian Monarchy*, vol. 1 (Princeton: Princeton University Press, 1995), 222.

58. Victoria E. Bonnell, *Iconography of Power: Soviet Political Posters under Lenin and Stalin* (Berkeley: University of California Press, 1997), 199.

59. Victor Shklovsky, *Mayakovsky and His Circle* (London: Pluto Press, 1974), cited in Dawn Ades, "Function and Abstraction in Poster Design," in *The 20th-Century Poster*, ed. Dawn Ades (New York: Abbeville Press, 1984), 49.

60. Nicoletta Misler, "Caricatures and Posters of Vladimir Lebedev," *Journal of Decorative and Propaganda Arts* 5 (Summer 1987): 60–75.

61. Denisov, *Voina i lubok*, 4–5.

62. Jahn, *Patriotic Culture*, 83.

63. Jahn, *Patriotic Culture*, 177.

Part 3

Figuring the Body in
the Context of War

9

Images of Femininity in American World War I Posters

How did the First World War affect women's struggle for equal rights? Historian Susan Grayzel identifies this as a "historical conundrum": "On the one hand, women in many participant nations . . . gained basic voting rights in its immediate aftermath that they had never possessed before. On the other hand, their overall economic and social status showed few, if any, notable transformations." Whether historians emphasize change or stasis, Grayzel notes, they agree that the war's totality and modernity changed the nature of the relationship between women and war. Women became members of the home front, participating in the war and feeling its effects in unprecedented ways. Because it involved them so extensively, the war triggered "heated public debates about women's social, cultural," economic, "and political roles."[1] These debates took place across a range of media and locations, from the newspaper to the pulpit and into the public square. But they can be seen nowhere more clearly than in posters.

War posters have been described alternately as portraying "thoroughly traditional" roles for women and as the site of a breakthrough for an entirely new figure, the "Emancipated Girl." One historian concludes that posters "reflect agreement about the appropriate war roles for women," while another argues that they vary "to the point of self-contradiction."[2] Even after reducing the question of woman's place to two dimensions and confining it to the boundaries of a poster, it remains difficult to resolve.

Looking at the variety of war posters in which women appear, one is immediately struck by both the sheer number of them and the range of femininities they portray.[3] The range has its limits—with the important exceptions discussed by Jennifer Keene in this volume, known American posters limit their depictions to white women. Thus, they offer selective and idealized images of American womanhood. Together, these idealized female figures did the symbolic work of selling the war. As Martha Banta observes in *Imaging American Women*, "Once the focus is placed on national allegories, females are the figures that count."[4] Why that is and what consequences it wrought are the questions pursued in this essay. In search of answers I analyze the various and contradictory ways images of women function in American World War I posters. But while I agree that posters idealize femininity and use it to sell the war, my findings differ from those of previous scholars, who have treated the question cursorily or focused on the images' "conservative" objectives and legacies.[5] In contrast, I argue that American World War I posters reflect more radical possibilities for female subjectivity. Some testify to the important and new roles real women took up during the war. To be sure, many war posters seek to discipline their female viewers, while others portray idealized or commodified images of women for the pleasure of the male gaze. The posters that stake new claims for women as workers and contributors to the war effort are undoubtedly fewer in number. However, contradictions in and among images of femininity, read within the context of their historical moment, signal that the category of "woman" was incoherent and unstable, and thus malleable. Posters reveal that "woman" did not have a single "place," nor were the differences between masculinity and femininity as fundamental as they were supposed to be. Even when images attempt to fix their subjects along stereotypically feminine lines, they betray the slipperiness of gendered identities. That open-endedness invited both men and women to imagine femininity in powerfully new, and newly powerful, ways.

In other words, posters were not just *illustrations* of women's status during the war; they also functioned as *instruments* of the changes affecting that status. The home front came into existence in large part through the dissemination of propaganda by mass media. No one could ignore the war or imagine it only involved male soldiers. Posters everywhere insisted that women were both needed and threatened, that they themselves constituted the nation whose life was at stake. Posters redefined the ways femininity could be imagined and was experienced. As we shall see, many American women took posters as evidence that their contributions to the war effort were essential and used posters to advertise and justify their war work.

My conclusion emerges from reading images of women cumulatively across the range of available posters and considering how they work together in a mutually referential aggregate and in relation to their larger historical context. Posters were not consumed in isolation, and their "messages" were not delivered univocally. In the totality of known posters, several contradictory types of femininity appear with regularity: allegorical figures (Columbia and the Statue of Liberty, for instance); female victims of the war ("Poor Little Belgium"); commodified, sexually objectified figures offered as enticements for men in uniform; home-front consumers, producers, and laborers who contribute to the war effort; and, most radically for the time, uniformed war workers. These broad categories offer a wide range of activities and identifications to female viewers and offer male viewers a range of ways of imagining women. Each representational "type" seems designed to convey a particular message to a particular audience and is taken up in detail in this essay. Despite the clear differences among types, however, single images frequently employ the imagery or logic of competing kinds of femininity. Particular posters can credibly be assigned to different categories. Although Martha Banta only identifies two categories and so does not address the full range of representational types, her observation that "images from one category start to infiltrate the emotional shadows of the other group" remains essential.[6]

As categories of femininity merge in and across war posters, their messages become more complicated. This complication begs careful analysis, since it directly contradicts the simplicity for which most people valued the poster medium. Walton Rawls reminds us that posters were seen as useful vehicles for propaganda precisely because they could "communicate essential information rapidly and efficiently"; Adolf Hitler appreciated American and British posters' immediacy, which they achieved through the use of "stereotyped formulas."[7] But their messages, both to and about women, were neither consistent nor simply stereotypical.

In the United States women were not only flat figures on posters; they also disseminated and consumed information as members of the home front. The U.S. Food Administration archives reveal that women ratified some visions of female work and citizenship and used them to justify uses of female authority. In this instance, at least, posters were part of a campaign that changed the relationship between women and the state.

"The Amazon Warrior"

Feminine imagery has functioned for centuries as a vehicle of allegory in Western art. Art historical precedent, then, partially explains why this imagery did so much symbolic work during the war. Much poster imagery differs little from that found in paintings and public monuments of the prewar decades. This is particularly the case for the female figures such as Columbia, Liberty, Victory, and the Statue of Liberty, who symbolize the nation.[8] These figures, both in the imposing, physically powerful version that Banta discusses as the "Amazon Warrior" and in the more delicate "Frozen Goddess" that Ann Uhry Abrams identifies in turn-of-the-century painting, descend from the classical period and its subsequent European adherents.[9] As Marina Warner reminds us, iconographic representation of abstract principles in feminine allegory has its origins in verbal rhetoric, which follows the rules of grammar: in Greek, Latin, and many of the languages that derive from them, many abstract nouns (including chastity, virtue, knowledge, spirituality, faith, hope, charity, prudence, justice, fortitude, temperance, and wisdom) are feminine in grammatical gender. Artists therefore personified these abstract concepts with female forms. What began as an accident of grammar persisted and by the nineteenth century had become formulaic.[10]

When World War I began, artists from every combatant nation put this formula to use. As Maurice Rickards noted in *Posters of the First World War*, "the role of female as government spokesman . . . was common to the war effort of all the belligerents"; and in particular, the "figures of Britannia, Germania and Italia (not to mention sundry other national females), [and] Marianne of France [were] on instant call throughout the war."[11] The United States was no exception. Within this formula, virginal or masculine female figures embody national identity and ideals in seemingly timeless and universal visual terms. Unlike recognizable historical leaders (such as Napoleon or Abraham Lincoln), these timeless goddesses do not have reputations subject to historiographic change, nor do they belong to any faction within the nation. Neoclassical iconography allowed nations to lay claim to universal ideals (for instance, justice) that existed as it were outside of history. It allowed recently founded nations to trace an imaginary heritage to ancient times via a classical visual tradition.

Such imagery pretends to represent the universal, not the particular. In American posters it portrays whiteness as the rule and ignores difference among various (class, regional, racialized) constituencies within the nation. (That such a figure could be offered up as a "universal" symbol of America seems naive or problematic today, given our increased awareness of the particularity of whiteness as a privileged racial category.) Yet internal differences may have fueled the appeal of this imagery and made all the more enticing its invitation to the imagined national community to see itself embodied in a classical, supposedly universal icon. During the war American illustrators worked in this tradition to make the United States' sovereign identity intelligible within a recognizable and venerated visual language.

Despite the power these warrior-goddesses wield, they did not necessarily offer women empowering self-images. While some have claimed that "the most inspirational messages" were expressed through allegorical females, who combine "women's inner strength and outer beauty into a mystical force," I would argue that such images would not necessarily have inculcated a sense of agency in female viewers.[12] Consider Kenyon Cox's "The Sword Is Drawn, the Navy Upholds It!" as a paradigmatic example (fig. 38).[13] This female figure looks physically powerful, entirely self-sufficient, austere, impartial, and dispassionate. In other words, she shares nothing with the various ideological norms of femininity in the late nineteenth and early twentieth centuries: physical frailty (be it imagined in Victorian rotundity or the more modern ideal of slenderness);

dependence upon men; or a sentimental, impulsive, and emotional nature. Her muscular arms, broad shoulders, deemphasized breasts and waist, and phallic sword describe a physical power that in every other discursive context at this time was understood as masculine.

The dual classicism and masculinity that constitute this figure's appeal establish her distance from actual women and thus limit the extent to which female viewers should see her power as something they might themselves wield. She embodies a navy that had traditionally excluded female participation (though this would change in the course of U.S. involvement in World War I). The contradiction is clear: allegorical female figures embody a nation's power, despite women's lack of power within it. They provide emblems of national strength in an era when dominant gender norms denied the normalcy or desirability of women's physical strength or civil authority.

In other words, the Amazon Warrior is not a woman but a man in drag. Americans could disguise their imperial aggression by cloaking it in feminine garb. Though this imagery dominated the Chicago World's Fair in 1893 through the incarnation of Daniel Chester French's sculpture *The Republic*, Banta notes that it became even more popular after the Spanish American War because "gigantic female forms now expressed the sense of national destiny; they redefined the nature of the protective zeal that went with the new moral and territorial imperialism."[14] Banta reads a gendered split in American self-imagery in such images, which did the work of balancing "the paradox of feminine virtue and masculine power" that Americans wanted to claim as their special prerogative in the international sphere.[15] The classical female figure seems disinterested, not greedy for conquest. She is above politics. Imagining their nation's agenda as one pursued by such a goddess allowed Americans to overlook the rapacious aspects of U.S. foreign policies. The self-deception she enables works in other ways as well: not only does feminine imagery avoid connotations of masculine aggression—it also avoids connotation of actual soldiers, fighting, wounding, and death. The female figure is invulnerable precisely because she cannot fight. Such imagery distances the viewer from the details of American involvement in imperial and world wars, inviting them to see the nation's "progress" as an abstract idea rather than as a particular campaign involving costs in human lives and material.

The self-deceptive power of allegory may explain the preponderance of this imagery despite the fact that it was singled out

PEARL JAMES

by some poster design experts as ineffective. In their pamphlet *How to Put in Patriotic Posters the Stuff That Makes People Stop— Look—Act!* Horace Brown and Matlock Price caution would-be poster designers to avoid such imagery. "To impel people to act, action must be depicted. A design of allegorical nature, as for example, a sublime figure of 'Democracy' seated on a throne, with the nations of the earth passing before her in review might, conceivably, fail to sell a single thrift stamp. It may be pleasing, but leaves the holder with no specific impulse," they explain.[16] Another implicit reason for the ineffectiveness of this imagery, in their account, is because it appeals to no particular, defined group. It is simply too abstract. Despite such official disfavor, this imagery abounds in World War I posters, only to disappear during World War II.[17]

In some instances allegorical figures are eroticized, and they consequently become less abstract. In American World War I posters the sexual appeal common to commercial advertising frequently enters the visual field. The categories of feminine imagery overlap and infiltrate each other. We see an instance of this in Harrison Fisher's "I Summon You to Comradeship in the Red Cross" (see fig. 21, chapter 4). This figure is decidedly not an Amazon warrior, nor is she Aphrodite or Eve. Her genealogy can be traced to modern advertising rather than to European painting or beyond it to ancient Greece. The expression, gesture, and graphic line of Fisher's female figure have the look of "the Gibson Girl," made popular by Charles Dana Gibson, or other versions of "the American girl" drafted by advertising illustrators such as Howard Chandler Christy and James Montgomery Flagg. Fisher's pencil-drawn girl has exchanged the stern look and physical power of the Athena-like figures of European tradition for a plaintive expression, delicate features, and windblown hair. Such changes transformed the allegorical feminine imagery appearing in European posters, and updated American imagery from twenty years before, in both artistic and cultural registers.

The result has an interesting effect: images such as Fisher's bring historical women into play in a way that depictions of the Amazon Warrior do not. That is, the ad campaign girl looks like a contemporary girl, who may be idealized as being slender or having unblemished skin, who is eroticized in order to sell the product she symbolizes, but who refers to women and appeals to them as consumers. As analogous figures do in commercial advertisements, this poster girl invites the female viewer "to play a vicarious, scripted role as protagonist in the ad."[18] If some posters' female figures are untouchable, "universal," classical warrior goddesses, many more are, like Fisher's, drawn in the softer lines in which American women had been trained to see themselves. In these instances the cultural work done by female figures to symbolize the nation through a denial of history and of historical actors is oddly undermined.

As John Berger explains, eroticized and objectified female figures enable the male gaze, inspiring feelings of power and possession. At the same time, they appeal to women, who learn to see themselves in the images. By looking at images, women develop a double consciousness that enables them to anticipate how they will be seen and so to dress and perform accordingly.[19] Women can also choose not to identify with eroticized images or refuse to be visually consumable according to the gestures, expressions, and dress featured in advertisements.

Because of its eroticism, then, Fisher's poster girl appeals to both men and women. But her appeal goes beyond eroticism. She stands in front of the Capitol building, wears the flag, and seems to speak for the nation. More precisely, the poster's text suggests that she speaks for a real person who has a recognizable body of his own, Woodrow Wilson. Wilson's words are, in turn, uttered on behalf of the American Red Cross—an organization founded by a woman who had famously expanded the roles women could play during war. (The organization was long associated with Clara Barton, even though its female leadership was mostly replaced by men during the First World War.) The female figure appeals on at least two grounds: erotically, she catches the (male) viewer's eye; patriotically, she compliments the (female) viewer's capacity to contribute meaningfully to the war effort. Thus, if Fisher's figure is an abstraction who embodies a nation that did not recognize women as full participants, she nevertheless makes an appeal to real women, whose work was worth soliciting and recognizing as "comradeship." An eroticized figure speaks for the nation's male president and for an organization built by "serious" women. The image, then, manifests several contradictions in the gendered ways war work was being imagined and solicited.

Damsels in Distress

The next category of femininity—woman as victim—appears nearly as often as warrior-goddesses and seems to provide an important counterpoint. Many posters represent the violence of war through the visual metaphor of a raped, mutilated, or murdered woman. (Following the sinking of the *Lusitania*, Fred Spear made an iconic figure of the violence of war in his depiction of a drowned woman and child in his poster "Enlist.") What could be more different from "timeless," classical figures? Yet the victimized woman is also very much a fantastic construction with a complex appeal, despite the attestations of reality that frequently accompany these depictions. Certainly, there were female casualties. Yet posters that depict female victims depend not on factual evidence but upon sexual fantasy and gender (and in some cases racial) stereotypes.

Adolph Triedler's "Help Stop This" is a well-known example. In it an enormous German soldier strides across a ruined landscape, a gun in one hand and a bloody knife in the other. He crushes a semiclad, bloody woman underfoot. This poster won the first prize in the War Saving Stamps Poster Competition. Its perceived strength was its "strong suggestion" and "general appeal," which made it capable of doing what all good war posters should do: "*bring[ing] the issue home* to the civilian."[20] Posters were supposed to use simple and clear means to convince viewers of the urgency of the war effort. (This was a particularly hard sell in the traditionally isolationist and geographically distant United States.) Images that present the war not as a conflict between opposed masses of armed men but as a sexual assault on an innocent, unarmed, defenseless woman, often by an animalistic male aggressor, seemed to offer an effective solution. A famous example with racist overtones is H. R. Hopps's "Destroy This Mad Brute" (see fig. 11, chapter 2).

Such imagery had "general appeal" because it served to energize both male and female viewers to support the war effort. Graphic depictions of mutilated women told female viewers that German aggression could bring them sexual and physical harm. Though such images construct women as narrative objects—passive vessels upon which brutal males have acted—and quite abject ones at that, they nevertheless invite female viewers to cast themselves in analogous roles and speak with a sense of urgency generated by the fear of victimization.

The more explicit appeal of the damsel in distress, however, goes out to the male rescuer, the active, honorable man who will come to her defense. In most of these images, that viewer remains safely out of the poster's frame. His place in the wartime economy of wounded and dead bodies is left unspecified. The realities of warfare—the injury he would risk himself and the injury he would inflict on others—are elided in such images. Through selection and emphasis, posters in this category tell the viewer that vulnerability is, by definition, a female predicament. In this abstraction women do not enjoy the power of masculine martial strength.

Many have analyzed the cultural work these images do to energize their male viewer.[21] Equally important but often overlooked are the ways in which this imagery functions to deny male vulnerability—an urgent task in the context of recruiting men to go to fight in the potentially deadly, disfiguring, and psychically damaging conditions that existed at the fighting front. The metaphoric representation of war as a threat to women is both extremely common in American war posters and highly unrepresentative of what the war was actually like. Most of those killed and wounded in World War I were, after all, men. But reminding male viewers of that fact did not make for very successful enlistment campaigns, and posters picturing male injury and death are few and far between. In American posters, injury is frequently feminized.

One poster that purports to represent an actual event rather than an allegorical one provides an interesting—because exceptional—illustration of the problem. Hoyle's "They Crucify" (fig. 39) appeals directly to American manhood to defend women. Unlike many posters that personify war victims as females, though, Hoyle's admits that men too receive wounds—it is one of the rare posters that includes a male victim. But the poster's several framing devices seem designed to minimize that admission.

The poster's most important design element is composition: the female figure is the central one, the one who draws our gaze. The other victims frame her own more spectacular, and more visible, wounds. Her centrality is also established through color, which is not only eye-catching but also rhetorically overdetermined in red, white, and blue. In contrast, the man and baby's drab colors almost make them fade into the

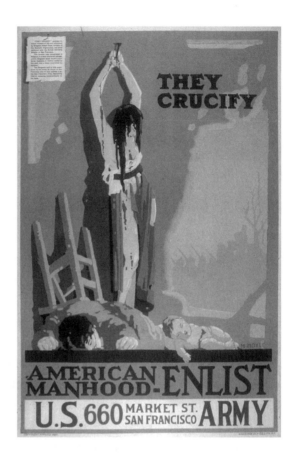

flat graphic background. The baby looks more fully three-dimensional, perhaps because a little hand enters the viewer's space at the bottom of the image. The image of the male body, in contrast, seems extremely flat and two-dimensional. Consequently, the spectacle of male injury is the most thoroughly contained of the three.

Another important framing device is the poster's use of narrative testimony. The "notice" in the poster's upper-left hand corner reads:

"They Crucify" portrays an actual incident of the war, witnessed by Sergeant Allen Goad, formerly of the Seaforth Highlanders, but since stationed with the British recruiting mission in San Francisco.

The atrocity was perpetrated in Belgium, in a shell shattered cottage, where Sgt. Goad found a murdered husband, a mother nailed to the wall, and a babe mutilated by bayonet.

The Sgt. told of the experience to the artist, M. Hoyle, of San Francisco, who in turn painted it for the San Francisco Army Recruiting District, adhering conscientiously to the facts.

This text asserts that despite the bodily threat going to war would seem to entail, soldiers are essentially tourists. Being a soldier will require witnessing violence but not experiencing it in the flesh or committing it on the flesh of others. The male viewer is safe, a spectator rather than a participant.

The essential differences between men and women in wartime asserted in such images of female victimization did not hold up in the actual experience of the war. For obvious reasons, the bodies wounded and victimized in World War I were predominantly male. Men who fought were seldom able to exert the kind of heroic masculine agency that posters invite them to imagine, particularly because of trench warfare and the use of modern technologies (machine guns, long-range and high-volume artillery bombardment, and poison gas). Combat testimony and historical narratives suggest that mechanized warfare inculcated feelings of powerlessness, enclosure, and vulnerability—feelings culturally understood as the symptoms that beset women.[22] Portraits of female vulnerability function to deny and displace male vulnerability and to engender a notion of difference (women are victims, men are actors and defenders) that the war threatened to make untenable. Yet, as Hoyle's poster and others I have analyzed elsewhere suggest, images often retain traces of the denied or displaced spectacle of male injury.[23]

Although some posters do display and consecrate male wounds, the trope of male victimization appears much less frequently than its female double.[24] Portraying male wounds ran the risk of *im*mobilizing male viewers, who might identify with the male victim and see him not so much as an object whose need was empowering but as a projected version of what might happen to them on the battlefield. Images of wounded female figures function to draw the nation's gaze toward an object that is both strange (as a victim of "inhuman atrocity") and familiar (the female body is pervasively figured as weak and passive), in order to divert awareness away from the spectacle of wounded male bodies.

Reading images that use women as victims of German rape and aggression as metaphors for the war within the larger context of 1914–18 frames them as distortions, allowing us to imagine the cognitive dissonance they may have generated in some viewers. Then as now, the images with the most potential to energize their viewers are those that entangle fear with desire, those that tease by keeping blatant contradiction just out of conscious awareness, those that activate a viewer's repressed psychic content. These posters did this on a variety of levels, not least because they insisted on an essential difference between men and women at the same moment that the larger historical context was undermining that difference.

Commodified Femininity: The Christy Girl

Another prominent type of femininity is the commodified coquette who offers herself as a sexual reward to recruits. Of course, because posters have their roots in advertising, many categories of femininity are—sometimes subtly—commodified and eroticized, even if that is not their primary purpose. It is admittedly artificial to discuss these categories in isolation, and this is especially true of the commodified sexual object.

PEARL JAMES

Fig. 40. Howard Chandler Christy, "Gee!! I Wish I Were a Man," 1918. Model Isabelle Rogers sports a man's naval uniform: enlisted dress blues with rank insignia of petty officer first class. The original watercolor is at the U.S. Naval Academy Museum in Annapolis MD. Museum of the City of New York.

Indeed, she bears certain resemblances to the figure of the female victim. Images of the coquette reiterate the female passivity/male activity binary opposition inherent in depictions of female victimization, and similarly eroticize the war. Howard Chandler Christy produced some of the most famous examples of this widespread imagery (fig. 40). Scholars have argued that this imagery flatters and reassures men and restricts the ways women can imagine themselves. The Christy Girl, according to Anne Classen Knutson, "reaffirms the American man's strength and virility, while guaranteeing normalized postwar gender relationships through her commodified sexuality and stereotypical preoccupations with love and marriage."[25] However persuasive, this claim oversimplifies matters.

Just as the damsel in distress does, this female figure conjures up and motivates a male viewer. (One version of "Gee!! I Wish I Were a Man" speaks directly to the male viewer with the caption "Be a Man and Do It.") The poster's caption defines femininity as lack: "I," the female image declares, cannot do things men do. She can don the uniform, but her cross-dressing visibly fails—there is no mistaking her for a man (or for even a "mannish" woman). She remains different from the man she supposedly wishes to be, or, to read more accurately the poster's visual language, the man she wishes *for, desires*. Her curve-accentuating pose, her plunging neckline, and her sidelong, coquettish gaze issue a sexual invitation. The image's commodification of female sexuality is incontrovertible.

Yet if this Christy Girl, as Knutson suggests, represents simply "a traditional ideal of woman as girlfriend, wife and mother who d[oes] not venture out into the masculine sphere in any threatening way," then the poster's challenge would not be meaningful.[26] The figure's provocation is based on two factors that do make her a potential threat in men's sexual and economic spheres. First, she has an implied sexual agency. Feminists can question the authenticity of this agency and posit that this is not an accurate portrait of female desire. The Christy Girl is a male fantasy. Nevertheless, despite her fantastic genealogy, this female figure expresses desire. That, in and of itself, makes her something of a threat. Moreover, she wants "a man," but not just *any* man; she is an agent in an economy of desire, who can appraise men and choose for herself. She can reject civilian men at will. The Christy Girl is one version of the "New Woman," whose sexual independence seemed both new and threatening. Second, this image plays with the fantasy that

PEARL JAMES

women could act as men by wearing uniforms and joining the navy. In 1917 this fantasy became a reality. This figure's cross-dressing conveys erotic play, but it needs to be read in a larger context of actual uniformed female war work.

Although it might seem that the Christy Girl appeals only to men, and only in nonthreatening ways, we should not isolate this kind of imagery from other posters that depict more active or "serious" kinds of femininity.[27] People did not consume these images in a vacuum. Other posters, perhaps hung next to this very image, informed viewers that women could and should participate in the war in uniform. Its contemporary audience must have had an increasingly ironic perspective on Christy's "Gee!!" poster as women did in fact join the navy. Women were recruited, wore uniforms, and contributed vital service to the nation's armed forces.[28] Looking back at the image, we can see that the possibility that women could do men's work serves here to motivate and challenge its male viewer. The multiplicity of armed services referred to in this version of the poster ("I'd join the Navy, Naval Reserve, or Coast Guard") specifies that service takes many forms. This Christy Girl is herself a figure for the consumer of poster images: she has been seeing recruiting images aimed at men, and she wants what she wants because of them. How can the viewer be sure that her gaze will not turn, next, to posters asking *her* to enlist?

"For Every Fighter a Woman Worker"

The Christy Girl shared physical and ideological space with another figure, the Woman Worker. World War I posters pictured women making contributions to the war effort in traditional and new ways: knitting, canning, cooking; nursing and driving near the front; working in uniform, either in factories or for the armed services and volunteer organizations. These images claimed new ground for female labor. Even posters that show women doing traditional labor such as cooking worked to create a modern feminine subjectivity: they sought to incorporate and nationalize their female audience. These images played an important role in the creation of what historians call "total war"—the militarization and mobilization of civilian life and the emergence of the home front. Even by staying at home and within a traditionally feminine domestic sphere, women could contribute, and poster images told women to think of themselves as participants in the war.

Visually, many of the posters addressed to women on the home front look entirely traditional. For instance, W. T. Benda's Red Cross poster "You Can Help" depicts a woman knitting. A slender woman, with long hair swept back into a bun, sits in a chair and looks down at her knitting. Both her clothes and her averted gaze convey modesty. Yet even this traditionally feminine, modest, and quotidian activity, the poster's legend insists, can help win the war. Lloyd Harrison's poster for the Food Administration makes a similar claim. It depicts a woman mixing hominy, surrounded by plates of home-baked corn muffins and cakes. Its legend declares: "Corn—the food of the nation. Serve some every meal. Appetizing, nourishing, economical."[29]

Nowhere does the poster explicitly mention the war, and so it resembles a simple advertisement for a commodity, corn. But simple appearances can be deceiving. This is not an ad for a brand-name corn but for corn as "the food of the nation." Wartime food shortages in Europe threatened the Allies' ability to fight, and American troops would need their own food supply. Wheat flour and sugar were both in high demand, and the U.S. Food Administration urged Americans to adopt local substitutes that did not ship as well, including corn, potatoes, honey, maple syrup, and sorghum. The public was encouraged to eat perishable fruit and vegetables in place of products made with flour. The success of the USFA campaigns depended largely upon women, the primary consumers and housekeepers. Harrison's poster places women in the kitchen but places the kitchen on the front line. According to its logic, the war cannot be won without the efforts of women in the home. Christy's poster "In her wheatless kitchen she's doing her part to win the war" reiterates this logic, as does another often-reprinted poster by J. Paul Verrees for the National War Garden Commission, which invites women to "Can Vegetables, Fruit, and the Kaiser too." (Verrees depicts a bust of the kaiser compressed into a jar. The kaiser's spiked *Pickelhaube* helmet is placed jauntily over the top of the jar, offering a visual pun on the "Kaiser Brand Unsweetened" pickles.) Even as these images assert women's place in the domestic sphere, they covertly modernize, nationalize, and professionalize women's roles. Despite their traditional imagery they contribute to a fundamental shift in the way women's work could be understood.

The radical aspect of these posters is, I grant, hard to see in their images. Michele J. Shover and Anne Knutson, who have both made insightful and authoritative analyses of women in World War I posters, discount their potential as feminist texts. Shover insists that World War I posters offered viewers "familiar" and "nonthreatening images of women." Posters advocated a "war effort role for women" that was "thoroughly traditional: service-support-sacrifice." For her, the value contemporary feminists saw in these portrayals is "ironic," since poster images "constitut[e] a substantial reaffirmation of women's traditional roles."[30] This reading underemphasizes the extent to which such posters both modernize and bestow national importance on feminine labor, and it does not take into consideration the larger context of which these posters were the sign.

Many posters produced by the Food Administration, the National War Garden Commission, and other governmental agencies disseminated information in order to rationalize the domestic realm of kitchens, parlors, and gardens. They educate their female audience in the new science of domestic economy. Many posters adapt the advertisement's direct address to female *consumers* to address an audience of female *workers*, exhorting them to practice home economy in a scientific way and to make their housework contribute to the war effort.

While we can still appreciate the appeal these posters make to a female viewer, equally important are the largely forgotten circumstances in which real women encountered them in 1917 and 1918. Women were not only viewers but also distributors, exhibitors, and makers of such posters. In order to reach its audience, the USFA enlisted women themselves to convey the conservation message. They compiled lists of librarians, teachers, boy and girl scout leaders, university extension home economics teachers, women's club members and directors, "Four-Minute Men" (public speakers, many of whom were women), in addition to store owners, theater owners, grain elevator operators, and so on, complete with names and telephone numbers, for each state. They used these lists to enjoin individuals to carry and implement their message. As a result thousands of women went from house to house, asking other women to sign and display pledges to reduce their use of wheat and sugar. "Home Demonstration Agents" were made responsible for translating posters' advisories to individuals. When Glenn Merry (a member of the Iowa State Council of National Defense) wrote to Washington for help, Federal Food Administrator J. F. Deems replied, "This is a woman's movement. . . . This campaign is being conducted by the Women's Committee of the State Council of Defense, which has a chairman in every county in the state. They are already at work. . . . See Mrs. E. E. Sutphen at Davenport. Write or wire her to get her women together for a meeting."[31] As this wire makes clear, the USFA found it efficacious to work directly with women's organizations.

This "women's movement" took place both in and outside the home. When the fair came to town, women were responsible for Food Administration exhibits. The USFA addressed and conceived of them as experts: "The central exhibit is the information booth. . . . A competent person should be in charge here all the time, someone capable of answering questions on food subjects and one well posted on the general situation [of food distribution among the Allies]. She should wear the Hoover costume and pledges should be at hand and visitors urged to join," ran the instruction letter. Though organizers received directions about how to arrange their exhibits, the Food Administration began by asking them to select a chair from their ranks, "all matters of final decision being referred to her." Designs called for "the ingenuity of the individual in arranging the exhibit."[32] In other words, women were given a measure of jurisdiction over the message they delivered. Washington hoped to learn from them: women were enjoined to report back about their posters, exhibits, and speeches. Women responded with hundreds, perhaps thousands, of letters back to Washington, many with photographs or hand-drawn sketches of the posters that they had made and displayed. Mrs. Jesse Hastings of Delaware County, Iowa, described the hand-made posters that appeared in her exhibit: "Large posters made by cutting beautiful pictures from magazines were used. One poster displayed a flower show and at the foot a loving couple, with a big sign reading 'If you must tell it, tell it in Flowers, not Candy.' . . . Other signs were 'Use more fresh fruit,' 'Use more vegetables,' 'Back up your cannon by the use of The Canner.'"[33] Although we cannot look upon these posters ourselves, we can be certain that they were amply seen in 1918—Hastings reports that "Over 3500 people visited the booth during the week"—and we can infer something from their manufacture and display, which records suggest were typical. Women felt called upon as patriots, and they answered that call. They had something to tell male viewers (don't buy candy), and saw housework (done by "the Canner") as an equivalent of fighting the enemy (with "the cannon"). They ratified the Food Administration posters—personalizing the USFA message and translating its mandates into local idioms, including recipes—through a variety of performances and behaviors, in both private and public. Indeed, these exchanges of information fundamentally transgressed the traditional boundary of public and private upon which so many ostensible differences between men and women were based. It was not easy to imagine women as passive, dependent, and emotional while watching them show one another how to rationalize their work for the public good.

In many instances women performed the roles advertised in posters for live audiences, dressed the part of posters for exhibitions, and were photographed working alongside war posters. They looked the part and, in doing so, asserted the veracity of poster images: posters refer to real women—here is the proof, they seem to say (fig. 41). But some performances also suggest the power women could exercise as actors and as interpreters of the script posters offered to them. In one photograph of a USFA fair exhibit in Iowa (fig. 42) the two demonstration agents differ from the image of the female consumer displayed on posters in their booth. One important difference is their dress and appearance, which marks the demonstration agents as uniformed workers rather than leisured, private consumers. But more important, the poster offers a two-dimensional and allegorical (negative) image of woman, while the flesh-and-blood agents embody actual (positive) roles women could play in the war effort. As little as we know about this image, it testifies to the fact that real women could choose to

PEARL JAMES

Fig. 41. Women work a booth for the Third Red Cross Roll Call, Kansas City, Missouri, 1919. Accession no. 82.12, National World War I Museum, Kansas City, Missouri.

adopt some, and not all, of the scripts and images that were offered to them.

Several posters use visual means to compare female non-combatant contributions to the war effort with those made by male soldiers. Recalling Christy's "Gee!! I Wish I Were a Man," many enact a visual flirtation with the possibility of women taking on male roles. One Land Army poster from 1918, in both its visual organization and its textual inscription, plays with the possibility of similarity between men and women, with the possibility that women can replace or work as men (fig. 43). Part of the pleasure of viewing it (and posters like it) emerges from the interpretive game of comparing and differentiating masculinity from femininity. The female figure wears androgynous clothing—her waist and the length of her hair are alike

Fig. 42. U.S. Food Administration posters tell viewers to "Save on Sugar" and that "Sugar Means Ships" in an exhibit at a fair in Iowa. Box 1, Audio-Visual material, Record Group 4, Records of the U.S. Food Administration, 1917–1920 (Iowa), National Archives and Records Administration—Central Plains, Kansas City, Missouri.

obscured. For this is a relatively "mannish" female worker, whose Land Army uniform includes overalls rather than the more frequently pictured skirts and puttees. More interestingly, the poster's visual organization recalls the sequencing of still photographs to capture motion, made famous by Eadweard Muybridge. In other words, the poster plays with the possibility that the woman laboring in the field could turn into the soldier on the battlefield by raising her farm tool and turning her gaze to the east. The soldier's gesture merely intensifies the latent possibility of her physical stance, rather than being fundamentally different from it. The poster's motto verbally echoes this visual possibility: "Get Behind the Girl He Left

PEARL JAMES

Behind Him" places the soldier and the woman in a repeating chain, in which one replaces the other. Similarly, the imperative to "Join the Land Army" evokes the logic of male recruiting posters and insists on the continuity between the work of these two "armies."[34]

Ernest Hamlin Baker's "For Every Fighter a Woman Worker" (fig. 44) stakes out a similar claim for women and their contributions and anticipates the appearance of Rosie the Riveter during World War II. Baker takes a visual motif that had been used in several war posters across several combatant nations to show the unification of national populations of *men* as

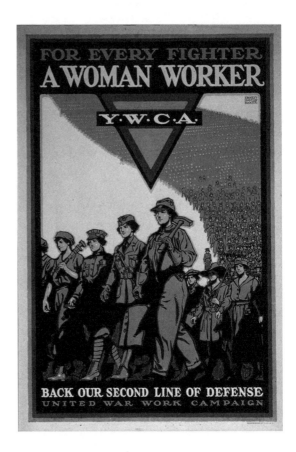

Fig. 44. Ernest Hamlin Baker, "For Every Fighter a Woman Worker," 1917–18. These figures' uniforms identify them as industrial workers, members of the Land Army, Motor Corps, and other organizations. Political Poster collection, US 486, Hoover Institution Archives.

they joined the army. Indeed, Baker himself produced a similar poster in which the parading figures are male and carry the flags of different service organizations. But this time the same visual motif depicts women workers. Their uniforms indicate their different professional roles (industrial laborer, street car conductor, Motor Corps driver, Land Army worker, and so on) in winning the war. These women have left the domestic sphere to take on jobs once thought of as male. It is important to note that the largest individual figure, in the poster's closest foreground, marching directly beneath the point of the triangle pointing down from the poster's lettering, carries

PEARL JAMES

a sledgehammer and wears a worker's jersey with pants, flat-heeled boots, and heavy-duty gloves. All the women either have short hair or confine their hair to a cap. The poster's motto states an equation in which men and women make equal contributions: "For Every Fighter a Woman Worker."

Such images promote anything but the traditional femininity that previous scholars have claimed is the rule in World War I posters. While Knutson grants that some posters depict women in "serious" roles, she minimizes their importance, arguing that they appealed only to women. "Serious images of women never appear in recruiting posters aimed at men," she states.[35] But arguing that a poster appealed only to one audience or another seems problematic. Returning momentarily to Baker's image, one notes that literally, of course, it appeals both to men and to women. Its request to "Back Our Second Line of Defense" asks a collective national audience, regardless of sex or gender, for money. More important, it makes its appeal in visually cross-gendered terms. I have already pointed out its similarity to many recruitment posters aimed at men. Viewers had seen its visual motif repeatedly and knew how to read it from having looked at male recruitment posters. To realize that is to realize, once again, that posters issue complex appeals to a range of viewers and that poster viewers are promiscuous: they look at many posters, whether or not they are the intended audience for a particular image. It would be strange to claim that men would not have found this image appealing, since at least from a middle distance, it looks exactly like images designed to recruit them. Like the Land Army poster, this poster's flirtation with gender-crossing constitutes its primary visual interest and gains its meaning by playing against and expanding its viewer's expectations of what women do and how they look.

The range of available evidence suggests that definitions of female labor shifted dramatically during the war. In addition to those who enlisted in the armed forces, many women were mobilized by volunteer organizations such as the Red Cross, the Salvation Army, and the YMCA/YWCA. According to historian Susan Zeiger, "women's work at the front was much more than a simple extension of their participation in the civilian labor force. It was also military or quasi-military service and therefore had profound implications for a society grappling with questions about the nature of women and their place in the public life of the nation, in war and peacetime."[36] Posters helped break new ground for what women could do and how they could look, depicting uniformed women working close to the front in capacities once reserved for men. Posters make the wartime (re)definitions of femininity visible. If women could do things they were not supposed to be able to do, were they still women? And how, if at all, did they still differ from men? Depictions of cross-dressing and other visual similarities raise these questions for their viewers.

In the face of such evidence, Knutson concludes that posters tried to divorce femininity from new kinds of female labor. Posters depicting women at the front "feature women in practical, mannish uniforms that delete all trace of the sexual."[37] Ample evidence supports her claim, including Clarence Underwood's "Back Our Girls Over There," a poster depicting an army switchboard operator in France. She wears a hat that obscures her hair, and she is engrossed in her work, which involves modern technology. She is not obviously eroticized. Knutson concludes that this imagery was designed to appeal to women as potential recruits and to broker a compromise: in exchange for new economic and social status, women would have to sacrifice. These images suggest "that women can only experience . . . male activities if they shed their sexuality"—that they must stay within a feminine sphere or risk being unattractive.[38] Thus, these depictions of women stop short of offering women new possibilities because they depict opportunity as coming at the price of femininity.

In addition to this grim cultural logic, however, there are other ways of interpreting the desexualization of female war work in some images. The mobilization of women alongside men threatened to destabilize two of the propaganda campaign's cultural myths: the stoic male hero and the damsel in distress. In fact, the presence of female hostesses in France was predicated on male dependence on women and on a notion that women were necessary to the strength and viability of the American Expeditionary Force (AEF). Male soldiers, it was argued, would naturally be homesick; and American women could comfort them. This reasoning, however, led to an inevitable concern for propriety.

In response, the Salvation Army, Red Cross, and hospitality services of the armed forces supervised the interactions of American soldiers and their female support corps and tried to desexualize depictions of their interactions. The kind of bond Salvation Army "Lassies" and other female support corps were supposedly able to offer male soldiers was continually figured as a sibling or maternal one. "American women . . . were expected to provide the troops with a wholesome but winning distraction from French prostitutes or lovers," Susan Zeiger writes; by their presence, American women could comfort soldiers and help them observe the AEF's "policy of sexual continence" against venereal disease.[39] In other words, women working at the front had to walk a thin line between being feminine (comforting) but not too feminine (alluring)—they had to enact their difference from soldiers while still being their "chums."

Many posters are structured by a need to define American women as fundamentally different from French women, who were imagined either as posing a sexual threat—both moral and physical—to American soldiers or as icons of the defeminization war work would wreak. The latter impression was offered up in a widely circulated photograph and accompanying essay by Alonso Taylor, that depicted the heroic but back-breaking work done by rural French women. Edward Penfield rendered the photograph's image in 1917 in "Will you help the women of France?" and it became one of the most celebrated of all war posters (see fig. 6, introduction). Posters calling American women to go to France studiously avoided these visual possibilities. American service and volunteer women had to be pictured as "envoys of the American home front, representatives of the mothers, wives, and sisters left behind," and as such were pictured in terms of "sentimentality and homey comfort" rather than sexuality or overt defeminization.[40]

And yet, maintaining that balance in posters proved a fairly difficult task, at least insofar as many images portray women workers as at once serious, professional, and physically appealing. We can take an example from Howard Chandler Christy, whose poster for the Motor Corps—as Knutson admits—features an independent female figure who works without losing her feminine allure (fig. 45). This 1918 Christy Girl has a buttoned-up collar but a sensual expression. Her slim waist is accentuated, but by a Sam Browne belt, which was worn by AEF troops after their arrival in France. Her hands are delicate, but she grasps a stretcher, which reminds the viewer of the physical aspects of her job and her proximity to the fighting. She is not a sexual reward for a soldier but instead wears military insignia and does a kind of soldiering herself.

This and dozens of other images offered women novel and positive scripts. They informed viewers about the challenging jobs women could take on. The Motor Corps posters, for instance, glamorize what was in fact a difficult job: women who drove in France worked hard hours on bad roads, they did their own maintenance, and they worked alone close to the

Fig. 45. Howard Chandler Christy, "The Motor Corps of America," 1918. The driver carries what looks like a stretcher and wears a Sam Browne belt, which places her overseas. Yale Manuscripts and Archives Collection.

THE
MOTOR CORPS
OF
AMERICA

front. Civilian Motor Corps work was similarly rigorous, even if it did not entail the danger of being near the front. The posters that solicited female volunteers did so through portraits of female ambition, independence, and responsibility. They show women handling machinery, answering for themselves, being serious and professional rather than friendly and hospitable. But they do not make these women mannish, unattractive, or asexual. These images depict female agency in ways that ignore the contradictions surrounding women workers at the time and thus invited actual women to do the same.

Conclusion

Images of women appeared in many—and many of the most striking—American war posters. To be sure, part of why female figures appeared so often was because sex sells, and war posters grew out of advertising. But such a neat formulation oversimplifies the ways in which femininity was pictured and the kinds of symbolic work female figures were enlisted to do. Commodified female sexuality and the enticing spectacle of women threatened by rape both energized male viewers. Other types of femininity served other rhetorical purposes: allegorical, masculinized images of women promised to unify a nation and could embody the nation's invulnerability precisely because in fact women could not fight. But other images of women appealed more directly to female viewers' wartime roles, which illustrators and poster producers—male and female— recognized as important. To win the war, women had to do their traditional work but also step into *new* places. Posters cajoled them to do both.

Understanding the social consequences of these images requires grappling with the range and complexity of these visual messages and examining contradictions among them. This complexity destabilizes firm ideas about woman's "place." The multiplicity and contradictoriness of the posters have a surplus effect that is liberating for women; these images are too many and too complicated for their subjects to be subsumed under a single rubric or regime of the gaze.

Perhaps because of the suspicion to which propaganda is subject, historians have predominantly described these posters as playing a conservative social role. But others have seen them as instrumental in sustaining women's wartime and postwar struggle for equality:

> Job shifts occasioned by wartime economic circumstances . . .
> [gave] American women greater latitude for choosing work than
> they had ever had. . . . Working women . . . seized opportunities
> for changing jobs, petitioned the government for fairer labor
> policies, struck at their workplaces for better pay and conditions,

PEARL JAMES

joined trade unions, and challenged the authority of their bosses [. . .] When male co-workers, foremen, unions, and even social reformers attempted to block the aspirations of these women workers, the newly heightened awareness of their own worth made them a substantial collective force with which to be reckoned. Many women took literally the wartime propaganda which corresponded to their own experience and hopes, that the rhetoric of democracy and human dignity should have meaning in women's work.[41]

We may never obtain the detail we desire about just how women interpreted the wartime propaganda campaign. But it is surely too simple to relegate posters to a "fantasy world" that, because its "bravura" and "heroic image[s] reached for the timeless and the sublime," were less instrumental in social change than photographs depicting the realistic or everyday woman.[42] Nor should we conclude that the contradictory messages paralyzed viewers into accepting the most traditional images as the most realistic or desirable ones.[43] Despite the restriction inherent in some of the roles played by women in posters, posters told women that their roles were important, that they were many, and that it was up to them to play these roles.

Notes

1. Susan R. Grayzel, *Women and the First World War* (New York: Longman, 2002), 4–5.

2. The earliest essay to treat the subject in useful detail is Michele J. Shover's "Roles and Images of Women in World War I Propaganda," *Politics and Society* 5, no. 4 (1975): 468–86. She asserts that posters "reflect agreement" that women should play a "war effort role . . . that was thoroughly traditional" (471, 473). Peter Conrad Frank's curatorial essay, *Women of the World War I Poster* (Middletown CT: Wesleyan Center for the Arts, 1981), and Anne Classen Knutson's excellent dissertation, "Breasts, Brawn and Selling a War: American World War I Propaganda Posters 1917–1918" (PhD diss., University of Pittsburgh, 1997), support Shover's interpretation. In a less scholarly fashion, Barbara Jones and Bill Howell describe the advent of the "Emancipated Girl" in wartime media in *Popular*

Arts of the First World War (New York: McGraw Hill, 1972), 131. Martha Banta argues that images of women during this period, including those found in posters, "vary" and contradict themselves; see her *Imaging American Women: Idea and Ideals in Cultural History* (New York: Columbia University Press, 1987), 32.

3. Precise numbers remain elusive since no complete collection of poster images exists, nor do we have precise evidence of how many copies of known images were made, in what sizes, or how they were displayed.

4. Banta, *Imaging American Women*, 567.

5. Shover, "Roles and Images of Women," 472. Despite the general usefulness of Banta's argument, she treats posters in insufficient detail. See, for instance, the following note.

6. Banta's categories: "One is the Amazon Warrior (called for official purposes Columbia, Liberty, or America). The other is the Protecting Angel (labeled as the Red Cross Nurse, the Rescue Mission lady, the YWCA girl, or the women in the Land Army)" (Banta, *Imaging American Women*, 562). These two categories do not distinguish adequately the various and contradictory images of femininity that the posters put in circulation.

7. Walton H. Rawls, *Wake Up, America! World War I and the American Poster* (New York: Abbeville Press, 1988), 11. He quotes Hitler's *Mein Kampf.*

8. These various entities can often be distinguished through iconography: Columbia frequently stands astride the globe or wears the flag; Liberty also holds the flag but sometimes bares a breast or wears a Phrygian cap; Victory holds a sword; the Statue of Liberty wears her pointed crown and often holds her tablets; the Republic often wears a laurel wreath. But they all draw on a single generic femininity, and some composite figures contain numerous icons.

9. See Banta, *Imaging American Women*, especially chaps. 9 and 10; and Ann Uhry Abrams, "Frozen Goddess: The Image of Woman in Turn-of-the-Century American Art," in *Woman's Being, Woman's Place: Female Identity and Vocation in American History*, ed. Mary Kelley (Boston: G. K. Hall, 1979), 93–108.

10. Marina Warner, *Monuments and Maidens: The Allegory of the Female Form* (New York: Vintage, 1996), 64, 199. Warner chronicles the origins of the tradition in Greek and Roman art and wryly notes, "Congruity with the female character was hardly ever adduced" (64). Yet the tradition of personifying these concepts in feminine form, in accordance with their grammatical gender, persisted. "Occasionally," she notes, "artists ignored grammatical gender in favor of male images," but "such inversions are unusual; and the tendency to personify in the feminine became more and more marked rather than decreased . . . : it was a formula." "The rediscovery of the classical gods" in fourteenth-century Europe "assisted in the widening divergence between the use of the female form as a symbol and woman as a person": "the Greek and Roman deities . . . were no longer actors in a continuously ritual performance of their stories, in which the

PEARL JAMES

audience could also join; nor were they commonly represented in the mien of the men and women of the time. Their history belonged in the past, where they were perceived as reflections of an ideal, distant culture" (199–200). By the late nineteenth century, "the allegorical convention had set so hard that it provided a solid foundation" for artists who could innovate upon it in various ways, including those who integrated modern elements, such as, in France, a female personification of "the telephone" (85).

11. Maurice Rickards, *Posters of the First World War* (London: Evelyn, Adams and Mackay, 1968), 11, 25.

12. "Women in War: A Touring Exhibit of World War I Posters from the Collection of the Liberty Memorial Museum, Kansas City, Missouri, July, 1985" (Kansas City MO: Mid-America Arts Alliance, 1985). Exhibition catalog, no author.

13. "The Navy" draws on numerous iconographic figures: her Phrygian cap connects her to Liberty, while the garland in her hair and eagle on her breastplate denote the Republic, the sword denotes Victory, and, like the Statue of Liberty, she holds a tool in one hand and bears a text in the other.

14. Banta, *Imaging American Women*, 515.

15. Banta, *Imaging American Women*, 519.

16. Matlock Price and Horace Brown, *How to Put in Patriotic Posters the Stuff That Makes People Stop—Look—Act!* (Washington DC: National Committee of Patriotic Societies, n.d., ca. 1917–18), 11.

17. Knutson provides ample evidence from the press that allegorical imagery was sharply and widely criticized. She concludes that "it was not these sober types of woman as allegory that the middle-class public wanted, but rather the sexy and commodified images of femininity that emerged from the 'lower' realms of advertising and magazine illustration" ("Breasts, Brawn," 160). Christina S. Jarvis notes the disappearance of this imagery and its replacement, during World War II, with a newly masculinized Uncle Sam; see her *The Male Body at War: American Masculinity during World War II* (Dekalb: Northern Illinois University Press, 2004), 35.

18. Roland Marchand, *Advertising the American Dream: Making Way for Modernity* (Berkeley: University of California Press, 1985), 12.

19. John Berger, *Ways of Seeing* (New York: Viking Press, 1972).

20. Price and Brown, *Patriotic Posters*, 11–12; emphasis in the original.

21. Knutson discusses this image with insight in her dissertation, "Breasts, Brawn." See also Nicoletta F. Gullace's *"Blood of Our Sons": Men, Women, and the Renegotiation of British Citizenship during the Great War* (New York: Palgrave Macmillan, 2002); both Gullace's and Albrinck's essays in this volume; and, for an argument that develops an account of how racial signifiers work alongside masculinity in such images, Gail Bederman, *Manliness and Civilization: A Cultural*

History of Gender and Race in the United States, 1880–1917 (Chicago: University of Chicago Press, 1995).

22. Certainly, American experience of World War I differed from the British, French, and German experience. The American Expeditionary Force (AEF) did not endure years of trench warfare; on the contrary, the arrival of the AEF largely coincided with the return to a war of movement. Nevertheless, motifs of enclosure, passivity, and physical vulnerability are prevalent in American fictional and historical accounts, particularly in the descriptions of being below ship in submarine-infested waters, surviving artillery bombardment and gas attacks, and in depictions of incarceration, hospitalization, and amputation. See, for instance, Hervey Allen's memoir *Toward the Flame*, or well-known World War I American novels and plays, including Lawrence Stalling's *Plumes* and *What Price Glory*, Thomas Boyd's *Through the Wheat*, Cummings's *The Enormous Room*, Dos Passos's *Three Soldiers*, or Hemingway's *A Farewell to Arms*.

23. See Pearl James, "From Trench to Trope" (PhD diss., Yale University, 2003).

24. A few notable exceptions, in addition to the images discussed in this volume by John Kinder, include Cyrus Leroy Baldridge's "Pvt. Treptow's Pledge," US 1235; Walter Whitehead's "Come On," 1918, US 1031; McClelland Barclay's "Second Red Cross Fund," US 175; and, from England, Frank Brangwyn's "Put Strength in the Final Blow," UK 4040; all are in the Poster Collection, Hoover Institution Archives.

25. Knutson, "Breasts, Brawn," 169–70.

26. Knutson, "Breasts, Brawn," 170.

27. Knutson, "Breasts, Brawn," 182–83.

28. Lettie Gavin reports that the navy enlisted approximately 11,000 women. They wore naval uniforms and received pay equal to that of men in the same ranks. For the most part they performed clerical tasks in offices, mostly in Washington DC. See her *American Women in World War I: They Also Served* (Niwot: University of Colorado Press, 1997). See also Susan Zeiger, *In Uncle Sam's Service: Women Workers with the American Expeditionary Force, 1917–1919* (Ithaca NY: Cornell University Press, 1999).

29. Lloyd Harrison, "Corn, Food of the Nation," date unknown. Color, U.S., 20 x 30 inches, Yale Manuscripts and Archives Collection.

30. Shover, "Roles and Images of Women," 473.

31. Telegram to Glenn M. Merry dated October 4, 1917, folder "Merry," box 8, Record Group 4 (U.S. Food Administration) for Iowa, National Archives and Records Administration—Central Plains, Kansas City MO (hereafter cited as Record Group 4).

32. "Working Plans for Food Conservation Exhibit Prepared by the United

States Food Administration, March 1918," folder "Exhibits" (1 of 2), box 75, Record Group 4.

33. Typed letter addressed to J. F. Deems, U.S. Food Administration, September 12, 1918, folder "Fairs—Exhibits," box 75, Record Group 4.

34. Regarding the cultural crisis that women in uniform provoked in Britain, see Susan R. Grayzel, "'The Outward and Visible Sign of Her Patriotism': Women, Uniforms, and National Service during the First World War," *Twentieth Century British History* 8, no. 2 (1997): 145–64; and Lucy Noakes, "'Play at Being Soldiers'? British Women, Fashion, and Military Uniform in the First World War," in *British Popular Culture and the First World War*, ed. Jessica Meyer (Leiden and Boston: Brill, 2008), 124–45.

35. Knutson, "Breasts, Brawn," 183.

36. Zeiger, *In Uncle Sam's Service*, 3–4.

37. Knutson, "Breasts, Brawn," 183.

38. Knutson, "Breasts, Brawn," 184–85. She does suggest that some posters offer a way out of this double bind, particularly those such as E. A. Foringer's famous "Greatest Mother of All" image for the Red Cross. Mothers are allowed to be both feminine and powerful.

39. Zeiger, *In Uncle Sam's Service*, 56.

40. Zeiger, *In Uncle Sam's Service*, 57.

41. Maurine Weiner Greenwald, *Women, War, and Work: The Impact of World War I on Women Workers in the United States* (Westport CT: Greenwood Press, 1980), 45.

42. Banta, *Imaging American Women*, 573–74.

43. In their analysis of images of women in advertising during World War II, Susan Alexander and Alison Greenberg draw just such a conclusion. Just as during the First World War, advertisements of the Second "offered women inherently contradictory messages about work and home, in one ad urging them to go to work for the war effort and in the next pushing cold cream as the way to stay 'lovely' for the men." Alexander and Greenberg argue that "the contradictory messages . . . had an overall detrimental effect on the women of that era, ensuring that above all else they persevere in taking care of their men"; see "You Must Go Home Again: Duty, Love, and Work as Presented in Popular Magazines during World War II," in *Modernism, Gender, and Culture: A Cultural Studies Approach*, ed. Lisa Rado (New York: Garland Publishing, 1997), 101–10, quotes from 102.

10

Humanitarians and He-Men: Recruitment Posters and the Masculine Ideal

With a standing army eighteen times smaller than that of the Germans, Britain's most immediate task at the outbreak of the First World War was to build up its military. The nonpartisan Parliamentary Recruiting Committee (PRC) was quickly formed and given the job of calling eligible men to serve. For the first two years of the war, the PRC used a variety of initiatives to expand the armed forces, including door-to-door canvassing and recruiting rallies. However, our best records of the PRC's efforts lie in the print materials they produced. Working with advertisers and other artists, the PRC developed a series of recruiting posters and pamphlets that asked, called, and later demanded military service from British men.

These materials blanketed the nation, covering walls, windows, hoardings, tramcars, taxis, and kiosks in urban and rural areas alike. Although few photographs remain to confirm the prevalence of these images, stories and articles from the period refer to their ubiquity. In one story these posters haunt a clerk as he makes his way through town:

> "Your King and Country Need You . . . 100,000 Men Wanted . . . God Save the King!" The City clerk and his wife stared up at the big poster together. . . . He tried to avoid a daily reading of this . . .

message. He went round by the longer way to the station in the mornings. Then there was one posted up in that road, too. Gradually one began to meet them everywhere. Then came other messages—some pictured—all with that same direct stirring appeal—*more men.*[1]

The pervasiveness of these images was well established by the summer of 1915: "In every street, on every hoarding, at every railway station, all the art and artifice of the poster-designer and publicity-agent have been enlisted in the national cause. Everywhere striking placards, plain or coloured . . . emphasise and illustrate the urgent necessity of the call to arms."[2] One writer reports that the posters cover "the length and breadth of the land," while another claims that "there are acres of them."[3]

Using these publications, the British government orchestrated a range of voices to call its citizens to service. Even though the figure of the soldier was visually and verbally drawn and redrawn, the idealized outlines of the soldier himself remained constant throughout the recruiting campaigns. He was usually plucky, genial, and determined, happy to be serving his country and reveling in the camaraderie of his regiment. If he was in a tight spot, he exhibited courage; if he faced a serious challenge, he did so with resolve. In all nations in the First World War, press and propaganda praised the soldier for resisting invading armies, protecting women and children, defending the ideals of his homeland, and standing by his comrades in the face of danger. Together, these texts argued that military service exemplified not only one's patriotism but one's masculinity as well.

This is clarified by a further look at the clerk's story. When he sees the first poster, he assumes "an air of manly authority" as he assures his wife that Kitchener will resolve the conflict in short order and that his service will not be necessary.[4]

However, his defiance of the poster's call makes him feel guilty, and in his efforts to avoid the appeal, he seeks more circuitous routes to the train station. By the second page of the story, he begins to succumb to the poster's pressure and, in a strange turn, asks "for his wife's tape-measure."[5] Finding that he does not meet the physical criteria for enlistment, he then "hunt[s] up his old dumbbells" in order to shape his body into the form required by the War Office.[6] Once he achieves a more robust physique, he volunteers and is accepted for service. This story, for all its predictability, clearly demonstrates the links between patriotism and masculinity in the discourse surrounding the soldier. The clerk cannot maintain his air of "manly authority" once the wartime definition of masculinity begins to circulate in his community. He is restored only when he brings his body and his behavior into compliance with the authoritative definitions of manliness communicated through the recruiting posters.

Lacking a conscription system in 1914, British recruiters used posters, pamphlets, and leaflets to persuade many men like the clerk to enlist in the military. While archivists such as Philip Dutton and Nicholas Hiley have each compiled useful guides to the themes and history of the PRC campaign, in this essay I demonstrate that the arguments about military service in British recruitment posters relied upon gendered arguments that developed and changed in response to other cultural discourses and needs at the time. Specifically, I reveal the ways these government-sponsored posters and leaflets worked with other resonant cultural images and vocabulary to articulate and proscribe a definition of militant masculinity for British men, a definition that initially appealed to a national tradition of courage, honor, and glory but later used shame and coercion to question the virility of the unenlisted man.

"Remember Belgium": The Moral Necessity of Military Service

While one could point to any number of documents that articulate the meanings of "masculinity" and "femininity" in a specific time and place, I make use of the PRC's campaign in this study because it is a rare example of a centralized authority on gender roles. First of all, War Office records confirm that the publication and distribution range of PRC materials was vast, with almost 12 million copies of 140 different posters, 34 million leaflets, and 5.5 million pamphlets printed and distributed by May 1916.[7] Furthermore, the PRC's materials made use of authoritative speakers and authoritative content. They bore the stamp of the PRC and often employed images or quotations from state representatives, including Lord Kitchener, Lord Roberts, and Prime Minister Asquith, thus presenting their arguments as institutional truths. This is clear in the story already related; the poster speaks to the clerk using the authority of Kitchener's voice and seems to leave the clerk no recourse for resistance.

Other encounters with these posters brought similar reactions. For example, in an unpublished memoir Maisie Richards remembers seeing such texts around her village: "The little town became busy—posters calling for recruits were everywhere. Kitchener's eyes glared at you, and the words: 'Your King and Country needs you' *hit out.*"[8] Another young woman who later served as a member of the Women's Army Auxiliary Corps speaks of one poster's effectiveness: "I was walking along wondering what to do when I saw a Large Poster asking for Women to join the Army & help win the War. The Picture had a Woman in Uniform & said, 'Your Country needs '*you*.' That settled it for me. . . . I thought that is what I'll do—I'll go & help win the war."[9] Both women identify the posters as compelling attention and allegiance; both report feeling small in the presence of the poster, whether due to Kitchener's glaring eyes or to the size of the poster itself. As a result, both women suggest that the posters themselves carried an indisputable authority, much as they did in the clerk's story.

In the early days of the war, PRC posters focused on the moral urgency of service and utilized a masculine ideal that equated military service with defending women and children. This argument relied on a dichotomization of two types of masculinity. To use Jean Bethke Elshtain's terms, the British soldier was represented as the Just Warrior, a primarily defensive figure, honorable in deed and noble in intent. In contrast, the German soldier was represented as a ferocious and rapacious fighter, a primarily aggressive figure whose goals were uncivilized and whose activities were inhumane. These two versions of masculinity were the first to emerge in the construction of the conflict, taking shape around Germany's advance through Belgium. Respected papers such as the *Times*, more sensational tabloids, and the PRC constructed the invasion in decidedly and violently gendered terms; all portrayed small and defenseless Belgium as feminine, while representing Germany as hypermasculine and barbaric. Stories of bombed civilian houses and of raped and mutilated women and children circulated through the press and horrified the British public, especially after the Siege of Antwerp in October 1914.[10] By constructing German soldiers as barbaric, the stories made space for the construction of British soldiers as noble and heroic, able to assert their own masculinity in a more protective way.

Many early recruiting posters used the reports in the press to construct visual arguments that impressed the viewer with the moral imperative of service. In one poster an ogre-ish man stands on the body of a slain woman (who is sexualized by the exposure of her breast) and is about to step on an infant; clippings from newspaper articles and officers' letters accompany the graphics and tell of Germans attacking and mutilating women (PST 6066). By November 1914 the PRC had established the recurring enlistment phrase "Remember Belgium," pairing it with illustrations of women and children fleeing the destruction of their homes. PRC poster 16 explicitly positions the British soldier within this field (see fig. 8, chapter 1). In the center of the poster, beneath the "Remember Belgium" slogan, stands a fighting man in khaki, his rifle resting on the ground, his eyes looking toward the viewer. Behind him to the left a fire destroys a village and sends black smoke billowing across the sky. To the right a woman flees with two children—an infant and a toddler. While she looks back over her shoulder, the toddler looks forward and reaches a small hand toward the man in khaki. At the bottom of the poster appears the command "Enlist To-day." The message is clear: to remember Belgium is to remember the alleged immorality of the German armies and to take up arms against them.

This poster uses two structural devices to imply that enlistment is a moral option for defeating barbarity. First, fighting is depicted as a humanitarian act—as helping women and children—thus disguising the brutality that the soldier will have to participate in and endure. Framing battle in this way, the image depicts the government's appeal through the outstretched hand of the child, covering national interests with personal ones. The second structural device involves the positioning of the soldier. Standing as a barrier between the fire on the left and the fleeing family on the right, this image of the fighting man suggests that enlistment will directly protect women and children. Just as the soldier in the poster stands between the family and the fire raging behind them, so the viewer will be able to stand between other innocents and German barbarism. This poster employs the same arguments about gender as the most prevalent atrocity stories did. The "volume of demand" for this poster marks it as the second most popular poster of the campaign, with 140,000 copies distributed.[11]

One of the reasons that this poster and others like it were popular is that they were so familiar, using codes of militant masculinity that predated Britain's 1914 declaration of war. As Eric Leed and Paul Fussell have pointed out, and as Jay Winter reminds us elsewhere in the present volume, British men had grown up with ideals of battlefront heroism, ideals introduced by stories of St. George and the Dragon, of King Arthur and Sir Lancelot, of Henry V, of the Spanish Armada, and more recently of colonial conquest.[12] British culture had long associated military activity with the abstract ideals of "honor" and "courage," and the PRC used these ideals to craft the British officer in Belgium as a masculinized man of honor and as protector of the weak. Believing it was important to "issue posters that would stimulate and not depress" the populace, the Publications Subcommittee of the PRC avoided more explicit reference to the atrocity stories, choosing to "set its face resolutely against depicting scenes of a gruesome character" and to focus in a more uplifting way on the character of the men who served.[13] Reviews of the poster campaign suggest this was a wise move, with some arguing that the most appealing posters were those possessing "a delightful geniality."[14]

If representations of Belgium initially set the gendered terms of the war, they were soon joined by representations of a feminized home front, also in need of protection. Appeals often linked the fate of Belgium to the fate of Britain, suggesting that delay in enlisting could result in the invasion of England. As arguments shifted from defending a feminized Belgium to defending a feminized Britain, the PRC codified patriotic masculinity by asking for "brave" and "stalwart" men "to guard our dear ones from the ruthless barbarity with which the German invaders have treated the Belgian people."[15] Such propaganda

MEG ALBRINCK

reminded readers of the sexual dimensions of this conflict and called men to step into roles that would protect the bodies of British women. Leaflets told men to "remember that if they got the chance the Germans would destroy British homes as ruthlessly as they have destroyed Belgian homes," and a variety of materials insisted that female loved ones were also at risk.[16]

This shift was a relatively simple one, especially after the German navy shelled the British coastal town of Scarborough in December 1914. The PRC published posters using language similar to that noted earlier, calling British men to "REMEMBER SCARBOROUGH" and to condemn the German attacks on "defenceless women and children" (PRC 29). One poster in particular clearly builds on representations of Belgium, showing a small girl holding an infant in front of a ruined house (fig. 46). Beneath, the caption reads: "It was the Home of a Working Man. Four People were killed in this House including the Wife, aged 58, and Two Children, the youngest aged 5. 78 Women & Children were killed and 228 Women & Children were wounded by the German Raiders."[17]

The caption is interesting for several reasons. First, it represents the bombing as an attack upon the home of the "Working Man," while refusing to acknowledge any male deaths. By visually presenting a small girl and ambiguously gendered infant as the sole survivors of the attack and by referring only to women and children in the casualty reports, the poster and historical accounts feminize the civilian population. This poster conflates the discourse of personal insult with the discourse of German barbarism in order to suggest that the attack marks a violation of women and children similar to that seen in Belgium. Not only has the man been insulted by being attacked in his home; his women and children have also been violated by the advance of German shelling missions and by the breakdown of the physical barriers between private and public spaces.

Fig. 46. F. Foxton, "Men of Britain! Will you stand this?" 1915. The poster depicts damage to "the Home of a Working Man. Four People were killed in this House including the Wife, aged 58, and Two Children, the youngest aged 5." Political Poster collection, UK 197, Hoover Institution Archives.

The homeless children and the damaged wall in this poster point toward a dual message of exposure and rape. The children are exposed to the dangers of the outer world, no longer protected by the walls of the home. The home and (by association) its women have been torn apart, with the penetration of the outer walls pointing to the violation of both the home and the women who dwell there. Thus the poster informs British men that the Germans are not just insulting the men themselves; they are physically assaulting their women as well. Not only do the safety and sanctity of women's bodies come to play an important role in recruiting British men, but such action also moves the Germans outside the acceptable role of Just Warrior and presents the British government with ample justification for counterattack.

MEG ALBRINCK

These recruiting materials used the same rhetoric to approach women as well, encouraging them to recognize the danger of their position by linking the fate of Belgium to their own fates and suggesting that women who hoped to remain pure and to protect their children needed to send their menfolk to the recruiting office. In March 1915 the PRC published both a poster (no. 69) and a leaflet (no. 31) addressed "To the Women of Britain," which asked the following questions:

1. You have read what the Germans have done in Belgium. Have you thought what they would do if they invaded this Country?
2. Do you realise that the safety of your home and children depends on our getting more men *now*?[18]

In this and other examples, the PRC used its central position to coordinate a recruiting blitz on the British people, maximizing its impact by using the same text in the large and more distant genre of posters as well as in the more personally addressed form of the leaflet. This technique was used primarily for posters that were banner style or text only, but a variation was done with the most popular recruiting posters. As Hiley reports, the eleven illustrated posters that were most appealing to the people were also distributed as cigarette cards in August 1915, a technique ensuring that the recruiting imperatives came off of the hoardings and directly into the hands and pockets of those the War Office needed most.[19]

As the war dragged on and disquieting reports from the trenches found their way back to England, material suggesting that enlistment would accomplish noble and heroic aims began to be questioned in significant ways. Some questioned the logic of these appeals.[20] Others criticized the approach taken. While the PRC's first posters seemed primarily crafted with reference to government decrees and calls to arms, posters as early as those produced in the winter of 1914–15 referenced a broader context, including reports in the newspapers (both respectable and sensational), propaganda, advertising, and jingoist poetry. For some, the PRC's reliance upon advertising styles was insulting.[21] "There they are, an appeal to the nation to risk its life and an appeal to the public to drink only So-and-So's wine-tonic cheek by jowl! . . . It vulgarises and depopularises the war to the enrichment of the least scrupulous of the parasites on industry. For every recruit drawn to the ranks by these fly-papers, ten have been disgusted and driven away, though perhaps without knowing why."[22] Critics were disgusted that "advertising for people to go to a war is just like advertising for people to buy a popular cigarette or a new boot polish."[23] For whatever reason, the discourse of patriotic honor was not powerful enough; resistance emerged as fewer and fewer men elected to fight for their nation.

Thus, while these campaigns can give us a glimpse of the cultural discourses on gender and patriotism, we should not confuse the campaigns' goals with their results. In other words, these materials should be read as proposed arguments for patriotic behavior, not as evidence reflecting the existence of such behavior nor as evidence reflecting the internalization of these arguments. The failure of the voluntary enlistment campaign as a whole helps demonstrate this point. The gradual decline of voluntary enlistment throughout 1915 and the eventual move to conscription in 1916 suggests that the recruiting campaigns were not as persuasive as the government had hoped. Despite the fact that almost four million British men had volunteered for service by 1916, this number was inadequate for a war against Germany, a nation that had mobilized eleven million by 1918. However, before instituting conscription, the government made one last attempt. Moving to a rhetoric of coercion in mid-1915, the PRC began to suggest

MEG ALBRINCK

that the unenlisted man would suffer social embarrassment and personal guilt if he did not serve.

"Be a Man": Deploying the Rhetorics of Shame and Coercion

While appeals to honor and duty may have been effective in the early months of the war, growing frustration with the British Army's losses resulted in declining enthusiasm for enlistment. Needing more recruits in early 1915, the PRC shifted its recruitment strategies, moving from appeals to the unenlisted man's sense of duty and honor to denigrations of his patriotism, masculinity, and virility. While the goal of both strategies was the same, the earlier campaigns were more positive in their celebration of the man who enlisted voluntarily; in contrast, the later campaigns are more pointed and judgmental in their critiques of the man who had not yet joined up.

From the campaign's very beginning, the PRC had reminded men that their status as citizens of the Empire could be questioned if they did not enlist. Leaflets told unenlisted men they were not "true Britons" if they did not heed the call of their country, and posters proclaimed that "the only road for an Englishman" was one of service, preferably service in a war-torn area like Belgium.[24] Recruiting pamphlets argued that "every true-born Englishman" needed to serve, with one leaflet directly calling, "Boys! Be British! Enlist Now."[25] The links between enlistment and national identity suggested that unenlisted men could not consider themselves true Englishmen.

Nor could they consider themselves men, later rhetoric insisted. At first this designation was merely implied, as the masculinity of the fighting man was held up for admiration and respect. Joining the armed forces, pamphlets and leaflets noted, allowed one to feel more masculine. A privately printed 1915 pamphlet called *Obey That Impulse Now* tells men to go and get a khaki uniform: "You'll feel that you are a man, and that you are playing your part in the world of men," the text insists.[26] Another 1915 pamphlet suggests that joining up will make men feel masculine in years to come: "Do your bit and when it's all over . . . you'll be able to say 'THANK GOD I TOO WAS A MAN.'"[27] These materials are generally positive, advertising the benefits of service; however, they also indirectly attack the masculinity of the noncombatant, suggesting that manhood is achieved only through enlistment.

It did not take long for the PRC to employ an even more direct strategy. As recruiting numbers continued to dwindle, the PRC began to direct the unenlisted man to consider his reputation with three groups: his children, his peers, and women in general. Often this type of appeal asked the man to consider his place in British tradition and to "maintain the honour and glory" of British manhood. One PRC poster calls men to "Justify the faith of your fathers, and earn the gratitude of your children."[28] Poet "J.C." uses the image of children in "Rally to the Flag" to tell men to carry on the tradition they have inherited: "Come at the call of your children! Remember that in years to come, / You must leave them a name as stainless as that which your fathers won."[29] Savile Lumley's famous poster depicts a worried father of two, faced with the question: "Daddy, what did *you* do in the Great War?" (fig. 47).[30] His son, playing with toy soldiers on the floor at his feet, is clearly undisturbed by the implications of "playing war." However, the man's troubled expression suggests that he is distressed by the idea of conflict and that he realizes his noncombatant past will not impress his children. Such appeals emphasized men's duty to their fathers and to their children and insisted that men earn their place in the patriarchal tradition.

However, as some have pointed out, many resented this strategy, feeling the approach was akin to "bullying by poster."[31] A less offensive approach (but a problematic one nonetheless)

Fig. 48. Laura Brey, "On Which Side of the Window are *You*?" 1917. Brey's poster is an appeal to American men. Yale Manuscripts and Archives Collection.

who delay, And—*The Others*. To which do you belong?" (PRC 103). In this poster, the unenlisted man becomes an unmentionable "Other," measured as lacking against the norm of the patriotic enlisted man.[34]

This "othering" was not a uniquely British technique. The same kinds of strategies appeared in other Allied documents, particularly American ones. A 1917 American poster employs the same binaries of space and gender to feminize the man who does not enlist (fig. 48). The American poster clearly echoes a PRC poster from March 1915, which positions a woman, a

refugee, and her child within the interior of the home as they watch the local battalion march off to war (fig. 49). Using a parallel structure, the American poster positions a man in civilian attire in the place originally occupied by women and children; outlined against an illuminated window, he looks passively at the marching troops and flowing American flag outside. The poster enacts visually what the slogans suggest syntactically: watching this parade is a passive, feminine activity, but participating in the parade is a masculine one. The interior private space is also marked feminine whereas the exterior public space is marked masculine. These divisions are

MEG ALBRINCK

confirmed by the poster's slogan—"On Which Side of the Window are *You*?"—words proposing that the private sphere is not an appropriate place for a man who should be serving his country.[35] Indeed, here and in other examples, the unenlisted man is feminized by his delay.

Such posters also suggested that the unenlisted man was physically more feminine than his military counterpart.[36] Like the man in the American poster, the civilian man in a July 1915 PRC poster is slighter in build than the enlisted men in the illustration (fig. 50). In contrast to the hard features and muscular builds of the other men, the suited man has slimmer shoulders, more delicate features, and a softer jawline. In fact, he is more closely aligned physically with the women and the boy scout in the scene. With his hands in his pockets, the businessman does nothing to contribute to the work that connects the laborer at the bottom of the poster to the military figures at the top; he is separate, not only by his inactivity, but also by his placement in the field. The man clearly cannot answer the poster's question affirmatively—he is not "in this" endeavor at all. In one fell swoop, he is feminized and infantilized by his build, and his patriotism is questioned.[37]

If unenlisted men were deemed feminine and unpatriotic, such discourse suggested, their sexuality became suspect as well. Even though the British soldier was portrayed as a noble man who would defend women's honor, he was also depicted as a distinctly virile male specimen. Peter Paret, Beth Irwin Lewis, and Paul Paret suggest that "the identification of virility with war was most explicit in countries that relied on volunteers."[38] Britain being one such country, British recruiting appeals and the media encouraged men to believe that they would be more sexually appealing to women if they were in uniform. H. C. Fischer and E. X. Dubois explore this phenomenon in their 1937 *Sexual Life during the World War*: "love of uniforms is closely related to the feminine worship of strength. A military uniform not only brings out to the best advantage the physical qualities of the wearer, but also suggests strength and courage, and in the eyes of most women it constitutes the hall mark of virility."[39] The cultural mythology surrounding the warrior emerges clearly in this passage. Although Fischer and Dubois's conclusions about the sexual desires of women are not well documented and tend at times toward misogyny, their arguments speak to the persistent romanticization of the soldier-hero. Even after the antiwar sentiments of the interwar years, the appearance of such works on the eve of the

Second World War suggests that the myth was hardy enough to be recalled when the enlistment of British men was once more required.

In the early months of the 1914–18 war especially, this argument took shape in the growing concern over "khaki fever," "outbreaks" of sexual activity that centered around military bases and training camps. As historian Angela Woollacott reports, "Young women, it seemed, were so attracted to men in military uniform that they behaved in immodest and even dangerous ways."[40] Jessie Pope wrote several poems celebrating the sexiness of men in uniform.[41] For example, in "Comrades in Arm-Lets," she notes that the popular uniform "takes the feminine heart by storm, / And wins soft glances, shy or warm." In "True Blue" she records the "coloured" history of women's affection for men in uniform, beginning with the "scarlet fever" over the king's uniform, moving into adoration of the "Heroic hue" of khaki, and ending with women's fondness for the most recent addition, air force blue: "feminine allies adore it," she remarks. In "The Beau Ideal," Pope notes that a man "Must be in shabby khaki dight" to attract the young Rose's attention. Popular culture deemed the actions of the men in khaki heroic; thus it was no surprise that women were attracted to the man in uniform. The British man was told in no uncertain terms: if he were not outfitted by the armed forces, he was not appealing—a direct challenge to his relations with the opposite sex.

The norms of heterosexuality linked the fighting man to sexual virility, a theme that surfaced frequently in material praising men in uniform. In addition to calling unenlisted civilian men "unpatriotic" and "unmasculine," recruiting posters also implied that such men "were not only cowardly, but also impotent."[42] Indeed, in the social sense, this was true to some degree. Organizations like the Baroness Orczy's Women's

Active Service League asked women to refrain from granting any attention to men who would not enlist. To join this league women were required to sign a form pledging the following: "At this hour of England's grave peril and desperate need I do hereby pledge myself most solemnly in the name of King and Country to persuade every man I know to offer his services to his country, and I also pledge myself never to be seen with any man who, being in every way fit and free for service, has refused to respond to his country's call."[43] Such forms equate military service with sexual soundness; if a man would not serve, he would not receive sexual attention.

This service league and its pledge form were not isolated examples. A 1915 leaflet asked "mothers" and "sweethearts" to think about why their men had not enlisted. If the woman was holding back her boy or lover out of concern for his safety, the leaflet argued, then "the shame of your Country rests upon YOU."[44] However, if the man could not be persuaded to go, then the leaflet counseled the woman to "*Discharge him* as unfit!" A poster of the same period makes the comparison even more direct, saying: "If your young man neglects his duty to his King and Country, the time may come when he will *neglect you*. Think it over—then ask him to join the army *to-day*."[45] This poster conjures the threat of neglect and advises women to view the unenlisted man's rejection of national demands as the potential rejection of their own; if he won't listen to the king, will he listen to his woman? Both of these publications insist that only those men who fight are worthy of sexual attention. Posters encouraging female viewers to judge unenlisted men as inferior, possibly even impotent, once more illustrate the twinned rhetorics of patriotism and gender.

Such logic resulted in the addition of appeals to women in recruiting materials, urging women to remind their men to act on the ideals of duty, responsibility, and honor. For women to

MEG ALBRINCK

be "true women," they needed to know their men were "true men." As one PRC leaflet explains, "It is a hard thing to part with son, or husband, or lover; but *no true woman* who thinks of what is at stake will hold her man back. *Women, urge your men to respond to the call.*"[46] True men are those who fight; if a man did not fight, his gender identity and that of the women in his life would be called into question. The discourse of gender thus encouraged each British citizen into roles and activities that ensured the performer's gendered identity and helped anchor the gender identities of his and her loved ones.

The most visible manifestation of this recruitment appeal was the "white feather" campaign. In August 1914 Admiral Charles Penrose Fitzgerald encouraged women to hand white feathers to every able-bodied man who was not wearing khaki, the idea being to humiliate the unlucky fellow into joining up.[47] The gesture often threw men into agonies of self-doubt. Some men would have served if able but were not admitted because of occupational or health reasons. Vera Brittain's uncle was an officer at a London bank and was not allowed to serve because of his status as an "indispensable." In a letter to her, he writes, "I am getting more and more ashamed of my civilian togs . . . and I shrink from meeting or speaking to soldiers or soldiers' relatives, and to take an ordinary walk on Sunday is abominable."[48] His embarrassment and shame are echoed in other literary works of the era, including F. Frankfort Moore's 1915 novel *The Romance of a Red Cross Hospital.*[49] The novel is primarily about a young woman who founds a hospital in memory of a lover she believes is dead, but the lover himself serves as an interesting figure in his inability to serve in the army. After he has been rejected by the military because of a heart condition, he reflects upon his "shame," calling his condition a "crime," and fearing the scorn and derision that will follow when he is labeled a wretch and a shirker.[50] Worried about how his fiancée will react, he anticipates "active jeers, definite abuse, sardonic sneers" and reports feeling impotent because of his inability to serve.[51] The narrator notes that patriotic women "affirmed in public that girls should feel it a disgrace to be seen talking to a man who was not wearing khaki, and patriotic rhymesters addressed their taunting indiscriminate doggerel to men who had not enlisted, insisting on their sweethearts cutting them dead. Coroners' inquests gave proof of good men goaded to suicide by patriotic persecution of this stamp."[52] In this passage, the narrator emphasizes that women are the ones who inflict punishment. Women insist that girls should only be seen with soldiers, and women write poetry insulting the civilian man.

The white feather campaign serves as an interesting counterpoint to the argument that posters and leaflets operated as the most famous recruiting tools of the time. Even though the white feather was at times given in error and its direct effects are virtually impossible to trace, it has gained near legendary status in historical and literary representations of recruiting techniques and the home front during the First World War.[53] However, it is important to note that the white feather—with all its cultural connotations—was "studiously avoided" by the PRC in its official posters.[54] This is somewhat atypical of the PRC, which frequently mined popular culture for images and slogans that could link its call for soldiers to some of the most easily recognizable figures and icons of the time. (Examples include posters using the famous "Scrap of Paper"; images of John Bull and St. George; and famous quotes from Shakespeare's *Macbeth*, Lord Kitchener, and the prime minister.)[55] Surely the iconography could have been easily and efficiently used; a poster employing a simple white feather on a green background would have spoken volumes to the men and women on the home front. However, the PRC chose to avoid associating itself with the more intensely criticized white feather campaign, even though the aims of both groups were the same. Perhaps they sensed that this would have been going too far. Indeed, Hiley argues that the later attempts at coercion through shame were much less popular than the earlier calls to noble and moral action. This unique illustration suggests a division between arguments overtly used by the government and those heavily utilized by private organizations.

In the formation of Kitchener's Army and in the transition to postwar peace, multiple sources united to offer the British man a portrait of masculine heroism. In the initial stages of the war his war service was aligned with humanitarian relief as he stood between the innocent Belgians and the savage Germans. This definition changed as the war progressed, becoming over time an exhibition of his masculinity and virility. Examining the progress of these developments offers insight into the negotiations that often frame dialogues between national and personal interests.

It is important to clarify once more that the existence of these messages does not necessarily prove that all men and women believed them. As mentioned, such messages reflect national ideals but not necessarily actual behavior. To read the rhetoric as evidence of historical reality is to ignore the resistance it inspired, whether in the more overt forms of nonenlistment and conscientious objection or in the more indirect guise of shell shock and malingering. As late as August 1915 a survey "revealed that 2,179,231 single men of military age (18 to 40) were not yet in the armed forces."[56] John Morton Osborne notes that there was no evidence that enlistment figures rose after the raid on Scarborough, nor even after reports of Belgian atrocities or the use of poison gas by the Germans.[57] That the posters and leaflets became more insulting as the war dragged on may reflect, as Dutton suggests, "the disappointment of the recruiting organisation in the failure of their audience to respond."[58] However, even if the posters did not produce the desired results, they were affecting popular conceptions of masculine duty and personal concepts of gender identity. Such arguments shaped individual perceptions of selfhood and identity during the war years and in the postwar years as well. As soldiers worked to match these images and arguments to the harsh realities of war, the resulting disjunction produced reactions ranging from simple disillusionment to more complex iterations of psychopathology.

Notes

1. E. M. Bryant, "His Call to Arms," *Windsor Magazine* 41 (May 1915): 817, 818. The poster referenced is probably that indexed as PST 0581 by the Imperial War Museum in London (hereafter IWM); it appeared in August 1914. The IWM's poster collection is housed in its Department of Art, and all posters mentioned refer to samples found in this collection. All IWM posters are assigned a four-digit number preceded by the poster code "PST." Posters issued by the PRC also have numbers indicating the sequence of production. Thus each PRC poster in the IWM collection has two numbers: the first is its PRC number, and the second is its IWM catalog number. To distinguish PRC posters from those issued by other sources, I have provided only the PRC number when available for all PRC posters and the IWM catalog number (PST) for all others. I rely throughout on the timeline of publication developed by Nicholas Hiley.

2. "2,500,000 Posters: Their Success as Recruiting Agents," *Daily Chronicle*, June 24, 1915, 3.

3. "Recruiting by Poster: A Remarkable Patriotic Campaign," *Windsor Magazine* 42 (June 1915): 3; "On the Hoardings," *Advertising World* (November 1915): 466.

4. Bryant, "His Call to Arms," 817.

5. Bryant, "His Call to Arms," 818.

6. Bryant, "His Call to Arms," 818.

7. War Office 106/367, Publications 6, available at the National Archives, Kew.

8. D. M. Richards, P328, Department of Documents, IWM.

9. L. Downer, 79/15/1, Department of Documents, IWM. This story is a rare example that correlates enlistment with a specific poster; in most cases it is virtually

impossible to determine which posters influenced which recruits. However, a combined analysis of distribution statistics and discussions of specific posters by the media or private citizens allows us to see which posters were seen most positively by the general public. Nicholas Hiley has developed a list of the fifteen posters that were printed most.

10. These stories were investigated by a government Committee on Alleged German Outrages, which published its findings in May 1915. The report, commonly known as the Bryce Report, is best remembered for its 300-page appendix, which includes accounts of destruction, assaults, mutilations, mass rapes, and executions of male civilians, Red Cross workers, prisoners, women, and children. While this report certainly established in British minds a barbaric image of the enemy Germans, it did not appear until very late in the PRC campaign and thus is not primarily responsible for the images that appeared in the poster art of the time.

11. War Office 106/367, Publications 7.

12. For further discussion, see essays by Jay Winter and Stephen Goebel in this volume.

13. War Office 106/367, Publications 4.

14. "Recruiting by Poster," 4; "2,500,000 Posters," 3.

15. PRC leaflet, 6, Pamphlet Collection, Department of Printed Books, IWM. The PRC issued two series of publications—one set called "leaflets" and the other called "pamphlets"—and each set is numbered separately. In general, the leaflets are 1–4 pages long, while the pamphlets are longer. All leaflets and pamphlets, unless otherwise noted, are from the Imperial War Museum's Pamphlet Collection.

16. PRC leaflet 7. See also PRC poster 39 and PRC leaflet 24.

17. "REMEMBER SCARBOROUGH," PRC poster 29; "It was the Home of a Working Man," PRC poster 51.

18. "To the Women of Britain," PRC poster 69; PRC leaflet 31.

19. Nicholas Hiley, "'Kitchener Wants You' and 'Daddy, What Did You Do in the Great War?': The Myth of British Recruiting Posters," *Imperial War Museum Review* 11 (1997): 42.

20. See C. F. G. Masterman, "Why the Workman Enlists," *Nation* (September 11, 1915): 762–63.

21. See Hiley, "'Kitchener Wants You,'" for a thorough discussion of this linkage.

22. "Notes of the Week," *New Age*, September 3, 1914, 411.

23. "Secrecy: The Public Is Told Nothing," *Daily Mail*, April 19, 1915, 4.

24. PRC leaflet 7; PST 0349.

25. PRC pamphlet 33; PRC leaflet 28.

26. *Obey That Impulse Now*, ([London?]: n.p., 1915), IWM Pamphlet Collection.

27. *Have YOU got a mother, a sister, a girl or a friend worth fighting for?* (London: June 1915), EPH C Recruitment, Documents Collection, IWM.

28. "Maintain the honour," PRC poster 18; "Justify the faith," PRC poster 68.

29. J. C. *Recruiting Poems Published during the Progress of the Great War 1914–1918*. Dungannon, U.K.: Tyrone, 1919.

30. "Daddy, what did *you* do in the Great War?" PRC poster 79. Hiley suggests that this poster did not capture the public's attention in the same way that it has captured that of contemporary critics. Arguing that the British people saw Lumley's approach as vulgarly tied to advertisement, Hiley notes that posters like this one "are famous because we want them to be famous, not because they give us access to the dominant emotions of the recruiting campaign" (55)—a point worth noting.

31. "Recruiting by Poster," 3.

32. "You're proud of your pals," PRC poster 43; "Do you feel happy?" PRC poster 62; Brangwyn, "At Neuve Chapelle," POS-Gt. Brit. B73, no. 14, Prints and Photographs Collection, Library of Congress.

33. "Why are *you* stopping?" PRC poster 27; "Think! Are you content?" PRC poster 38; "Come into the ranks," PRC poster 74; "It is far better to face the bullets," PRC poster, no number.

34. "There are three types of men," PRC poster 103.

35. Laura Brey, "Enlist. On Which Side of the Window are *You*?" Yale Manuscripts and Archives Collection; E. V. Kealey, "Women of Britain say—'*Go!*',", PRC poster 75.

36. The only exception to these constructions of male identity was the example of the laborer. In both figure 50 (PRC 112) and other posters (e.g., PRC 85c), the laborers' square jaws and muscular forearms mark them as visually similar to the soldiers.

37. "Are *you* in this?" PRC poster 112.

38. Peter Paret, Beth Irwin Lewis, and Paul Paret, eds., *Persuasive Images: Posters of War and Revolution from the Hoover Institution Archives* (Princeton: Princeton University Press, 1992), 50.

39. H. C. Fischer and E. X. Dubois, *Sexual Life during the World War* (London: Aldor, 1937), 61.

40. Angela Woollacott, "'Khaki Fever' and Its Control: Gender, Class, Age and Sexual Morality on the British Homefront in the First World War," *Journal of Contemporary History* 29 (1994): 325.

41. Jessie Pope, *Jessie Pope's War Poems* (London: Richards, 1915), and *More War Poems* (London: Richards, 1915).

42. Paret et al., *Persuasive Images*, 50.

43. Baroness Orczy, "To the Women of England, the Answer to 'What Can I Do?" *Daily Mail*, September 4, 1914.

MEG ALBRINCK

44. In Maurice Rickards and Michael Moody, *The First World War: Ephemera, Mementoes, Documents* (London: Jupiter, 1975), n.p.

45. "If your young man neglects his duty," PST 4903.

46. PRC leaflet 23.

47. For further readings of this campaign see Nosheen Khan, *Women's Poetry of the First World War* (Brighton, U.K.: Harvester, 1988), 79–83; and Nicoletta F. Gullace, "White Feathers and Wounded Men: Female Patriotism and the Memory of the Great War," *Journal of British Studies* 36 (1997): 178–206.

48. Vera Brittain, *Testament of Youth: An Autobiographical Study of the Years 1900–1925* (1933; repr., London: Virago, 1978), 307.

49. For examples, see poems by Oliver Wendell Holmes ("The Sweet Little Man") and Helen Hamilton ("The Jingo-Woman").

50. F. Frankfort Moore, *The Romance of a Red Cross Hospital* (London: Hutchinson, 1915), 133–34.

51. Moore, *Romance of a Red Cross Hospital*, 143, 148.

52. Moore, *Romance of a Red Cross Hospital*, 134–35.

53. See Gullace, "White Feathers," for a full bibliography of both contemporaneous and contemporary reactions to the campaign.

54. "Recruiting by Poster," 4.

55. "Scrap of Paper," PRC posters 7, 15, 17; John Bull, PRC 125; St. George, PRC 108; *Macbeth*, PRC 52; Lord Kitchener, PRC 21; prime minister, PRC 98.

56. John Gooch, "The Armed Services," in *The First World War in British History*, ed. Stephen Constantine, Maurice W. Kirby, and Mary B. Rose (London: Edward Arnold, 1995), 189.

57. Quoted in Philip Dutton, "Moving Images? The Parliamentary Recruiting Committee's Poster Campaign, 1914–1916," *Imperial War Museum Review* 4 (1989): 56.

58. Dutton, "Moving Images?" 52.

Iconography of Injury: Encountering the Wounded Soldier's Body in American Poster Art and Photography of World War I

World War I produced injury on a previously unimaginable scale. Along the Western Front—the vast network of entrenchments and redoubts that snaked its way from the Atlantic Ocean to the Swiss border—the sight, smell, feel, and taste of opened bodies was ubiquitous. The dead hung on nets of barbed wire, rotted half-buried in shell craters. Some soldiers were obliterated entirely, atomized in the creeping artillery barrages that preceded infantry assaults. Others were violently dismembered, their limbs, skulls, fingers, even teeth transformed into deadly projectiles. The widespread introduction of new, increasingly efficient killing and maiming technologies resulted in the devastation of an entire generation of European youth. In fifty-two months of bloody fighting, the war would claim the lives of more than 9.5 million men. Twenty million more were severely wounded, while 8 million veterans returned to their homes permanently disabled because of injury and disease.[1]

Although American casualties paled in comparison to those of other nations, they were by no means insignificant. Over the course of U.S. involvement in World War I (April 6, 1917–November 11, 1918), more than fifty thousand "doughboys" died from combat-related injuries (a figure even more horrific if we recall that U.S. forces only spent about two hundred days in the field). Tuberculosis, influenza, and other infectious diseases killed sixty thousand more, many of whom perished in training camps or on transport ships long before reaching European shores.[2] For the survivors the physiological and psychological effects of the Great War would linger well beyond its end. Over 224,000 Americans were wounded in battle, the vast majority by shrapnel from German artillery.[3] Moreover, nearly all of the 1.3 million Americans who saw action suffered some kind of injury, from routine maladies such as "trench foot" and muscle fatigue to more serious ailments resulting from gas attacks and relentless bombardment. By the end of 1919, 179,578 army servicemen had been officially discharged because of disease and nonbattle injuries, and over 930,000 servicemen applied for disability benefits within the first five years of the war's end.[4] Despite rapid advances in military medicine and transportation, more than two hundred thousand American veterans remained permanently disabled as of 1920.[5] Countless others would suffer from undiagnosed psychological ailments for decades after returning home.

An ocean away from the fighting, few American civilians encountered (were able to touch, smell, hear, see) their nation's war-wounded bodies in the flesh. Throughout World War I, many in the United States remained sheltered from the realities of wartime injury to an extent that would have been difficult, if not impossible, in the urban centers of Europe. Unlike their European counterparts, the bulk of America's injured soldiers were not shipped home until after the Armistice was signed. Even then, many of America's most severely wounded—despite spending months, sometimes years, in rehabilitation centers—were never fully reintegrated into civil society. Thousands were permanently cloistered in military hospitals and government-run soldiers' homes, hidden away from public eyes.

As a result, both during World War I and afterward, Americans' encounters with wounded and disabled soldiers were largely mediated through cultural productions, especially poster art, magazine illustration, and photography. While the Committee on Public Information, the U.S. government's propaganda arm during World War I, rigorously censored photos of America's dead and dying throughout much of the conflict, there was no shortage of injury-themed visual culture.[6] Indeed, in the absence of the soldiers themselves, images of woundedness disproportionately shaped Americans' understanding of the social and political meanings of war-produced impairment. Besides recovering the contexts, contents, and conventions of the Great War's iconography of injury, this essay examines how the wounded soldier's body was constantly reimagined in American visual culture. As we shall see, propagandists, charity organizations, rehabilitation advocates, and antiwar activists all employed images of woundedness, although to very different ends. Collectively, they offered a diversity of interpretations of wartime injury and America's obligations to its disabled veterans. With notable exceptions, however, they also managed to decontextualize soldiers' injuries—to detach them from both the life struggles of disabled soldiers and the historical context in which they came into being.

Overall, I have chosen to focus on three broad constructions of war-injured soldiers in World War I–era visual culture. The first, manifested most prominently in American Red Cross membership posters and magazine art, presented a sentimental vision of combat injury, portraying the wounded soldier as a helpless victim in order to spur donations on his behalf. The second, often figured in rehabilitation poster photography, represented a markedly different vision of the injured soldier's body. Here the wounded soldier emerged as a self-reliant actor, ready (with the help of prosthetics and vocational training) to resume his normative role as a productive citizen. I conclude by briefly examining a pair of antiwar photo albums of the 1920s and 1930s. In contrast to wartime propagandists, antiwar photo editors mobilized fears about bodily disfigurement in order to critique the brutality of modern war. Although this study is in no way exhaustive, I believe it offers a representative view of strategies for imagining the wounded soldier in American poster art and photography of World War I. Furthermore, it shows how the wounded soldier's body figured as a site of ideological and aesthetic contestation both during the war and beyond.

Sentimental Bodies: The Wounded Soldier in American Red Cross Posters

In his now classic study *Posters of the First World War* (1968), Maurice Rickards locates images of the war-wounded in the second stage of what he deems the "basic structure of the apparatus of persuasion." According to Rickards, government calls to aid wounded soldiers (along with orphans, injured civilians, and refugees) invariably came in the middle of World War I propaganda campaigns—after the mobilization of men and money, and before the appeal for women workers and economic sacrifice on the home front.[7] The identification of wounded soldiers' bodies with those of orphans, injured civilians, and refugees is significant, in that all four groups were routinely (and interchangeably) presented as helpless victims of wartime tragedy. Moreover, as Rickards points out, the dissemination of images of hurt bodies (especially those of soldiers) had to be carefully controlled. Released too early in the conflict, they might lead the viewer into a state of "premature despondency," fearful that the war would be impossible to win.

Issued too late, they might fail to convey the government's appreciation of wartime sacrifice.[8]

As Rickards's own book documents, pictorial images of wounded or permanently disabled soldiers were integrated into the propaganda campaigns of all of the belligerent nations. In the United States they were showcased most frequently in the recruitment posters and magazine art of the American Red Cross. It should be no surprise that of all wartime organizations, the Red Cross would make the greatest use of imagery of woundedness. According to its congressional charter, the American Red Cross had an obligation to "furnish volunteer aid to the sick and wounded of armies in time of war."[9] Before the United States' entry into World War I, the organization worked extensively with international branches (including those of the Central Powers) to provide emergency assistance to both civilians and combatants. As early as September 1914 the relief ship *Red Cross* had set out from New York Harbor with physicians, nurses, and medical supplies for the beleaguered populations of Europe. Over the next four years American Red Cross volunteers and administrators set up hospitals, cantonments, and camps across both fronts to serve the needs of the wounded and civilian refugees.

With the United States' entry into the war, both the size and the daily operation of the American Red Cross changed radically. On May 10, 1917, Woodrow Wilson replaced the organization's largely female leadership with a group of businessmen, known henceforth as the War Council. By June the Red Cross had embarked on an ambitious publicity campaign to swell its membership ranks and raise an unprecedented 100 million dollars. Spearheaded by the War Finance Committee and its publicity advisor Ivy L. Lee, often called the "Father of Public Relations," the campaign established a pattern that would be followed over the course of the war. Public speakers,

JOHN M. KINDER

promotional films, billboard advertisements, electric signs, parades, public auctions, and posters extolled the virtues of Red Cross work, glorified Red Cross volunteers, and chided those who failed to sacrifice for the greater good.[10]

Under the influence of Ivy Lee and other corporate leaders, Red Cross poster art rigidly adhered to conventions and standards established by prewar advertising firms. Commercial poster artists had fine-tuned a variety of techniques for using pictorial imagery to stimulate desire, mold popular opinions, and mobilize public actions. Industry handbooks stressed simple, eye-catching designs, coupled with bold color schemes and memorable taglines. In addition, posters were supposed to arouse the viewer's sympathy by deploying "human interest" imagery: in other words, images designed to stimulate nostalgia or a sense of familiarity. Advertisers were explicitly warned against using "negative suggestion" to move merchandise. According to one text, poster art should avoid arousing "a feeling of distaste, fear, or horror" in the viewer (i.e., the sort of emotions that pictures of "disfigured hands and feet" might produce). Far more effective, advertisers believed, were pleasurable images that would leave viewers with positive memories of the product or idea they were attempting to sell.[11]

Advertisers' strategy of trafficking only in uplifting or wholesome images played a pivotal role in shaping the depiction of wounded soldiers in Red Cross poster art. Albert Sterner's "We Need You" (1918; fig. 51), for example, is typical in its efforts to frame wartime injury in the most nonthreatening context possible. His head wrapped in an immaculate white bandage, his eyes gently closed, Sterner's soldier appears to be resting peacefully. The poster offers no hint that he is suffering from his injuries (or that he ever did). In fact, other than the bandage, which was the most common signifier of wartime woundedness, there is little suggestion that the soldier has incurred

Fig. 51. Albert Sterner, "We need you," 1918. As in most Red Cross posters, the patient is overshadowed by a nurse tending to his every need. Political Poster collection, US 160, Hoover Institution Archives.

any bodily damage whatsoever. As in most Red Cross posters, the patient is overshadowed by a number of motherly Red Cross nurses tending to his every need. His body has been removed from the company of men (the gendered sphere long associated with war making) and transplanted to a convalescent space inhabited only by women. Although soldiers continued to represent powerful social ideals of manhood throughout the war years, this one is a silent, even passive figure, wholly dependent upon his female caregivers. Lacking the muscular sensuality so common in representations of America's fighting men, he has also been thoroughly de-eroticized, resembling less a grown man than a helpless child.

Like the most popular Red Cross poster of World War I, A. E. Foringer's Pieta-themed "The Greatest Mother in the World" (ca. 1917), which features a Red Cross giantess cradling a diminutive wounded soldier in her arms, Sterner's "We Need You" recasts nurses' war work within the gendered conventions of maternal care. More important, the poster (as with most Red Cross art) is designed to appeal solely to the noninjured; that is, those who managed to escape the war without bodily harm. The viewer, perhaps a potential volunteer, is meant to recognize herself in the bourgeois assistant or in the white-robed nurses, not in the wounded soldier. Although such posters were intended to convey a clear message in a matter of seconds, this image encourages a more leisurely contemplation. Absent is the sense of awkwardness, distress, and guilt that accompanies—and renders traumatic—most encounters of the nondisabled with the bodily impaired. Here, the gaze of the wounded soldier is averted, leaving him vulnerable to (unnoticed) inspection. Moreover, the soldier himself is less an enfleshed being (who bleeds, cries, stinks, and suffers) than a flat caricature, endowed only with the ability to cultivate pity in those who view him.

While Red Cross poster art must allude to the mutilation of soldiers in war in order to incite donations, ultimately it works to keep the viewer's potential fear of unwhole bodies at bay. One prominent strategy for doing so involves presenting war-related disability within what Rosemarie Garland Thomson has called a "visual rhetoric of sentimentality." Sentimental images, argues Thomson, often establish the relation between the viewer and the viewed in spatial terms. By placing disabled figures below the viewer's gaze, they construct an impaired subject as "sympathetic victim or helpless sufferer needing protection or succor." This technique diminishes disabled figures in order to evoke compassion (and monetary contributions) from the viewer.[12] In the context of Red Cross art, the sentimental provides a visual framework in which seeing injury is not only socially acceptable but the duty of all good-hearted Americans. However, it is important to recognize that sentimental images, though frequently used to garner support for disability charities, are not designed to destigmatize the bodily impaired. On the contrary, they are only effective if disabled figures remain powerless, dependent upon the benevolence of the nondisabled viewer.

Other representational strategies commonly employed in Red Cross posters also work to mitigate the viewer's unease when encountering wartime injury. One popular technique entails stripping the wounded men of all nationalist markers. In posters such as Albert Herter's "In the Name of Mercy Give" (ca. 1917), which once again depicts a motherly nurse clutching a languid wounded soldier, the identity of the patient is strikingly ambiguous. He is not a member of a particular army but a generic figure whose anonymity distances him from the viewer's social and political history. Even more frequent, however, is the practice of omitting all tangible evidence of bodily injury. In Red Cross poster art, the actual site of injury—the fleshly location where war has left the soldier's body anomalous, scarred, torn, empty—is always hidden from view. The soldier's injured or disabled state is signified through the circulation of icons (crutches, bandages, closed eyes, reclining postures, etc.), but the wound itself is denied signification.

The combined effect of these strategies—sentimentalizing the wounded, keeping them anonymous, and hiding evidence of injury—is to disassociate the wounded soldier's current appearance from the war itself. Indeed, even when the war is directly referenced, the battlescapes of Red Cross posters bear little resemblance to the miserable environment in which so many American soldiers lived, fought, and died. Often the field of battle is sterile and empty, save for the bandaged soldier himself. Sometimes wounded soldiers are simply framed against a field of white, with few visual clues to suggest that their injuries are a result of combat. Furthermore, Red Cross poster artists ignore (or intentionally misrepresent) one of the most salient aspects of World War I: that soldiers were injured en masse. In the densely populated trenches of both sides, getting wounded (or killed) was invariably a group activity.

This estrangement from the historical experience of the war is further compounded by the practice of placing the wounded in allegorical contexts. In many war posters and illustrations, wounded soldiers are aided by symbolic figures from America's national mythos. Typical of this trend would be Charles Dana Gibson's "Columbia's Greatest Task," published in the September 1917 issue of the *American Red Cross Magazine*, depicting a flag-draped Columbia helping a neatly bandaged soldier away from the scene of battle.[13] One month later the newspaper illustrator Oscar Cesare would offer a similar lithograph, this time replacing Columbia with a stern-faced Uncle Sam.[14] However, the wounded soldier's interaction with the imaginary was not limited to nationalist icons. Many posters and illustrations depict struggles between Red Cross nurses and Death itself— usually personified as the Grim Reaper—over the bodies of injured men. By figuring wounded soldiers within a visual vocabulary of legend and myth, all such images further remove the viewer from the mechanized carnage taking place across the Atlantic. They also make the suffering of actual wounded soldiers seem that much more unreal.

Of course, sentimental images of wartime injury were not limited to Red Cross poster art. The Salvation Army, the Knights of Columbus, and other organizations authorized nearly identical depictions of wounded soldiers, as did the propaganda agencies of all of the belligerent nations. Publications such as the *American Red Cross Magazine* regularly featured images from allied poster campaigns, many of which included equally gauzy depictions of the war-wounded. Yet it is important to distinguish the images discussed thus far from those that actually allude to disabled soldiers' lives after the war. In most American Red Cross posters, there is no mention of the fact that war-produced impairment—or, more specifically, public prejudice against such impairment—would leave many wounded soldiers economically and socially disadvantaged. Unlike in Europe, where similar images of the wounded (especially the blind) were regularly mobilized to raise money for veterans' relief, the link between woundedness and dependency was downplayed in the United States. Only after the war were images of the wounded systematically used by the Disabled American Veterans and other organizations as a lever for securing compensation for wartime injury. However, even these tended to reaffirm bodily impairment as the root "cause" of soldiers' disabled status and not, as many disability scholars would argue, their thwarted access to the resources of civil society.[15]

Independent Bodies: Wounded Soldiers in Rehabilitation Photography

Fortunately, not all Americans were satisfied with sentimental attitudes toward disabled people, especially toward the war-wounded. Throughout the late 1910s a growing coalition of Progressive reformers, social scientists, and business leaders urged the public to adopt "a new psychology toward the handicapped," one that approached the problem of the wounded soldier (as it came to be called) in a rational and systematic manner.[16] The Progressives' solution was in many ways revolutionary. Rejecting the notion that wounded soldiers were permanent charity cases, they called for the physical and social rehabilitation of all injured veterans, with the goal of returning as many as possible to their prewar lives. Although rehabilitationist impulses predated World War I, the mass carnage

JOHN M. KINDER

in Europe prompted a renewed interest in providing the war-wounded not only with immediate medical care but with "physical reconstruction," vocational training, and career counseling. Rehabilitation was supposed to offer disabled veterans a more meaningful social existence by fully reintegrating them into civil society. According to one advocate, rehabilitation "goes far beyond the mere undertaking to return the war-cripple to useful employment. It looks toward bringing him back into our common life with a soul not only undiscouraged, but strengthened; with capabilities developed, if possible, beyond what they were before he sacrificed himself for us all; with the happy consciousness that he holds his place in his own right, by his own ability."[17]

No organization did more to publicize the goals of rehabilitation than the Institute for Crippled and Disabled Men, founded in New York City in 1917. Under the direction of Douglas C. McMurtrie, a prominent historian of printing and a spokesman on behalf of the disabled, within the first year of the war's end the Institute published more than fifty different pamphlets, broadsheets, and monographs on rehabilitation work. With the help of AT&T and other private utilities, it distributed six million copies of McMurtrie's flyer "Your Duty to the War Cripple" in customers' phone and gas bills in 1918 alone. Between 1917 and 1920 Institute staffers gave over three hundred public lectures and lantern slide shows on the movement to rehabilitate America's fighting men. The Institute also distributed a set of eighteen 28 by 42-inch posters offering photographic evidence of rehabilitation's ability to transform the war-wounded from helpless cripples into productive citizens.[18]

Unlike the Red Cross posters discussed earlier, Institute posters (along with journals devoted to the rehabilitation of wounded soldiers) largely eschew illustration or advertising graphics in favor of stark black-and-white photography. This choice is significant. Since the development of the daguerreotype in 1839, photography had played a critical role in solidifying the professionalized discourses of the new social sciences and establishing the body as a site of technical intervention. Medical, public health, and rehabilitation discourses all relied heavily on photography to justify their own practices and to support their claims of expertise.[19] Indeed, in the wake of World War I, photography became the primary medium for displaying the rehabilitated wounded soldier to the nondisabled public.

Whether found in Institute posters, hospital newspapers, or medical journals, rehabilitation photography was meant to appeal to the war-injured viewer and those in contact with him on a regular basis. This goal had an indelible impact on both the content and representational strategies found in rehabilitation photography. Common to all rehabilitation photography, for example, is a rejection of sentimentality. Unlike most Red Cross art, rehabilitation photography presents the wounded soldier on the same spatial plane as the viewer. In many cases the wounded soldier actually meets the viewer's gaze head on, establishing him not as an object of pity but as the viewer's social equal. Sometimes the wounded soldiers depicted in rehabilitation photography seem to be aware of the camera's presence. The majority are posed to highlight their bodily independence, their ability to work, play, and care for themselves without the help of others. Those who fail to meet the viewer's gaze simply appear to be too busy to concern themselves with the stares of others.

As with all rehabilitation photography, the Institute of Crippled and Disabled Men's poster campaign legitimates a narrative of bodily and cultural reconstruction, a transformation of both the corpus of the wounded man and the general public's

　　　　　　　　　　　　　　　　　　JOHN M. KINDER

Fig. 52. Institute for Crippled and Disabled Men, "Future Members of the Fourth Estate," 1919. Prints and Photographs Division, LC-USZC4-7375, Library of Congress.

attitudes toward disabled people. Combining "realistic" photographic images and seemingly dispassionate captions, Institute posters offer a novel way of seeing the war-injured—not as helpless victims or even icons of courage but as independent workers, unhampered by bodily impairments. In posters such as "Future Members of the Fourth Estate" (1919) (fig. 52), which contains images of war amputees learning to operate a monotype caster in a print shop, wounded soldiers are depicted as self-sufficient, capable of supporting themselves with their own labor. In contrast to Red Cross art, which often presents the wounded as incapacitated or unconscious,

Institute posters show wounded soldiers as upright and active, without the need of feminine supervision and care. Although women played a critical role in the rehabilitation of wounded soldiers, they are largely absent from rehabilitation photography. This absence is crucial to the success of rehabilitation discourse in severing the popular association between wartime injury and physical dependency—an association reiterated in Red Cross art.[20] By transporting wounded soldiers from the feminine sphere of convalescence to the masculine sphere of the industrial or agricultural workplace, Institute posters re-insert them into the gendered hierarchy of American social relations. Furthermore, rehabilitation photography attempts to teach wounded soldiers (and the noninjured public) to re-imagine the war-injured body as functionally, if not constitutionally, "whole."

In doing so, rehabilitation photography relies upon one of the key tenets of liberal individualist ideology—the link between bodily autonomy, masculinity, and socioeconomic independence.[21] With the rise of the modern factory in particular, men's abilities to perambulate, work long hours, and discipline their movements were intimately tied to their economic viability. Bodies that could not be regulated or standardized—including those of earlier generations of disabled veterans—often found few opportunities on the scientifically managed factory floor. Rehabilitation photography offers visual "proof" that the value of the rehabilitated soldier's labor had not been diminished by wartime injury. Moreover, in reassuring the disabled viewer of his own secure future, rehabilitation photography allows the disabled soldier to recognize himself not as a suffering body but as an independent agent with unimpeded access to market relations. This (mis)recognition also extends to nondisabled viewers, who are given a visual grammar to reimagine the disabled soldiers they might encounter in everyday life.

The fantasy of the functionally "complete" body exhibited in rehabilitation photography is often dependent upon the presence of organ-extending technologies—machines designed not only to supplement the injured soldier's corporeal "deficiencies" but to extract untapped labor power from the wounded body itself. Unlike Red Cross art, rehabilitation photography is saturated with images of machines. Some photographs feature the instruments designed to restore the wounded soldier's body to a state approaching biophysical "normalcy" (e.g., braces, exercise equipment, crutches, prosthetic hooks, masks, glass eyes). Others foreground the industrial machinery used by rehabilitated soldiers once they have reentered the workplace. The technophilia manifested in rehabilitation photography was common throughout postwar rehabilitationist discourse, which placed great faith in the ability of technology (and the experts who manipulate it) to make up for what the injured body "lacked." Writing in the government-sponsored rehabilitation journal *Carry On* in 1918, the author Herbert Kaufmann opined, "How much of a body does a man need to earn a living in this year of wheels and wires? . . . What with telephones, elevators, motor cars and like couriers and carriers, a respectable remnant of the human frame can overcome most of the handicaps of mutilation."[22]

In rehabilitation photography the wounded soldier emerges as part of an assemblage, a machine system, which extends beyond the injured body itself. Some men's bodies appear to be plugged into freestanding machines, as in the Institute poster "No Longer Out of a Job" (1919), which depicts amputees operating a tin cutter and a fountain pen maker. More often, however, the wounded soldier's body is fitted to make itself more suitable for mechanomorphic interfaces, new linkages between bodies and machines, flesh and metal. According to the caption of "At Work Again/Back to the Farm" (1919), an Institute poster showing French amputees engaged in both industrial and agricultural labor, "Physical handicaps are made up for so far as possible by modern artificial appliances—'Working Prostheses' they are called—which replace the missing limb. Men in the mechanical trades are fitted with chucks in which can be fitted interchangeably the various tools of their calling." Rehabilitation photography presents prosthetic technologies (whether located on the body itself or independent of their users) as capable of making the body "complete" again, if not even more functional than it was before injury. Never mentioned, of course, are the body-reducing technologies (i.e., rifle and artillery systems, machine guns, barbed wire, mines) responsible for the soldiers' mental and physical impairments in the first place.

Despite their obvious enthusiasm, advocates of rehabilitation recognized that images of wounded soldiers were potentially disturbing to viewers unused to looking at war-injured bodies. Rarely do poster makers or journal editors allow images of rehabilitation to stand alone, to address the viewer without uplifting captions to rein in possible misreadings of the photographic messages. Indeed, in its attempt to mitigate the viewer's possible uneasiness about looking at injured soldiers, rehabilitation photography shares much in common with Red Cross poster and magazine art. Rehabilitation photography regularly employs the same signifiers of woundedness (immaculate white bandages, crutches, etc.) as found in sentimental depictions of the war-injured soldiers. With the obvious exception of amputees, who were overrepresented in both photographic and pictorial depictions of America's war-wounded, soldiers featured in rehabilitation photography display little evidence of wartime injury. Wounds are strategically kept out of view; at most, one only sees an empty sleeve, never an actual stump, scar, or gaping orifice. Rehabilitation photography also avoids all imagery that suggests the pain of wartime injury—or the mental and physical anguish that accompanies the rehabilitation process itself. By displaying only rehabilitation's success stories, moreover, rehabilitation photography estranges the viewer from the experiences of soldiers whose bodies were so mangled that rehabilitation was hardly an option. Equally lost in the photographic record of rehabilitation are those whose bodies, even when made "functional," would never be socially acceptable—in particular, soldiers with facial wounds, burns, or scarification from disease.

In its attempt to distinguish impairment from disability, rehabilitation photography imbues the wounded soldier with a sense of dignity, even normalcy, that is absent from much of World War I propaganda. Although some images direct the viewer's attention to the mark of bodily anomaly (an extended prosthetic hook, the absent-presence of a lost limb), others give little hint that their subjects are functionally impaired. And yet, rehabilitation photography remains complicit in the mass production of injury and, as such, works to make modern war socially acceptable. Whereas Red Cross art, for the most part, ignores war's inscription on the soldier's body, rehabilitation photography narrates the erasure of wartime injury—the reconstruction of the wounded soldier's body into a productive worker-machine. Photographs of rehabilitation are offered as evidence that even those who suffered the most from war-produced injury could leave their pain behind and rejoin the nondisabled as if nothing had happened. In their effort to destigmatize bodily nonconformity, images of rehabilitation alienate the viewer from the trauma of wartime disability and its long-term effects. Read in the context of postwar rehabilitationist discourse, such images suggest (incorrectly, it turns out) that wartime injury might leave America's soldiers physically altered but not socially or economically disadvantaged.

Horrific Bodies: Wounded Soldiers in Antiwar Photo Albums

As memories of World War I turned increasingly bitter, both Red Cross art and rehabilitation photography found themselves in competition with a different visual interpretation of the wounded soldier's body—one meant to shock and disgust the viewer into rejecting modern war altogether. By the late 1920s and early 1930s, both Europeans and Americans were deeply cynical about the viability of modern war making as a means of conflict resolution. Corruption within the Veterans' Bureau, which was charged with overseeing all rehabilitation programs, and the skyrocketing costs of medical care for America's permanently disabled veterans, further soured the public on the Great War's legacies. This atmosphere was sympathetic to pacifists and other critics of modern war, who soon began to distribute photographic images of the war's horrors on a mass scale. Never as widely disseminated as Red Cross poster art and rehabilitation photography, such images were nonetheless a powerful tool of antiwar activists throughout the interwar years, especially as threats of new conflicts loomed on the horizon. Wielding photographs of wartime casualties, antimilitarists hoped to remind future generations of what was easily forgotten: that, in Elaine Scarry's words, "the main purpose and outcome of war is injury."[23]

Perhaps the most famous collection of such images, *War against War!* (*Kriege dem Kriege!*), was assembled by Ernst Friedrich, a German conscientious objector and founder of Berlin's International Anti-War Museum, in 1924.[24] Originally published in four languages (German, English, French, and Dutch), *War against War!* is a montage of more than one hundred and eighty photographs—along with other visual artifacts—detailing the

JOHN M. KINDER

barbarism of modern conflict. Among the photographs are images of mass graves, razed forests, skeletal victims of disease, and mutilated soldiers and civilians. Many of the most frightening images were drawn from German medical archives, where they had been precluded from public circulation both during the war and after. Friedrich's editorial strategy throughout *War against War!* involves juxtaposing photographs of wartime carnage (including images of dead, maimed, and disfigured bodies) with patriotic discourse and propaganda images. The effect is to expose—with devastating irony—the lies and moral hypocrisy that allowed the war to flourish. In the face of the human, cultural, and environmental consequences of World War I documented in the book, militarist propaganda appears not only misguided but obscene. In Friedrich's words, the book provides "a picture of War objectively, true and faithful to nature."[25] Its photographs of opened bodies—some hardly recognizable as human—are offered as indisputable evidence of the need to abolish war in the future.

Similar in both form and content is *The Horror of It: Camera Records of War's Gruesome Glories,* a lesser known though equally powerful photo album first published in the United States in 1932.[26] The book was edited by Frederick A. Barber, author of the later antiwar primer *"Halt!" Cry the Dead* (1935), and prefaced with introductions by modernist theologian Harry Emerson Fosdick and feminist Carrie Chapman Catt. Its ninety-one photographic images, drawn from military archives in the United States, France, Great Britain, and Germany, are interspersed with antiwar poetry and bordered with acidic captions meant to unmask the discrepancies between jingoistic platitudes and the misery World War I produced. According to Fosdick, the book is "a hard-headed answer to the common charge made against peacemakers that they are soft-headed idealists."[27] An antidote to romanticized visions of modern war, *The Horror of It* is intended to "stop the mouths of those who think war a moral tonic, or a glorious tradition, or an inspiration to useful patriotism, or a way of advancing human progress."[28]

Like its German counterpart, *The Horror of It* is a catalog of war's destruction, a visual chronicle of war's capacity to unmake the civilized world. Beginning with a photograph of an unattached hand covered in dirt and surrounded by upturned roots, the collection documents the mass bloodshed and material devastation of World War I in ghastly detail. Images of bombed-out cemeteries, broken monuments, mountains of empty shell casings, slaughtered cavalry horses, and war-ravaged cities are positioned side by side with photographs of war refugees, starving children, executed prisoners, and open graves. The most repellent images, however, tend to focus on the war-mangled bodies of soldiers. In "A Mother's Son," for example, a dead soldier is pictured on a capsized table. His right arm is shredded, his chest is torn open, and what looks like intestines are snaking out of a hole in his side. Some photographs reveal the soldier's body in a state of decomposition, covered in insects or rotting in abandoned dugouts. Others show only the skeletal remains of soldier's bodies—their skin hardened, their bones bleached in the sun.

War's injured survivors are prominently featured in *The Horror of It* as well, although they bear little resemblance to the representations disseminated during wartime. Throughout the collection, images of soldiers' facial wounds, gross bodily disfigurement, scars, and naked stumps—all of which were avoided in Red Cross art and rehabilitation photography—are common. Several photographs of the wounded, including the haunting "Living Death" (fig. 53), are also found in *War against War!*, evidence of their widespread iconicity. This particular image shows a soldier's face in profile, his nose, teeth, lips, and upper palette having been sheared away by shrapnel. Such images

JOHN M. KINDER

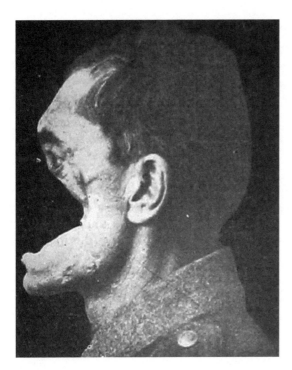

Fig. 53. "Living Death," from Frederick A. Barber's *The Horror of It: Camera Records of War's Gruesome Glories* (New York: Brewer, Warren, and Putnam, 1932).

force the viewer to confront what modern war does to human flesh—to acknowledge that the meeting of technology and the soldier's body is not always benign but can be traumatic, destructive, and frequently disabling.

This applies especially to photographs intended to expose the false promises of rehabilitationists. In the ironically titled "Reconstruction," seven former soldiers, their faces mangled almost beyond recognition, stare blankly at the camera lens (some are missing their eyes). Though it shares much in common aesthetically with rehabilitation photographs, the overall effect of the image is decidedly different from those reproduced in Institute posters. Its purpose is to terrify viewers, not reassure them. Although we might pity these men, the photograph itself suggests little we can do to help. War's inscription on these veterans' faces is permanent. Despite advances in prosthetic masks and skin grafts, such men would never be able to slip unnoticed back into society; they would always remain outsiders, hideous reminders of a war most people wanted to forget.

In the text's multiple introductions, contributors to *The Horror of It* proclaim an abiding faith in the power of photographic technology to cut through distorting ideologies. Carrie Chapman Catt optimistically suggests that with the proliferation of photographic images, war's cruelty can no longer be disguised. "Blessings on the camera," she writes, "which now for the first time in the history of the world, provides the means of teaching youth the terrible, undeniable facts of war. The camera tells the truth, speaks all languages and can cross all frontiers."[29] According to the book's creators, photography offers an unmediated transposition of historical reality: it lays bare "war's plain, stark, ugly meaning."[30]

Such claims notwithstanding, Barber's placement of images, captions, and poems is carefully orchestrated in order to maximize antiwar critique. One typical strategy is to foreground the destruction of the wounded body by offering "before" and "after" photographs on opposing pages, contrasting images of corporeal integrity with ones of ruptured, diseased, maimed, and dead soldiers' bodies. This compositional technique, common to both *War against War!* and *The Horror of It*, is best exemplified in the placement of two photographs near the end of Barber's collection. The first, captioned "Those Who Went," shows a group of smiling German soldiers, waving goodbye from a departing train; the corresponding photograph, "And Came Back," displays a row of amputees in bathing suits, their stumped legs fully exposed to the viewer. Their facial expressions suggest that they are disgruntled, having lost the sort of patriotic spirit exhibited when they went off to war. It is doubtful, of course, that the two photographs show the same group of men. However, this fact detracts little from the rhetorical impact of the images. The message to the viewer is clear: men leave for war not only inspirited but bodily whole; upon returning, they are helpless cripples, embittered and disfigured, hardly distinguishable from the rest of the war's detritus.

And yet, no matter how much we might admire the sociopolitical protest driving collections such as *War against War!* and *The Horror of It*, we also have to acknowledge the ways they continue to stigmatize corporeal anomaly and mobilize the viewer's fears about his or her own bodily disfigurement. Atrocity photographs mark the wounded soldiers' bodies as grotesque or horrific, tragically altered by war's dehumanizing violence. These are bodies to be deplored—bodies that should never have come into being—produced by an unthinkable aberration that must be eradicated. In Friedrich's and Barber's collections, wounded and disabled soldiers are presented not only as products of World War I but as metonyms of its horrors and inhumanity. As such, they constitute what Julia Kristeva has called the *abject*, that which must be recognized and expelled so that the rest of us can continue living.[31] Moreover, although photo albums such as *War against War!* and *The Horror of It* are designed to undermine the discourses and social practices that legitimate wartime injury, they can do little to alleviate the suffering of those already wounded. Instead, both albums deploy images of impaired bodies to teach a lesson to those without injury. They are meant to serve as a warning to nondisabled viewers: if you continue to fight wars, you too will be killed, disfigured, or disabled for life.

Conclusion

The productions I have discussed—Red Cross poster art and magazine illustration, rehabilitation photography, and antiwar photo albums—were not the only venues for displaying the wounded soldier's body in World War I–era visual culture. Wounded soldiers were frequently found in stereographic images, in veterans' benefits campaigns, and in popular film. However, even in these various media, representations of America's war-wounded generally adhered to at least one of the three visual typographies described earlier. Wounded soldiers were displayed as passive icons, tragic victims in need of public sympathy. They were constructed as independent, even heroic, citizen-workers whose return to postwar life marked the triumph of science over sentiment. They also came to symbolize the horrors of modern war, in particular its devastating effect on the human body. These conventions continue to structure how wounded or disabled soldiers' bodies are figured in American visual culture. In light of this fact, the work of many disability scholars has been to break the hegemony of these conventions and to reimagine disabled soldiers—indeed, all disabled people—not as icons or cultural markers but as actual people, irrespective of bodily impairment.[32]

For scholars of World War I visual culture, moreover, the images I have discussed suggest a number of lessons. First and foremost, they remind us that depictions of the war-wounded were not absent from wartime visual culture but were—in the case of Red Cross art and rehabilitation photography—often highly sanitized, distancing their viewers from the realities of wartime injury. In addition, they show that no group exercised absolute authority over public representations of the wounded soldier's body; on the contrary, such images were taken up by a variety of groups, often with vastly divergent interests. Further, in surveying the Great War's injury-themed visual culture, one cannot help but be struck by the paucity of images devoted to shell shock and other forms of psychological trauma. During World War I more than a hundred thousand U.S. service personnel were evacuated for psychological or neuropsychiatric ailments; many of them exhibited no

JOHN M. KINDER

outward signs of bodily damage.[33] Yet, with the exception of a few rehabilitation photographs and antiwar films, postwar image makers made little effort to find a visual grammar to articulate the Great War's psychological legacies. As a result, war disability continued to be associated with physical impairment, while shell shock—the form of injury most closely associated with the Great War—was rendered largely invisible in postwar American visual culture.[34]

Most important of all, the images I have discussed suggest wounded soldiers' inability to shape their own public image. Despite the flood of interest in visualizing wartime injury, the social absence of actual wounded and disabled soldiers meant that they were almost always displayed for the consumption of the nondisabled: to encourage charity donations, generate support for government-sponsored rehabilitation programs, and frighten the noninjured into rejecting war as a means of conflict resolution. Even rehabilitation photography, which addresses the war-disabled viewer directly, does so in order to promote the nondisabled's vision of what the war-injured can become. To understand how the war-injured saw themselves— how they imagined their own suffering, self-displayed their own somatic legacies of war—we would have to turn to a different set of sources (sketchbooks, diaries, "performances" of everyday tasks, etc.), few of which were meant for widespread public consumption. In short, the iconography of injury that inundated World War I poster art, magazine illustrations, and photography was largely the creation of those who escaped the war unscathed, who witnessed war's devastation in the bodies of others but not in their own.

Notes

1. Deborah Cohen, "Will to Work: Disabled Veterans in Britain and Germany after the First World War," in *Disabled Veterans in History*, ed. David A. Gerber (Ann Arbor: University of Michigan Press, 2000), 295.

2. For statistics about American casualties, see Robert H. Zieger, *America's Great War: World War I and the American Experience* (Lanham MD: Rowman and Littlefield, 2000).

3. John Maurice Clark, *The Costs of the World War to the American People* (New Haven: Yale University Press, 1931), 182.

4. Clark, *Costs of the World War*, 188; K. Walter Hickel, "Medicine, Bureaucracy, and Social Welfare: The Politics of Disability Compensation for American Veterans of World War I," in *The New Disability History: American Perspectives*, ed. Paul K. Longmore and Lauri Umansky (New York: New York University Press, 2001), 238.

5. David A. Gerber, "Introduction: Finding Disabled Veterans in History," in *Disabled Veterans in History*, ed. David A. Gerber (Ann Arbor: University of Michigan Press, 2000), 19.

6. On government attempts to censor images of American casualties in World War I, see Susan D. Moeller, *Shooting War: Photography and the American Experience of Combat* (New York: Basic, 1989).

7. Maurice Rickards, *Posters of the First World War* (London: Evelyn, Adams and Mackay, 1968), 3.

8. Rickards, *Posters of the First World War*, 2. For numerous examples of such images, also see Walton H. Rawls, *Wake Up, America! World War I and the American Poster* (New York: Abbeville Press, 1988).

9. "The Obligations of the American Red Cross to the Armed Forces of the United States," *American Red Cross Magazine*, December 1915, 380.

10. Robert J. Berens, *The Image of Mercy* (New York: Vantage Press, 1967), 48–61. For detailed, albeit largely uncritical, surveys of the Red Cross during World War I, see Henry P. Davison, *The American Red Cross in the Great War* (New York: Macmillan, 1920), and Foster Rhea Dulles, *The American Red Cross—A History* (New York: Harper, 1950).

11. Herbert Cecil Duce, *Poster Advertising* (Chicago: Blakely Printing Company, 1912), 174–75. For a broader, historicized discussion of advertising techniques in America, see Jackson Lears, *Fables of Abundance: A Cultural History of Advertising in America* (New York: Basic Books, 1994).

12. Rosemarie Garland Thomson, "Seeing the Disabled: Visual Rhetorics of Disability in Popular Photography," in *The New Disability History: American Perspectives*, ed. Paul K. Longmore and Lauri Umansky (New York: New York University Press, 2001), 341.

13. Charles Dana Gibson, "Columbia's Greatest Task," *American Red Cross Magazine*, September 1917, frontispiece.

14. Oscar Cesare, "The Modern Crusader," *American Red Cross Magazine*, October 1917, frontispiece.

15. On the social (rather than medical) construction of disability, see Colin

Barnes, Mike Oliver, and Len Barton, eds., *Disability Studies Today* (Cambridge: Polity, 2002); and David T. Mitchell and Sharon L. Snyder, eds., *The Body and Physical Difference: Discourses of Disability* (Ann Arbor: University of Michigan Press, 1997).

16. Captain Arthur H. Samuels, "Reconstructing the Public," *Carry On*, July 1918, 16.

17. "They Shall Be Made Whole," *American Red Cross Magazine*, September 1918, 50.

18. John Culbert Faries, *Three Years of Work for Handicapped Men: A Report of the Activities of the Institute for Crippled and Disabled Men* (New York: Institute for Crippled and Disabled Men, 1920), 70–75.

19. John Tagg, *The Burden of Representation: Essays on Photographies and Histories* (Minneapolis: University of Minnesota Press, 1993), 1–31.

20. On the feminization of dependency in modernity, see Nancy Fraser and Linda Gordon, "A Genealogy of *Dependency*: Tracing a Keyword of the U.S. Welfare State," *Signs: Journal of Women in Culture and Society* 19, no. 2 (Winter 1994): 309–36.

21. See Mary Klages, *Woeful Afflictions: Disability and Sentimentality in Victorian America* (Philadelphia: University of Pennsylvania Press, 1999), 1–9.

22. Herbert Kaufman, "The Only Hopeless Cripple," *Carry On*, October–November 1918, 22.

23. Elaine Scarry, *The Body in Pain: The Making and Unmaking of the World* (New York: Oxford University Press, 1985), 63.

24. Ernst Friedrich, *War against War!* (Seattle: Real Comet Press, 1987).

25. Friedrich, *War against War!* 21.

26. Frederick A. Barber, ed., *The Horror of It: Camera Records of War's Gruesome Glories* (New York: Brewer, Warren, and Putnam, 1932). Similar collections include *The Absolute Truth* (American Field Service, 1920), *No More War* (Paris: Imprimarie Coopérative Lucifer, 1934), and *The Tragedy and Horror of War*, the press booklet for the 1933 antiwar documentary *Forgotten Men*.

27. Harry Emerson Fosdick, foreword, in *The Horror of It: Camera Records of War's Gruesome Glories*, ed. Frederick A. Barber (New York: Brewer, Warren, and Putnam, 1932), 7.

28. Fosdick, foreword, 8.

29. Carrie Chapman Catt, foreword, in *The Horror of It: Camera Records of War's Gruesome Glories*, ed. Frederick A. Barber (New York: Brewer, Warren, and Putnam, 1932), 11.

30. Fosdick, foreword, 7.

31. For a full discussion of the metaphor of the abject, and its connection to opened bodies, see Julia Kristeva, *Powers of Horror: An Essay on Abjection*, trans. Leon S. Roudiez (New York: Columbia University Press, 1982).

32. Recent texts working in this direction include Michael Oliver, *The Politics of Disablement: A Sociological Approach* (New York: St Martin's Press, 1990); David Hevey, *The Creatures Time Forgot: Photography and Disability Imagery* (London: Routledge, 1992); and Lennard J. Davis, *Bending over Backwards: Disability, Dismodernism, and Other Difficult Positions* (New York: New York University Press, 2002).

33. U.S. Office of the Surgeon General, *The Medical Department of the United States Army in the World War*, vol. 10 (Washington: Government Printing Office, 1927), 1.

34. Even at the time, some observers were aware of the fact that the "invisibly wounded"—including men suffering from psychological trauma and disease—were frequently overlooked in post–World War I visual culture: "Among the wounded, the empty sleeve and the sightless eye, the visible scars, are bound to be more or less of a compensation in themselves. Where is there a heart that does not swell with gratitude toward the soldier bearing the outward signs of his war sacrifices? And even when the injuries are hidden by the clothing, the wound chevron on the right sleeve tells the story and stirs the heart. . . . Ask the mother of the boy who developed tuberculosis in the army. To her his wound is as real and as glorious as that of her neighbor's boy." "What about the Tuberculosis?" *Carry On* 1, no. 8 (May 1919): 22–23.

JOHN M. KINDER

JEFFREY T. SCHNAPP

Epilogue

olitical posters serve as a bridge between the new public sphere constituted by mass communications and the
streets and squares that are the theaters of modern mass
politics. They were (and in many developing countries they remain) among the visual protagonists of the industrial metropolis, layered many high and many deep on kiosks and walls like
the strata of a sociopolitical geology in which plate-tectonic
shifts are measured in weeks rather than millennia. Pointing
backward to the broadsheets of the eighteenth century and
forward to the flickering pixels of late twentieth-century television advertising, these agents of mass persuasion come into
their own with the widespread diffusion of industrial chromolithography at the conclusion of the nineteenth century.

   The emergence of posters as a dominant feature of the early
twentieth-century cityscape cannot be explained by invoking
technological factors alone. Aloys Senefelder's discovery of lithography dates back to 1798. Godefroy Engelmann patented
chromolithography thirty years later. By the mid-nineteenth
century, a wholesale mechanization of paper production was
under way, and the costs associated with color printing began to
diminish due to the accelerated drying times obtained through
the blending into printing inks of solvents like benzene.

However significant, none of these developments guaranteed the rise to prominence of posters in general and of political posters in particular. Rather, posters triumphed within the broader setting of that second industrial revolution, which saw an explosion of new forms of mass communication in response to the cultural, sociopolitical, and economic needs created by industrialization, by the growth of literacy rates, and by the extension of suffrage to ever greater sectors of the population in modern nation-states. Sellers of goods, providers of services, entertainment venues, publishers, the state, protest movements, and labor unions—to mention but a few social actors—all required an inexpensive, fast, and efficient conduit to the multitudes: multitudes equipped with highly variable degrees of visual and verbal literacy; multitudes who could not always be counted upon to read daily newspapers; multitudes on foot and riding public conveyances, distracted and on the move. Before the advent of radio and television, that conduit was largely provided by posters.

As the essays in this volume amply demonstrate, World War I marks a key threshold with respect to the role assumed by political posters. The reasons are adduced by every contributor: the distinctive challenges that the first fully mechanized war posed to the governments of modern nation-states; their need for recruitment campaigns to enroll ordinary citizens into mass armies; their reliance upon bond campaigns launched on the domestic front to support the war effort; their struggle to maintain the public's faith in the face of the sheer scale and brutality of the war's carnage. These challenges were shared by the governments of every combatant nation. (The addition of Italy, Austro-Hungary, Canada, Australia, and Japan to the book's mix would leave the picture unaltered.) Yet behind these global challenges there are local stories to be told: stories of how specific artistic traditions inflect or deflect the messages

JEFFREY T. SCHNAPP

of political poster art, of how the soldier-heroes whom posters celebrate are inscribed into genealogical myths stretching back to the nation's beginnings, of how enemies are not just dehumanized in the generic sense but also transformed into an Other that is irreducibly opposed to the national Self. Within these local stories are embedded tales more local still: of visual or verbal twists and turns added by individual artists, of works produced by independent groups and communities in tension with more mainstream state-sponsored messages.

The concept of propaganda does little to capture the complex layerings just evoked. If propaganda aims to "paralyze thought, to prevent discrimination and to condition individuals to act as a mass," then the corpus of works examined here surely qualifies as propagandistic.[1] Yet to reduce it to mere propaganda, assuming (which I do not) that *mere* propaganda even exists, would be to miss the nuances, ambivalences, and even artistry that the essays are careful to tease out. Some things are beyond dispute—that World War I posters were weapons in a battle for public opinion, that they were deployed to propagate myths of collective redemption and damnation, that the artists who created them operated under sometimes severe ideological and artistic constraints. To acknowledge this instrumentality, however, is not to deny the need for carefully drawn distinctions between effective and ineffective, imaginative and hackneyed, mainstream and less-than-mainstream iterations of poster art. Nor is it to diminish recognition of the inaugural role, for instance, that posters performed in contributing to the formation of a new verbal-visual language of mass persuasion: a language that had to communicate efficiently in already semiotically oversaturated urban environments as well as compete with both rival media and commercial counterparts. Interpreting World War I posters means grappling not only with overarching instrumentalities but also with subtler textures of form, detail, and meaning.

The media landscape of the Great War was distinctive in three ways that directly condition the roles performed by posters. First, it was characterized by the increasing importance assumed by large-format illustrated news weeklies that were differentiating themselves from daily newspapers through an emphasis upon photographic features. Second, as mentioned in Jay Winter's contribution to the present volume, it saw the birth of the documentary cinema in the form of pioneering works like G. H. Malins and J. B. McDowell's 1916 *Battle of the Somme*: a cinema that, within three decades, would transform the very concept of "news." Third, it consecrated the triumph of telegraphically relayed forms of newspaper reportage, which claimed readers' attention based on the pretence of providing information that was increasingly "live," "fresh," and "direct from the front" (a cult of eyewitness reportage that found its natural prolongation in the unprecedented outpouring of war memoirs, testimonies, and war novels—written by everyone from footsoldiers to generals—gobbled up by home front readers even as the war was being fought). All three developments point to the beginnings of a documentarist, photo- or cine-journalistic model of mass communications that would transform the language of 1920s, 1930s, and 1940s posters. In the 1910s, however, this model still stood at a remove from poster art.

The World War I poster is typically a work that, for all its rhetoric of urgency and effort to achieve immediate impact, has little interest in staging effects of "liveness." Accordingly, it has little if any use for photography, not to mention film, drawing its models and sources instead from cartooning, commercial illustration, and the fine arts. Its communicative strategies are based on melding an act of the visual imagination—a painting

JEFFREY T. SCHNAPP

or illustration—to a hortatory verbal/typographical message—
a banner headline—rather than on the manipulation of rea-
lia carried out, for instance, in the photographic features of illustrated weeklies or in 1920s and 1930s posters based on the
practice of photomontage. All of this places World War I posters
squarely on the *mythmaking* (rather than on the documentary)
side of the media divide: entrusting them with the elaboration
of idealized images, allegories of the nation, and stereotypes of
the soldier, citizen, or collectivity; or of monstrous doubles—
the enemy combatant, the foe as faceless horde.

This mythmaking role inflects both the visual language of
the posters and their iconography. They become sites for the
development of hybrid pictorial languages that borrow from
folk traditions or outsider art (for instance, from children) in
order to dismantle dominant canons of representation and
give rise to nativist redactions of the modern. They become
staging grounds for prospective/retrospective myths like those
of the technobarbarian (viz., the Hun) and the soldier-knight,
analyzed in several essays.

Let us muse for a moment over the significance of the ubiquity of medieval knights in European World War I posters.
Knights figure prominently less as an icon of revolt against
the present or as a nostalgic evocation of a (mostly imaginary)
past than for the same complex reasons that medievalism informs so many nineteenth-century debates concerning modernity, from Romantic nationalist efforts to locate the origins of
modern nation-states in the Middle Ages to critiques of alien-
ated labor, like those variously put forward by the Arts and
Crafts movement, utopian socialists, and anarchosyndicalists,
for whom medieval models of production and social organization provide a potentially radical alternative to their indus-
trial-era descendants.

As interpreted by the graphic artists of the 1910s, the medieval knight is a composite figure. He conveys the defining values of a given (modern) national identity: composure and obedience (Germany); observance of a higher moral calling (England); the defense of Civilization (France). He places an ennobling veil of individual heroism, hand-to-hand and face-to-face combat, and warfare bound by laws of civility and even politesse over the harsh truth of faceless, lawless, mechanized, mass trench warfare. Yet he does so in a manner that merges retrospective with prospective fantasy. He is not dressed in actual fourteenth-century battle attire but instead in a gleaming steel version of *display* armor in what amounts to the creation of a distinctively contemporary type: the man of steel—a hyperbolically literal-minded counterpart to the armor-plated, blasé urbanite who, bombarded by the stimuli of the modern metropolis, builds his identity like a bullet-proof shell.[2] The realities both of mental life in the industrial city and of mechanized warfare have been displaced onto the surface of the warrior's body and transformed into an impermeable shield: a projectile able to pierce the armored surface of other modern warriors even as it fends off the storms of steel produced by automatic weapon fire, aerial bombardments, and barrages of artillery.[3]

It was once fashionable to situate such hybrid formations outside the mainstream of modernity: to exile them to outlying domains bearing labels like "reactionary modernism," "eclecticism," or "state propaganda" or simply to peel away "progressive" elements from "regressive" ones as if the latter were little more than the residue of history, soon to be cast asunder in the course of modernity's inexorable march toward the overcoming of myth and the triumph of reason. More recent decades of cultural historiography have cast doubts on such linear narratives and utopic hopes, finding instead eclecticism in even the most avant-garde expressions of culture; exploring

JEFFREY T. SCHNAPP

blurrings between left, right, and center; uncovering hitherto unsuspected continuities between high and low cultural forms. In keeping with this overall drift, political posters have moved from the sidelines to the center of contemporary attention. And they now make demands upon the contemporary viewer that transcend the discourses of collectors, historians of the graphic arts, and political historians. They demand a gaze that at once contextualizes and interprets, a gaze that looks from the standpoint of both surface and depth, a gaze that reads in the qualitative sense. Such is the gaze that the present collection casts on the posters of the Great War.

Notes

1. Sam Keen, *Faces of the Enemy: Reflections of the Hostile Imagination* (San Francisco: Harper and Row, 1988), 25.

2. I have in mind Georg Simmel's seminal account of urban subjectivity in "The Metropolis and Mental Life," in *Classic Essays on the Culture of Cities*, ed. Richard Sennett (New York: Appleton-Century-Crofts, 1969), 47–60, as well as a wide range of other phenomenologies of the industrial metropolis from Charles Baudelaire to Ernst Jünger. On this subject one may also consult chapters 6 and 7 of my *Staging Fascism: 18 BL and the Theater of Masses for Masses* (Stanford: Stanford University Press, 1996), 83–112.

3. The classic account of the new soldier-warrior-knight is that of Ernst Jünger, *The Storm of Steel: From the Diary of a German Storm-Troop Officer on the Western Front* (London: Chatto and Windus, 1929), elements of which are reworked into his later *Das Kampf als inneres Erlebnis* (Berlin: E. S. Mittler, 1933). That Jünger's modern warrior cannot be constrained within the realm of so-called "reactionary modernism" I take for granted, given its pertinence to everything from Joseph Stalin's self-styling as *Steel man* to comic superheroes such as Superman.

Aulich, James. *War Posters: Weapons of Mass Communication.* London: Thames and Hudson, 2007.

Aulich, James, and John Hewitt. *Seduction or Instruction? First World War Posters in Britain and Europe.* Manchester: Manchester University Press, 2007.

Baker, Steve. "Describing Images of the National Self: Popular Accounts of the Construction of Pictorial Identity in the First World War Poster." *Oxford Art Journal* 13, no. 2 (1990): 24–30.

Banta, Martha. *Imaging American Women: Idea and Ideals in Cultural History.* New York: Columbia University Press, 1987.

Barnicoat, John. *A Concise History of Posters: 1870–1970.* New York: H. N. Abrams, 1972.

Belgum, Kirsten. *Popularizing the Nation: Audience, Representation, and the Production of Identity in Die Gartenlaube, 1853–1900.* Lincoln: University of Nebraska Press, 1998.

Benton, Barbara. "Friendly Persuasion: Woman as War Icon, 1914–45." *MHQ: Quarterly Journal of Military History* 6, no. 1 (1993): 80–87.

Borkan, Gary A. *World War I Posters.* Atglen PA: Schiffer, 2002.

Bryant, Mark. *World War I in Cartoons.* London: Grub Street, 2006.

Buitenhuis, Peter. *The Great War of Words: Literature as Propaganda 1914–18 and After.* Vancouver: University of British Columbia Press, 1987.

Chenault, Libby. *Battlelines: World War I Posters from the Bowman Gray Collection.* Chapel Hill: University of North Carolina Press, 1988.

Cohen, Aaron J. *Imagining the Unimaginable: World War, Modern Art, and the Politics of Public Culture in Russia, 1914–1917.* Lincoln: University of Nebraska Press, 2008.

Compère-Morel, Thomas, ed. *Les Affiches de la Grande Guerre.* Péronne, Somme: Historial de la Grande Guerre, 1998.

Creel, George. *How We Advertised America.* New York: Harper and Brothers, 1920.

Curtis, Barry. "Posters as Visual Propaganda in the Great War." *Block*, no. 2 (1980): 45–57.

Czuray, Jörg, and Hans Pammer. *Plakate im Ersten Weltkrieg: Materialien zur Medienpädagogik zu 24 Dias für Geschichte, Politische Bildung und Bildnerische Erziehung.* Vienna, 1996.

Darracott, Joseph. *The First World War in Posters from the Imperial War Museum, London.* New York: Dover, 1974.

Denscher, Bernhard. *Gold gab ich für Eisen: Österreichsiche Kriegsplakate 1914–1918.* Vienna: Jugend & Volk, 1987.

Douglas, Roy. "Voluntary Enlistment in the First World War and the Work of the Parliamentary Recruiting Committee." *Journal of Modern History* 42, no. 4 (1970): 564–85.

Dutton, Philip. "Moving Images? The Parliamentary Recruiting Committee's Poster Campaign, 1914–1916." *Imperial War Museum Review* 4 (1989): 43–58.

Frank, Peter Conrad. *Women of the World War One Poster*. Middletown CT: Center for the Arts, Wesleyan University, 1981.

Fuglie, Gordon L. *Images of the Great War: 1914–1918*, ed. Lucinda H. Gedeon. Los Angeles CA: UCLA Publication Services Department, 1983.

Gallo, Max. *The Poster in History*. Trans. Alfred and Bruni Mayor. New York: American Heritage, 1974.

Gervereau, Laurent. *Terroriser, manipuler, convaincre! Histoire mondiale de l'affiche politique*. Paris: Somogy, 1996.

Ginzburg, Carlo. "'Your Country Needs You': A Case Study in Political Iconography." *History Workshop Journal*, no. 52 (2001): 1–22.

Grayzel, Susan R. *Women's Identities at War: Gender, Motherhood, and Politics in Britain and France during the First World War*. Chapel Hill: University of North Carolina Press, 1999.

Gregory, Adrian. *Last Great War: British Society and the First World War*. Cambridge: Cambridge University Press, 2008.

Gregory, G. H. *Posters of World War II*. New York: Gramercy Books, 1996.

Hammond, Michael. *The Big Show: British Cinema Culture in the Great War*. Exeter: Exeter University Press, 2006.

Hardie, Martin, and Arthur K. Sabin. *War Posters Issued by Belligerent and Neutral Nations 1914–1919*. London: A & C Black, 1920.

Haste, Cate. *Keep the Home Fires Burning: Propaganda in the First World War*. London: Allen Lane, 1977.

Hewitt, John. "Poster Nasties: Censorship and the Victorian Theatre Poster." In *Visual Delights: Essays on the Popular and Projected Image in the Nineteenth Century*, ed. S. Popple and V. Toulmin, 154–69. Trowbridge, U.K.: Flicks Books, 2000.

Hiley, Nicholas. "'Kitchener Wants You' and 'Daddy, What Did You Do in the Great War?': The Myth of British Recruiting Posters." *Imperial War Museum Review* 11 (1997): 40–58.

———. "Sir Hedley Lebas and the Origins of Domestic Propaganda in Britain 1914–1917." *Journal of Advertising History* 10, no. 2 (1987): 30–45.

Howell, Bill, and Barbara Jones. *Popular Arts of the First World War*. New York: McGraw-Hill, 1972.

Jahn, Hubertus F. *Patriotic Culture in Russia during World War I*. Ithaca NY: Cornell University Press, 1995.

Jobst-Rieder, Marianne, Alfred Pfabigan, and Manfred Wagner. *Das letzte Vi-vat: Plakate und Parolen aus der Kriegssammlung der k. k. Hofbibliothek.* Vienna: Austrian National Library, 1995.

Jones, Heather, Jennifer O'Brien, and Christopher Schmidt-Supprian, eds. *Untold War: New Perspectives in First World War Studies.* Leiden, Netherlands: Brill, 2008.

Karetsky, Joanne L. *The Mustering of Support for World War I by the Ladies' Home Journal.* Lampeter, Ceredigion, Wales: Edwin Mellen Press, 1997.

Keen, Sam. *Faces of the Enemy, Reflections of the Hostile Imagination.* San Francisco: Harper and Row, 1988.

Knutson, Anne Classen. "Breasts, Brawn and Selling a War: American World War I Propaganda Posters 1917–1918." PhD diss., University of Pittsburgh, 1997; Ann Arbor: University Microfilms International, 1998.

———. "The Enemy Imaged: Visual Configurations of Race and Ethnicity in World War I Propaganda Posters." In *Race and the Construction of Modern American Nationalism,* ed. Reynolds Scott Childress, 195–220. Boston: Garland Press, 1997.

Krass, Peter. *Portrait of War: the U. S. Army's First Combat Artists and the Doughboys' Experience in World War I.* Hoboken NJ: Wiley, 2007.

Laffin, John. *World War I in Postcards.* Gloucester: Alan Sutton Publishing, 1988.

Lasswell, Harold D. *Propaganda Technique in World War I.* Cambridge MA: MIT Press, 1971.

Liddiard, Jean, and Diana Condell. *Working for Victory? Images of Women in the First World War, 1914–1918.* London: Routledge and Kegan Paul, 1987.

Margolin, Victor. *American Poster Renaissance.* New York: Watson-Guptill Publications, 1975.

Metzl, Ervine. *The Poster: Its History and Its Art.* New York: Watson-Gutpill Publications, 1963.

Meyers, Jessica, ed. *British Popular Culture and the First World War.* Leiden, Netherlands: Brill, 2008.

Moody, Michael. "Vive La Nation! French Revolutionary Themes in the Posters and Prints of the First World War." *Imperial War Museum Review* 3 (1988): 34–43.

Moses, Montrose J. "Making Posters Fight." *Bookman* 47 (July 1918): 504–12.

Norris, Stephen. *A War of Images: Russian Popular Prints, Wartime Culture, and National Identity, 1812–1945.* DeKalb: Northern Illinois University Press, 2006.

Paillard, Rémy. *Affiches 14–18.* Paris: Rémy Paillard, 1986.

Paret, Peter, Beth Irwin Lewis, and Paul Paret, eds. *Persuasive Images: Posters of War and Revolution from the Hoover Institution Archives.* Princeton: Princeton University Press, 1992.

Pennell, Joseph. *Joseph Pennell's Liberty-Loan Poster: A Text-Book for Artists and Amateurs, Governments and Teachers and Printers, with Notes, an Introduction and Essay on the Poster by the Artist, Associate Chairman of the Committee on Public Information, Division of Pictorial Publicity.* Philadelphia: J. B. Lippincott Company, 1918.

Petrone, Karen. "Family, Masculinity, and Heroism in Russian War Posters of the First World War." In *Borderlines: Genders and Identities in War and Peace, 1870–1930,* ed. Billie Melman, 95–120. New York: Routledge, 1998.

———. "The Motherland Calls." In *Picturing Russia: Essays on Visual Evidence,* ed. Valerie Kivelson and Joan Neuberger, 196–200. New Haven: Yale University Press, 2008.

Price, Matlock, and Horace Brown. *How to Put in Patriotic Posters the Stuff That Makes People Stop—Look—Act!* (pamphlet). Washington DC: National Committee of Patriotic Societies, n.d. (ca. 1917–18).

Randall, Roy O., ed. *The Poster: War Souvenir Edition.* Chicago: Poster Advertising Association, 1919.

Rawls, Walton H. *Wake Up, America! World War I and the American Poster.* New York: Abbeville Press, 1988.

Reznick, Jeffrey S. *So Comes the Sacred Work: John Galsworthy and the Great War.* Manchester: Manchester University Press, 2009.

Rickards, Maurice. *Posters of the First World War.* New York: Walker and Company, 1968; London: Evelyn, Adams and Mackay, 1968.

———. *The Rise and Fall of the Poster.* New York: McGraw-Hill, 1971.

Rider, Mary. "Images of Propaganda: World War I and II Posters." *Queen City Heritage: Journal of the Cincinnati Historical Society* 41, no. 3 (1983): 31–36.

Robbins, Trina. *Nell Brinkley and the New Woman in the Early 20th Century.* Jefferson NC: McFarland, 2001.

Rosenfeld, Alla. "The World Turned Upside Down: Russian Posters of the First World War, the Bolshevik Revolution, and the Civil War." In *Defining Russian Graphic Arts: From Diaghilev to Stalin, 1898–1934,* ed. Alla Rosenfeld, 121–31. New Brunswick: Rutgers University Press, 1999.

Roshwald, Aviel, and Richard Stites, eds. *European Culture in the Great War: The Arts, Entertainment, and Propaganda, 1914–1918.* Cambridge: Cambridge University Press, 1999.

Roze, Anne. *Fields of Memory: A Testimony to the Great War.* London: Cassell, 1999.

Segal, Joes. "The Work of Art as a Mirror of National Identity: Public Debates on Art and Culture in Germany during World War I." *European Review of History* 4, no. 1 (1997): 9–17.

Sherman, Daniel J. *The Construction of Memory in Interwar France.* Chicago: University of Chicago Press, 1999.

Shover, Michele J. "Roles and Images of Women in World War I Propaganda." *Politics and Society* 5, no. 4 (1975): 469–86.

Sontag, Susan. "Posters: Advertisement, Art, Political Artifact, Commodity." In *The Art of Revolution: Castro's Cuba, 1959–1970,* ed. Dugald Stermer, not paginated. New York: McGraw-Hill, 1970.

Squires, James Duane. *British Propaganda at Home and in the United States from 1914 to 1917.* Cambridge MA: Harvard University Press, 1935.

Stanley, Peter, ed. *What Did You Do in the War Daddy? A Visual History of Propaganda Posters (a Selection from the Australian War Memorial).* Oxford: Oxford University Press, 1983.

Taylor, Philip M., and M. L. Sanders. *British Propaganda during the First World War, 1914–18.* London: Macmillan Press, 1982.

Timmers, Margaret, ed. *The Power of the Poster.* London: Victoria and Albert Publications, 1998.

Walton, Ruth. "Four in Focus." In *The Power of the Poster,* ed. Margaret Timmers, 146–71. London: Victoria and Albert Publications, 1998.

Weill, Alan. *The Poster: A Worldwide Survey and History.* Boston: G. K. Hall, 1985.

Welch, David. *Germany, Propaganda and Total War, 1914–1918.* New Brunswick: Rutgers University Press, 2000.

White, Stephen. *The Bolshevik Poster.* New Haven: Yale University Press, 1988.

Winter, Jay. "Nationalism, the Visual Arts, and the Myth of War Enthusiasm in 1914." *History of European Ideas* 15, nos. 1–3 (1992): 357–62.

———. "Propaganda and the Mobilization of Consent." In *Oxford Illustrated History of the First World War,* ed. Hew Strachen, 216–26. Oxford: Oxford University Press, 1998.

Wollaeger, Mark A. *Modernism, Media, and Propaganda: British Narrative from 1900 to 1945.* Princeton: Princeton University Press, 2006.

———. "Posters, Modernism, Cosmopolitanism: *Ulysses* and World War I Recruiting Posters in Ireland." *Yale Journal of Criticism* 6, no. 2 (Fall 1993): 87–132.

Women in War: A Touring Exhibit of World War I Posters from the Collection of the Liberty Memorial Museum, Kansas City, Missouri, July, 1985. Kansas City MO: Mid-America Arts Alliance, 1985.

Meg Albrinck is Interim Vice President for Academic Affairs and Dean of the College and an associate professor of literature and writing at Lakeland College in Sheboygan, Wisconsin. She has published articles on women's war narratives, Virginia Woolf, and Gertrude Stein and is working on a book-length study that explores the intersection of gender and genre in narratives of the First World War.

Richard S. Fogarty is an assistant professor of history at the University at Albany, State University of New York. He received his PhD in history from the University of California, Santa Barbara. He is author of *Race and War in France: Colonial Subjects in the French Army, 1914–1918* (Johns Hopkins University Press, 2008); "Race and Sex, Fear and Loathing in France during the Great War," *Historical Reflections/Réflexions Historiques* 34, no. 1 (Spring 2008); and "Between Subjects and Citizens: Algerians, Islam, and French National Identity during the Great War," in *Race and Nation: Ethnic Systems in the Modern World*, ed. Paul Spickard (Routledge, 2005).

Stefan Goebel is a senior lecturer in modern British history at the University of Kent at Canterbury and a visiting fellow at the Centre for Metropolitan History at the Institute of Historical Research, London. A graduate of the University of Cambridge, he has held postdoctoral research fellowships at Churchill College, Cambridge, and the Institute of Historical Research, London. He is the author of *The Great War and Medieval Memory: War, Remembrance and Medievalism in Britain and Germany, 1914–1940* (Cambridge University Press, 2007). He is working on a book on Coventry and Dresden in the aftermath of the Second World War.

Nicoletta F. Gullace is an associate professor of history at the University of New Hampshire. She is the author of *"The Blood of Our Sons": Men, Women, and the Renegotiation of British Citizenship during the Great War* (Palgrave, 2002). Her current research is on memory and citizenship before and after the Great War.

Pearl James is an assistant professor of literature at the University of Kentucky. She received her PhD from Yale University. Her essays on American modernist writers and the First World War have appeared in *Modern Fiction Studies, Cather Studies*, and *Modernism and Mourning*, ed. Patricia Rae (Bucknell University Press, 2007).

Jakub Kazecki studied German language and literature at the Adam-Mickiewicz-University in Poznań, Poland, and holds a master's degree in German from Dalhousie University, Halifax, Nova Scotia, and a PhD in Germanic studies from the University of British Columbia, Vancouver. His research interests include representations of war in twentieth-century German literature and visual arts, with a concentration on the relationship between humor and violence. He is currently an assistant professor of German at Central Connecticut State University in New Britain, Connecticut, where he teaches courses in German language, literature, and film.

Jennifer D. Keene is a professor of history at Chapman University in Orange, California. She is the author of *World War I* (Greenwood Press, 2006); *Doughboys, the Great War, and the Remaking of America* (Johns Hopkins University Press, 2001); and *The United States and the First World War* (Longman, 2000). Dr. Keene is the recipient of Fulbright, Mellon, and National Research Council fellowships. She is completing a project on African American soldiers during the First World War.

John M. Kinder is an assistant professor of American studies and history at Oklahoma State University. He earned his PhD in American studies from the University of Minnesota. His current book project, *Paying with Their Bodies: Disabled Soldiers in the Age of American Militarism* (University of Chicago Press, forthcoming), traces the relationship between U.S. foreign policy and Americans' anxieties about war disability.

Mark Levitch is a writer and editor at the National Gallery of Art. He is the author of *Panthéon de la Guerre: Reconfiguring a Panorama of the Great War* (University of Missouri Press, 2006) and recently completed his dissertation on French visual culture during World War I.

Jason Lieblang holds master's degrees in philosophy and German literature, both from the University of British Columbia, and is currently both a PhD candidate at the University of Toronto and an instructor in the Modern Languages Department at Kwantlen Polytechnic University, Surrey, British Columbia, where he teaches courses in German language, culture, and film. His research interests include the legacies of German Romanticism, the visual culture of the Weimar Republic, New German Cinema, and the sociology of masculinities.

Andrew M. Nedd is a professor of art history at the Savannah College of Art and Design. He specializes in Russian art of the late imperial period. He received his PhD in art history from the University of Southern California. His dissertation is entitled "Defending Russia: Russian History and Pictorial Narratives of the "Patriotic War," 1812–1912."

Jeffrey T. Schnapp holds the Rosina Pierotti Chair in Italian Literature at Stanford University. He has been awarded numerous fellowships by Fulbright, the NEH, the Getty Research Institute, the Guggenhiem Foundation, and the Andrew W. Mellon Foundation. He is the author and editor of numerous books, including *Building Fascism, Communism, Liberal Democracy: Gaetano Ciocca—Architect, Inventor, Farmer, Writer, Engineer* (Stanford University Press, 2004).

Jay Winter is the Charles J. Stille Professor of History at Yale University. He is the author or coauthor of many works, including *Socialism and the Challenge of War: Ideas and Politics in Britain, 1912–18; The Great War and the British People; The Fear of Population Decline; The Experience of World War I; Sites of Memory, Sites of Mourning: The Great War in European Cultural History, 1914–1918; Capital Cities at War: Paris, London, Berlin 1914–1919; The Great War and the Shaping of the 20th Century; Remembering War: The Great War between History and Memory in the 20th Century;* and *Dreams of Peace and Freedom: Utopian Moments in the 20th Century.*

INDEX

Page numbers in italic refer to illustrations.

Abrams, Ann Uhry, 277

Adler, Jules, 150

advertising, 4–6, 31–32, 135; and American posters, 120, 136, 345; and Banania campaign, 195–96, 205nn51–52; and British posters, 43–45, 322; effectiveness of, 16–17; and feminine imagery, 281–82, 311n43; and French posters, 177, 195–96, 205n51; and German posters, 112–13, 116

Africa, 67–68; Algeria, 180–83, 188–92, 194, 201; Senegal, 195. *See also* colonialism; race

African Americans, 33; and black newspapers, 212, 213, 215, 220; and civil rights agenda, 207–8, 209, 215, 218–19, 224, 232, 236–37; and community morale, 231; discrimination against, in the military, 208–9, 210, 212, 217, 220–21, 229–31, 232; enlistment rates of, 231–32; film depictions of, 210; and fundraising posters, 229–31; and government poster campaigns, 207, 208–15, 218–23, 225–29, 236–37; and jazz bands, 220; and patriotism, 207–8, 214, 233, 236; perceived "insolence" of, 224–25; and privately produced posters, 27–28, 33, 208, 215–18, 223–26, 228–37; and venereal disease lectures, 226–29. *See also* race

"The Aid of the Colonies to France" (exhibition), 179

Alexander, Susan, 311n43

Alexandre, Arsène, 158–59

Algeria, 180–83, 189–92, 194, 201. *See also* colonialism

"All Aboard!" (poster), *129*

allegorical images: criticism of, 309n17; feminine, 128, 175, 275, 276–82, 306, 308n8, 308n10, 309n13; and injuries, 349. *See also* imagery

All Quiet on the Western Front (Remarque), 88

"Amazon Warrior" imagery, 276–77, 280, 282. *See also* femininity

America: casualty numbers, 340–41; neutrality of, 117–19; "poster revolution" in, 113; and social class, 130. *See also* American posters

American Expeditionary Force (AEF), 303, 310n22

American posters, 5, 24–25; and advertising, 120, 136, 345; and allegorical images, 128, 275, 276–82, 306, 308n8, 308n10, 309n13, 309n17, 349; and American Red Cross, 342, 343–50, 357, 364; and anti-evolutionary themes, 68–69; and color, 113, 285–86, 345; and conservation themes, 6–9, 213–14, 221–22, 292–93; design of, 113, 115–16, 285, 345, 347–48; differences of, from German posters, 25–26, 111–17, 118, 120–36; and feminine imagery, 132–33, *134*, 273–94, 296, 297–307, 307n2; and Food Administration (USFA), 8–9, 12, *13*, *15*, 212–15, 218–19, 221–22, 236, 276, 292–97, *298*; in foreign languages, 210; and gender roles, 274–75, 283, 293, 300–303, 332–33, 336, 346–47; hand-made, 295–96; and "Hun" imagery, 71, 72–73; and injury depictions, 342–50, 364–65; and masculinity, 131–32, 279, 327–30; number produced, 209–10, 308n3; and philanthropic groups, 229–31, 232; and progressive narratives, 112, 126–28, 130–31, 133; and race issues, 27–28, 207–9, 210–11, 212–37, 279; and recruiting, 71, 72–73, 327–30; and rehabilitation photography, 350–58, 360, 364, 365; and sentimentality, 347–48, 349–50, 352; and slogans, 114; and text, 286–87; thrift stamp posters, 210–11, 225; war bond posters, *12*, *13*, *114*, 129, 210–12, 220–21, 370. *See also* America

American Red Cross, 282–83, 292, 302; posters of the, 342, 343–50, 357, 364

amputees, 356, 362–63. *See also* injuries

antiwar photo albums, 343, 358–63. *See also* photography

"Are you in this?" (poster), *329*

art, 21–22, 28; avant-garde, 150–51, 241,
243–44, 248, 249–50, 259, 268n36;
decorative arts, 147, 151–55, 157, 162–64,
166–68, 169n11; education, in France,
152–57, 158–59, 163, 167, 169n15; and
Exposition Internationale (1925), 166–67;
folk art, 3, 28–29, 158, 241–45, 247–49,
259, 262–63, 265; French schoolchildrens'
exhibition of, 147–48, 151–53, 154–56,
158–59, 168n4; Futurism (Russian), 243,
245, 248, 249–51, 259, 262; and gender,
26–27, 145, 159–60; neoprimitivism, 248,
249, 254, 260–61; primitivism, 242–43,
245, 249, 250, 251, 253, 262–63; realism,
248; Russian exhibitions of, 241, 252–53,
261–62
assimilation, 173–74, 192, 194, 201n2. *See
also* colonialism
atrocity reports, 67–68, 74–75, 206n59, 287,
316–18, 337n10. *See also* propaganda
Atwell, Ernest T., 213, 221
"At Work Again/Back to the Farm" (poster),
356
Aulich, James, 3, 6, 16, 43, 45, 135
Australian posters, 24–25; and "Hun" imagery, 71–73, 76n5; and recruiting, 71–72
"An Austrian went to Radziwill" (poster), 260
avant-garde art, 150–51; in Russia, 241,
243–45, 248, 249–50, 259, 268n36. *See
also* art

Babcock, R. F., 132
"Back Our Girls Over There" (poster), 302
Baker, Ernest Hamlin, 299–301
Baker, Newton E., 210
Banania, 195–96, 205nn51–52. *See also*
advertising
Banta, Martha, 274, 276, 277, 280, 308n6
Barber, Frederick A., 359–63
Barthes, Roland, 269n47
Barton, Clara, 283
Battle of the Somme (film), 48–49, 50, 372
"Beat Back the Hun" (poster), 67, 72
"Beat Back the Hun with Liberty Bonds"
(poster), *114*
Belgium, 71, 116–17, 287; cultural destruc-
tion in, 66; poster references to, 41–42,
44, 45, 316–17, 318–19, 321

"Below Warsaw and Grodna we smashed the
Germans" (poster), 260
Benda, W. T., 292
Benjamin, Walter, 57
Berger, John, 282
Bernard, Camille, 163
Bernhard, Lucian, 81, *82,* 113, 114–15
black community. *See* African Americans
black newspapers, 212–13, 215, 220. *See also*
African Americans
Bonnard, Pierre, 4
Boret, Victor, 147–49
Bowlt, John E., 248
Brangwyn, Frank, 326
Brey, Laura, 132, *327,* 329
Britain. *See* Great Britain
"Britain Needs You at Once" (poster), 98, *99*
British posters, 22–23; and advertising,
43–45, 322; and chivalry imagery, 95–102,
103; and coercion, 314, 322–36; and
color, 326; design of, 317–18, 326; differences of, from German posters, 19–20,
101–3; and "Hun" imagery, 24–25, 72–73,
75–76; and masculinity, 30–31, 33, 313–
14, 316–19, 323–33, 335–36; and national
identity, 41–43, 46–47, 54–57, 323; and
naval tradition, 38–39; and "othering,"
327–28; postwar, 51–53, 54–57; production of, 315, 318, 336n9; and recruiting,
17–18, 23, 24, 43–44, 98, 312–36; and
social class, 44–46, 50–51; and solidarity,
43, 52; and text, 319. *See also* Great Britain
Brittain, B. W., 232
Brittain, Vera, 333
Brooks, Jeffrey, 245, 252
Brown, Horace, 281
Bryce, James, 65
Bryce Report, 68, 337n10
Burliuk, David, 241

Callot, Jacques, 150
cartoons, 62, *63,* 67–68, 70, 76n5, 77n18
Catt, Carrie Chapman, 359, 362
Cesare, Oscar, 349
"A Chance Shot" (poster), 131, 132
Chekrugin, Vasilli, 241
Cheremnykh, Mikhail, 264
Chéret, Jules, 4
chivalry, 95–102, 103. *See also* knight imagery

Christy, Howard Chandler, 133, 281, 289–91, 293, 297, 304–5

"Christy Girl," 289–91, 304

chromolithography, 4, 369

cinema: documentaries, 47–50, 372; in foreign languages, 210; and injury depiction, 364; and slide lectures, 221

Circle for Negro War Relief, 231–32

Civil War (U.S.), 41, 220, 232

Claretie, Léo, 155

Clément-Janin, Noël, 162, 165

Coll, Joseph Clement, 115–16

Colley, Linda, 77n10

colonialism: and assimilation, 173–74, 192, 194, 201n2; British, 39–40, 318; French, 172–74, 178–201, 201n2. See also colonial soldiers

colonial soldiers: as shock troops, 197–99, 206n58; tirailleurs sénégalais, 184, 192–200, 205n51, 206n58, 206n62; troupes indigènes, 172, 174, 178, 179–80, 184, 187, 188, 190, 191–92, 193–201, 201n1, 203n20. See also colonialism; race

color, 20, 26; in American posters, 113, 285–86, 345; in British posters, 326; and chromolithography, 4; in French posters, 145, 146–47, 149–51, 155–56, 157–59, 167–69; printing, 369

Colored Americans (film), 210

"Colored Man Is No Slacker" (poster), 225–26, 228–29

"Colored Men" (poster), 218

"Columbia's Greatest Task" (poster), 349

"Come, German, come, come" (poster), 256

commemorations, public. See war memorials

Commission on Training Camp Activities (CTCA), 226–27

Committee on Public Information (CPI), 28, 119, 209–11, 212, 215, 236, 342. See also propaganda

Compton, Susan, 250, 251

conscription, 12–13, 73, 95, 98, 99, 314; of Algerians, 183, 190; in America, 226, 232; British, 322; and troupes indigènes, 183, 187, 190. See also recruiting

conservation (food) themes: in American posters, 6–9, 213–14, 221–22, 292–93; in French posters, 145–46, 147, 148, 149, 159, 161, 164, 168n2

Copse 125 (Jünger), 94

Cork, Richard, 255

Cossacks, 247, 257, 259. See also Russian posters

Cox, Kenyon, 278–79

Craig, A. U., 213, 214, 222

Creel, George, 119

Crispus Attucks Circle for War Relief, 229–31

Crow, Thomas, 244–45, 248

Crowley, David, 21

"Cultivons notre potager" (poster), 164

"Daddy, what did you do in the Great War?" (poster), 324, 325, 338n30

"damsel in distress" imagery, 275, 283–88, 306. See also femininity

"The Dawn of Hope" (poster), 232, 233

death tolls, 79, 340

decorative arts: in France, 147, 152–55, 157, 162–64, 166–68, 169n11; in Germany, 152, 153–54, 157. See also art

Deems, J. F., 294

Denisov, Vladimir, 246, 252, 263

Dennison, Franklin A., 217

design repetition, 10–14, 17–18, 19, 25, 72, 76, 137–38, 176–77, 327–28. See also propaganda

"Destroy This Mad Brute" (poster), 68–69, 71, 76, 77n20, 284

Deville, Alphonse, 151, 155–56

Dienst, Paul, 115

diffusionist narrative, 127. See also progressive narratives

disabilities, 341–42, 364; and compensation, 350; and rehabilitation photography, 350–58, 360, 364, 365. See also injuries

Disenchantment (Montague), 99–100

Division of Pictorial Publicity (DPP), 119, 209–10. See also Committee on Public Information (CPI)

Douanne, G., 148

Douglass, Frederick, 216

draft. See conscription

Dubois, E. X., 330

Du Bois, W. E. B., 217–18, 231, 237

Dunbar, Paul L., 216

Duncan, Otis B., 217

Düsseldorf Academy of Art, 112

Dutton, Philip, 18, 314, 336

Dyson, Will, 70

École des Beaux-Arts, 152, 202n4
"Economisons le pain en mangeant des pommes de terre" (poster), *147*, 164
Elshtain, Jean Bethke, 316
"Emancipation Proclamation" (poster), 215–18
empire. *See* colonialism
Engelmann, Godefroy (Godefroi), 4, 369
England. *See* Great Britain
Erler, Fritz, 90, *91*
Europe, James, 220
"Exhibition of Original Icon Paintings and Lubki" (exhibition), 253
exhibitions: "The Aid of the Colonies to France," 179; Exposition Internationale des Arts Décoratifs et Industriels Modernes, 166–67; French schoolchildrens' art, 147–48, 151–53, 154–56, 158–59, 168n4; Musée Galliera (1917), 151–53, 154–56, 158–59, 163, 168n4; Russian art, 241, 252–53, 261–62; "War and Publishing" (posters), 241, 261. *See also* art
Exposition Internationale des Arts Décoratifs et Industriels Modernes, 166–67

Faivre, Jules Abel, 150
Fehr, H. C., 97
femininity, 29–30, 36n36, 160; and allegorical imagery, 128, 175, 275, 276–81, 306, 308n8, 308n10, 309n13, 309n17; and American posters, 132–33, *134*, 273–307, 307n2; commodification of, 288–91; contradictions in images of, 274–76, 281–83, 306–7, 307n2, 308n6, 311n43; and damsel in distress (victim) imagery, 275, 283–88, 306; and desexualization, 302–4; in German posters, 126, *127*; and the home front, 318–20, 326; and sexualization, 132–33, *134*, 281–83, 288–91, 306; and war work imagery, 291–305, 306–7.
See also gender roles; masculinity; women
films. *See* cinema
Fischer, H. C., 330
Fischer, Joschka, 137–38
Fisher, Harrison, 133, *134*, 281–83
Fitzgerald, Charles Penrose, 333

Flagg, James Montgomery, *11*, 128, 132, 133, 281
folk art, 3, 28–29, 243–45, 247–49, 259; French, 158; and *lubok*, 241–43, 244–45, 247–48, 262–63, 265. *See also* art
food. *See* conservation (food) themes
Food Administration. *See* U.S. Food Administration (USFA)
"For Every Fighter a Woman Worker" (poster), 299–301
Foringer, A. E., 346–47
Fosdick, Harry Emerson, 359
"Four-Minute Men," 210, 221, 294
Foxton, F., 319, *320*
Frampton, George, 101
France, 42, *45*, 86, 303; and art education, 152–57, 158–59, 163, 167, 169n15; birth rate in, 160; decorative arts in, 147, 152–55, 157, 162–64, 166–68, 169n11; and French Colonial Army, 201n1; and gender roles, 159–61; and "Golden Age" of posters, 4, 174–75, 202n3; morale in, 148–49; national identity in, 172–73, 174; population of, 203n20; and soldiers' benefits, 184–86. *See also* French posters
Franco-Prussian War (1870–71), 178, 190
French, Daniel Chester, 280
"The French Allies have a wagon full of defeated Germans" (poster), 254–55
French posters: and advertising, 177, 195–96, 205n51; and colonial imagery, 27, 173–74, 178–96, 198–201; and color, 145, 146–47, 149–51, 155–56, 157–59, 167–68; and conservation themes, 145–46, *147*, *148*, 149, 159, 161, 164, 168n2; design of, 145–47, 149–51, 165–66, 167–68, 175–76, 202n4; and emotional candor, 175–76; "Golden Age" of, 4, 174–75, 202n3; history of, 174–78; and Marianne (symbol of Third Republic), 175, 179–80, 277; and patriotism, 151–52, 154, 186, 191; postwar, 52–53; and race, 173–74, 179–80, 184, 188–90, 192–200; repeated themes in, 176–77; schoolgirls' exhibition of, 145–47, 149–51, 159, 161–62, 163–66, 167–68; and slogans, 185, 195–96; and solidarity, 26–27, 174; and text, 185–87; and war loans, 177, 180–81, *182*, 183–84, 191, 192, 196. *See also* France

Friedrich, Ernst, 358–59, 360, 362–63

fundraising, 229–31, 344–45, 347, 351, 364, 365

Fussell, Paul, 2, 55, 77n7, 97, 318

"Future Members of the Fourth Estate" (poster), 353

Futurism (Russian), 243, 245, 248, 249–51, 259, 262. *See also* art

Gavin, Lettie, 310n28

"Gee! I Wish I Were a Man" (poster), 289–90, 297

gender roles: and American posters, 274–75, 283, 293, 300–303, 332–33, 336; in American Red Cross posters, 346–47; in France, 159–61, 162–65, 167–68; and German posters, 125–26; and the home front, 318–21, 326; and male vulnerability, 285, 287, 310n22; and rehabilitation photography, 354. *See also* femininity; masculinity; women

German posters, 90–91; and advertising, 112–13, 116; design of, 112–13, 114–15; differences of, from American posters, 25–26, 111–17, 118, 120–36; differences of, from British posters, 19–20, 101–3; and knight imagery, 82–83, 88; mailed fist imagery, 80–81, 82, 83; and masculinity, 90–91, 126; and medieval imagery, 25–26, 122; and regressive narratives, 112, 120–22, 124, 133; *Stahlhelm* (steel helmet) imagery, 87–91. *See also* Germany

"Germans! Although you are mighty, you will not see Warsaw" (poster), 257

Germany, 5–6, 42; and anti-modernism, 64, 68; and army size, 322; birth rate in, 160; and "corpse conversion factory," 74–75; death toll, 79; and decorative arts, 152, 153–54, 157; and fascism, 137; and *Materialschlacht*, 79, 80–81, 87, 89, 103; and militarism, 53, 73, 81, 102; morale in, 117; patriotism in, 117, 125; population of, 178–79, 203n20; and racial heritage, 64–65; veterans in, 82–83, 89, 94, 103; war memorials in, 83–87. *See also* German posters

Gervereau, Laurent, 206n62

Gibson, Charles Dana, 281, 349

Gilbert, Sandra, 62–63, 65

Gilson, E., 67

Ginzburg, Carlo, 18, 21

Girouard, Mark, 96

Goad, Allen, 287

Goncharova, Natalia, 244, 248–50, 251, 261

Gordetskii, Mikhail, 241

Grasset, Eugène, 174

Grayzel, Susan, 273, 310n34

Great Britain, 5–6; and cinema, 47–50; and civil society, 95–96; and colonialism, 39–40, 318; death toll, 79; and the "Lost Generation," 53–54; and militarism, 38–39, 110n91; and national identity, 41–43, 46–47, 54–57, 323; and popular culture, 42–43, 46–50, 53–54, 56–57, 96; and recruiting, 17–18, 23, 24, 43–44, 98, 312–27; social classes in, 44–46, 50–51; street theater and posters in, 9; veterans in, 83; and volunteer soldiers, 41–42. *See also* British posters

"The Greatest Mother in the World" (poster), 346–47

Greenberg, Alison, 311n43

Guenther, Lambert, 299

Guillaume, Eugène, 152, 153, 156–57, 159, 169n15

Haag Convention of 1907, 123

"Halt!" Cry the Dead (Barber), 359

"Halt the Hun" (poster), 65–66

hand-made posters, 8, 27, 33, 295–96

Hardie, Martin, 15–16

Harris, Ruth, 71

Harrison, Lloyd, 292–93

Hastings, Mrs. Jesse, 295

"Helft uns siegen!" (poster), 90, *91*

"Help Stop This" (poster), 67, 283–84

"Help the Women of France" (poster), 12–14, 304

"Help Us to Win! Sign Up for the War Loan" (poster), 123

Herter, Albert, 348

Hewitt, John, 3, 6, 16

Hiley, Nicholas, 18, 314, 321, 335, 336n1, 336n9, 338n30

Hitler, Adolf, 134, 276

Hobsbawm, Eric, 242

Hohlwein, Ludwig, 113

Holland, Henry Scott, 101

"Home Demonstration Agents," 294–95, 296–97

home front: connection of, to war front, 14, 46; development of, 2, 3, 7; imagery, *45*, 46, 47, 50–51, 318–20, 326; and women, 273, 275, 292–94, 296, 318–20, 326

Hopps, H. R., 68–69, 76, 77n20, 284

The Horror of It (Barber), 359–63

Hosaeus, Hermann, 91–92

Hosking, Geoffrey, 246

Hoyle, M., 285–87

Hughes, Ted, 56–57

"Huns": history of term, 61–62; imagery, 63–66, 67, 69, 71–73, 75–76, 76n5. *See also* race

Hüppauf, Bernd, 89

Huss, Marie-Monique, 161

Hynes, Samuel, 37, 50, 55, 56, 100

iconography, 309n12; and American posters, 74, 119, 342, 365; and British posters, 17, 19, 79–80; and French posters, 151; and German posters, 19, 79–80, 121; neoclassical, 278; and race, 62, 64; and recruiting posters, 43; similarity of, between countries, 19–20; and war memorials, 90, 101. *See also* imagery; *lubki*

icons: in Russian art, 242–43, 244, 249, 252–53. *See also* art

imagery, 24; Abraham Lincoln, 215–16, 217, 218, 224, 232–33; African American, 210–11, 215–18, 220, 222, 223–29, 232–35; antiwar, 358–63; Belgium, 41, 316–19, 321; and children, 161, 324; and chivalry, 95–102, 103; classicism, 279, 280; and death, 52–53, 77n18; and desexualization, 302–4; and the Fatherland, 125; of females as victims, 275, 283–87; German "Hun," 24–25, 63–66, 67, 69, 71–73, 75–76, 76n5; "German Ogre," 62, *63*, 71–72; home front, *45*, 46, 47, 50–51, 275, 318–20, 326; injuries and disabilities, 31, 285–88, 342–65; and iron, 79, 80–87, 93–94, 102–3; knights, 79–80, 82–84, 85, 88, 96–103, 122, 373–74; lone soldier, 8–9, 191, *193*; Lost Generation, 54–56; machines and rehabilitation, 355; mailed fist, 25, 80–81, *82*, 83; medieval, 25–26, 121–22, 318, 373–74; and memories,

37–38; nation as body, 124–26; peasants (Russian), 243, 247, 252, 253–55, 258–62; Rosie the Riveter, 299; self-reliant disabled, 353–56, 364; sexualized, 68, *69*, 70–71, 132–33, *134*, 206n62, 275, 281–83, 288–91; *Stahlhelm* (steel helmet), 87–93, 107n41; swords, 120; *troupes indigènes*, *172*, 179–80, 184, 187; Uncle Sam, 128–30, 137, 228–29, 309n17, 349; and venereal disease, 225, 226–29; and violence, 31–33, 124–25, 234–35, 257; war workers, 275, 291–94. *See also* femininity; iconography; masculinity; themes

Imaging American Women (Banta), 274

imperialism. *See* colonialism

Imperial War Museum, 16, 34n5, 336n1

India, 39–40, 75

industrialization, 1, 252, 360; and craft production, 152; and warfare, 41, 62–63, 79, 121

injuries, 50, 340–42; and allegorical images, 349; and antiwar photo albums, 343, 358–63; and compensation, 350; depictions of, 31, 285–88, 342–50, 363–65; and Red Cross posters, 342, 343–44, 345–49, 357, 364; and rehabilitation photography, 350–58, 360, 364, 365

Institute for Crippled and Disabled Men, 351–56. *See also* injuries

International Anti-War Museum, 358

interwar period, 51–52, 53, 54–55, 56–57

"In the Name of Mercy Give" (poster), 348

iron fist. *See* mailed fist imagery

"I Summon You to Comradeship in the Red Cross" (poster), *134*, 281–83

"Is your home worth fighting for?" (poster), *45*

Jaeger, Louisette, 164

Jahn, Hubertus, 247, 265

Jarvis, Christina S., 309n17

Johnson, Henry, 234–35

Johnson, James W., 231

"Join the Navy" (poster), 132

Jonas, Lucien, *182*, 198–200, 206n60

Jones, James, 235

Jourdain, Frantz, 154–55, 158–59, 171n51

Jünger, Ernst, 90, 93–95, 107n41, 375n3

"Kameraden zeichnet die VII^te. Kriegsan-
leihe" (poster), *88*
Kaufmann, Herbert, 355
Kealey, E. V., *328*
Keegan, John, 52
Keen, Sam, 243
Keith, Jeannette, 12–13
Kennedy, M. D., 75
Kipling, Rudyard, 39–40
Kitchener, Lord, 17–18, 21, 137, 313,
315–16
Klunk, Brian, 126
knight imagery, 79–80, 88, 96–100, 122,
373–74; and British posters, 98–100,
101–2; and war memorials, 82–84, 85,
100–101, 102–3. *See also* imagery
Knutson, Anne Classen, 68–69, 77n20, 119,
289–90, 293, 301, 302, 304, 309n17
Kriegserlebnis, 83, 89, 90, 102, 103
Kriegswahrzeichen zum Benageln, 83–87. *See also*
war memorials
Kristeva, Julia, 363

Land Army (poster), 297–99
Larionov, Mikhail, 249, 250, 251, 253
"The Last Blow Is the 8th War Loan"
(poster), 120
Lee, Ivy L., 344–45
Leed, Eric, 318
Leete, Alfred, 17
Lentulov, Artistakh, 241
Lewis, Beth Irwin, 330
Leyendecker, Francis Xavier, 132
Liberty Loan war bond posters, *12, 13, 114,*
129, 211–12, 220–21
Liberty Memorial Association, 16
Lincoln, Abraham, 215–16, 217, 218, 224,
232–33
Lindsay, Norman, 71–72
literature, wartime, 94–95, 99–100, 107n41
lithography, 4, 369
Little, Arthur, 235
Livshits, Benedikt, 250
Lloyd, Jill, 242
Lloyd George, David, 81
"Lost Generation," 53–56
Louvain, Belgium, 66–67
lubki, 28–29, 261–65; and battle imagery,
257; as folk art, 241–43, 244–45, 262–63;

history of, 245–48, 250–53, 267n13. *See
also* Russian posters; Segodniashnii Lubok
(Today's Lubok)
lubochnaia literatura, 245. See also *lubki*
Lumley, Savile, 324, *325*, 338n30
Lunn, Joe, 206n58
Lutaud, Charles, 194

Maiakovskii, Vladimir, 241, 250, 253–55,
256–57, 259, 260, 262, 264
mailed fist imagery, 25, 80–81, *82*, 83. *See
also* imagery
Main, U. S., *10*
Malevich, Kazimir, 241, 249, 253–55, 256,
259, 260–63
male vulnerability, 285, 287, 310n22. *See also*
gender roles
Malins, G. H., 48, 372
Maliutin, Ivan, 264
Mamontov, Savva, 247
"Mangez moins de viande pour ménager
notre cheptel" (poster), *146*
Mangin, Charles, 203n20
Marchand, Roland, 16–17, 31–32
Marianne, 175, 179–80, 277. *See also* allegorical images
Marshall, Logan, 66
masculinity, 29–30, 36n36; and American
posters, 131–32, 279, 327–28; and British posters, 30–31, 33, 313–14, 316–19,
323–33, 335–36; feminization of, 328–30;
and French posters, 164; and German
posters, 90–91, 126; and heroism, 40–41,
287, 303, 318, 330–31, 335; and patriotism, 313–14, 318–19, 322, 323, 327,
329–30, 332; and virility, 330–33, 335. *See
also* femininity; gender roles; imagery
Masefield, John, 97
Mashkov, Ilia, 241
mass communication, 1, 5, 369–70, 371–73.
See also propaganda
matériel, war (*Materialschlacht*), 79, 80–81, 87,
89, 103. *See also* "modern" war
Mather, Frank Jewett, 66
Matyushin, Mikhail, 262
McDowell, J. B., 48, 372
McMurtrie, Douglas C., 351
memorials. *See* war memorials

"Men of Britain! Will You Stand This?"
(poster), 319, *320*

Merry, Glenn, 294, 310n31

militarism, 38–39; in Germany, 53, 73, 81,
102; in Great Britain, 38–39, 110n91

miscegenation, 69, 71. *See also* race

Misler, Nicoletta, 264

Mitchell, W. T. J., 8

modernism, 65–66, 69–70, 96, 374–75; and
art, 242, 244

"modern" war, 1–2, 41, 62–63, 69–70, 77n7,
79, 85, 102–3, 287; and brutalization,
105n19; and trench warfare, 46, 94, 100,
191, 310n22; and Western Front, 41, 87,
90, 103, 191, 234–35, 340

Montague, C. E., 99–100

Moor, Dmitrii, 264

Moore, Aldwin, 230

Moore, F. Frankfort, 333–34

Morgan, J. H., 64

"mother Russia," 247, 257. *See also* Russian
posters

motifs. *See* themes

Moton, Robert R., 215

Motor Corps, 304–5

movies. *See* cinema

Mucha, Alphonse, 4

Müller, Hans-Harald, 94–95

Musée Galliera exhibition (1917), 151–53,
154–56, 158–59, 163, 168n4. *See also*
exhibitions

Muybridge, Eadweard, 298

mythmaking, 56, 255–56, 257–58, 269n47,
373. *See also* allegorical images; imagery

nailing rituals, 84, 85, 94. *See also* war
memorials

Napoleon, 246, 252, 263, 269n52

narod. See peasants (Russian)

narratives: progressive, 112, 126–28, 130–31,
133; regressive, 112, 120–22, 124, 133. *See
also* themes

national identity, 2, 3, 124–25, 265n2; British, 41–43, 46–47, 54–57, 323; French,
172–73, 174; Russian, 28–29, 241–45,
246–49, 252, 253, 257, 259, 263–65

National Safety Council, 210–11, 225

National Security League, 119

Nazis, 76, 137

Negro Press Section (Food Administration),
213, 214, 221

neoprimitivism, 248, 249, 254, 260–61. *See
also* art

Neo-Primitivism (Shevchenko), 244

"Ne pas gaspiller le pain est notre devoir"
(poster), 164

nervous disorders. *See* psychological ailments

Nesbitt, Molly, 152

newspapers, 372; black, 212–13, 215, 220

Nicholas II (Czar), 259, 268n36

"No Longer Out of a Job" (poster), 355

Norris, Stephen M., 267n13

The One and A Half-Eyed Archer (Livshits), 250

"On Which Side of the Window are *You*?"
(poster), 132, 327, 329

Oppenheim, Luis, 125–26

Osborne, John Morton, 335

Osthaus, Karl-Ernst, 85

Our Colored Fighters (film), 210

"Our Colored Heroes" (poster), 234–36

pamphlets, 32, 51, 66–67, 210, 337n15;
atrocity, 67–68; international distribution
of, 74; recruitment, 314, 323–24; on rehabilitation, 351. *See also* propaganda

Paret, Paul, 330

Paret, Peter, 330

Parliamentary Recruiting Committee (PRC),
23, 98, 312, 321–22, 336n1, 337n15; advertising techniques used by, 321–22; and
coercion, 322–27, 329–30, 334–36; founding of, 314; and gender roles, 315–21,
326; and popular culture imagery, 324–25.
See also recruiting

"Patriotic War of 1812," 252, 263

patriotism: and African Americans, 207–8,
214, 233, 236; in French posters, 151–52,
154, 186, 191; in Germany, 117, 125; and
masculinity, 313–14, 318–19, 322, 323,
327, 329–30, 332; Russian, 246–47, 252,
257, 265

Paus, Herbert Andrew, 131

peasants (Russian), 243, 247, 252, 253–55,
258–62. *See also* Russian posters

Penfield, Edward, 12–14, 304

Pfeifer, Richard, *127*

philanthropic groups, 229–31, 232

photoengraving, 112

photography, 50; and antiwar photo albums, 343, 358–63; "Battlefield Gothic," 50; censorship of, 342; rehabilitation, 350–58, 360, 364, 365

Picard, Marthe, *146*

poetry, 51–52, 55, 331; antiwar, 331, 359

Poole, Ross, 124

Pope, Jessie, 331

popular culture (British), 42–43, 46–50, 53–54, 56, 96

Poster Advertising Association, 5

Posters of the First World War (Rickards), 3, 5, 18–19, 26, 111, 277, 343–44

postwar posters, 51–57

"Potatriots" poster, 6–7

Powell, Robert Baden, *329*

Price, Matlock, 281

Price, Montrose J., 31

primitivism, 63–64, 68–69, 74; and art, 242–43, 245, 249, 250, 251, 253, 262–63. *See also* art

progressive narratives, 112, 126–28, 130–31, 133

propaganda, 5–9, 28, 33, 359; and African Americans, 207–19, 221–26, 229, 236–37; and atrocity reports, 67–68, 74–75, 206n59, 287, 316–18, 337n10; and Committee on Public Information (CPI), 28, 119, 209–11, 212, 215, 236, 342; and cultural destruction, 66–67; and cultural traditions, 20; effectiveness of, 5, 17–18, 133–38, 140n46, 276; and government poster contests, 148–49, 151–52, 159–60, 162, 166; international dissemination of, 74–76; and "othering," 327–28, 371; pro-German, 117, 138n11; purpose of, 243, 371; and race issues, 28, 64–66, 67–68, 73–74, 173–74; and social class, 50–51; and thematic repetition, 10–14, 17–19, 177; and war memorials, 80; and women's rights, 306–7. *See also* imagery; themes

Prop Art (Yanker), 136

Prost, Antoine, 52–53

psychological ailments, 341, 364–65, 368n34; shell shock, 83, 84–85, 335, 364

Punch (magazine), 62, *63*

"?" (poster), 71–72

race, 67–68, 173–74, 278, 284; and Algerian

stereotypes, 188–92, *193*, 206n59; and American posters, 27–28, 207–9, 210–11, 212–37, 279; and Banania advertising, 195–96, 205nn51–52; and French posters, 173–74, 179–80, 184, 188–90, 192–200; and "Huns," 24–25, 62, 64–65, 67–69, 73, 75–76, 76n5; and West African stereotypes, 192–200, 201; and women, 274. *See also* African Americans; colonial soldiers

Radishchev, Alexander, 245

Raemaekers, Louis, 76n5

Rawls, Walton H., 3, 276

recruiting, 370; and American posters, 71, 72–73, 327–30; and Australian posters, 71–72; and British posters, 17–18, 23, 24, 43–44, 98, 312–36; and pamphlets, 314, 323–24. *See also* conscription

Red Cross. *See* American Red Cross

"A red-haired, uncouth German" (poster), 259

Redslob, Edwin, 92

regressive narratives, 112, 120–22, 124, 133

rehabilitation photography, 350–58, 360, 364, 365. *See also* photography

Remarque, Erich Maria, 88

"Remember Belgium" (poster), *44*

Renesch, E. G., 215–16, 223, 225–26

Rhodes, Cecil, 64–65, 77n11

Richards, Maisie, 315

Rickards, Maurice, 3, 5, 18–19, 26, 111, 175, 201, 277, 343–44

Roberts, Mary Louise, 160

Roberts, Needham, 234–35

Roerich, Nikolai, 248

Rogers, Isabelle, *289*

The Romance of a Red Cross Hospital (Moore), 333–34

Romberg, Maurice, 192, *193*

Roosevelt, Theodore, 118, 131

Rosie the Riveter imagery, 299

rotary printing, 112

Rovinskii, Dimitrii, 247

Russia, 81, 245; and Civil War (1919–22), 264–65; crafts of, 253; and military management, 256–58; and "Patriotic War of 1812," 252, 263; patriotism in, 246–47, 252, 257, 265; and Russo-Turkish War (1877–78), 267n13. *See also* Russian posters

Russian posters: exhibitions of, 241, 261–62; motifs of, 243, 246, 253–62; and national identity, 28–29, 241–45, 246–49, 252, 253, 257, 259, 263–65. *See also* Russia

Russian Telegraph Agency (ROSTA), 264–65

Russo-Turkish War (1877–78), 267n13

Sabin, Arthur K., 15–16

Said, Edward, 77n10

Salvation Army, 302, 303, 349

Sassoon, Siegfried, 52, 55

"A Sausage Maker came to Lodz" (poster), 253–54, 259

Scarry, Elaine, 358

Schnug, Leo, *88*

Scott, Emmett J., 210, 220–21

Section Photographique et Cinémato-graphique, 179

Seduction or Instruction? (Aulich and Hewitt), 3, 6, 16, 43

Segodniashnii Lubok (Today's Lubok), 28–29, 264–65; and folk art, 245, 253–54, 262–63; founding of, 241–42; motifs used by, 243, 246, 253–62; and national identity, 251, 252, 253–54, 263; text and image, 250, 253–55, 262, 264. *See also* Russian posters

Senefelder, Aloys, 4, 369

Senghor, Léopold Sédar, 195, 205n51

Seton-Watson, Hugh, 259

Sexual Life during the World War (Fischer and Dubois), 330

shell shock, 83, 84–85, 335, 364. *See also* psychological ailments

Sherman, Daniel, 80

Shevchenko, Aleksandr, 244

Shklovsky, Victor, 264

shock troops, 197–99, 206n58. *See also* colonial soldiers

Shover, Michele J., 293

"Sign Up for the 8th War Loan" (poster), 126

Silver, Kenneth, 156

Simmel, Georg, 375n2

Simons, Paul, 149, 152–54, 155–57, 158, 159, 169n15

sizes, poster, 9

Slavophiles, 244

slogans, 114, 137, 185, 195–96, 205n52,

326, 328–29, 345. *See also* text

Smith, Anthony D., 265n2

Smith, Helmut Walser, 127

social classes, 44–46, 50–51, 135–36; in America, 130; in France, 163; in Germany, 93, 116, 122; in Great Britain, 101–2

"Soignons la basse-cour" (poster), *148*

solidarity, 22–23, 38; and British posters, 43, 52; and French posters, 26–27, 174

Sombart, Werner, 82

Sontag, Susan, 11, 14, 21

Spear, Fred, 283

Spingarn, Arthur, 231

steel helmet (*Stahlhelm*) imagery, 87–93, 107n41

Steinlen, Théophile-Alexandre, 150

stereotypes, 174, 176–77; of African Americans, 209; of Algerians (North Africans), 188–92, *193*, 206n59; and "childlike" colonials, 178, 179–80, 184, 194–96; of West Africans, 192–200, 201; and women as victims, 283–84. *See also* race

Sterner, Albert, 345–46, 347

Storey, Moorfield, 231

Storm of Steel (Jünger), 94–95, 375n3

Strothmann, Frederick, *114*

"Sus Bonos de la Libertad ayudarán á fin con esto" (poster), 74

"The Sword is Drawn, the Navy Upholds It!" (poster), 278–79

Taylor, Alonso, 12, 304

Telegraph Agency of the Soviet Union (TASS), 265

"Tell That to the Marines" (poster), *11*, 132

text, 37, 50–51, 185–87, 286–87, 319; and Russian posters, 250, 253–55, 262, 264. *See also* slogans

themes: barbarism, 62, 65, 67–68, 128, 319; conservation (food), 6–9, 145–46, *147*, *148*, 149, 159, 161, 164, 168n2, 213–14, 221–22, 292–93; empire, 172, 174, 178–87, 200–201; exoticism, 188–91, 192, *193*; Germanic, 121, 137; national unity, 117; reality of battle, 243, 246, 256–57; repetition of, 10–14, 17–19; Russian peasant, 243, 247, 252, 253–55, 258–62; savagery and primitivism, 62, 67–69. *See also* imagery

"These Men Have Come Across" (poster), 132

"They Crucify" (poster), 285–87

"3rd Army: 7th War Loan" (poster), 120–21

Thomson, Rosemarie Garland, 347

thrift stamp posters, 210–11, 225

"The Tidal Wave" (poster), 115–16

tirailleurs sénégalais, 184, 192–200, 205n51, 206n58, 206n62. *See also* colonial soldiers

Titzmann, Michael, 121

Toulouse-Lautrec, Henri de, 4, 154–55, 174

trench warfare, 46, 58n6, 94, 100, 191, 310n22. *See also* "modern" war

Triedler, Adolph, 283–84

troupes indigènes (indigenous troops), 178, 184, 187, 201n1, 203n20; and assimilation, 172–73, 191–92; and race, 188, 190, 193–201; stereotypes of, 174, 179–80. *See also* colonial soldiers

"True Blue" (poster), 223–25

Tupitsyn, Margarita, 251

"U-Boot-Spende" (poster), 115

Uhland, Ludwig, 86–87

Uncle Sam images, 128–30, 137, 228–29, 309n17, 349. *See also* imagery

Underwood, Clarence, 302

United States. *See* America

"The United States Army Builds Men" (posters), 131–32

urbanization, 1, 2, 5, 252, 369–70, 375n2

U.S. Food Administration (USFA), 8–9, 12, 13, 15, 276; and African American campaigns, 212–15, 218–19, 221–22, 236; and women workers, 292–97, 298

Uvarov, Sergei, 269n52

Vasnetsov, Viktor, 247–48

venereal disease, 225, 226–28, 303

Vernet, Yvonne, 147, 164

Verrees, J. Paul, 293

veterans, 82–83, 89, 94, 103, 358; benefits for, 184–86, 231, 343, 350, 364; and war charities, 84

Villain, Henri, 181

Vincent, S., 164

Vinogradov, Nikolai, 252–53

violence: in films, 48–49; in posters, 31–33. *See also* imagery

volunteers, soldier, 23, 99; in Great Britain, 41, 42, 98. *See also* conscription

Wake Up, America! (Rawls), 3

"Wants You" (poster), 17, 21

War against War! (Friedrich), 358–59, 360, 362–63

"War and Publishing" (exhibit), 241, 261

War and the Lubok (Denisov), 252

war bond posters, 12, 13, 114, 129, 210–12, 220–21, 370. *See also* war loan posters

war loan posters: French, 177, 180–81, 182, 183–84, 191, 192, 196; German, 90, 91. *See also* war bond posters

war memorials, 80, 83, 90–92, 93, 102–3; in Great Britain, 97, 98, 100, 101; *Kriegswahrzeichen zum Benageln*, 83–87; and *Stahlhelm* (steel helmet), 89

Warner, Marina, 277

War Office, 315, 321

War Posters (Aulich), 135

War Posters Issued by Belligerent and Neutral Nations (Hardie and Sabin), 15–16

Washington, Booker T., 216–18

Washington, George, 223, 224

Watkins, J. S., 71

"We are the Russians and there are more and more of us" (poster), 258

"We Beat Them and Sign Up for the War Loan!" (poster), 124

Weill, Alain, 4, 202n3

"We Need You" (poster), 345–46, 347

Western Front, 41, 87, 90, 103, 191, 234–35, 340. *See also* "modern" war

"What a boom, what a blast the Germans made at Lomza" (poster), 261–62

"white feather" campaign, 333–35

Wilhelm II (Kaiser), 61, 81

Willette, Adolphe, 150

"Will you fight now or wait for this" (poster), 71

Wilson, Woodrow, 119, 223, 224, 232, 282–83, 344

Winnington-Ingram, Arthur, 100

Witt-Schlumberger, Marguerite de, 160

women: in armed forces, 291, 302, 310n28, 315–16; artists, 26–27, 145, 159–61, 162–66, 168; differences between French and American, 303–4; and equal rights,

women (*continued*)
   273, 306–7; as "Home Demonstration
   Agents," 294–95, 296–97; and home
   front, 273, 275, 292–94, 296, 318–20,
   326; and manual labor, 51; as war work-
   ers, 291–305, 306–7. *See also* femininity;
   gender roles
"Women of Britain Say–Go!" (poster), *328*
"Women of Queensland!" (poster), 71
Women's Active Service League, 331–32
Women's Committee of the State Council of
   Defense, 294

Woollacott, Angela, 331
World War II, 25, 38, 76, 137, 281, 299,
   309n17, 311n43, 331
Wortman, Richard, 263
wounds. *See* injuries

"You Can Help" (poster), 292
"Your Country's Call" (poster), 42, *43*, 46, 47

Zeiger, Susan, 302, 303

Studies in War, Society, and the Military

Military Migration and State Formation
The British Military Community in
Seventeenth-Century Sweden
Mary Elizabeth Ailes

The State at War in South Asia
Pradeep P. Barua

An American Soldier in World War I
George Browne
Edited by David L. Snead

Imagining the Unimaginable
World War, Modern Art, and the Politics
of Public Culture in Russia, 1914–1917
Aaron J. Cohen

The Rise of the National Guard
The Evolution of the American Militia, 1865–1920
Jerry Cooper

The Thirty Years' War and German
Memory in the Nineteenth Century
Kevin Cramer

Political Indoctrination in the U.S. Army
from World War II to the Vietnam War
Christopher S. DeRosa

In the Service of the Emperor
Essays on the Imperial Japanese Army
Edward J. Drea

The Age of the Ship of the Line
The British and French Navies, 1650–1815
Jonathan R. Dull

You Can't Fight Tanks with Bayonets
Psychological Warfare against the
Japanese Army in the Southwest Pacific
Allison B. Gilmore

A Strange and Formidable Weapon
British Responses to World War I Poison Gas
Marion Girard

Civilians in the Path of War
Edited by Mark Grimsley and Clifford J. Rogers

Picture This
World War I Posters and Visual Culture
Edited and with an introduction by Pearl James

I Die with My Country
Perspectives on the Paraguayan War, 1864–1870
Edited by Hendrik Kraay and Thomas L. Whigham

North American Indians in the Great World War
Susan Applegate Krouse
Photographs and original documentation
by Joseph K. Dixon

Citizens More than Soldiers
The Kentucky Militia and Society
in the Early Republic
Harry S. Laver

Soldiers as Citizens
Former German Officers in the Federal Republic
of Germany, 1945–1955
Jay Lockenour

Army and Empire
British Soldiers on the American Frontier,
1758–1775
Michael N. McConnell

*The Militarization of Culture in the
Dominican Republic, from the
Captains General to General Trujillo*
Valentina Peguero

*Arabs at War
Military Effectiveness, 1948–1991*
Kenneth M. Pollack

*The Politics of Air Power
From Confrontation to Cooperation in Army
Aviation Civil-Military Relations*
Rondall R. Rice

*Andean Tragedy
Fighting the War of the Pacific, 1879–1884*
William F. Sater

*The Grand Illusion
The Prussianization of the Chilean Army*
William F. Sater and Holger H. Herwig

Sex Crimes under the Wehrmacht
David Raub Snyder

*The Paraguayan War
Volume 1: Causes and Early Conduct*
Thomas L. Whigham

*The Challenge of Change
Military Institutions and New Realities, 1918–1941*
Edited by Harold R. Winton and David R. Mets

To order or obtain more information on these
or other University of Nebraska Press titles,
visit www.nebraskapress.unl.edu.